# Beyond the Desktop Metaphor

# Beyond the Desktop Metaphor

## Designing Integrated Digital Work Environments

edited by Victor Kaptelinin and Mary Czerwinski

The MIT Press
Cambridge, Massachusetts
London, England

MIT Press books may be purchased at special quantity discounts for business or sales promotional use. For information, please email special_sales@mitpress.mit.edu or write to Special Sales Department, The MIT Press, 55 Hayward Street, Cambridge, MA 02142.

This book was set in Sabon by Omegatype Typography, Inc., and was printed and bound in the United States of America.

Library of Congress Cataloging-in-Publication Data

Beyond the desktop metaphor : designing integrated digital work environments / Victor Kaptelinin and Mary Czerwinski, editors.
p. cm.
Includes bibliographical references and index.
ISBN-13: 978-0-262-11304-5 (hc : alk. paper)
ISBN-10: 0-262-11304-X (hc : alk. paper)
1. Human–computer interaction. 2. User interfaces (Computer systems). 3. Microcomputers. I. Kaptelinin, Victor. II. Czerwinski, Mary P., 1960–.

QA76.9.H85B539 2007
004.16—dc22 2006046846

10 9 8 7 6 5 4 3 2 1

# Contents

# Acknowledgments

This book is the result of a collective effort made by researchers who share an interest in "post-desktop" interactive environments. The editors would like to thank all the chapter authors for their dedication, time, and generous intellectual contribution. The MIT Press supported our vision of the book and helped us bring it to fruition. We would also like to thank Chip Bruce, Jonathan Grudin, Kristo Ivanov, and Eric Stolterman for their help, support, and insightful discussions. Our thanks also go to our employers—Umeå University and Microsoft Research—for supportive environments that provided us with the freedom to work on this book. Many other people and institutions—too many to be listed on this page—contributed to this book in one way or another. The editors are thankful to all of them.

# 1

# Introduction: The Desktop Metaphor and New Uses of Technology

Victor Kaptelinin and Mary Czerwinski

The objective of this book is to present and discuss new approaches to designing next-generation digital work environments. Currently the most pervasive computer systems, such as Microsoft Windows and Mac OS, are based on the desktop metaphor. For many users and designers, these are the only digital work environments they have ever known. It is all too easy to assume that the desktop metaphor will always determine our experience of computer systems. The present book challenges this assumption. Its point of departure is an understanding that desktop systems as we know them may well represent a temporary—if hugely successful—phase in the development of interactive environments. Future systems may further develop, modify, or even abandon the metaphor. The book is an attempt to systematically explore a range of issues related to the design of interactive environments of the future, with a special focus on new design solutions, concepts, and approaches that could be employed in "post-desktop" systems.

Systems based on the desktop metaphor emerged on a massive scale as the first general-purpose work environments "for all" in the early 1980s (Smith et al. 1982). The designers' intentions were to support the individual user of a stand-alone computer—typically in the context of a traditional office environment—mostly in launching applications and storing and retrieving documents. Desktop systems provided coherent, no-nonsense environments for these types of activities and proved to be an enormous success.

Today, however, the life of a typical computer user is very different. To carry out their everyday tasks, people often use a range of technologies, such as desktop and laptop computers, PDAs (personal digital assistants), and smartphones, and employ various types of information objects, such as files, email messages, URLs, and contacts, to collaborate and communicate with each other. Information work requires the integration of information from a wide variety of sources, cutting across multiple applications and colleagues. Empirical studies and logical analyses indicate that traditional desktop systems do not provide sufficient support for information workers in real-life contexts characterized by collaboration, multitasking, multiple roles, and diverse technologies (e.g., Plaisant and Shneiderman 1995; Kaptelinin 1996; Dourish et al. 1999; Czerwinski, Horvitz, and Wilhite 2004).

## The Trouble with the Desktop Metaphor

A key factor in the original success of existing desktop systems was a set of intuitively clear underlying principles that rendered a consistent mental model of the digital workspace as a whole. The desktop provides a space for displaying the content of currently active documents in overlapping windows, while the hierarchical file system facilitates access to stored documents and tools. Users can rely on their knowledge of a typical office environment to make informed guesses about how individual objects and features of a desktop system can be employed to carry out the task at hand.

Workspaces based on the desktop metaphor are not monolithic. The user can create any number of subspaces by setting up new folders and rearranging existing ones. These subspaces make it possible to keep groups of files (and, if necessary, subfolders) separate from each other. Even though such organization is rigid, not reflecting the changes of the importance of documents over time (as opposed to piles of papers; see Malone 1983) and the dynamics of a user's cognitive processes (Lansdale 1988), it allows simple, intuitive navigation within the file system as a whole. Therefore, desktop systems provide relatively well-integrated environments for *handling files by individual users* of personal computers.

However, even within this application scope, it has become evident that the desktop metaphor has inherent limitations. One of the problems designers of desktop systems have continually been struggling with is that of *combining information access and information display*—that is, simultaneously supporting (a) access to information objects and (b) displaying the visual representation of the content of those objects.

As opposed to its source domain, the physical office, the desktop metaphor is based on using the same surface—the screen—for both displaying and accessing information. Physical desktops can be cluttered with individual documents and piles of papers, but we do not need to clear up these desktops to get to file cabinets, drawers, or bookshelves. People typically do not have to choose between making visible a desk or a file cabinet; they can see both and use them independently of each other. The users of modern information technologies, on the other hand, have to use the same screen space for finding information objects and for viewing their content. Both locating a document on a disc and editing the document make use of the same physical surface of a computer screen.

Perhaps the most apparent features differentiating modern desktop systems from early ones are the elaborate sets of tools developed by designers over the years to help users combine information access and information display. Users of early systems had to clear an area of the screen by moving, resizing, or closing open windows in order to view and access objects located on the desktop. Modern systems, such as Microsoft Windows XP or Mac OS X, allow access to the computer's content without ever selecting objects on the desktop. The user, for instance, can always open the "Documents" folder from the Start menu (Microsoft Windows XP) or a Finder window (Mac OS X).

A significant advancement of the desktop metaphor for personal computers was the introduction of the taskbar in Microsoft Windows (for a discussion of similar tools for X Windows, see LaStrange 1989). Not only do open windows obscure objects located on the desktop, they also conceal each other—just as papers placed on a physical desktop conceal other papers from view. As opposed to its physical counterpart, the virtual desktop lets the user view a list of all open documents and make any one of them visible by selecting it from the list. If it were possible to do this in the physical world, such a feature would definitely be appreciated by many people using physical desks!

Despite the apparent progress in the design of desktop systems over the last decades, combining information access and information display remains a problematic issue. Arguably, an obstacle to more effective solutions is the inherent limitations of the desktop metaphor. The very name "desktop" implies a single, limited physical surface used as a window to all of the resources of a virtual environment. However, current technological developments offer a much wider range of possibilities. Multiple, large-screen, and ambient displays, as well as new input and sensing technologies, open up new possibilities for combining information access and information display. Some of these new possibilities are presented in this book.

In addition, the desktop metaphor itself appears to be somewhat inconsistent. Desktop systems can be viewed from two different perspectives that correspond, respectively, to (a) the logical structure of a virtual environment, and (b) how that environment is perceived by the user. From the logical point of view, the top level of a virtual space, the entry point from which other parts can be accessed, is a collection of storage devices available to the user (for instance, what is displayed in the "My Computer" folder of Microsoft Windows). The desktop, from this perspective, is just a folder on one of these devices. However, from the subjective perspective of the user, the entry point to the system is the desktop. Usually, other components of the environment, including the "My Computer" folder, can be reached from the desktop. It appears this inconsistency may be confusing to some users (see Ravasio and Tscherter, this volume).

Another recurrent problem with desktop systems is multitasking. On the one hand, desktop systems provide support for some of the key activities of managing several task contexts. As already mentioned, users of desktop systems can conveniently organize their files into a hierarchical structure that matches the structure of their tasks. Also, Apple Macintosh System 7 and Microsoft Windows 95 made it possible for users of personal computers to enjoy a feature previously available only to users of workstations—working with several applications at the same time. Yet these successes in supporting multitasking underline the inherent limitations of desktop systems in selectively displaying sets of task-related information objects. This can be illustrated with the following example. Imagine that files related to two different tasks—task A and task B—are properly organized into two different folders, and the user can conveniently access these folders. Even in this simple case, switching from one task to another could be problematic. The user should either (a) close all documents related to task A and open documents related to task B, which can be tedious, especially if the user has to frequently switch back and forth between the tasks, or (b) keep all documents open, which can cause constant distractions. If the user needs to work with many open documents to accomplish these tasks, neither strategy can be considered optimal.

An obvious solution to the problem of the selective presentation of task-related information is employing multiple, task-related desktops along the lines proposed by developers of the Rooms system (Henderson and Card 1986). However, the only successful example of implementing the idea of multiple desktops have been window managers for UNIX based systems, which support switching between a predetermined number of desktops. As for the more pervasive operating systems for personal computers, such as MS Windows and Mac OS, multiple (virtual) desktops have not become widely popular with users.

Therefore, even within a narrowly defined scope of application —individual users working with files on stand-alone computers—the desktop metaphor manifests apparent limitations. Problems with the desktop metaphor were further aggravated by the use of email and the Internet as tools for communication and information sharing. These developments resulted in multiple information hierarchies within a single virtual environment (Dourish et al. 1999). Moreover, these hierarchies were not equally supported by the functionality of desktop systems. What emerged was the file as a first-class citizen, while individual email messages or instant messages were not. For example, it is relatively easy to select a disparate group of files to copy, backup, transfer to another device or move, but this is not necessarily as easily handled with email. Consider the example of email attachments—they must be explicitly saved or placed in a folder first, before having a permanent place or being easily manipulated in a group fashion.

And, the heavy usage of the World Wide Web and search engines makes it easy for users to send URLs or website material as content in an email, but again access and permanent storage of that content is not quite as easy as it is for files. Most of the time, users must dig through long lists of email looking for the one that had the attachment, or the website information in it. New search engines for personal files and web browsing make it easier to leverage metadata about the content of email, files, and websites during search, but these systems may not be suitable as replacements for the computer desktop.

Finally, with a more mobile work force, it is becoming increasingly important that the user be able to access his or her information bits at any time, from any device. Once again, the desktop metaphor breaks down here, as each device has its own look and feel, but must somehow synchronize with the alternate environments.

To sum up, the development of desktop systems over the last two decades has revealed limitations of the desktop metaphor. In particular, the metaphor does not provide adequate support for the access to information objects along with the display of the content of those objects, multitasking, dealing with multiple information hierarchies, communication and collaboration, and coordinated use of multiple technologies.

## Toward Integrated Digital Work Environments

Limitations of systems based on the desktop metaphor were recognized by human–computer interaction (HCI) researchers quite early, approximately at the time when the systems became widely used. That recognition sparked debates in the HCI community and stimulated the development of novel approaches. Now, two decades later, one can clearly see a continuous line of research and development originating from early HCI studies and growing over the years. In the 1980s, influential work was done by Malone (1983), Henderson and Card (1986), and Lansdale (1988). The Rooms system (Henderson and Card 1986) was probably the first important milestone in exploring design alternatives to traditional desktop systems. Selected highlights of the next decade of development include the Pad++ system (Bederson and Hollan 1994), personal role management (Plaisant and Shneiderman 1995), Norman's activity-based computing (Norman 1998), an "anti-Mac" interface debate in the *Communications of the ACM* (Gentner and Nielsen 1996), the Lifestreams system (Fertig, Freeman, and Gelernter 1996), and a discussion of user practices of finding and filing computer files in the *SIGCHI Bulletin* (Barreau and Nardi 1995; Fertig, Freeman, and Gelernter 1996).

Around the turn of the century the trickle of novel approaches, prototypes, and working systems challenging the desktop metaphor turned into a steady, ever increasing flow. The emergence of pervasive computing as a distinct field further stimulated the search for new design solutions for interactive environments (e.g., Arnstein et al. 2002; Voida et al. 2002; Judd and Steenkiste 2003). New organizing principles were proposed as alternatives to a single work surface combined with a hierarchical, spatiological structure of embedded containers, underlying traditional desktop systems. Novel approaches were based on different foundational concepts, including (but not limited to): time (Fertig, Freeman, and Gelernter 1996), logical attributes (Dourish et al. 1999), people (Nardi et al. 2001), tasks and projects (Robertson et al. 2000; Voida et al. 2002; Arnstein et al. 2002; Kaptelinin 2003), and collective activities (Christensen and Bardram 2002).

Currently, these approaches are fairly loosely related to each other. Even though there are more and more cross-references between them, each of these approaches predominantly positions itself relative to the desktop metaphor rather than to other alternatives to the desktop. However, recent developments indicate that there are both theoretical and practical reasons for increased coordination between individual research efforts.

Each of the novel systems and approaches challenging or extending the desktop metaphor also contributes to the exploration of a common set of more general research issues. In this book we tentatively define these issues as involving the "design of integrated digital work environments." By "integrated" environments we mean *environments based on a coherent set of underlying principles supporting a coordinated use of tools and resources across various tasks and contexts.* The words "digital" and "work" are used here in a broad sense. "Digital" primarily means reinventing the virtual world, but its use in this book also implies taking into account both digital and physical environments. "Work" covers any higher-level activity that is part of defining what an information worker considers as his or her primary role or function, but also includes learning, leisure, and so forth.

From a practical perspective, the limited impact of novel approaches on the everyday use of technology probably means that no single concept or system can be considered a "silver bullet." The development of stimulating and supportive integrated digital work environments requires coordinated efforts from a variety of disciplines and perspectives. Therefore, identifying commonalities and interrelations between current studies of integrated digital work environments has not only conceptual but also practical implications for the design of these environments.

## The Themes and Structure of This Book

The intention of this book is to discern the analysis and design of integrated digital work environments as a distinct area of HCI research and to support the consolidation of this emerging field. The book provides a comprehensive overview of the state-of-the-art of the most relevant research and makes an attempt to facilitate the coordination of this research.

Individual chapters of the book are related to each other in several ways. Perhaps the most apparent common feature of all contributions is that each of them addresses problems with the desktop metaphor. The section above entitled "The Trouble with the Desktop Metaphor" concludes with a list of limitations of traditional desktop systems. Each of the items on the list can be mapped to research questions or design solutions in at least one of the chapters:

**Information Access versus Information Display** Two systems, presented in the book, Scalable Fabric (Robertson et al.) and Kimura (Voida et al.), combine a workspace displaying task-related information objects with a peripheral representation facilitating access to other objects and other tasks. The approaches differ in whether the peripheral representations are scaled-down images displayed on the same screen (Scalable Fabric) or dynamically generated montages displayed on other surfaces (Kimura).

**Multitasking** Several of the chapters included in this book—Robertson et al., Plaisant et al., Voida et al., Bardram, and Kaptelinin and Boardman—have chosen to emphasize information workers' tasks, roles, projects, or activities. Because multitasking is becoming so common in our daily lives, and based on the observation by all of these authors that there is so little support for it in the desktop metaphor, the systems described in these respective chapters have been designed to better enable the user to find information relevant to a specific task, quickly start, and then reacquire tasks after interruptions.

**Multiple Information Hierarchies** Supporting the integration of different information hierarchies is a key issue in most chapters. Four general design solutions are presented in the book: using the same logical attributes across different types of information objects (Freeman and Gelernter, Karger); linking information objects to roles, contacts, or projects (Plaisant et al., Robertson et al., Fisher and Nardi, Voida et al., Kaptelinin and Boardman); organizing windows into groups (Robertson et al.); and maintaining a uniform structure across existing hierarchies (Kaptelinin and Boardman).

**Communication and Collaboration** The book describes several examples of how personal work environments can be designed to facilitate collaboration. The proposed solutions include organizing digital resources around: (a) the roles of the user (Plaisant et al.), (b) the structure of social interactions of the user (Fisher and Nardi), and (c) distributed activities the user is involved in (Bardram). In the last case, work environments are personal in the sense that they support an individual carrying out his or her share of an activity as a whole. However, they can also be considered mediators of collective activities. One of the objectives of the system proposed by Bardram is to make it possible for different users to fill in and carry out a collective activity, when necessary.

**Coordinated Use of Multiple Technologies** Several chapters describe systems supporting the coordination of work carried out on different computing devices (Voida et al., Bardram). More contributors mention such support as a direction of future development of their approaches.

Thus, dealing with limitations of existing desktop systems is a common feature of the book as a whole. Another common feature of the book is its design orientation.

The book gathers under a single cover a wide range of influential approaches and systems. A dozen of them are described in the book firsthand by their developers: ABC, ContactMap, GroupBar, Haystack, Kimura, Lifestreams, Personal Role Management, Scalable Fabric, Soylent, Task Gallery, UMEA, and WorkSpaceMirror. A few other systems, though not presented by their developers, are discussed extensively, as well. One of the chapters (Ravasio and Tscherter) does not present a novel system developed by its authors, but the analysis presented is firmly grounded in the design of an existing desktop system.

The design orientation of the book does not mean a preoccupation with concrete technological artifacts at the expense of conceptual analysis. In the spirit of HCI research the book integrates "activities directed at understanding with those directed at design" (Carroll and Rosson 1992).

The book combines technological and conceptual exploration in three different (but related) ways. First, novel systems and their analyses are used to illustrate a *design solution*, a strategy that can be implemented in a range of systems. Second, concrete designs provide evidence that a new *concept* is needed to properly understand and support users of technology. In particular, several chapters make the case for using "activity" as a foundational concept in design. Third and finally, systems and designs provide ammunition for general *reflections* on the fate of the desktop metaphor and integration in digital work environments. Accordingly, the book is organized into three parts.

The five chapters that make up parts I and II describe systems that illustrate novel approaches to designing digital work environments. The chapters suggest a range of organizing principles, according to which work environments can be organized: by time (Freeman and Gelernter), by relationships and properties (Karger), by tasks (Robertson et al.), by people (Fisher and Nardi), and by roles (Plaisant et al.).

Part I, "Designing Out of the Box," discusses how work environments can facilitate access to information that in traditional desktop systems is stored in opaque containers, that is, folders. The proposed solutions are illustrated with a variety of systems: Lifestreams (Freeman and Gelernter), Haystack (Karger), the Task Gallery, GroupBar, and Scalable Fabric (Robertson et al.).

The underlying ideas of the design approaches presented in part II, "The Social Dimension of Personal Environments," by Plaisant et al., and Fisher and Nardi, is that the organization of personal work environments should reflect the social context of work and support the individual's participation in collaborative activities.

The two chapters of part III, "From Tasks to Activities," discuss the notion of activity as a conceptual tool for designing integrated digital environments. The discussion is illustrated with examples of concrete systems: Kimura (Voida et al.) and activity-based computing (Bardram).

Part IV, "Reflections on the Desktop Metaphor and Integration," includes two chapters that deal with general issues: an analysis and discussion of how users make sense of the desktop metaphor (Ravasio and Tscherter), and a comparison of application-centered integration and workspace-centered integration (Kaptelinin and Boardman).

Main issues raised in the book and directions for future research are discussed in the concluding chapter by Moran and Zhai, "Beyond the Desktop Metaphor in Seven Dimensions."

The book is one of the first to provide a systematic overview of design-based HCI research on integrated digital work environments. But it is not just an anthology of already existing systems. Its genre can be more appropriately defined as a *collective exploration of the design space of new-generation digital work environments.*

The chapters making up the book report on the latest research results from the contributors, including technological advancements, empirical evaluations, and innovative applications of their approaches. The authors elaborate on the rationale behind their systems, the strengths and limitations of their approaches, users' experiences with the systems, how the systems address problems with existing digital environments, how they compare to other novel approaches, and how the underlying ideas can be used to benefit information workers in the design of future digital work environments.

Taken as a whole, the book provides a glimpse into how the everyday use of information technologies to support information workers may look in the not-so-distant future. We hope that these systems inspire the next generation of integrated digital work environments that provide real solutions to users' needs in this domain.

## References


Arnstein, L., Hung C.-Y., Franza, R., Zhou Q.-H., Borriello, G., Consolvo, S., and Su, J. (2002). Labscape: A smart environment for the cell biology laboratory. *Pervasive Computing* 1 (3): 13–21.

Barreau, D., and Nardi, B. (1995). Finding and reminding: File organization from the desktop. *ACM SIGCHI Bulletin* 27: 39–43.

Bederson, B., and Hollan, J. (1994). Pad++: A zooming graphical interface for exploring alternate interface physics. In *Proceedings of the 7th Annual ACM Symposium on User Interface Software and Technology (UIST'94),* pp. 17–26. Marina del Rey, California, November 2–4.

Carroll, J. M., and Rosson, M. B. (1992). Getting around the task-artifact cycle: How to make claims and design by scenario. *ACM Transactions on Information Systems* 10(2): 181–212.

Christensen, H., and Bardram, J. (2002). Supporting human activities—Exploring activity-centered computing. In Borriello, G., and Holmquist, L. E. (eds.), *Proceedings of the 4th International Conference. UbiComp 2002,* pp. 107–116. Lecture Notes in Computer Science 2498. Berlin: Springer.

Czerwinski, M., Horvitz, E., and Wilhite, S. (2004). A diary study of task switching and interruptions. *Proceedings of the 2004 ACM Conference on Human Factors in Computing Systems (CHI'04),* pp. 175–182. Vienna, Austria, April 24–19.

Dourish, P., Edwards, W., LaMarca, A., and Salisbury, M. (1999). Presto: An experimental architecture for fluid interactive document spaces. *ACM Transactions on Computer–Human Interaction* 6: 133–161.

Fertig, S., Freeman, E., and Gelernter, D. (1996). "Finding and Reminding" reconsidered. *ACM SIGCHI Bulletin* 28: 66–69.

Gentner, D., and Nielsen, J. (1996). The anti-Mac interface. *Communications of the ACM* 39: 70–82.

Henderson, A., and Card, S. (1986). Rooms: The use of virtual workspaces to reduce space contention in a window-based graphical user interface. *ACM Transactions on Graphics* 5: 211–243.

Judd, G., and Steenkiste, P. (2003). Providing contextual information to pervasive computing applications. In *Proceedings of the IEEE International Conference on Pervasive Computing (PERCOM)*, pp. 133–142. Dallas, Texas, March 23–25.

Kaptelinin, V. (1996). Creating computer-based work environments: An empirical study of Macintosh users. In *Proceedings of the 1996 ACM SIGCPR/SIGMIS Conference*, pp. 360–366. Denver, Colorado, April 11–13.

Kaptelinin, V. (2003). UMEA: Translating interaction histories into project contexts. In *Proceedings of the 2003 ACM Conference on Human Factors in Computing Systems (CHI'03)*, pp. 353–360. Ft. Lauderdale, Florida, April 5–10.

Lansdale, M. (1988). The psychology of personal information management. *Applied Ergonomics* 19: 55–66.

LaStrange, T. (1989). An overview of twm (Tom's Window Manager). Http://www.lastrange.com/work/twm.pdf/.

Malone, T. (1983). How do people organise their desks? Implications for the design of office information systems. *ACM Transactions on Office Information Systems* 1: 99–112.

Nardi, B., Whittaker, S., Isaacs, E., Creech, M., Johnson, J., and Hainsworth, J. (2002). Integrating communication and information through ContactMap. *Communications of the ACM* 45: 89–95.

Norman, D. (1998). *The Invisible Computer: Why Good Products Can Fail, the Personal Computer Is So Complex, and Information Appliances Are the Solution.* Cambridge, Mass.: MIT Press.

Plaisant, C., and Shneiderman, B. (1995). Organization overviews and role management: Inspiration for future desktop environments. In *Proceedings of the 4th IEEE Workshop on Enabling Technologies: Infrastructure for Collaborative Enterprises (WET-ICE'95)*, pp. 14–22. Berkeley Springs, West Virginia, April 20–22.

Robertson, G., van Dantzich, M., Robbins, D., Czerwinski, M., Hinckly, K., Risden, K., Thiel, D., and Gorokhovsky, V. (2000). The Task Gallery: A 3D window manager. In *Proceedings of the 2000 ACM Conference on Human Factors in Computing Systems (CHI 2000)*, pp. 494–501. The Hague, the Netherlands, April 1–6.

Smith, D., Irby, C., Kimball, R., Verplank, W., and Harslem, E. (1982). Designing the Star user interface. *Byte* 7: 242–282.

Voida, S., Mynatt, E., MacIntyre, B., and Corso G. (2002). Integrating virtual and physical context to support knowledge workers. *IEEE Pervasive Computing* 1: 73–79.

*Window Managers for X: The Basics* (n.d.). Http://xwinman.org/basics.php/.

# I

# Designing Out of the Box

# Introduction to Part I

In physical offices it is not uncommon to store documents and tools in opaque containers, such as drawers, file cabinets, binders, or cardboard boxes. People often start working on a task by finding the things they need through locating appropriate containers and checking what is inside. Arguably, shuffling through nontransparent containers is an inefficient and frustrating way to manage work environments (see, e.g., Freeman and Gelernter, this volume). In desktop systems there are no bookshelves, walls, or large desks; the only directly viewable surface is the desktop, so people are forced to do even more searching through opaque "boxes." The chapters in part I suggest a number of ways to overcome this problem with traditional desktop systems and facilitate access to potentially useful information (see table I.1). They include creating subsets of chronologically organized information objects (Freeman and Gelernter), enabling the development of flexible and dynamic personal information environments

**Table I.1**
An Overview of Design Approaches Presented in Part I

| Chapter | Author(s) | System | Organizing Principle |
|---|---|---|---|
| Chapter 2 | Freeman and Gelernter | *Lifestreams* | Time and search |
| Chapter 3 | Karger | *Haystack* | Relationships and attributes |
| Chapter 4 | Robertson, Smith, Meyers, Baudisch, Czerwinski, Horvitz, Robbins, and Tan | *Task Gallery*<br>*GroupBar*<br>*Scalable Fabric* | Tasks (explicit)<br>Tasks (implicit)<br>"Focus plus context" |

by defining and using relationships and attributes (Karger), organizing information objects around explicitly or implicitly defined tasks, and placing potentially useful objects on the visual periphery of a working area (Robertson et al.).

Part I opens with Freeman and Gelernter's chapter on the Lifestreams project, which clearly articulates the need for transparent information storage. The chapter is a personal and historical account by the creators of the Lifestreams system. The concepts in this system, which organizes a user's information bits along the time axis and emphasizes search, predate many of the search engine ideas that seem so groundbreaking today. Freeman and Gelernter's perspective of how the system's design was considered back before web-based searching was available provides a delightful historical frame not only for Lifestreams but also for many of the systems that followed.

The aim of the Haystack system, presented in a chapter by Karger, is to give users maximum control in creating their personal information environments. The system allows the individual to select various information objects of interest, record their properties, and organize the objects in a way that is appropriate to his or her needs. The system is envisioned as a powerful tool that supports the development of a highly personalized information space where the person can keep, describe, structure, view, or search all of his or her information.

The chapter by Robertson, Smith, Meyers, Baudisch, Czerwinski, Horvitz, Robbins, and Tan describes three systems—GroupBar, Task Gallery, and Scalable Fabric—that can gracefully complement the user interfaces of existing desktop systems. Their designs do this with representations that help the user organize collections of resources around higher-level tasks in order to be able to switch conveniently between these collections. Each of these systems explores a different way of supporting the user: extending the functionality of the regular Microsoft Windows taskbar to organize windows into groups, which are implicitly defined tasks (GroupBar); providing a quasi-3D representation facilitating access to a set of 2D workspaces (the Task Gallery); and employing a "focus plus context" visualization (Scalable Fabric).[1]

Part I outlines a variety of paths that can be taken in the design of digital work environments. The diversity of presented approaches also poses a challenge to future research and development. Can any of the proposed solutions be employed as the single basis for design? If not, how can different approaches be combined with each other and the desktop metaphor? Arguably, some of the approaches can complement each other productively. It appears that some strengths of Lifestreams, such as providing a historical context, and Haystack, such as giving the user control over defining, recording, and managing properties, can be combined within a single system. The Task Gallery, GroupBar, and Scalable Fabric can be easily incorporated into existing desktop systems. However, more work is needed to determine how (and if) an integration of the approaches can result in further development in the design of digital work environments.

## Note

1. Another example of a system that uses peripheral visualizations is Kimura, described in chapter 7.

# 2

# Beyond Lifestreams: The Inevitable Demise of the Desktop Metaphor

Eric Freeman and David Gelernter

In 1994, we undertook what we considered a radical approach to fixing our electronic lives by creating an alternative to the desktop metaphor. Our approach, Lifestreams (Gelernter 1994; Freeman 1997), is a software architecture for managing personal electronic information. The approach was radical in the sense that Lifestreams threw out filenames, folders, and static filing and replaced them with a simple data structure: a time-ordered stream of documents combined with a few powerful operators for locating, organizing, summarizing, and monitoring information. Our prototype implementation at Yale University realized many of the system's defining features and allowed us to experiment with the model's key ideas. Later, commercial releases implemented a narrower set of Lifestreams' features, yet met real-world needs and saw limited but successful production use, which at some sites still continues—although our commercial effort has run its course.

Over ten years later one only has to look as far as Apple's "iApps" (and other projects and products) to see many Lifestreams features in action. We don't claim that our work influenced, directly or indirectly, the various vendors whose products include features that were introduced, described, and promoted in the context of Lifestreams. We only claim that the Lifestreams system was a remarkably accurate predictor of future developments. We claimed all along that Lifestreams's defining features were natural and would end up eventually in standard commercial information management systems. This is happening today; as a result there is some renewed interest in our early work. In this chapter we'll look back at our research in alternative desktop metaphors. We will describe the Lifestreams project: our initial motivations, the basis for those motivations in the industrial psychology and HCI communities, the research system, reactions to the system in the mid-1990s, and Lifestreams in today's context. Finally, we'll point out Lifestreams-like functionality in today's applications and operating systems.

## Motivations: Flashback to 1994

Both of us lack the necessary talent (or patience) for organization. In 1994, the chaos of our real desktops could only be matched by our computer desktops and file systems.[1]

We both realized that, short of hiring a whole secretariat, there was no hope for our physical workspaces. But we knew that there had to be a better way of managing our software desktops. While we admired the desktop metaphor (and were avid Macintosh users), we were sure that the desktop would be incapable of scaling up to meet the coming deluge of information from a networked world; for that matter, it had already failed us both. Files (an invention of the 1950s), hierarchical storage (of the 1960s), and the desktop metaphor (of the 1970s) were brilliant inventions, but were all created before the PC was ubiquitous, email was essentially universal, and the World Wide Web was spun. The desktop metaphor, which attempts to simplify common file operations by presenting them in the familiar language of the paper-based world (paper documents become files, folders become directories, deletion is handled via the trashcan icon) had important advantages—particularly for new users (even though it was still necessary to explain to new users just *how* the electronic desktop is like a real one, why and how each "piece of paper" has to be named, how to eject a CD, and so forth). But the desktop metaphor also constrained our future software design choices.

We were willing to concede that we were not typical computer users. But we knew that our frustrations were shared by some, in fact many, possibly even *most* computer users. To support (or discredit) our conjecture we turned to the human–computer interaction (HCI) and human factors communities where we encountered the work of Mark Lansdale, Thomas Malone, and others. We looked for evidence in areas where we thought the desktop was problematic, especially in naming, filing and finding, archiving, reminding, and summarizing.

**Filing and Finding**

Lansdale's (1998) work studied the processes of recall, recognition, and categorization in an attempt to propose software frameworks that have a basis in psychological theory. His work builds on Malone's seminal study of the way people use information: *How Do People Organize Their Desks? Implications for the Design of Online Information Systems* (1983). Malone aimed in this study for a "systematic understanding of how people actually use their desks and how they organize their personal information environments," in an attempt to improve electronic systems.

Both researchers studied categorization, which Lansdale described as "the problem that lies in deciding which categorizations to use, and in remembering later exactly what label was assigned to a categorization." This topic was particularly important to us because it was directly related to creating directories and filing documents—mainstays of the desktop metaphor. Malone's work suggested that categorizing information might be the hardest information-management task people encounter. Lansdale found that "quite simply, information does not fall into neat categorizations that can be implemented on a system by using simple labels." The work of Dumais and Landauer (1983) identified two specific reasons for this: (1) information falls into overlapping and fuzzy categories, and (2) it is impossible for users to generate categories that remain unambiguous over time. Lansdale went further and, based on empirical evidence, concluded that people are "not good at categorizing information," and that forcing users to do so is a "flawed psychological process."

The difficulty of categorizing information, and the lack of reward for bothering, typically leads users (Malone discovered) not to file information at all, in order to overcome "the difficulty of making a decision between a number of evils, and avoid the consequences of having made it." This conclusion suggests in turn that two user tasks (filing and finding) are hard and cumbersome for a good reason: most people are not good at these activities.

Note also that users are forced to categorize information in another subtle way: by means of filenames. Lansdale's work has shown that names are an ineffective way of categorizing information. Although names can be mnemonic devices, over time their value decays. Carroll (1982) found that, within a short period, a user's naming patterns became inconsistent, leading to retrieval difficulties.

### Archiving

Old information is generally less valuable than new—yet it is often essential. We can all recall occasions when we've needed information we remember having trashed only last month. Unfortunately, today's software systems do not make it easy to archive personal information. Nor do they provide a convenient method for retrieving what has been archived. Whittaker and Sidner (1996) quote one user describing his difficulties: "I'm reluctant to archive junk . . . I know that the consequence of archiving junk is to make it that much harder to find good stuff. . . . " The result: users are left to invent their own schemes or use third-party applications. Neither method is apt to yield satisfactory performance on retrieval tasks.

Worse, users often delete old information rather than be forced to deal with the implications of storing it or inventing archiving schemes (Erickson 1991; Barreau and Nardi 1995). This is unfortunate and painfully ironic. Computers should make it much easier and cheaper to archive information. Today virtually anyone who wants a terabyte of storage can have it. Hardware is carrying out its obligations, but software (as usual) lets the user down.

### "Reminding"

Malone (1983) pointed out the importance of "reminding" in our paper-based systems and suggested that reminding be included in software. Yet desktop systems still provide little support for reminding. Although many time-management, scheduling, and to-do list applications have come to market, they don't provide general solutions to the reminding problem.

In more recent work, Barreau and Nardi (1995) observed that desktop computer users often use a file's location on the desktop as a critical reminding function. At the end of the day, for instance, a Macintosh user may leave files on his desktop as a reminder of work to be done next morning. Others leave email messages in their in-boxes (Whittaker and Sidner 1996) for the same reason. Lansdale found this behavior largely idiosyncratic. We have noticed that such a location-based method of reminding is easily undermined. In any case, since the desktop metaphor has no inherent semantic notion of reminding, users who leave electronic documents lying around in "strategic locations" are merely coping, on the fly. Presumably our software should be able to do better than this.

### Summarizing

Summarizing is a vital information-processing task. Summaries abbreviate a document or collection of documents and reduce the amount of information a user must process (Klark and Manber 1995). They also allow users to "gain access to and control the flood of information"; "summaries save time" (Hutchins 1995) in the end.

Summarizing information is obviously not new—yet today there are few electronic systems that support automatic summarization. Current desktop systems provide no general purpose support for summaries; they leave the job to special-purpose applications.

We believe this lack of support has occurred, in part, because of the current, narrow application-centric view of desktop computing—work has focused on developing tools within applications rather than on globally improving users' access to information at a systems level. Summaries are available to users through special-purpose products such as Intuit's Quicken, which allows the creation of overviews for financial information. But users need summaries for more routine purposes too.

## Beyond the Desktop Metaphor

We prefer to approach software design not by *metaphorics*, but by Nelson's (1990) concept of *virtuality*. Metaphorics is a method of building software based on comparisons of software to objects or machines in the real world (e.g., to the physical desktop in the world of office furniture). Metaphorics are useful in some contexts, but can also cramp design: once the metaphor has been chosen, every part of the system has to play an appropriate part within the metaphor. When designers are forced to add unexpected functions to the metaphor (e.g., to eject a CD) the solutions can be confusing or even ridiculous. (Why should dragging a CD icon to the trash cause the CD to eject? The user doesn't want to *throw away* the CD.) Nelson argues that "adherence to a metaphor prevents the emergence of things that are genuinely new."

Virtuality, on the other hand, is the construction of unifying ideas that can be embodied in rich graphic expressions and are no mere metaphors for a preexisting physical system, ideas that can rather lead (as Nelson argues) to the invention of new organizing strategies. This was our goal in designing Lifestreams: to provide a simple, unified system that is easily grasped by users and is unconstrained by any real-world metaphor.

To create a unified model we began with the following guiding principles, driven first by our own design sense and secondarily by the results we found in the HCI and human factors communities.

**Storage should be transparent** Naming a file when it is created and stuffing it in a folder are two prime examples of pointless overhead. Names should be invented only when users feel like inventing them. In the real world, "formal documents" (chapters, papers, grant proposals, books, poems) typically have names, but "informal documents" (drafts, letters, lists, calculations, reminder notes) typically do not. As computing becomes increasingly ubiquitous, an ever-larger proportion of our electronic documents are "informal," and the requirement that we invent names for each one of them becomes ever more ludicrous. When you grab a piece of paper, there is no need for you to give it a name or decide where to store it before you start writing. On the electronic desktop, many (arguably most) filenames are not merely pointless (e.g., "draft1.doc," "draft2.doc") but useless for retrieval purposes. Folder names, for their part, are effective as retrieval cues only for as long as users remember them—which is often not very long.

**Folders and directories are inadequate organizing techniques** Our electronic desktops are too faithful to the paper-based world: they force each document to be stored in exactly one folder. (At least this is true for novices; only experts are familiar with concepts like file aliases—and using them is clumsy even for experts.) In the electronic world, documents can and should be allowed to live in more than one place at one time. In a Lifestreams system, for example, a Powerpoint presentation on Lifestreams might live in the "Lifestreams" folder, the "presentations" folder, and the "current tasks" folder simultaneously. Conventional software systems force users to store information in static categories (namely, directories). But often we can't tell where information belongs until we need it. (Notes about a meeting to discuss an application called Zowie for the Mac, where Smith, Piffel, and Schwartz were present, might be stored—in a conventional system—in the folder called "Zowie," or maybe one called "Mac applications." In retrospect you might need to consult your records of all meetings that Piffel attended. But suppose you didn't know that at the time. For this obvious reason, the brain categorizes memories dynamically and not statically. I can ask you to recall "all meetings that took place in room 300" even if you never consciously classified meetings by room numbers.) In short, information should be organized as needed, not *a priori* at the time it is created. Directories should be created *on demand,* and documents should belong to as many directories as appropriate.

**Archiving should be automatic** Current systems fail miserably at data archiving (especially in comparison to paper-based systems). In the desktop metaphor it is the user's responsibility to create an archiving scheme and follow it. Faced with this task, many users simply throw away old data rather than archiving it (and then trying to remember how to locate it once it's been archived). Software should let documents to age gracefully and be archived when they are less frequently used—but allow users to retrieve any archived item quickly.

**Computers should make "reminding" an integral part of the desktop experience** It has been known for some time that reminding is a critical function of computer-based systems (Malone 1983); yet this functionality is still delivered only in third party applications such as calendars and task managers, and is not yet part of our integrated electronic environments. User studies have pointed out the many coping strategies users rely on to achieve some kind of reminder functions (this holds even for users who depend on third-party applications). Reminding should be a basic function in any electronic information system.

**Personal data should be available from anywhere, to any device, and compatibility should be automatic** In 1994, we knew that users would need to access, view, and manage their information from many network-connected devices. At the time this included emerging tablet computers, which led the way to PDAs (personal digital assistants) such as the PalmPilot and Microsoft's PocketPC. Today, we have a whole new set of network-enabled devices, dominated by the cell phone. Personal electronic information should be available to us on any net-enabled device, regardless of which one we choose. It follows that our information-management model must scale not only to a high-resolution PC display but also to small, low-resolution devices.

**The system should provide a means of summarizing a set of documents into a concise overview** An important aspect of managing information is the capacity to construct a "big picture" view of that information. For example: a time series of mutual fund closing quotes can be summarized in a historical graph. A set of songs can be summarized in a playlist that can be printed for a CD jewel case. A set of pay stubs and payments can be summarized in a partially completed tax return. And so on. "Summarize" can (and ought to) be an exceptionally powerful function if we define it imaginitively. Our software should include a sophisticated summarize routine, and enable higher-order operations (such as data mining and analysis) that use summarized data as input.

With these guiding principles in hand, let's look at the Lifestreams model.

## The Lifestreams Model

Let's start with the basic data structure of the Lifestreams model: a *lifestream* is a time-ordered stream of documents that functions as a diary of your electronic life. ("Document," meaning electronic document, is defined in the broadest possible way: a photo, video, audio, or application call all be "documents.")

Every document you create or receive is stored in your lifestream (see figure 2.1). The tail of your stream contains documents from the past (perhaps starting with your electronic birth certificate). Moving forward from the tail toward the present, your stream contains more recent documents—papers in progress, for example, or new electronic mail. Each document is stored at the time you first created or first received it. Thus all documents (pictures, correspondence, bills, movies, voice mail, and software) are stored at appropriate points along the way. Moving beyond the present into the future, the stream contains documents you *will* need: reminders, appointments, calendar items, to-do lists.

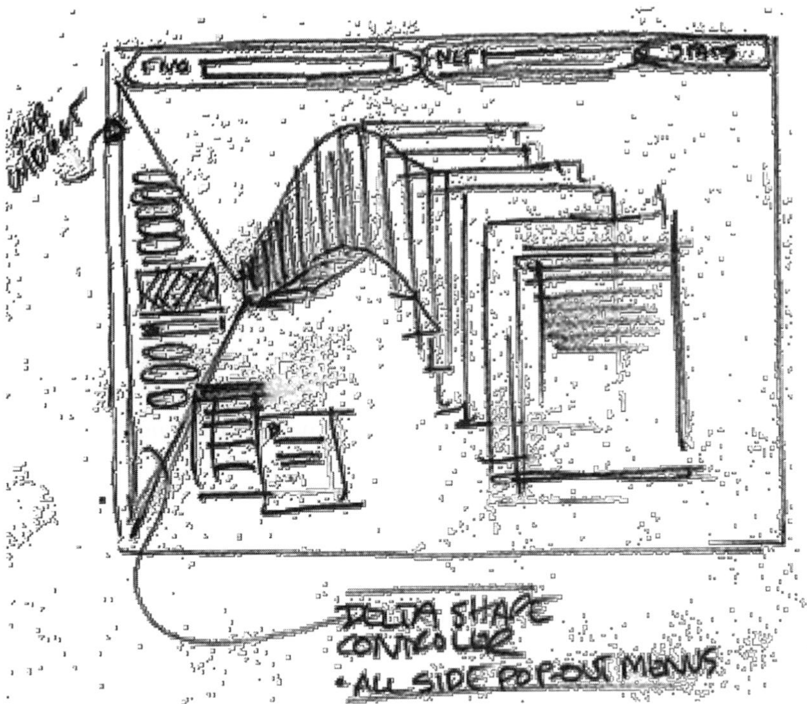


**Figure 2.1**
An early conceptual drawing of a lifestream.

To this model we add a small number of operations that, combined with the time-ordered stream, accomplish transparent storage, organization through directories on demand, archiving, reminding, and summaries—in a natural way.

To create documents, users use one of two operations: **new** and **copy**. **New** creates a new, empty document and adds it at the head of your stream. (Every stream has a now-line, marked by the current time. As the stream ages, the now-line moves steadily farther away from the tail—i.e., from the very first document in the stream. **New** creates an empty document and adds it to the stream at the now-line.) **Copy** takes an existing document, creates a duplicate, and adds it to your stream at the now-line. The source document in the **copy** operation can live in a different stream; **copy**, in other words, can be used to transfer a copy of a document between streams. Creation is always "transparent" because documents, by default, are always added to the end of the stream (at the now-line) and don't have to be named (unless the user chooses to name them) or be stuffed into a folder.

Lifestreams are organized on the fly with the **find** operation. **Find** prompts for a search query, such as "email from Piffel" or "Leigh Nash mp3s," and creates a *substream*. Substreams present a "view" of the stream as a whole—a view that contains all documents that are relevant to the search query. Substreams are different from conventional directory systems: users don't place documents into static substreams (although in some circumstances they can add documents to substreams by hand). Instead, virtual groups of related documents are created as needed, on the fly.

Documents aren't actually stored in substreams. A substream is a temporary collection of documents that already exist on the main stream. Substreams may overlap; they can be created and destroyed on the fly without affecting the main stream or other substreams.

Substreams are more than merely the result of a search operation. **Find** doesn't merely return a list of results; **find** creates a new data structure, namely, a substream. If you allow a substream to persist, it will collect new documents that match your search criteria as you create them or they arrive from outside. In consequence the substream is a natural way of monitoring information—it acts not only as an *organizational device* but as a *filter for incoming information*. For example: a substream created with the query "find all documents created by Piffel" would collect new emails from Piffel as they arrive.

The last operation, **summarize**, takes a substream and compresses it into an overview document. The shape and content of this overview document depends on the type of documents in the substream. If a substream (for instance) contains the daily closing prices of all stocks and mutual funds in your investment portfolio, the overview document might contain a chart showing the historical performance of your securities, and your net worth. If a the substream contains a list of tasks you must complete, the overview document might be a prioritized "to-do" list. If the substream contains all mp3s of "Leigh Nash," the overview might be a printable playlist à la iTunes.

**Chronology as a Storage Model**

One of the most common questions (and criticisms) of Lifestreams has always been: "why use creation time as the basis for storage? Isn't some other metric more useful? Isn't creation time too constraining?" Some realizations of the Lifestreams model allow you to re-sort the stream by some other key—title, size, whatever you want. But this is beside the point. The real point is this: human beings live their lives in time; their experiences exist in time; a Lifestream is explicitly *an electronic diary*. It's not just a file cabinet for information; it tracks your daily experience as it unfolds. Such a record is inherently useful—that's why people keep journals and diaries.[2] The stream adds historical context to everything it contains; like a diary, a stream documents the flow of your work, business transactions, thoughts—a function that is largely missing in today's operating systems. Often we need not merely isolated documents from the past; we need to see the context in which those documents were created. Often we can't understand a year-old document (a one-line email, a brief note, incomplete records of a meeting) unless we can see the context from which it emerged.

Historical context can in fact be crucial in an organizational setting (Cook 1995). But most current systems do little to track when, where, and why documents are created and deleted.

Note that a time-based stream also gives us three natural categorizations for documents: past, present, and future. The "present" portion of the stream is the zone at and immediately behind (i.e., older than) the now-line. It holds "working documents"; this is also where new documents are ordinarily created and incoming documents are placed. As documents age and newer documents are added, older documents recede from the user's view and are "archived" in the process. (Here we mean archiving in the conceptual sense; users don't have to worry about old information cluttering their desktops or getting in the way. If at some future point they need the archived information, it can be located using **find.**) The "future" portion of the stream allows documents to be created in the future. "Future creation" is a natural method of posting reminders and scheduling information. The system allows users to dial to the future and use the **new** operation to deposit a document there—a meeting reminder, say. The "future" is a particularly convenient way to deal with email that arrives at a point when you're too busy to respond. You can copy such a message into the future—into "tomorrow morning," for example. Tomorrow morning the copy will appear at the now-line; the email serves as its own reminder. (Yahoo has added a function similar to this Lifestreams operation.)

### Unification

As we mentioned earlier, our goal was to provide a simple, unified system that is easily grasped by users and solves the problems of filing, finding, reminding, archiving, and summarizing. The interested reader should refer to previous writings, in particular the Lifestreams dissertation (Freeman 1997), for details. But it is important to consider how the model achieves our goals.

First, naming. In Lifestreams there is no such concept. Lifestreams stores information transparently: any time a document is created or received, it is automatically added to the stream. This procedure reduces the overhead of creating information (which, as we mentioned, is one of a user's most difficult and ultimately least-productive tasks). Users are freed to concentrate on the task at hand instead of the name, folder, disk, machine, or network location of a particular document or data item.

Second, filing. Lifestreams keys information storage to *the time the information is created or arrrives* and organizes information *in the context in which it arrived or was created*. How? To organize information, the user does a **find**, which creates in effect a virtual directory (a substream). Unlike directories or folders, substreams don't pigeon-hole information into specific locations. Documents can exist in multiple substreams at once. By eliminating naming and filing, the Lifestreams model reduces the overhead of creating information, improves recall, and makes retrieval easier. Lifestreams' method of organizing documents has a second advantage: once you create a substream, you can allow it to persist and become (automatically) a filter or monitor, accumulating any new documents that happen to match its search criterion.

Reminding is one of Lifestreams' most novel features. By extending the stream into the future, the system allows documents to be created, copied, or placed in the future—and when their time rolls around, these documents become natural reminders. (We'll see how this works in the interface shortly.) Lifestreams, we believe, is the first general-purpose information model to treat reminders as first-class entities and to provide a metaphor that naturally accommodates reminding.

Lifestreams also solves the conceptual "archiving problem" by means of its time-organized stream. As documents age, they move out of the user's view (again we'll see how an interface might handle this shortly), and recede into the stream's past. The result is a natural means of moving data out of view as it is no longer needed, while keeping it available for future retrieval.

Lifestreams also provides a new opportunity for users to exploit relationships and global patterns that exist in document collections by offering an architectural framework for creating executive summaries and overviews. Lifestreams itself isn't concerned with data mining or the many algorithms for summary-creation. Instead it provides an enabling data structure over which such analysis can be accomplished. Our Yale prototype provided several means of generating summaries, but this area remains largely uninvestigated—and was not included in our commercial system.

Another way to think about the unifying aspect of Lifestreams is to consider how a few simple operations allow you to manage your whole electronic life. The same operation that creates a substream (**find**) also creates your mailbox, your web bookmarks, your entire set of Powerpoint presentations, and everything else in between. Consider a substream that includes all documents that include the word "lifestreams"—it will include documents you created, documents you were sent, web bookmarks for Lifestreams pages, all email that mentions lifestreams, and so on. In each case, if you can create a substream, you can create a persistent filter that continues to collect new documents. We'll also see shortly how you can see at a glance how much new information has collected in any substream—as if you were checking email. And at any time you can peek into the future to see what's coming up, or take a spin in the past with a simple click of the mouse; and clicking **summarize** on any stream gives you a context-sensitive overview.

## The Lifestreams Interfaces

The development of the Lifestreams interface was one of the most important and challenging aspects of the project. Creating a new interface involves navigating a large design space which we have only begun to explore.

Our Yale research prototype consisted of a client/server architecture that ran over the Internet. The server was the workhorse of the Lifestreams system. It managed one or more streams, storing all stream documents and substreams. Each interface acted as a client and provided views of the stream.

As we'll explain, our interface presented a definite look and feel for a stream. But we were actually agnostic regarding the appearance of the interface; we envisioned many different possibilities. In fact we believed that the look and feel of the interface would differ radically over a wide range of computing platforms, from set-top boxes to high-end workstations. But each interface would support the basic operations. (Again, one goal of the model was to support interfaces that handled many different devices with dramatically different capabilities.)

Our Yale work explored four interface implementations: an X Windows client, a pure text command line client, a PDA implementation, and a web browser implementation. The X Windows interface provided a rich graphical interface (for the time); it implemented the full range of operations functionalities. The ASCII interface also implemented the complete Lifestreams model, but with a text-based, mail-like interface. The PDA version was implemented on the Apple Newton; it provided rudimentary stream access, given the Newton's lack of internal memory and low bandwidth. The later commercial versions of Lifestreams were focused mostly on web browsers, but included a fair amount of support for cell phones and more modern PDAs.

Describing the interfaces and their functionality in detail is far beyond the scope of this chapter. But we'll examine the X Windows interface and touch briefly on others. The X Windows interface may appear crude next to today's GUIs, but its functionality remains unmatched—even by the commercial Lifestreams implementations!

### The X Windows Interface

Our X Windows interface is shown in figure 2.2. The interface is based on a visual representation of the stream metaphor (and is reminiscent of early Lifestreams sketches such as the one in figure 2.1). Users can slide the mouse pointer over the document representations to "glance" at a thumbnail of each document's content, or use the scroll bar in the lower left-hand corner to scroll forward or backward in time. All interface feed-

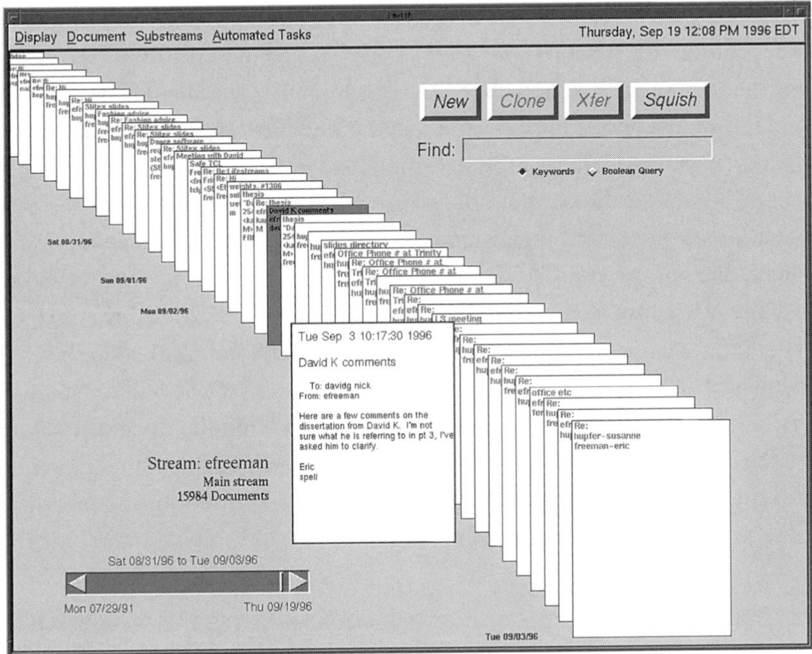


**Figure 2.2**
The X Windows interface of Lifestreams.

back (scrolling through time included) was immediate and close to real time.

We used color and animation for important document features. A red border meant "unseen" and a bold one meant "writable." Open documents were offset to the side to show that they were being edited. External helper applications were used to view and edit documents, which sped up the learning process significantly for Lifestreams users—they could use applications they were familiar with (such as emacs, xv, and ghostview) to create and view documents, while using Lifestreams to organize and communicate documents. Lifestreams (the document-organization model) was orthogonal to the document-creation and document-viewing applications.

Incoming documents slid in from the left side via animation, with a "swoosh" sound. Newly created documents popped down from on top and pushed the stream backward by one document into the past. To view (or edit) a document, the user simply clicked on its representation.

The interface prominently displayed the primary system operations—**New, Clone** (our original term for "copy"), **Xfer** (i.e., transfer—copy to another stream), **Find, Squish** (meaning summarize), and a few useful secondary operations as buttons and menus. The **New** button created a new document and added it to the stream. **Clone** duplicated an existing document and placed the copy on the stream. **Xfer** prompted the user for one or more addresses and then forwarded a document (to another stream or email, as appropriate).

**Find** was supported through a text-entry box that allowed the user to enter a boolean search query (or keyword search). **Find** resulted in the creation and display of a new substream, as shown in figure 2.3. In this figure we've searched for the terms "david and meme," and the documents that match the query constitute the substream. If a new document that matches this query arrives in the meantime, it slides right into the substream—just as it would have slid into the main stream.

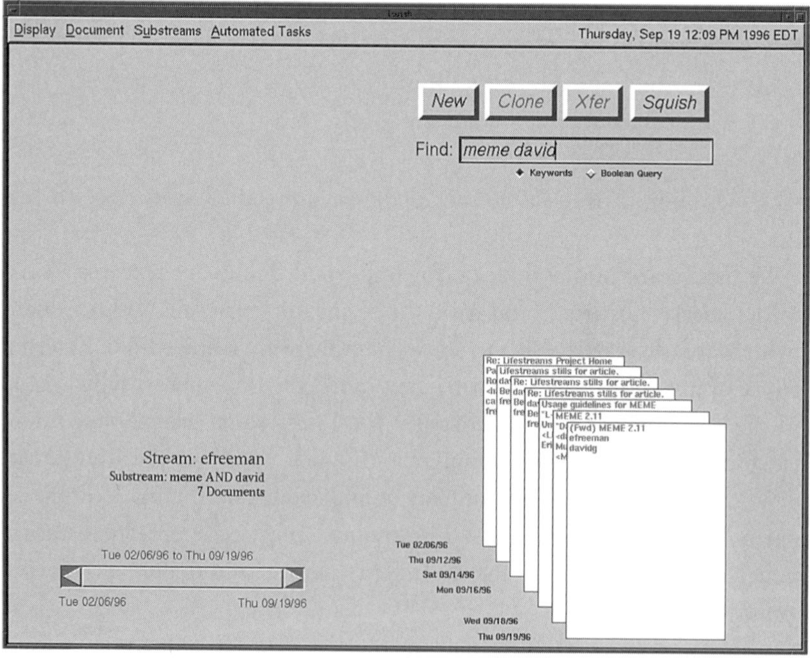


**Figure 2.3**
Creation and display of a new substream.

Menu operations were used to select persistent substreams, create summaries, and travel through time (an operation we'll explain shortly). Figure 2.4 shows the Substreams menu, which is divided into three sections. The first contains a list of operations that can be performed on substreams (such as **Remove**). The next contains one entry labeled "Your Lifestream," and focuses the display on your entire Lifestream (i.e., all of your documents). The last lists all of your substreams. Note that substreams can be created incrementally—which results in a nested set of menus. In this example, the nested menus were created by first creating a substream "lifestreams and david" from the main stream, then incrementally creating two substreams from this substream: "scenarios" and "ben." Finally, the substream "pda" was created from the "scenarios" substream. Semantically, this incremental substreaming amounts to a boolean AND of each new query with the previous substream's query.

While this may look like a classic hierarchy of information, note that the same document may appear in many streams. A substream can be removed at any time with the **Remove** menu item, but if it is left to persist

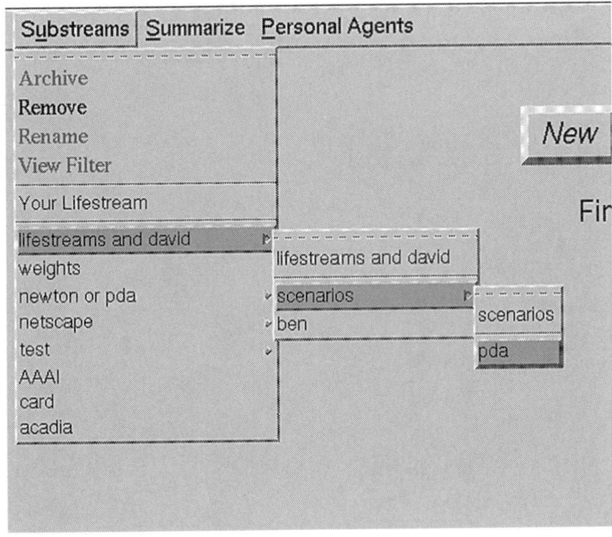


**Figure 2.4**
The Substreams menu.

it will continue to accrue new documents that match its search criteria as they are added to the main stream.

Lifestreams displays the time in the upper right hand corner of the interface. This time display also acts as a menu (figure 2.5) that allows the user to set the interface time to the future or past via a calendar-based dialogue box. Imagine a cursor always pointing to the position in the stream such that all documents (see figure 2.6) beyond that point toward the head have a future timestamp and all documents before it, toward the tail, have a past timestamp. As time progresses this cursor moves forward toward the head; as it slips past "future" documents they are added to the visible part of the stream, just as if a new document had arrived.

The effect of setting the time to the future or past is to reset the time-cursor temporarily to a fixed position designated by the user. Normally the user interface displays all documents from the past up to the time-cursor. Setting the time-cursor to the future allows the user to see documents in the "future" part of the stream. Creating a document in this mode (i.e., "in the future") results in a document with a future timestamp. Once the user is finished time-tripping, he can reset to the present by selecting the "Set time to present" menu option in the time menu.

Figure 2.7 demonstrates the summary operation (in this version, called **Squish**); this figure shows a summary of a substream that contains daily

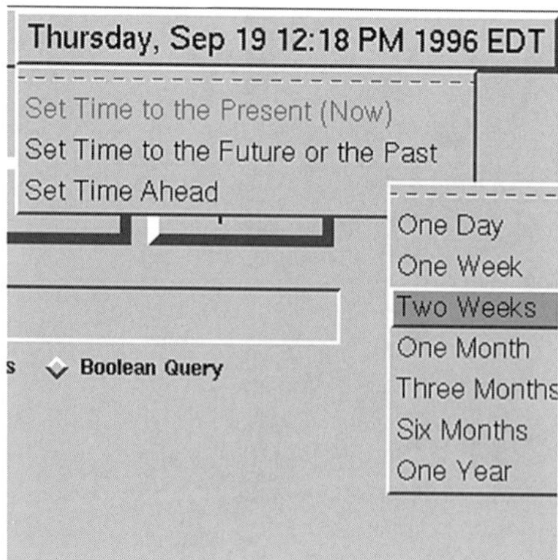


**Figure 2.5**
Setting the interface time.

closing values of stocks from an early Internet portfolio service. The summary graphs these values over time.

Summaries are context sensitive, so while a lifestream may have many summaries available, only the summaries that are relevant to a particular substream are presented to the user as possible operations. In this implementation, the **Squish** button has actually changed to "Squish stocks" to indicate that a specific summary is available. If multiple summaries are appropriate then the user is presented with a list of choices. Finally, if no summaries are appropriate then the **Squish** button remains grayed out.

## Common Tasks

Lifestreams can be used to accommodate common computer tasks, such as communication, creating reminders, managing scheduling, tracking contacts, and managing personal finances (to name a few). For instance, using email in Lifestreams is not much different from what users are already accustomed to. To send a message, the user creates

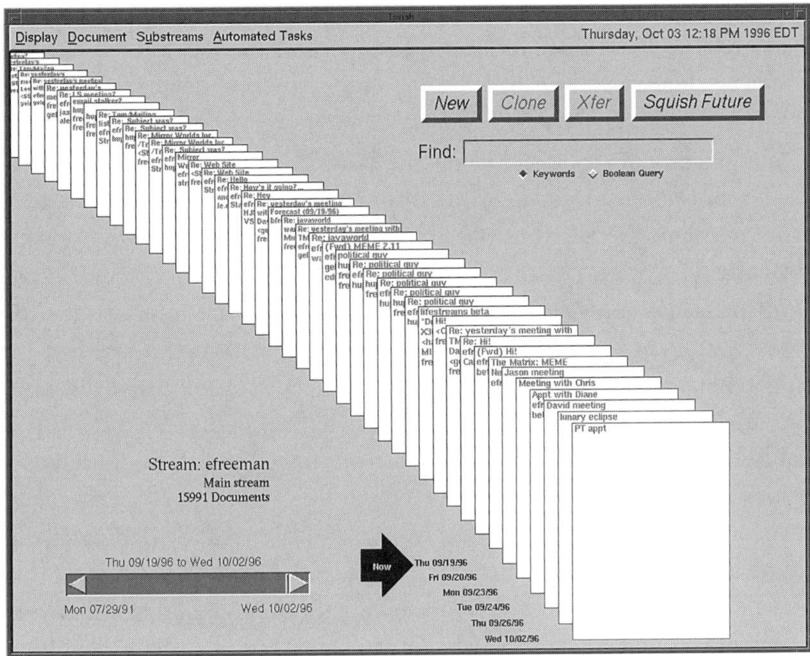


**Figure 2.6**
Displaying documents having a future timestamp.

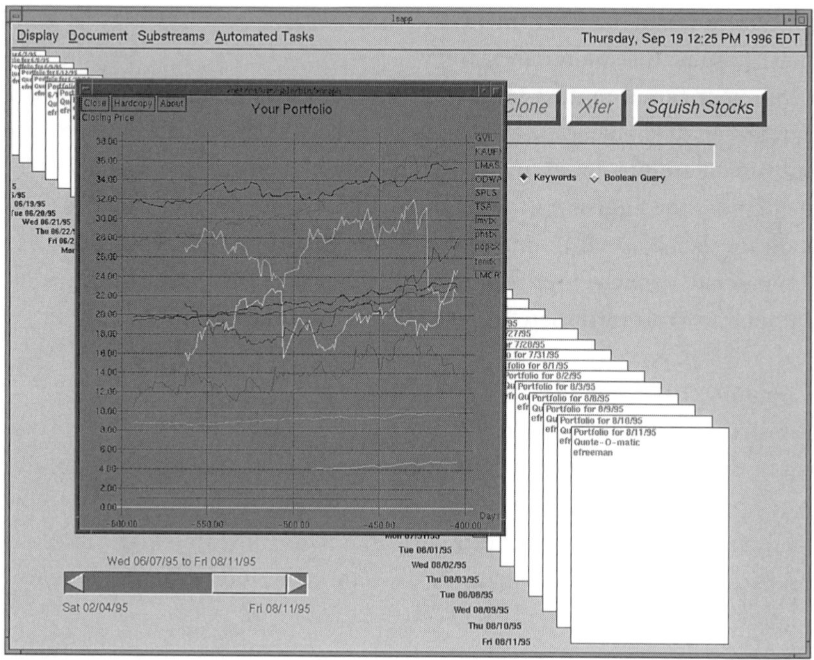


**Figure 2.7**
The summary operation.

a new document (by clicking on the **New** button) and then composes the message using a favorite editor. The message can then be sent with a push of the **Xfer** button. Similarly, existing documents are easily forwarded to other users, or documents can be cloned and replied to. While all email messages (incoming and outgoing) are intermixed with other documents in the stream, the user can easily create a mailbox by substreaming on documents created by other users; or, users can take this one step further and create substreams that contain a subset of the mailbox substream, such as "all mail from Bob," or "all mail I haven't responded to."

As another example, reminders can easily be created by dialing to the future and depositing documents that act as reminders (we automated this into one step in the prototype). A user can also send mail that will arrive in the future. If he "dials" to the future before writing a message, then when the message is transferred it won't appear on the recipients' stream until either that time arrives or they happen to dial their interface to the set creation date. In the present, the document will be in the stream data structure but the interface won't show it. We used this feature to send mail to the future to post reminders to others about important meetings, department talks, and so on. Because they appear "just in time" and don't require the user to switch to yet another application, these reminders are more effective than those included in a separate calendar or scheduling utility program.

There are many other examples of common tasks covered in the dissertation and we refer the interested reader there, as a detailed description would fill an entire chapter in itself.

### Alternative Interfaces

As we've mentioned in passing, one of the goals of the Lifestreams model was to scale to the capabilities of devices other than desktop computers. In contrast, how do you work with the desktop metaphor from a cell phone? Further, we wanted to provide a universal data structure over which many types of interface could be explored. In addition to the text-based and PDA implementations, we also did a fair amount of exploration of other interfaces in implementation and on paper. For example, figure 2.8 shows a fully functional calendar interface, implemented as a senior project at Yale (Larratt-Smith 1996), that provides an alternative to the "stream view" interface. This interface was particularly handy for reminding and scheduling tasks.

We also envisioned more ambitious interfaces that, at the time, were beyond the current technology (as well as our own graphical coding skills). One example, seen in figure 2.9, was created by Jim Dustin, a graphical designer working with us in 1997, and looks remarkably like a modern-day Apple OS X application.

In sum, while our interface experiences were quite diverse and varied, the space of user-interface designs still remains largely untapped.

## Analysis

While many of the motivations and ideas behind Lifestreams are common sense today, in the early to mid-1990s they were considered a bit fringe. In an interview with *Technology Review,* David Gelernter described Eric Freeman's work as follows: "it was a risky, radical departure and not an

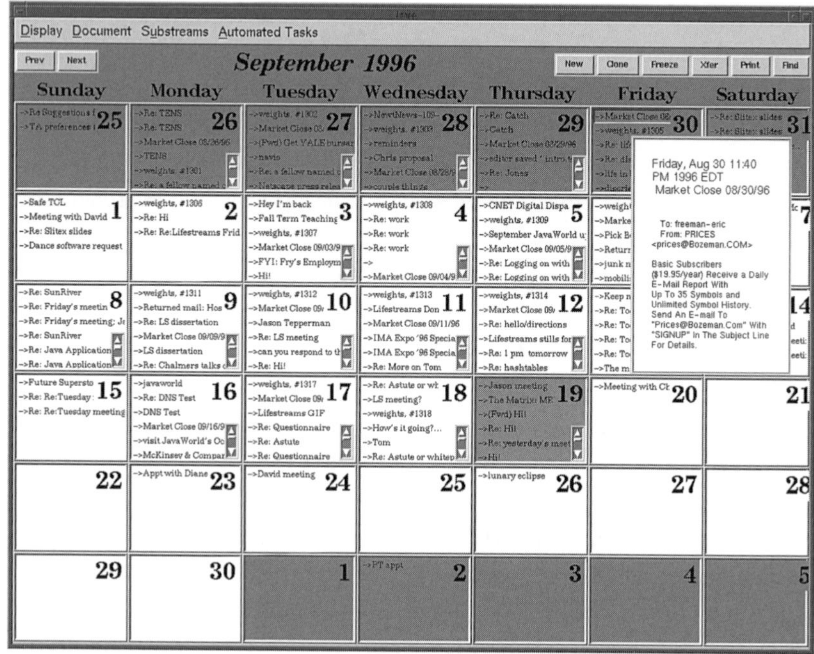


Figure 2.8
The calendar interface.

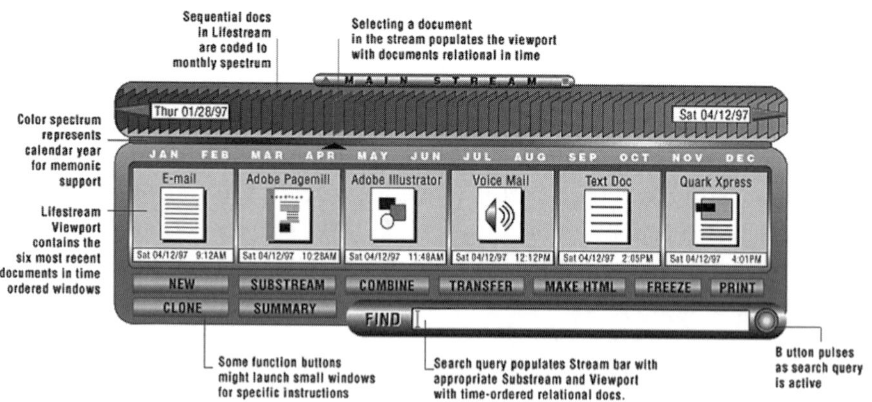


Figure 2.9
An alternative Lifestreams interface.

incremental improvement" (*Technology Review* 1999). While David has a talent for compliment, nevertheless, undertaking Lifestreams in a largely theoretical computer science department (with no faculty members in the HCI community) certainly felt dangerous.[3]

While we were concerned with the faculty's acceptance of the work, in general we were far more concerned with the reaction of everyday users. Our feedback on Lifestreams came largely from three populations: a small user base in the computer science department itself (we recruited not only technically savvy users, but also the department's administrative employees), a population of people who had heard about Lifestreams in the popular press but had never used the system, and a fairly large population of individuals in the computer and financial industries who we approached and gave demos to in our attempts to raise capital for a post-Ph.D. business venture.[4] Most of our analysis came from the group of administrative staff at Yale, who used our prototype for an extended period of time.

To measure user satisfaction we relied on the *Questionnaire for User Satisfaction* (QUIS), a standardized usability testing tool available for licensed use from the University of Maryland. Users had an overall high subjective reaction to the system. The following user comment reflects a high level of satisfaction and was consistent with many of the reactions we received from the other populations:

> The concept (of Lifestreams) appealed to me immediately on two levels. First, because I know myself that I naturally order and recall events in my life according to time cues, that "memories" become less important to my daily activities the further in the past they recede (yet retain punch and applicability at discrete moments when recalled because of similarity to current events), and that I find it so incredibly annoying not to be able to recall something that might be applicable because the "index" to that memory has been lost, or that a relevant document is no longer available because it has been thrown away (just weeks before to remove "clutter" or save space).

Users also quickly "got" the system, scoring (in QUIS) most highly on the system's ability to be quickly learned. One user, who was part of Yale's administrative staff, spoke directly to this point (underline in original response):

> The time at which I started using Lifestreams was at the beginning of the semester, my busiest time. . . . All this considered, I was still bowled over by all of the ways it could, and did, make my job easier in a very short period of time.

We also saw evidence that the system did have an effect on users' views of managing electronic information:

> the time I now spend on this system of mine has really changed. I hate hunting through this "tree." It is cumbersome at best and annoying at least. I have seen a better way. I didn't realize how much time I spend searching for documents.

Beyond our user study, we also found the system itself "hit home" with many who had never even used the system but had read about it in the popular press. Email like the following were quite common:

> I have so much stuff coming in my "InBox" daily, whether it's incoming e-mail, snailmail, phone messages, articles, or what-have-you; that there's not really time to organize it all. Rather, as you quite convincingly point out, I'd rather just STORE it all (since storage is cheap!) and access only what I want when I want to access it.

In addition to the QUIS surveys, we also instrumented Lifestreams in order to capture a quantitative measure of the effectiveness of the system. Overall, data suggested that substreams were an effective and efficient mechanism for locating information (although certain improvements could have been made with better indexing technology). You'll find these issues and others, such as the variety of user styles we saw when observing users of the system, detailed in the dissertation.

In sum, Lifestreams appeared to elicit a highly positive subjective reaction from those who used the system, but also from those who just envisioned using it. More quantitative analysis suggested further that in fact Lifestreams was efficient as a means of managing information. That said, while these results were promising, there remained much to be done in terms of studying the utility of Lifestreams among users, particularly in comparison to the traditional desktop.

### Differing Opinions

One of the most interesting discussions on Lifestreams (or perhaps more accurately, its foundations) was a short public debate in *SIGCHI Bulletin* with Deborah Barreau and Bonnie Nardi based on their studies (which examined users of the desktop metaphor and drew conclusions based upon their work habits).[5] Barreau and Nardi's (1995) study was particularly interesting to us because they observed many of the same user behaviors we had. More specifically, their study, performed over 22 subjects, noted the following similarities among desktop users:

- a preference for location-based search for finding files (in contrast to logical, text-based search);
- the use of file placement as a critical *reminding function*; and
- the "lack of importance" of archiving files.

This was also interesting to us, because at face value, it obviously contradicts our initial conjecture (as well as the previous work of Lansdale and Malone). While we believed their findings were valid, we found the extrapolation from *user behavior* to *user preference* misleading. Steven Steinberg (1997) commented in *Wired* magazine that from our perspective this study was "like studying people listening to the radio and deciding that they didn't want pictures."

That's exactly how we saw it—of course users in 1995 preferred location-based search (that is, finding files by the folder they are located in) to logical search; what choice did they have? While there were certainly some tools for text-based search on the desktop at that time, they were crude at best. Today, with the "Googlization" of the desktop (and nearly ten years of user education through using WebCrawler, Infoseek, Altavista, and now Google), it seems preferences may be changing.

In terms of location-based reminding, this was an excellent result and shows the user's need for reminding as a core function. But, concluding that location was the best ways to accomplish this was premature. As we've said before, surely there are better ways.

Last, to claim that archiving files wasn't important seemed, again, to be a result of the lack of support in current systems at that time. Archiving files is obviously valuable, especially if we can find ways to make the process transparent and improve means of locating archived materials.

Finally, Barreau and Nardi (1995) observed one additional aspect of their subjects, noting their

- use of three types of information: ephemeral, working, and archived.

We still find this an interesting and important conclusion; we believe *ephemeral*, *working*, and *archived* to be crucial classifications for desktop information, and these classifications provide clues to which abilities our software systems need to support to manage these different types of information.

### Commercial Efforts

Lifestreams, although of limited commercial success to date, nevertheless experienced modest sales and a devoted user base, many of whom are still using the system today. These commercial systems were aimed primarily at corporate and enterprise users (although they still supported personal information) and present the Lifestreams interface in a web browser.

Since the primary author left the company in 2000, exposure to this customer base is quite limited; however, user reactions to the commercial system were largely positive and mirror the Yale user studies. Post mortems on factors that have limited Lifestreams acceptance (beyond any marketing or business development factors) have uncovered issues of integration with existing corporate systems (such as Outlook/Exchange and Lotus Notes) as well as the underlying operating system. This last point shouldn't be taken lightly: Lifestreams is very much an integral part of the desktop information environment, and any attempts to bolt on this functionality in an application or utility will never be as powerful (or as accepted by users) as having Lifestreams-like models implemented as an integral part of the operation system (both Microsoft and Apple seem to be moving in this direction of integrating many lifestreams-like functionalities at the OS level).

## Lifestreams Today

In the late '90s when we were busily working on our own Lifestreams startup, we claimed that even if our efforts failed, *our idea would become mainstream, because it was such a natural idea*. Looking around the landscape today, our company is dead, but many of the ideas are blossoming nicely—considering such projects as Haystack, Chandler, MyLifeBits, parts of Microsoft's Longhorn, Apple's Spotlight and iApps, and the Google desktop (to name only a few). Some of these projects were influenced directly by Lifestreams. But there is a more powerful force at work too: the management of information demands an underlying model that is more capable than the desktop metaphor. We live our lives in time. Lifestreams was, is, and will continue to be inevitable.

Our contribution was (secondarily) the recognition and identification of problems inherent in the desktop metaphor (based on seminal work of researchers like Malone, and our own observations), and mainly our proposal of a new model that breaks away from the constraints of that metaphor. Today, things are moving in the right direction. The Google desktop suggests that users are starting to internalize new models for information management.

Search has become the holy grail of the desktop. The leading search companies are moving into desktop search as a way to extend their reach, and operating systems makers are moving aggressively in this direction as well. Integrating search into the desktop environments is by no means a new development—Microsoft has been pursuing WinFS in fits and starts for over more than ten years—but this time, something is different: everyone thinks it's important.

Why is there a growing interest in desktop search? Many attribute this interest to the "googlization" of the desktop. The thinking goes: If my desktop is becoming as complex and hard to navigate as the web, why not apply the principles that work on the web to my desktop? It's not a bad idea, and its early success clearly demonstrates a need for new technologies (and possibly new metaphors) that can help us manage our electronic lives.

But is "desktop search" what we're really after? Will it allow us to finally manage the deluge of information pouring into our desktops? We didn't think so in the early '90s, and we don't think so now. Our claim is: To fully deal with the problem, we need to break away from the desktop metaphor and move to a new model that removes the overhead and design constraints imposed by the desktop. Search on the desktop is a step in the right direction; by moving in that direction, we've gained something valuable: an alternative model for how users might take back control of their electronic lives. Over the last decade, web search has in fact primed users for a different style of managing their electronic lives. However, as we have seen, we're not there yet; search is a necessary component of such a model; but it won't be sufficient by itself. Search is only a solution when you know what you're looking for. Our guess is that people know what they're looking for maybe around half the time. The rest of the time, they don't need a good search engine; they need a good "browse engine," a good display. Lifestreams remains the best "browse engine" we've ever encountered.

As we've covered in detail in this chapter, there is much to be improved on beyond mere capture and retrieval because the desktop *is failing us* and *will continue to do so* in the areas of categorization, reminding, archiving, and summarization.

Moving away from the desktop metaphor will be a slow process—users have a lot invested in the current interface; however, as the deluge of information continues to accelerate so will the pressure to move past it. In 2006, we are still largely in the same position we were in 1994: our desktops are a mess. But we're hopeful our work and the work of others has started us down a path that leads beyond the desktop metaphor. And (as we like to point out), you may not have heard the last of Lifestreams.

## Acknowledgments

Our sincerest thanks to Elisabeth Freeman, Frank Weil, and Tom Carulli for their contributions to this chapter.

## Notes

1. To illustrate that we're not exaggerating for dramatic effect, in late 1995 *Wired* magazine dispatched two New York photographers to Yale University to do a photo shoot for an upcoming feature article. We expected the worst: they'd put us in some zany and embarrassing pose that we'd never live down. On schedule, the photographers arrived and began looking around the computer science department for good locations to shoot. They walked into David's office, set up a tripod, which extended nearly to the ceiling, and took a photo of David's desk. They then promptly left without saying a word.

We can only guess that they felt the desktop photograph communicated more about what we were trying to do than our pictures ever would. Sure enough, you can find that image in the February 1996 *Wired* magazine (full page no less).

2. It's interesting to point out that we made the statement "such a record is inherently useful which is why people keep journals or diaries" in '95 and felt we needed to add a parenthetical comment that "at least people used to keep journals." Over the last couple of years an interesting phenomenon has occurred: weblogs. Now keeping a time-ordered dairy of our lives is once again becoming common, this time on the web. We can't help but notice that some of our early browser-based implementations were very close to current weblog systems (perhaps it's time we take them in the direction of Lifestreams and allow your entire electronic life to be captured in a, presumably private, log).

3. Eric Freeman was fortunate to have Ben Bederson as an outside advisor and the work benefited immeasurably from this. In addition Ben's participation provided the credibility needed to convince the Yale faculty that the HCI aspect of the work was of value.

4. Note that raising venture capital in the middle of finishing a Ph.D. can provide an effective means of getting your work in front of a lot of people.

5. Apparently *Wired* magazine thought it would make its Lifestreams article more interesting by implying this debate was a contentious one. Nothing could be further from the truth. In fact we enjoyed the debate immensely and, although we disagreed with their conclusions, learned much from Barreau and Nardi's work.

## References

Barreau, D., and Nardi, B. (1995). Finding and reminding: File organization from the desktop. *ACM SIGCHI Bulletin* 27: 39–43.

Carroll, J. M. (1982). Learning, using, and designing filenames and command paradigms. *Behaviour and Information Technology* 1 (4): 327–346.

Cook, T. (1995). Do you know where your data are? *Technology Review* (January).

Dumais, S. T., and Landauer, T. K. (1983). Using examples to describe categorizes. In *Proceedings of the 1983 ACM SIGCHI Conference on Human Factors in Computing Systems (CHI'83),* pp. 112–115. Boston, Mass., December 12–15.

Erickson, T. (1991). Designing a desktop information system: Observations and issues. In *Proceedings of the 1991 ACM SIGCHI Conference on Human Factors in Computing Systems (CHI'91),* pp. 49–54. New Orleans, Louisiana, April 27–May 2.

Freeman, E. T. (1997). The Lifestreams software architecture. Ph.D. dissertation, Yale University Department of Computer Science, May 1997. Available at http://www.cs.yale.edu/homes/freeman/lifestreams.html/.

Gelernter, D. (1994). The cyber-road not taken. *Washington Post* (April 3): C1.

Hutchins, J. (1995). Introduction to text summarization. Dagstuhl Seminar Report, IBFI, Dagstuhl.

Jones, W. P., and Dumais, S. T. (1983). The spatial metaphor: Experimental tests of reference by location versus name. *ACM Transactions on Office Information Systems* 4 (1): 43–63.

Klark, P., and Manber, U. (1995). Developing a personal internet assistant. In *Proceedings of ED-Media 95, World Conference on Multimedia and Hypermedia,* pp. 372–377. Graz, Austria, June 18–21.

Lansdale, M. (1988). The psychology of personal information management. *Applied Ergonomics* 19 (1): 55–66.

Malone, T. (1983). How do people organize their desks? Implications for the design of office information systems. *ACM Transactions on Office Systems* 1 (1): 99–112.

Nelson, T. (1990). The right way to think about software design. In Laurel, B. (ed.), *The Art of Human–Computer Interface Design,* pp. 235–243. Boston: Addison-Wesley.

Larratt-Smith, A. (1996). A calendar interface for Lifestreams. Technical report, Senior Project, Department of Computer Science, Yale University, May 1996.

Steinberg, S. G. (1997). Lifestreams. *Wired* 5: 148–151, 204–209.

The Technology Review TR100. (1999). *Technology Review* (November/December).

Whittaker, S., and Sidner, C. (1996). Email overload: Exploring personal information management of email. In *Proceedings of the 1996 ACM SIGCHI Conference on Human Factors in Computing Systems (CHI'96)*, pp. 276–283. Vancouver, British Columbia, Canada, April 13–18.

# 3

# Haystack: Per-User Information Environments Based on Semistructured Data

David R. Karger

## Introduction

Every individual works with information in his or her own way. In particular, different users have different needs and preferences in regard to

- which *information objects* need to be stored, retrieved, and viewed;
- what *relationships and attributes* are worth storing and recording to help find information later;
- how those relationship and attributes should be *presented* when inspecting objects and navigating the information space;
- what *operations* should be made available to act on the presented information; and
- how information should be gathered into *coherent workspaces* in order to complete a given task.

Currently, developers make such decisions and hard-code them into applications: choosing a particular class of objects that will be managed by the application, deciding on what schemata those objects obey, developing particular displays of those information objects, and gathering them together with relevant operations into a particular workspace. The Haystack project takes a different approach. We posit that no developer can predict all the ways a user will want to record, annotate, and manipulate information, and that as a result the applications' hard-coded information designs interfere with users' abilities to make the most effective use of their information.

Our Haystack system aims to give the end user significant control over all four of the facets mentioned above. Haystack stores (i.e., references to) arbitrary objects of interest to the user. It records arbitrary properties of the stored information, and relationships to other arbitrary objects. Its user interface flexes to present whatever properties and relationships are stored, in a meaningful fashion.

To give users flexibility in what they store and retrieve, Haystack coins a *uniform resource identifier (URI),* naming anything of interest to the user—a digital document, a physical document, a person, a task, a command or menu operation, a view of some information, or an idea. Once named, the object can be annotated, related to other objects, viewed, and retrieved.

To support information management and retrieval, a Haystack user can record arbitrary (predefined or user-defined) *properties* to capture any attributes of or relationships between pieces of information that the user considers important. Properties of an object are often what the information users are seeking when they visit the object. Conversely, they may help users find the objects they want: the properties serve as useful query arguments, as facets for metadata-based browsing (Yee et al. 2003), or as relational links to support the associative browsing typical of the World Wide Web.

Haystack's user interface is designed to flex with the information space: instead of using predefined, hard-coded layouts of information, Haystack interprets *view prescriptions* that describe how different types of information should be presented—for example, which properties matter and how their values should be (recursively) presented. View prescriptions are themselves customizable data in the system, so they can be imported or modified by a user to handle new types of information, new properties of that information, or new ways of looking at old information. Incorporating a new relationship or even a new type of information does not require programmatically modifying the application or creating a new one; instead, an easy-to-author view prescription can be added to describe how to blend the new information seamlessly into existing information views.

Beyond letting users customize the information they work with, Haystack lets users customize their information-management activities. By taking a "snapshot" of partially completed dialogue boxes, a user can create specialized operations to act on their data in common ways. At a higher level, a variation of the view prescription approach is used to define *workspaces* for a particular user task, describing which information objects are involved, how they should be laid out, and what operations should be available to perform on them. With Haystack's unified information model, any heterogeneous set of objects can be brought into a coherent visualization appropriate for a given task.

The need to flexibly incorporate new data types, presentations, and aggregations is not limited to individual users. As is demonstrated by this volume, researchers keep proposing beneficial new attributes, relationships, and data types. Plaisant et al. (this volume) propose to tag all information objects with a "role" attribute that can be used to determine under which circumstances a given information object is relevant, and which operations on it should be available. Fisher and Nardi (this volume) propose that information management will be improved by recording and displaying linkages from information objects to the people relevant to those objects. Freeman and Gelernter (this volume) advocate recording and presenting information according to the access time of all of a user's information objects. The essays all make good cases, suggesting that each is correct *some of the time*. The Haystack system demonstrates an infrastructure that would make it much simpler to incorporate such new ideas in a single system as they arise, and invoke each of them at the appropriate times, as opposed to crafting new and distinct applications (and convincing users to migrate to them) for each new idea.

## Principles

Haystack's design is guided by a number of principles and concepts. Many of them seem obvious and almost wasteful to assert. But all of them might be debatable, so we attempt to justify them in our motivation section below.

**Universality** Users should be able to record any information object they consider important or meaningful, and should be able to seek, find, and view it later.

**The centrality of metadata and relationships** Much retrieval of objects is based on recalling specific attributes of the objects and their relationships to other objects. Thus, the system must be able to record whatever attributes and relationships matter to the user, display them, and support their use in search and navigation.

**One information space** There should be no *a priori* segregation of a user's information by "type" or application. Rather, all information should exist logically in a single space. Users should be able to group and relate any information objects they choose.

**Personalization** No developer can predict what kinds of information objects a user will want to store, or what attributes and relationships will be meaningful to them for retrieval. Thus, the system must let the end user define new information types and properties, and adapt to be able to store, present, and search using those types and properties.

**Semantic identity** There should be only one representation of a particular information object in the data model (as opposed to having distinct representations stored by different applications). Any visible manifestation of that object should be "live," offering access to that object (as opposed to, say, simply acting as a dead text label for an object that must be located elsewhere).

**Separate data from presentation** The development of multiple views of the same information object should be encouraged, so that the right view for a given usage can be chosen. It should be possible to use each such view to be used in whatever contexts are desired, instead of restricting each view to certain applications.

**Reuse presentations** Many types (such as "email message") are instances of more generic types ("message") that have other incarnations (newsgroup posting, instant message, telephone call) and to which many attributes (sender, recipient, subject) and operations (reply, forward) apply uniformly. We should design views to apply generically when possible, so that the user can ignore differences that are irrelevant to their information-management needs.

This chapter explains the motivation for these principles and describes the system we have built to apply them.

## A Tour of Haystack

To begin exploring Haystack's design, we take a brief tour through an end user's view of Haystack. In figure 3.1 we see a screen shot of Haystack managing an individual's inbox. As is typical of an email application, Haystack shows the user's inbox in the primary browsing pane. The layout is tabular, with columns listing the sender, subject, and body, among other things. Less usual is the fourth "Recommended categories" column, which the user added to the display by dragging the Recommended Categories view from the message on the lower right into the inbox column header. As is usual, the collection includes a "preview" pane for viewing selected items, which is currently collapsed.

While the Haystack inbox looks much like a typical email display, it contains much more. Some of the items in the inbox are not email messages. There are stories from Really Simple Syndication (RSS) feeds, and even a representation of a person—perhaps placed there as a reminder that the user needs to meet with him. The RSS message has a sender and a date, but the person does not. This is characteristic of Haystack: rather

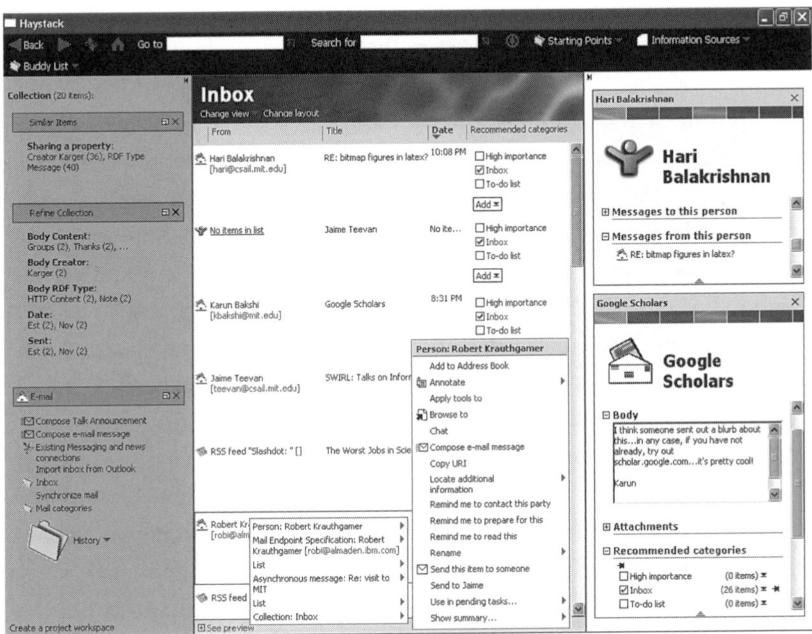


**Figure 3.1**
Haystack viewing a user's inbox collection. A person and an email message are displayed to the right. The user right-clicks on the name "Robert Krauthgamer" to open a context menu of person-relevant operations.

than being inextricably bound to an "email reader application," the inbox is a collection like all other Haystack collections, distinguished only as the collection into which the user has specified that incoming email (and news) be placed. It is displayed using the same collection view as all other collections. Any items can be part of the inbox collection, and will be properly displayed when the inbox is being viewed. This means that the inbox can serve as a general purpose "to-do list." Bellotti et al. (2003) observe that many users have forced email into this role but have had to cope as a result with the constraint that only email could be in their to-do list; Haystack does away with the constraint.

It is also worth noting that RSS was a "late arrival" in Haystack. The view showing the inbox was created before RSS was developed. When we made the decision to include RSS stories as a new type of information to be handled by the system, we did not make any change to the user interface. Instead, we simply added a *view prescription*—a small annotation explaining which attributes of an RSS object were worth seeing—and Haystack was immediately able to incorporate those stories as shown in the figure. This is standard for Haystack: new types of information, and new attributes of information, do not force modifications to the visualization tool. Instead, lightweight annotations give Haystack sufficient information to seamlessly incorporate new types and attributes among the existing data.

On the right-hand side of the screen is a clipboard-like "holding area" for arbitrary items; it currently contains an email message (about Google Scholars) and a person (Hari Balakrishnan). Various aspects of the message are shown, including the body, attachments (currently collapsed), and recommended categories. Displayed aspects of the person include messages to and from them; others, such as address and phone number, are scrolled out of view.

The bottom of the left panel of figure 3.1 shows that the "email" task is currently active, and lists various relevant activities (composing a message) and items (the inbox) that the user might wish to invoke or visit while performing this task, as well as a history of items that the user previously accessed *while performing this task* (expanded in figure 3.2). The tasks can be invoked, and items visited, by clicking on them.

Indeed, the user can click on any item on the screen in order to browse to a view of that item—the individual messages, the various individuals named as senders or recipients, or any of the "recommended categories."

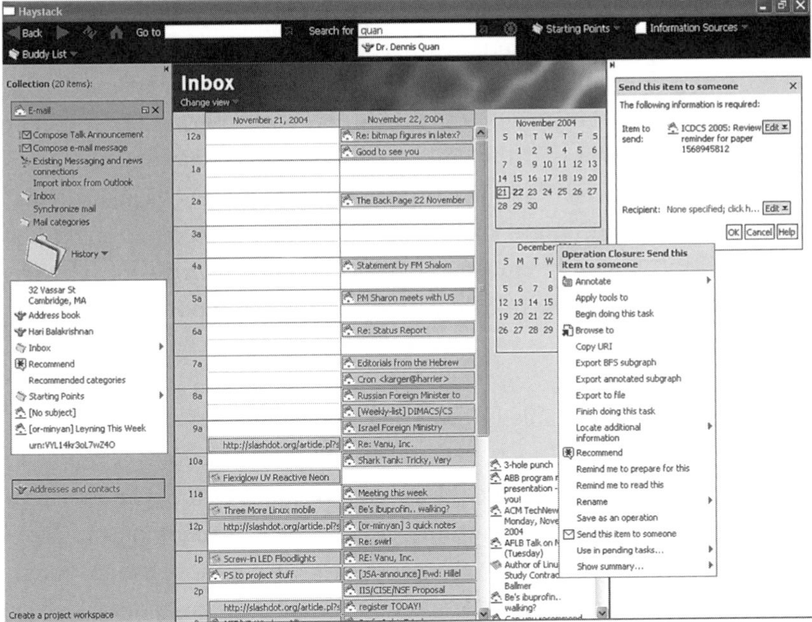


**Figure 3.2**
Invoking "send this item to someone" in Haystack. The inbox collection is displayed in the calendar view. We show three distinct open menus—the task-specific history, the result of a search for "Quan," and the context menu for an operation—though in actual use only one would remain open at a time.

Similarly, the user can right-click on any visible item in order to invoke a context menu of operations that can be applied to that object. The user right-clicks on one of the people listed as a message sender and a menu (and submenu) opens up listing operations that might be invoked for that person, such as sending him an email message, initiating a chat, or entering him in the address book. The operations are not limited to those typical of an email application; rather, they are the ones applicable to the object being viewed. One of the operations, "Send to Jaime," was created by the user because he performs that operation frequently. He saved a partially completed "Send this to someone" operation; Haystack automatically recognized that this new operation was applicable and added it to the context menu.

Finally, the user can drag one item onto another in order to "connect" those two items in an item-specific way—for example, dragging an item onto a collection places the item into the collection, while dragging an item into a dialogue box argument (see figure 3.2) field binds that argument to the dragged item. These three actions—click to browse, right-click for context menus, and drag and drop—are pervasive. They can be invoked at any time upon any visible object in a uniform fashion.

A "browsing advisor" in the left pane suggests various "similar items" to those in the collection—such as items created by Karger, or type of message—and ways to "refine the collection" being viewed—for example, limiting to emails whose body contains certain words, or that were sent at a certain time.

## Motivation: Personalizable Information Management

Before embarking on a detailed discussion of the design of the Haystack system, we attempt to motivate the design by elaborating on the problem we are trying to solve. We observe that current applications strait-jacket users into managing information in ways that may not be natural for them, and argue that good information-management tools must give users more control over what kinds of information they store and how they visualize and manage it.

### Impersonal Applications

The Haystack project is motivated by the observation that different people have distinct and often idiosyncratic ways of managing their information. For example, I use a traditional subject classification for my books (with many exceptions for books that are in heavy use). My wife arranges her books chronologically by birth date of the author. A friend groups her books by color. Each of these three organizations works well for its owner, reflecting what he or she remembers about the relevant books, but would fail for many other people.

This variability in physical organization is squeezed into conformity in the management of digital information.[1] Instead of our bookshelves, current applications are one-size-fits-all: someone else has decided on the right "organizing principles," and we are stuck using them whether we like them or not. The application's choices may be "optimal" with respect to some hypothetical average user, but always seem to miss certain attributes a given individual would find useful. In a typical email program, we can sort only by the application's predefined fields such as subject, sender, date, and perhaps importance, but not by more idiosyncratic features such as sender's age, "where I was when I read this," number of recipients, importance of sender, or "needs to be handled by such-and-such a date."

Sometimes, the desired information is in fact recorded in the application but no appropriate interface is offered to make use of it. For example, although all modern email clients track the threading/reply-to structure of email messages, Microsoft's Outlook Express 6 does not permit a user to display or sort according to the number of messages in a given thread. So if what I remember about an email message is that it generated much discussion, there is no easy way for me to exploit that information to find the message. Mozilla Thunderbird does have this capability, because an application developer decided it was worth incorporating. And although the information is present to answer the question, neither tool lets me display or sort messages according to how long it has been since I have heard from the sender.

In other cases, the problem starts even earlier, when information a user cares about cannot even be *recorded* in an application. Email programs do not contain a "due by" field for email messages. Although MP3 music files come with ID3 tags for recording various sorts of metadata, there is no field or representation for a user to record the dance steps associated with a given piece of music. And while photographs come with metadata fields, none of them is designed to hold a pointer to the email message that was used to send me (and tell me about) the photo. Neither Microsoft's nor Thunderbird's address-book tools allow me to include a photograph of a given contact. As an academic, I might even want address-book entries for my colleagues to contain descriptions of, and links to, some of their papers I have read. But there is no "publications" field in typical address books, because the application developers did not think it worth including.

In many cases, one could try using one of the generic "note" or "comment" fields available as a last resort, but this abandons all opportunity for the application to use those fields in a meaningful way. Although I could write down the filename of a photo of a given contact, I couldn't see that photo when looking at their address book entry—instead I would have to manually seek out and open the named file. And even if I recorded my colleagues' publications in an address book "custom" field, I wouldn't be able to use the address book to select those colleagues who have published in a given conference. If I record a "due by" date as text in the comment field of an email message, I would likely not get the due-date result I desire when I sort by that field, since such fields are generally sorted lexicographically. To fix this problem I would have to invent and remember a specific "backward" representation of dates (year-month-day, with careful attention to always using two digits for date and month).

### Unification

A common reason that an application does not record a given type of information is that the information is considered a "different application's job"—a developer could argue that recording publications seems a job for a bibliography tool, not an address book, or insist that answering an email by a certain date should be handled by your to-do list or calendar instead of your email program. After all this passing the buck, we may grant that the information a user needs is stored in *some* application, but it is not possible to gather it all into one place and use it together, or even to navigate easily from one piece in one application to a different piece in another application. If my calendar shows that I have to deal with a certain email, I have to go find the message in my email program before I can deal with it. Such data fragmentation can also lead users to record duplicate information in multiple applications, which can then lead to inconsistencies when the user changes one but not all copies of that information. If a follow-up message arrives eliminating the need for a response, I might forget to delete it from my to-do list (especially as it would involve more work to get from the email message to the corresponding to-do item). Our recent article on data unification (Karger and Jones 2006) discusses this issue at great length.

Difficulties multiply with more applications. Many people make use of an email-reading client, a music-management tool, a photo album, a calendar, and an address book. The email client and address book may be somewhat linked, but the other applications manage their own data independently. Now consider the plight of an entertainment reporter following the music industry. She exchanges emails with musicians, schedules interviews with them, attends scheduled concerts where they play certain songs, and writes reviews and interviews. It seems likely that such a user would want to

• associate emails about a certain interview with the interview article she is writing;

• link musicians to messages from them (as is demonstrated in the "Person" object in the clipboard of figure 3.1), concerts they played, songs they performed, and photographs they are in;

• "caption" performance photographs of musicians with the song being performed in the photo;

• place songs or albums in a calendar according to release date; and so on.

At present, while each item of interest is managed by *some* application, none is aware of the other item types or applications. The applications' internal models are not expressive enough to refer to the other item types (except through English-language "comments") and their user interfaces do not display the linkages that interest the user, or bring together the related objects into a single coherent representation. The system does not know that the artist noted in the ID3 tags of a song is the same one mentioned in the address book. The best the reporter can hope for is to open all the relevant applications for this data simultaneously, at which point the information she actually cares about is lost in a clutter of other information less relevant to their particular task. The reporter must struggle to take applications targeted to certain tasks and "repurpose" them for a new task. She would likely prefer an application targeted specifically at her task.

In a study of users' desktop environments, Ravasio, Guttormsen-Schär, and Krueger (2004) observed that users are themselves aware of this issue: "the systematic separation of files, emails and bookmarks was determined by three users to be inconvenient for their work. From their points of view, all their pieces of data formed one single body of information and the existing separation only complicated procedures like data backup, switching from old to new computers, and even searching for a specific piece of information. They also noted that this separation led to unwanted redundancy in the various storage locations."

This fragmentation of related information across applications blocks an important information-seeking strategy. In a recent study (Teevan et al. 2004), we highlighted the important role played by *orienteering* in the quest for information. Rather than giving a precise description of their information need and expecting the computer to "teleport" them directly to the relevant object, users often orienteer, starting somewhere "near" the object in their information space, then navigating to the object through a series of local steps. When related information is spread across multiple applications that are not "linked," it becomes impossible for users to follow natural orienteering paths.

### New Data Types

Beyond adding information to existing types, users may also discover a need for brand new types of information. Sometime this may be an enrichment of an existing application. For example, calendar programs often let one record the location of an event. But this record is merely a text string. A user might want a richer representation that incorporates directions to the location, a map of it, a list of nearby hotels, or a link to the site's web page if it exists. At other times, a user may create a new type from scratch. Our music reporter may realize that she wants to record and retrieve information about concerts—where they happened, who else attended, who played, how good they were, how many people were arrested, and so on. Where should she place this information?

Existing applications are even worse at incorporating new types of information than they are at extending existing types. They offer no widgets for displaying the new type, no operations for acting on it, and no slots to attach it to other information objects in the application. Faced with this situation, users often turn to a spreadsheet, creating a tabular record in which each row is an "item" and each column corresponds to some attribute of the new information. This "poor man's database" does give some ability to work with the information: users can sort on a column to find all information with a given value of some attribute. But the presentation is necessarily generic, without any of the task- or data-specific presentations, menus, and operations that applications offer to facilitate work in specific domains.

### Personalization

Application developers could easily solve each of the specific problems mentioned in this section. An application developer could add a place for a contact's photo to the address book, or write an address book function that queried the email database and listed "messages from this person," or make live links from a photograph to an email message. One might even build a specialized data-management application for music reporters, complete with a new "concert" data type.

But there are far more application users than application developers, and each will have different needs for his or her application's information and presentation. Even if application developers could somehow keep up with all these individual wishes, the resulting applications would be cluttered with data and presentations that most people do *not* care about. Kaptelinin and Boardman (this volume) argue that efforts to serve all users within a single application bloat the applications to the point that they are no longer useful for their original intended task. And the set of desired attributes is surely a moving target: no matter how many kinds of information the developers fit into their application, there will be a user who decides he wants one more.

One, and perhaps the only, way to surmount this problem is to give end users themselves the ability to customize the data managed by their applications and the way it is presented. Such customization is already offered to some extent: most email programs, music managers, and file/directory explorers give users the ability to choose which columns (attributes) are displayed in the tabular view of their displayed collections. But this customization is limited mainly to tabular/aggregate views; the user has less control over the presentation of single information objects. When it comes to adding and then working with *new* data types and attributes, much less support is offered—often, the ubiquitous and generic textual "comment" field is the only place to hold a user's new information type.

## Lessons from the Web

The World Wide Web would appear to address many of the problems we have outlined with today's applications. On a web page, users can record any information they want about any type of object. To add a new information attribute, users just type it into the existing web pages—no applications need to change. They can link to other web pages, regardless of the type of object that the other web page describes—there are no "partitions by application." The web is thus ideally suited for orienteering: a search engine will generally take one to the right neighborhood, from which a series of helpful links can be followed to the desired information.

Should users then abandon applications and move all their data to the web? Hypothetically, a user could create a separate web page for each email message, each directory, each music file, each calendar appointment, each individual in their address book, and so on. Editing these pages, the user could indicate arbitrary relationships between their information objects. Feeding these web pages to a tool like Google would give users powerful search capabilities; combining them with the orienteering opportunities offered by the user-created links would surely enhance users' ability to locate information.

Of course, such an approach could never work: it requires far too much effort on the part of the user. It is not clear that the payoff in better retrieval is worth the investment of organizational effort.[2] And the investment would be huge, given the current state of web content creation tools. Far more people consume web content than create it; they treat it as a read-only resource. And "read-only" should be taken literally—users generally inspect web pages by eye in order to extract their information, rather than feeding them to any sophisticated automated tools. Conversely, when people work with their own information, they manipulate and modify it in various ways. Such manipulation and modification needs to be easy, so each application should come with its own specialized interfaces and operations for manipulating the data it manages. We need to let users manage their information without forcing them to become website developers.

## Typing and Structure

Applications offer *structured* data models involving carefully defined types and relationships. These models make it easier for users to manipulate, navigate, and display information in natural ways than on the web. Many of the information objects people work with, attributes of them, and relationships between them have meaningful types. People constitute a type of object that tends to have attributes like name, address, and phone number. Mail messages constitute a type of object that typically has attributes like a sender and a receiver, both of which are often instances of the person type. And while the sender and receiver may both be people, these two attributes represent distinct roles with respect to the message that should not be confused.

On the web, it is typically left to the reader to adduce the types of objects and relationships. The type of an object being viewed may be implied by the title of the object, or by its exhibited attributes, or its placement in context. The types of the attributes are often indicated in English in the text preceding or anchoring links—thus, for example, the Internet Movie Database page for a given movie has headers like "Directed by," "Writing credits," and "Genre," introducing links to objects that exhibit those relationships to the given movie.

The drawback of such visual or English-language cues is that they can *only* be understood by a human. While this may be fine for basic orienteering, it prevents our applications from exploiting the implicit types to improve the presentation and retrieval of information. Depending on context, a user may not want to see *all* information about an object. To support email browsing, for example, mail tools generally offer a condensed view of (a list of) messages showing only sender, date, and subject. Such information is painful to extract from an arbitrarily human-formatted web page, but easily accessible from a structured data model. In this sense, web pages are much like the flexible comment fields available in many applications—able to record everything, but not in a way that can be used effectively by the supporting applications.

Storing information in structured form also enhances search capabilities. Individual applications typically exploit structure this way—for example, a music-playing application will let users arrange their music by composer, album, or performer. More generally, Yee et al. (2003) have argued that faceted metadata browsing, in which a user can choose to organize the corpus according to the value of chosen attributes, is an important information-retrieval tool.

While applications have always imposed such structure on their data, the web is heading in that direction as well. To support navigation and search, websites like the IMD (Internet Movie Database) store their information in structured form and then render it into human-readable form through the use of templates. Structured storage means that sites can offer "site search" tools that exploit the available metadata in richer ways than pure full-text search. For example, Epicurious.com lets users search and browse on various classes of recipe ingredient or cooking method—a kind of faceted metadata search (Yee et al. 2003).

But this move by websites to be more like data-specialized applications means that they run into some of the same problems that face those applications. Users often find that the attributes *they* consider important are not exposed for navigation, or not available at all. When the data users are in spans of multiple websites, no one site is able to offer them an aggregated view of the information, or support navigation that moves between the sites.

What we need, then, is an approach that fuses the information-flexibility of the web with the rich interactions supported by applications' structured data models.

### User Interface Consequences

We have laid out our motivation for letting end users make their own choices about their information models—what information objects, attributes, and linkages matter to them. Accepting such a position imposes interesting challenges on the user interface.

Perhaps the simplest task of a user interface is to display information. Using traditional application data models this is relatively straightforward. The developer considers, for each data type and display context, which features of that object need to be presented to the user. By considering the expected type of each feature, the developer determines some meaningful way to display each feature (such as a string, a number, a color, or an icon) and some effective aggregation of all the individual feature presentations.

But in our personalizable data model, much less can be assumed about the data that will be displayed. The user may start recording or connecting to novel information types, for which no presentation mechanism was developed. Even for expected information types, the user may have developed new relations, or violated the schemas of old relations, so that the developers' assumptions of what needs to be displayed become invalid.

It follows that a user interface for our flexible data model will need to be equally flexible, adapting its presentations to the actual, rather than planned, content of its data model.

The web browser may seem like a promising start in this direction—it makes no assumptions about the structure of the information it is presenting, but simply renders formatted HTML. But where does that HTML come from? One possibility is that it is produced by hand—but above, we have argued that it is implausible to record all user information in HTML.

Another possibility is to produce the HTML through the application of some templating engine to the underlying data model, as is done in many data-oriented websites. But this just pushes the problem down a level: current templates require the same strong assumptions about the structure of the data that limit applications.

Equally problematic is the "read-only" focus of web browsers. We need a user interface that also lets users *manipulate* their information with the ease they expect of typical applications.

### Summary

In this section, we have outlined our motivation for a semistructured data model that can adapt to the needs of any individual user, and for a user interface that can adapt to fit the data model, incorporating new information attributes, new linkages between information, and new types of information. In the remainder of this chapter, we describe our attempts to meet these goals in the Haystack system. After addressing the core data-modeling and user-interface issues, we discuss some of the opportunities such a system offers.

## Semantic Networks—The Haystack Data Model

Above, we have discussed the importance of letting users work with arbitrary information objects, and letting them record and use arbitrary new properties of those objects. Before we can think about an interface to support these activities, we need to develop a data model flexible enough to hold the information.

An effective generic representation supporting flexible information is a *semantic network:* a graph in which the nodes denote the information objects to be managed and the edges are labeled with property names to represent the relations we would like to record. An edge can directly represent only a *binary* relation, not one between more than two entities. However, the majority of relations we have encountered are binary, and higher-arity relationships can generally be represented by reifying the relationship (creating a new information object to represent a particular relationship tuple, and using binary connections from the tuple to the entities that participate in the relationship), so this binary restriction has not been a burden.

In addition to what we think of as relations, semantic network edges can also represent what we think of as "attributes," "properties," or "features" of an object, by creating a link, labeled with the attribute name, between the object and the value of the given attribute. This highlights the fact that from a formal perspective these concepts are equivalent to relations. While the user may maintain an intuitive differentiation (e.g., that properties are intrinsic to an object while relations connect the object to other distinct objects), we will avoid drawing this distinction in the data model, and instead carry it into the user interface that aims to present the data in a way that matches the user's intuition.

**Resource Description Framework (RDF)**

While the original version of Haystack (Adar, Karger, and Stein 1999) implemented its own semantic network representation, we have since adopted the *resource description framework (RDF)* propounded as a standard by the World Wide Web Consortium (Manola and Miller 2003). RDF meets our representational goals. It uses uniform resource identifiers (URIs) to refer to arbitrary information objects—these are much like URLs, but need not refer to information stored on a particular web server (and certainly need not resolve over HTTP). In RDF, information objects are referred to as *resources.* Relationships are referred to as *properties.* And specific assertions that a given property holds between two resources are referred to as *statements.* The two resources linked by the statement are referred to as the *subject* and *object* while the chosen property is called the *predicate.* Properties are also named by URIs, which allows us to make statements about the property—such as a human-readable name for it, or the assertion that each resource should have only one value for that property. Statements too can be reified and given URIs, to allow one to record, for example, who asserted a given statement.

RDF also supports a type system with inheritance. A **Type** property is reserved to specify that a given resource is of a given type. Some resources, of type **Class**, represent types; these are the typical objects of a **Type** statement. There is a (most generic) class called **Object**; all resources are instances of this class. Properties are asserted to be of type **Property**.

RDF lets users define a collection of types and properties appropriate to a given usage. These properties can all be defined in a single (RDF) file; if that RDF file is given a URL, then individual classes and properties in it can be referred to using a label syntax (**http://url/\#label**). The root URL is referred to as a *namespace* for the defined classes and properties. For example, the *Dublin Core* defines types such as **dc:document** and **dc: person** and properties such as **dc:author** and **dc:title** (here **dc:** is shorthand for the Dublin Core namespace, while each suffix labels a specific class or property in the namespace).

Building atop RDF, the *RDF schema language (RDFS)* and *web ontology language (OWL)* (McGuinness and van Harmelen 2003) can be used to define *schemata* for the classes and properties. RDFS and OWL are collections of properties and classes (defined in the RDFS and OWL namespaces) that can be used to assert typical schematic rules. For example, RDFS and OWL can be used to assert that the subject of a **dc:author** statement must be a **dc:document** and the object a **dc:entity**, or that a **dc:document** has at most one **dc:date**. We do not enforce schemata in Haystack; nonetheless, such schemata can be used to establish appropriate views of the information or to guide (but not force) users in filling in values.

**Why RDF?**

One might question our choice of RDF as opposed to either XML or a more traditional table-per-property relational database representation. In many ways, this question is unimportant. All three representations have equal expressive power. It is true that unlike traditional databases, RDF *can* be used without any schemata. However, RDF and OWL can be used to impose schemata on an RDF model if we so choose. RDF has a standard representation in XML (RDF-XML) and can also be stored in a traditional database (with one table of triples, or with one binary table per named property). Conversely, XML or database tuples can be represented in RDF. Of course, the choice of representation might have tremendous consequences for the *performance* of the system as it answers a variety of queries. However, the end user will likely neither know nor care which representation lies under the covers of the user interface.

Nonetheless, a few features of RDF led us to select it. The lack of (enforced) schemata, discussed below, is an appealing feature. The use of URIs (uniform resource identifiers) for all information objects provides a uniform location-independent naming scheme. Also appealing is the fact that RDF places all information objects on a level playing field: each is named by a URI and can become the subject or object of arbitrary assertions. This contrasts (positively) with XML's hierarchical representation of information objects, in which the root object is "special" and related objects are nested deep inside a particular root object. RDF is more in keeping with our belief that the information designer cannot predict which information objects will be of greatest interest to a given user. Shades of this same argument appear in Codd's (1970) seminal paper, where he argues that a hierarchical representation of information that is not fundamentally hierarchical introduces an undesirable *data dependence* that can trip up database users. A similar argument can be made regarding a relational database. Defining a database table with many columns suggests that those fields should be considered in aggregate, but various users may be interested only in some of those fields. We could offer to project onto a subset of columns, but RDF surrenders from the start to the idea that each individual column may be interesting in its own right and deserve its own table, thereby avoiding the whole question of how to project.

Yet another motivation for our adoption of RDF is its structural similarity to the World Wide Web. The power of the web comes from its links, which let users navigate from page to related page. Similarly, the semantic net highlights the linkage of objects rather than highlighting the relations as a whole. This is important for two reasons. First, it captures a notion of "locality." When a user is working with a particular information object, it is quite common for them to want to visit "adjacent," related information objects in the semantic network. Second, linkage is an appropriate emphasis given the important role orienteering plays in individuals' information-seeking behavior (Teevan et al. 2004). Rather than carefully formulating a query that precisely defines the desired information target, users often prefer to start from a familiar location, or a vague search, and "home in" on the desired information through a series of associative steps. In RDF, the statements connecting subject and object form natural associative links along which a user can orienteer from subject to object. The database perspective might be more appropriate if a user wished to formulate a complex query, reflecting operations such as "join" and "project" that can be expressed concisely in a database language such as SQL. However, typical users are not capable of working with such database query languages, so exposing these operations will be of limited value.

The various attributes displayed for each item in figure 3.1 are often just other information objects related by some predicates to the displayed object. Haystack's user interface lets the user click on any of those information objects in order to browse to them, providing support for orienteering. As will become clear when we discuss the user interface, RDF's single notion of "predicate" is made available to the end user in a number of ways—sometimes as a relationship to another object, and other times as an attribute of the current object. "Properties" or "attributes" of a given object and "relationships" between pairs of objects are all represented by predicates in the data model.

### A Semistructured Model

Beyond named relationships, structured data models often have *schemata* expressing knowledge of how different information objects and types will be related. For example, we might declare that the composer of a symphony will invariably be a person, or that any individual can be married to at most one other individual at a given time. Such schematic declarations are very useful. They can protect the user from errors in recording information, catching, for example, when a user swaps the composer and title while entering information about a new symphony. They can facilitate the presentation of information, letting the user deduce that only one line will be needed to present the spouse in an address book entry.

But these protections are at the same time restrictions imposed by a communal sense that might go against the desires of an individual. Consider someone with an interest in computer music: her attempt to enter a particular computer program as the composer of a symphony will be blocked if the above schemata are enforced. Similarly, a researcher of polygamous societies might find himself unable to view critical information in his records about people and their spouses.

Thus, although schemata may be of great *advisory* value, we argue against *enforcing* them. There must always be a way for the user either to modify the schema or violate it if, given fair warning, she concludes that is the best way to record relevant information. This perspective is a natural extension of the idea of letting the user record whatever information she considers important. If we are faced with the choice of violating a schema or refusing to let a user record information she cares about, we choose the former. Whereas developers may consider it unlikely for the sender of an email message to be an animal, and thus may schematize the sender as a person, a user may decide otherwise. Although documents typically have authors, a user might not care to record them. Semantic nets depend less on schemata than databases do: each named link can exist or not independent of any global schema.

A representation like this, in which it is possible to represent a database-type structure but the structure is not enforced, is known as a *semistructured* data model. While we have argued that a semistructured model is essential to supporting a user's recording of information, it poses some problems when it comes time to actually present or manipulate that information. But these are problems at the *user interface* level, which we should address there, instead of trying to solve them by restricting the *data model*. As we shall see there, schemata can play an important role in semistructured information management; the difference is that the schemata become *optional* and *advisory* instead of being enforced. Thus, semistructured information is best seen as "schema optional" rather than "schema free."

**Importing Data**

Although RDF is appealing, the majority of data is presently not in that form. Haystack generates RDF data by applying a collection of *extractors* to traditionally formatted data. At present we can incorporate directory hierarchies, documents in various formats, music and ID3 tags, email (through an IMAP or POP3 interface), Bibtex files, LDAP data, photographs, RSS feeds, and instant messages. Each is incorporated by an appropriate parser that is triggered when information of the given type is absorbed into the system.

Another outstanding source of semistructured data is the web itself. Many websites use templating engines to produce HTML representations of information stored in back-end databases. We have studied machine-learning techniques to automatically extract such information from the web pages back into structured form in RDF (Hogue 2004; Hogue and Karger 2005). In our approach, the user "demonstrates" the extraction process on a single item by highlighting it and labeling its parts; the system then attempts to induce the (tree-shaped) structure of HTML tags and data elements that represent the object on the page. If successful, it can recognize that structure on future pages and automatically perform the same extraction. Of course, Haystack does not care about where its RDF comes from, so other extraction methods (Muslea, Minton, and Knoblock 1999) can easily be incorporated.

## Viewing Information

Given the representational power of the data model, the next question is how it should be presented to users so that they can effectively view and manipulate the stored information. Simply modifying traditional applications to run atop the unified data model would offer some limited benefit—for example, by reducing the amount of information duplicated over multiple applications, and therefore reducing the amount of inconsistency among those duplicates. But it would leave users as constrained as before by the developers' sense of what and how information should be presented in various contexts. Instead, we must make it simple for the user interface to evolve according to the users' preferences and the data it is called upon to display. We achieve this goal through a recursive rendering architecture, in which essentially each object is asked to render itself and recursively makes the same request of other objects to which it is related (Huynh, Karger, and Quan 2002; Quan and Karger 2003).

### Views

Most elementary information-management applications present a hierarchical display of information on the screen. To display a particular object in a certain region of the screen, they subdivide that object's region into (typically rectangular) subregions, and use those subregions to display various attributes of the given object and to display other objects to which the object is related. Thus, a typical email application will present an email message by creating a region showing the sender, another region showing the subject, another region showing the body, and so on. The message might itself be in a subregion as part of a larger display of, say, a collection of messages, using distinct columns to present each message's (relationship to a) sender, subject, and date. The calendar view displays in each day a list of appointments, and the address book has a standard format for displaying an individual by listing properties such as name, address, phone number, and notes in some nicely formatted layout. The address itself may be a complex object with different subproperties such as street, city, and country that need to be laid out.

When applications are targeted at specific domains, they can assume a great deal about what is being displayed in their subregions. The sender of an email address will be a person; he will have a name and address that can be shown in the sender region of the display. An address-book entry will describe a person who has an address. In Haystack we do not wish to make such assumptions: our inbox contains RSS stories, which perhaps do not have the same sort of sender as an email message. But we can still apply the recursive display principle. We can construct a view of any object *X* by (i) deciding which properties of *X* and relationships to other objects need to be shown, (ii) requesting recursive rendering of views of the objects required by *X*, and (iii) laying out those recursively rendered views in a way that indicates *X*'s relation to them. As a concrete example, when rendering a mail message we might consider it important to render the sender; we do so by asking recursively for a view of the sender and then laying out that view of the sender somewhere in the view of the mail message. The recursive call, in rendering the sender, may recursively ask for a rendering of the sender's address for incorporation in the view of the sender.

The key benefit of this recursive approach is that the root view only needs to know about the root object it is responsible for displaying, and not about any of the related objects that end up inside that display. Incorporating RSS feeds into the inbox did not require a wholesale rewrite of a mail application; it simply required the definition of a view for individual RSS messages. Once that view was defined, it was invoked at need by the collection view showing the inbox.

### View Prescriptions

Formally, views are defined by *view prescriptions* that are themselves data in the model. A view prescription is a collection of RDF statements describing how a display region should be divided up and which constants (e.g., labels) and related objects should be shown in each subdivision. It also declares that certain standard graphical widgets such as scrollbars and text boxes should be wrapped around or embedded in the display.

When a view prescription is invoked, it will require some *context* in order to render properly. Most obviously, we need to know how much space the rendered object should occupy. It is often useful to pass another state, such as current colors and font sizes, down from the parent view in order to get a consistent presentation. This is done by dynamic scoping—the view has access to an environment of variables set by the ancestral view prescriptions in the recursive rendering process. It can examine those variables, as well as modify them for its children.

The key task of Haystack's interface layer is to decide which view prescription should be used to render an information object. At present, we take a very simplistic approach: we choose based on the *type* of object being displayed and the *size* of the area in which it will be shown. Each view prescription specifies (with more RDF statements) the types and sizes for which it is appropriate; when a rendering request is delegated, Haystack uses an RDF query to determine an appropriate prescription to apply. Type and size are the most obvious attributes affecting the choice of prescription; an issue of great interest that requires further research is to expand the vocabulary for discussing which views are appropriate in which contexts.

When matching against type, Haystack uses a type-hierarchy on information objects and selects a view appropriate to the most specific possible type. The type hierarchy lets us define relatively general-purpose views, increasing the consistency of the user interface and reducing the number of distinct prescriptions needed. For example, RSS postings, email messages, and instant messages are all taken to be subtypes of a general "message" type for which we can expect a sender, subject, and body (Quan, Bakshi, and Karger 2003). Thus, a single view prescription applies to all three types. To ensure that all information objects can be displayed in some way, Haystack includes "last resort" views that are always applicable. For example, the "small" last resort view simply displays the title or, if unavailable, the URI of the information object, while the "large" view displays a tabular list of all the object's properties and values (rendered recursively).

One might argue that our view architecture is remarkably impoverished, offering only rectangular hierarchical decompositions and delegation based on object type and size. While we agree that this is an impoverished architecture, we assert that it captures much of the presentational power of current (equally impoverished) information-management application displays, and hold up figure 3.1, which can pass as a typical mail client, as evidence. While matching the presentational capabilities of existing applications, our delegation architecture facilitates the incorporation of new data types and the cross-domain linkage of information.

One key improvement relative to existing applications is that views can be invoked anywhere. The right panel of figure 3.1 shows a "clipboard" of sorts, into which any information object can be dragged for display. Thus information about the individual "Hari Balakrishnan" can be inspected without launching an entire address book application; similarly, the email about "Google Scholars" can remain in view even if we choose to navigate away from our inbox and stop "doing email." This idea of getting at data without the enclosing application connects with the WinCuts technique propounded by Tan, Meyers, and Czerwinski (2004).

Our view architecture also makes it straightforward to offer multiple views of the same information object, allowing the user to choose an appropriate view based on their task. The center pane of figure 3.1 offers a "change view" drop-down menu. From this menu, the user can select any view annotated as appropriate for the object being displayed.

It is also important to recognize that at the base of the view recursion, the presentation of complex data objects can be delegated to special-purpose widgets. Haystack's view prescriptions would be inadequate for describing the presentation of a scatter plot and the interactive manipulations a user might want to invoke while viewing it, but a prescription can certainly specify that some "scatter plot widget" is the proper view to invoke when a scatter plot needs to be displayed. This approach could even allow the embedding of entire applications within Haystack, so long as they can be told what data object to focus on.

### Lenses

While it may suffice to display a list of attributes of a given object, the attributes often group naturally to characterize certain "aspects" of the information being presented. Such a grouping in Haystack is effected by defining a *lens*. Lenses add yet another layer to the presentation of information. Like views, lenses are described in the data model as being appropriate to a certain type of object. The person and mail message in the right pane of figure 3.1 are being displayed using a *lens view*. The lens view is applicable to *all* object types. It simply identifies *all* the applicable lenses for the given type, and displays each of them. Each lens has a title describing the aspect it is showing, such as "messages from this person."

Unlike recursively rendered views, these lenses are "reified" in that the user can visually address each one, choosing to expand or collapse it (with the small plus/minus sign adjacent to the lens name). The choice is stateful: the user's choice of which lenses to show is remembered each time the lens view is applied for that type of information object. This provides a certain level of view customization. Furthermore, many of our lenses are simple "property set lenses"—they are described by a list of which properties of the object they will show, and these properties are simply shown in a list. Users can easily modify these lenses by adding properties to or removing them from the list. Thus, if a user chooses to define a brand new property in his data model, it is straightforward for him to adapt the user interface to present that property.

Lenses can also be *context sensitive*. For example, some lenses might be present only when a given task is being performed. The "recommended categories" lens shown for the Google Scholars email message is present only when the user is performing the "organizing information" task. A "help" lens could aggregate useful information about any object, but should be visible only when the user is actually seeking help.

Users can further customize their views of information by manipulating lenses. For example, the fourth "recommended categories" column in the view of the inbox was created by dragging the "recommended categories" lens from the Google Scholars view onto the header of the inbox collection. This would be a useful action if the user wanted to quickly skim and organize his email based on the headers, without inspecting the details of each. This tabular collection view lays out one item in each row, and applies a lens in each column to determine what information to show in that column about the object in a given row. Any lens can be placed in a column of this collection view, allowing the user to construct a kind of "information spreadsheet" showing whichever aspects of the objects in the collection the user cares to observe.

### Collections

Collections are one of the most common data types people work with. Nearly every application offers tools for managing collections of its primitive elements: directory/folder managers for files, bookmark managers for web browsers, mail folders for email, and so on. Generally, these collections are limited to the type of object the given application "owns."

Under Haystack's unified data model, it becomes possible to aggregate arbitrary collections of information germane to a given task. Perhaps the closest analogue in existing desktop systems is the file manager. Directories are able to hold files of arbitrary types, meaning that the user can group files by task instead of by file type. The limitation, of course, is that such management can be applied only at the file level. Thus, items whose representation is wrapped up inside an application's data file, such as individual contacts in an address book or individual mail message in a mail folder, cannot be organized into heterogeneous collections. Haystack, by providing a uniform naming scheme for all objects of interest, extends the benefits of heterogeneous collections to arbitrary objects. We have already noted how, in figure 3.1, non-email objects such as RSS stories and people can be placed seamlessly into the inbox.

The availability of multiple views is particularly important for collections, which are perhaps the central nonprimitive data type in Haystack. Since collections are used for so many different purposes, many views exist for them. Figure 3.1 shows the standard row-layout for a collection, but also available are a calendar view (in which each item of the collection is displayed according to its date—this view is applied to the inbox in figure 3.2), a graph view (in which objects are shown as small tiles, and arrows linking the tiles are used to indicate a specific chosen relationships between them), and the "last-resort" view showing all properties of the collection and their values. Each view may be appropriate at a different time. The standard view is effective for traditional email reading. The graphical view can be used to examine the threading structure of a lengthy conversation. And the calendar view could be applied by the user to rearrange email according to its due date instead of its arrival time.

Yet another collection view is the menu. When a collection is playing the role of a menu, a left click drops down a "menu view" of the collection, which allows quick selection of a member of the collection. Implementing menus this way gives users the power to customize their interfaces: by adding to and removing from the collection of operations in a menu, users modify the menu. Users can similarly customize the pinned-in-place *task menus* in the left pane (such as the email task menu displayed in figure 3.1) in order to make new task-specific operations and items available.

Traditionally, drop-down menus are used to present collections of *operations*. While Haystack certainly does place operations in menus (see below), *any* object can be in the collections presented this way. Thus, the notion of lightweight access and putting a collection away is separated from the issue of access to operations. For example, as shown in figure 3.2, the results of a search in the search box at the top of the system are presented as a drop-down menu (but can also be navigated to for closer inspection and manipulation).

A particularly noteworthy collection view is the "check-box view" exhibited in the bottom right of the display. This forms a somewhat inverted view of collections, in that it shows which of the collections from a given *category set* the Google Scholars email is in. Checking and unchecking a box will add or remove the item from the given collection. Of course, the collection itself is live—items can be placed in the collection by dragging them onto the collection name, and the collection can be browsed to by a left click. But in a past study (Quan, Bakshi, and Karger 2003), we demonstrated that presenting the collections to users as checkable "categories" made a big difference in the way they were used. Many email users are reluctant to categorize email away into folders, fearing that any email so categorized will be lost and forgotten from their inboxes. Many mail tools allow a user to *copy* an email message into a folder and leave a copy behind in the inbox, but apparently users find this too heavyweight an activity. In particular, once two copies are made, the user may have trouble keeping them in sync—an annotation on one copy will not appear on the other. Checkboxes, on the other hand, feel like a way of annotating the message, rather than a putting away, and therefore encourage multiple categorization. In our study, users given the option to categorize with checkboxes made use of it, and found that it improved their ability to retrieve the information later. In the underlying data model, of course, the checkboxes represent collections like all others that can be browsed to (indeed, the inbox itself is one of the checkable categories).

### Creating New Views

We continue to explore ways to let users customize their information presentation. We have created a "view builder" tool that lets users design new views for given information types (Bakshi 2004). The users rely on menus and dragging to specify a particular layout of screen real estate, and specify which properties of the viewed object should be displayed in each region and what kind of view should be used to display them.

The representation of view prescriptions as data, rather than as code that is invoked with arbitrary effects, makes this kind of view definition feasible—it involves the simple manipulation of the view data. This work is still in its early stages; while the system has the view-construction *power* we want, we continue to seek the most intuitive interfaces offering that power to users. The current scheme requires explicit reference to properties, types, and views, which may be beyond the capabilities of many users. Ultimately, we aim for users to edit the views in place, manipulating the presentation of the information by dragging appropriate view elements from place to place. Such design "by example" is likely to be within the capabilities of more users.

Even with ideal tools, many users will likely be too lazy to design new views. However, the description of views as data means that, like other data, views can be sought out from elsewhere and incorporated into the system. We imagine various power users placing view prescriptions in RDF on websites where other users can find and incorporate them, much the way individuals currently define "skins" for applications such as MP3 players.

In the longer term, we hope to explore application of machine learning to let Haystack create and modify views automatically. By observing the way a user examines and manipulates information, the system may be able to hypothesize which attributes are actually important to a user in a given context, and construct views showing only those attributes.

At a higher level, the same view-construction framework can be used to design entire *workspaces*—collections of information objects laid out and presented in a specific way, to support the performance of a particular task. We discuss this issue in the section entitled "Workspaces."

## Manipulation

Besides viewing information, users need to be able to manipulate it. Most of Haystack's views offer on-the-spot editing of the information they present, as a way to change specific statements about an object. More generally, Haystack offers a general framework for defining *operations* that can be applied to modify information objects in arbitrary ways. Most operations are invoked by *context menus* that can be accessed by right clicking on objects. Particularly common operations are supported by a natural drag-and-drop metaphor.

### Operations

The basic manipulation primitive in Haystack is the *operation*. Operations are arbitrary functions that have been reified and exposed to the user. Each function takes some number of arguments. When the operation is invoked, the system goes about collecting its arguments. If the operation takes only one argument and the operation is invoked in a context menu, the argument is presumed to be the object being clicked. If more than one argument is needed, a dialogue box is opened in the right pane to collect the other arguments. Unlike in many traditional applications, this dialogue box is *modeless*. It does not force the user to finish filling it out before turning to other tasks. In particular, the user can use all of Haystack's navigation tools to seek and find the arguments he wishes to give to the operation (by dragging and dropping them onto the dialogue box) before invoking it.

Operations are objects that can be manipulated like any other objects in Haystack. In particular, users can drag operations into (menu) collections in order to make them accessible from wherever the user wishes.

### Invoking Operations

*Context menus* provide a standard way to access all the operations germane to a given object. Statements in the data model declare which operations are applicable to which types of objects; a right click leads to a database query that creates the collection of operations (and other items) that apply to the clicked object.

*Drag and drop* provides a way for a user to associate two information objects by dragging one onto the other. Dragging onto a collection has the obvious semantics of placing the object in the collection. Dragging onto a particular property displayed in a lens has the effect of setting the dragged object as a value for that property with respect to the object the lens is showing. Dragging into a dialogue box argument assigns the dragged item as an argument to the operation being invoked. More generally, a view can specify the operation that should be invoked when a specific type of object is dragged into the view.

## Customization

Like other data, operations can be customized by the user. In particular, the user can fill in some of the invoked operation's arguments, then "curry" the result, saving it as a new, more specialized operation (Quan, Huynh, Karger, and Miller 2003). For example, a user may take the standard "email an object" operation, fill in his boss's email address as the destination, and then curry it into a "mail this to my boss" operation. Since the curried operation takes only one argument (the object to send), it can be invoked in a right-click context menu with no need for any dialogue box. Once created, the new operation can be given a name and then dragged into various collections of commands (menus) so that it can be accessed when needed.

We are working to offer users more powerful operation customizations. In addition to currying operations, we would like to let users define new operations by composing existing ones—passing the result of one operation as an argument to the next. We are also exploring techniques like those we use to extract information from web pages (see the section "Importing Data") that let a user encapsulate web operations (accessed through web forms) as Haystack operations, which can then by accessed (and customized) through Haystack's interface without visiting the website.

Like views, operations offer an opportunity for arbitrary, fine-grained extensions of Haystack. Operations are defined in RDF, and so can be created and offered up by power users for download by any individuals who find them useful. Some operations may simply be carefully curried operations; others may include newly crafted database queries, or even arbitrary code.

## Example

Figure 3.2 shows what happens after a user invokes the "send this item" operation on a particular object. A dialogue box in the right pane gathers the necessary arguments, including the object to send (already filled in) and the person to whom it should be sent. To fill in that person, we show how the user might drop down the email-specific history in the left pane, listing items recently used while handling email. Since the desired recipient is not present, the user can perform a search in the search box in the top navigation bar. The (single) result matching this search appears in a drop-down menu. From there it can be dragged and dropped onto the dialogue box in order to indicate that it is the intended recipient. If the user has cause to believe that he will need to send this particular item to other individuals, he can drop a context menu from the dialogue box (shown) and select "save this as an operation" to create a new operation for which the item to send is prespecified, and only the intended recipient needs to be filled in. The resulting operation, which takes only a single argument (the intended recipient), will become available in the context menu that drops down when right-clicking any person. A complementary operation, in which the recipient is prespecified but the item to send is not, shows up as "Send to Jaime" in the context menu of figure 3.1.

## Tasks

Another concept we consider it crucial to model in Haystack is that of *tasks*. Without attempting a formal definition, we recognize that many people spend time engaged in what are commonly called tasks: dealing with their email, planning their day, writing a paper, surfing the web, shopping for an item, and so on. For each of these tasks, there is information the user will likely need to work with (the inbox for email, the calendar for day planning, the paper being written, and so on) and a collection of operations the user is likely to invoke while doing the task (sending a reply to an email message, scheduling an appointment, or spell-checking a document). Nowadays, it seems that people are often doing more than one task at a time; however, at most a few are likely to be kept simultaneously in mind.

### The Task Window

In Haystack, we are exploring two approaches to supporting tasks. The first is the task pane shown on the left of the figures. The task pane can display a collection of objects and operations useful for a given task. For example, in figure 3.1 we see an "E-mail" task window containing objects (such as the inbox) and operations (such as composing a message) relevant to the email task. The user can navigate to task-relevant objects, or invoke task-relevant operations, by clicking on them in the task window. The task window simply presents a collection, which can be manipulated like any collection. In particular, if the user decides that other objects or operations are frequently useful for the task, she can drag those items into the task-collection so that they will be accessible in the future. Of course, a user can also create brand new tasks and populate them with relevant items.

Also visible in the task windows is a *task-specific* history collection, containing the items accessed in the recent past *while the user was performing this task.* Unlike a generic history such as might be found in a web browser, the task-specific history does not become cluttered with irrelevant items visited while the user is performing other unrelated tasks. If there are items that a user accesses often while doing the given task, those items will tend to be found in the history. Thus, even if the user does not go to the trouble of customizing the task window to include items he needs for the task, the history provides a kind of automated customization accomplishing the same thing.

The task window is much lighter-weight than the typical application, but at the same time it is significantly more detailed than a "minimized" application. We believe that this middle ground can be very effective for multitasking users. Instead of cycling through the expansion and collapse of various full-screen windows as they try to work with information from multiple applications, users can keep a little bit of state from each of their tasks in view.

The task windows can be seen as similar to the dockable "toolbars" currently available in many applications. However, their modeling as standard collections means that users are free to incorporate any objects or operations they find useful.

Task windows become active in two ways. First, users may explicitly begin doing the task. For example, the user can select "E-mail" from the starting-point menu (top right) in order to invoke the task. Alternatively, a user can type "E-mail" into the search box, and select the "E-mail" task from the result set. This is analogous to launching an application: the user explicitly states that she wishes to begin the task. A second option is for the system to guess which tasks the user is engaged in. For example, in figure 3.2, a grayed-out "Addresses and Contacts" task is visible in the left pane. This is a sign that the system believes the user may be performing this task. If the user clicks on the grayed-out header, the task window will expand to show the items relevant to that task. At present, such guesses are hard-wired into the system—certain objects and types are explicitly associated (by an appropriate RDF statement) with certain tasks. For example, the inbox is explicitly associated with email, so any time the user navigates to the inbox, the email task is offered in the left pane. In the longer term, we see this problem of discovering which tasks a user is currently performing as a fruitful target for machine-learning research.

**Workspaces**

Our second approach to tasks is on a larger scale. A *workspace* is a (presumably rather large) region filled with (relatively detailed) views of various information objects that can be used to tackle a given task. For example, a traditional email application may present a region holding a collection of current messages, a region holding a particular current message, a region holding an address book, and so on. A user working on a paper about a particular research project may wish to gather and lay out the relevant research data, useful citations and documents, spell-checking functionality, and mail-sending operations to their co-authors (see the section entitled "Manipulation" on customizing operations). Continuing our main argument that developers cannot predict what workspaces end users will want, we would like to give end users the ability to create their own workspaces, deciding what pieces of information should be presented (and in what way) to let them carry out a given task.

Creating a workspace is much like creating a new view. While a view may be intended to apply to many pieces of information, a workspace is typically created once, for a single task. While a view typically presents information associated with the object being viewed, workspaces instead present information associated with the task to be performed—in a sense, the workspace can be seen as a view of the task.

Given their similarity, we can apply tools similar to those for the construction of views to the construction of workspaces. To construct a workspace, the user needs to choose a collection of items to be shown in the workspace, choose a view for each of those items, and determine how those views should be laid out in the workspace. Choice of items (creating a collection) and the selection of (predefined) views are already available as standard components of Haystack. We have designed a prototype tool for managing the layout of the items so as to create a workspace (Bakshi 2004).

Figure 3.3 shows a paper-writing workspace constructed with our drag-and-drop tools by assembling views that were also constructed with our

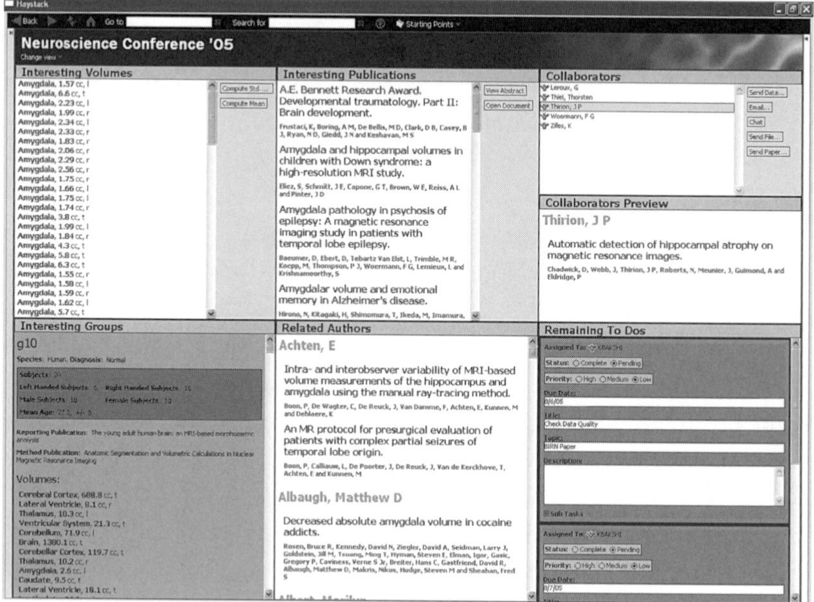


**Figure 3.3**
A workspace constructed by drag and drop. This workspace is specialized for writing a particular research paper, presenting research data, coauthors, and relevant references. The publication view was created with the similar view-construction tool.

drag-and-drop tools mentioned in the section entitled "Creating New Views."

## Search

Beyond reading and writing information, search is perhaps the key activity in information management. Haystack offers a number of search tools. We aim to make search both pervasive and lightweight—rather than dropping what they are doing and initiating a search, we want users to think of search as a "no-overhead" activity that is performed as part of regular navigation.

As we argued above, orienteering is a natural search mode. Should a plausible starting point be visible, we expect users to "hyperlink" their way from object to object, homing in on the one they are seeking. By placing user-definable task-specific collections of information in the left panel, we aim to maximize the chances that the user will find a good jumping-off point for their search.

### Text Search

At times, of course, no such starting point is clearly visible. A simple scheme to fall back on at that point is text search. Information objects are often associated with memorable text, such as a title, a body, or an annotation. Haystack's upper navigation bar includes a search box into which an arbitrary textual query can be entered. The results of this search are a collection. The collection is presented in the drop-down-menu view of a collection, which optimizes for rapid selection of an item in the common case where the search is successful. However, the collection of results can also be "navigated to" to provide the starting point for a more complex search.

In Haystack, text is associated with many items—not just traditional data, but other objects such as operations. Thus, a user can search to find (and then invoke in place) an operation by describing it—essentially dynamically specifying a menu of commands relating to the given description. It also becomes natural to use search at a fine grain to locate small items, for example, to locate a particular value to fill in as the argument to a dialogue box.

Unlike text search of traditional corpora, where the text associated with a given item is clear (the text in the file plus its metadata), the question of what text to associate with a given RDF resource is complex. It is natural to associate with a resource any text directly connected to it by a statement, but one might also imagine associating text located at greater distance along a chain of statements.

### Fuzzy Browsing

Much research has been done in the database community on search. Some (Bosc, Motro, and Pasi 2001) have even looked for ways to offer ranked or approximate matching, avoiding the off-putting "all or nothing" effect of Boolean database queries. However, as we argued above, attention needs to be given to orienteering, which manifests in search as an iterative process of query specification, inspection of the results, and refinement of the query. Orienteering along statements is natural to get from one resource to another, but when a user starts by issuing a query, she is faced with a *collection* of better or worse matches from which she needs to orienteer. Yee et al. (2003) have explored *faceted metadata browsing* as a way to let users orienteer through a collection of data by choosing to restrict certain attributes of the information.

In Haystack, we are exploring ways to bring orienteering tools from the text-search domain to the database domain (Sinha 2003; Sinha and Karger 2005). We propose to think of a resource's attributes and values (predicates and objects) as features of that resource that can be used for search and similarity estimation, much as the words in a document are used in text search. Put another way, we can think of associating to each item a "virtual document" containing "words" such as "author:yc1yb87Karger" and "Send-Date:012937" (note that URIs are kept in the terms in order to differentiate values that are lexicographically identical but semantically distinct). We can apply all the well-studied techniques of fuzzy text search to those virtual documents.

For example, given any item, we can define "similar items" to be those that share many of the same attribute values. These may well be worth displaying when we are looking at an item, as they will likely assist the user's orienteering. Text-search research suggests various *term-weighting* approaches to decide which attributes are "important" in deciding similarity—for example, extremely common attributes should likely be ignored. When it comes to the common search process of issuing queries, browsing the results, and modifying the query, the text-search community has also developed various *query refinement* and *relevance feedback* techniques that can be used to suggest next steps. It is just such suggestions that are presented in the left pane of figure 3.1.

### Database Search

We also offer a general-purpose "find" interface that lets people design a database query against the RDF model. At present it is limited to expressing constraints that specific predicates must take on certain values. We have invested relatively little effort in this interface, because we see the need to express a query in this way as a sign of failure of the more lightweight navigation tools. Instead of a generic query interface, we expect that specific useful queries will likely be packaged up by developers as operations (discussed above) that use domain-specific dialogues to capture the information necessary to formulate the query.

## Discussion

Having presented the Haystack system, we now turn to a discussion of some of our design choices and of some of the open questions that we continue to examine.

### Why a Semantic Network?

Our discussion of Haystack may lead one to ask why we use a database or structured model at all. The user sees almost no sign of the underlying database: tuples are never shown, and database querying is deprecated. One might think, given our focus on link traversal, we would be better off simply storing user information as HTML in some kind of "personal web."

On the contrary, we argue that a semistructured data model is absolutely critical to the design of a personalizable information-management system. Much of the data users work with clearly *is* structured, relying heavily on properties and relationships to other items. Unlike the web, in which each link must be manually labeled with a textual description of its role, a structured model gives a concise machine-readable way to indicate that role played by a certain class of links. Our view-rendering architecture can make use of that structure to render information objects in a variety of informative ways. And the representation of links in machine-readable form means that, even if complex database queries are beyond end users' capabilities, power users can package up complex database queries (as operations) and information presentations (as views and lenses) that can then be incorporated by typical users to increase the capabilities of their system. Even more generally, the structure available in the model makes it possible to write various autonomous agents that can import and manipulate data on behalf of the end user.

### Semantic Networks Are Universal

We also argue that a semantic network, and RDF in particular, offers a natural "universal data model" that should be adopted widely in the development of applications. The semantic network is rich enough to represent a tremendous portion of the information that users need to work with. At the same time, it is simple enough to be incorporated into any application design with very little effort. All that is needed is a mechanism for naming individual objects, and a representation for specific relationships connecting those named objects.

With such a representation, applications can easily make use of data created by other applications, even if they understand nothing else about those applications' semantics. An object name is enough to let an application create a live link to the object in another application. A relation connecting two objects can be exploited by an application without much understanding of the meaning of that link (as is the case on the web). Invariably, applications will hold some information that is too "complicated" to expose into the semantic network—the individual pixels of an image, or the fuzzy classification scheme of some complex data filer—but these can easily hide inside the individual information objects named in the network and be handled by applications that do understand the internals of those objects. Meanwhile, search tools can let users query on and browse the metadata represented by the semantic network without understanding the semantics of those relationships or the information objects to which they relate. Much like text or files, relations are universal enough to be worth giving a standard representation, so that cross-application tools (like clipboards and desktop search engines) can help to reduce the problem of data fragmentation across applications.

It is also worth noting that much of what each application does is just a straightforward manipulation of relations and attributes. Nearly every application offers some sort of "collection" framework, with the same drag-and-drop interactions for moving items among collections. Many offer "annotations"—customized fields that can be filled in with arbitrary text—again using similar interfaces. Offering these capabilities by application is a waste of the developer's effort, and also means that they cannot be used across applications. Given the essential simplicity of the intended data model manipulations, there is good reason to expose it at a system-wide level, much as the manipulation of files (and ASCII text) is exposed in existing systems.

### The Role of Schemata

While we rely heavily on a structured representation, the same is not obviously true of schemata. We allow the user to relate arbitrary objects in a schema-violating fashion—the author of a document can be a piece of furniture, the delivery date a person. And we allow users to craft arbitrary new relations to connect objects, without providing any schematic descriptions.

**On not using schemata** On the whole, we believe this schema-light approach is necessary in a personal information-management system. Given schemata, we must choose whether to enforce them or not. As with developers designing applications, we will invariably find users wanting to record information that will violate our schemata. At that point, we must choose whether to enforce our schemata and forbid users from recording information they consider important, or to allow for the violation of our schemas. Although the latter choice makes it challenging for us to design the structure of our system, the former defeats the fundamental goal: to let users record information they need. Mangrove (see Halevy et al. 2003) takes a similar tack, arguing that in practice schema will need to be crafted to fit existing data, rather than the reverse.

Of course, one might argue that the user does not know best. Perhaps enforcement can be couched as an educational experience that teaches users how they ought to be structuring their information. We suspect, however, that users are too set in their ways for such an approach to work. Even if an interface can steer users to *record* information the "right" way, we expect users returning to seek that information will look for it the "wrong" way that they original envisioned, and thus be unable to find it because it was recorded "right." We need to record information the way we expect users to seek it, even if we expect them to seek it incorrectly.

**On using schemata** Although we do not envision enforcing schemas, they nonetheless pervade Haystack. For the sake of consistency, we do attempt to steer users toward reasonable information schemata. We expect that the "preexisting conditions" established by the large number of schemata initially distributed with Haystack will lead to users having similar in-the-large knowledge representations, so that standard views, queries, and operations work with them.

Schemata play a particularly important role in the design of views. In particular, we make heavy use of **Type** assertions to decide on appropriate views and operations; a user with a highly nonstandard type system will also need a highly nonstandard interface to work with it. The choice of which attributes to display in the view of an object of a given type is also schematic—it expresses an expectation that those attributes will typically be available, and that other attributes will not (or will not be important). When users modify views, they are in a sense modifying the schemas associated with the viewed types. A key difference, however, is that the schematic constraints suggested by views are "soft." While a view implies that certain attributes are expected, the lack of one simply results in no information being displayed. We can see this in figure 3.1: while the inbox display suggests the need for a sender and date associated with each object, a person can be included in the collection, with the only consequence being some blank fields. Equally important is the fact that multiple views mean that, in a sense, different schemata can be imposed on the same object at different times, depending on the task the user is undertaking.

Although we do not enforce schema, the manipulation primitives of our user interface often make strong suggestions. Schematic annotations about whether a given property is single-valued or multi-valued affect the behavior of drag and drop: dropping on a single-valued field may *replace* the value of the property while dropping on a multi-valued field may incorporate an *additional* value for the property. Again, these suggestions are not rigidly enforced: with sufficient effort, a user can add a second value to a schematically single-valued attribute. At that point, views that assume single-valuedness may end up displaying only one of the two assigned values nondeterministically. Of course, there is always the opportunity for the user to modify the view to repair this flaw. And database queries, which address the data without the constraints imposed by views, can make full use of the multiple values.

Underlying our use of schemas is the general research question of how to make use of database schemata that are "usually true." We have already discussed ways that usually true schemata can facilitate the design of information views. At the programmer level, schemata let the developer write clearer code, as they can avoid complex case analyses for dealing with data. As a simple example, knowing that a given property is always present means that one can skip the code needed to deal with its absence. An intriguing question is to what extent usually true schemata can be used to maintain clear code. At present, Haystack operations are filled with various blocks of code dealing with schema exceptions—for example, an operation that sorts on dates needs to check explicitly whether each date is actually of type date. In other cases, operations fail silently when they encounter unexpected exceptions (arguably, this is reasonable behavior, effectively refusing to apply the operation to schema-violating data). One might hope instead to write code in which all schema violations are caught implicitly and branched off to some kind of exception-handling block. But this begs the question of describing that exception-handling code, and in particular giving clean descriptions of the ways the schema can be violated and of the desired defaults to apply when they are.

**Haystack Limitations**

Our use of Haystack has highlighted assorted limitations and flaws in the design. One significant flaw is "UI ambiguity." Given that every object on the screen is alive, it is sometimes difficult for the user interface to guess which object a user is addressing with a given click. Any point on the screen is generally contained in several nestings of hierarchically displayed objects, and when the user clicks it is unclear which level of the nesting he is addressing. For context menus, we resolve this problem by giving the author access to menus for *all* the objects nested at the click point. As can be seen in figure 3.1, the context menu offers access to operations on the email sender, on the email message of which that sender is a part, and on the inbox of which the email message is a part. When the user drags and drops an object, we make the heuristic decision to address the "most specific" (lowest in the hierarchy) objects at the click and drop points. This is often correct, but it sometimes leads to difficulties. For example, in order to drop an item onto a display of a collection, one must carefully seek out a portion of the collection display that is *not* owned by any recursively rendered member of the collection. Much research remains to be done on the best way to disambiguate UI actions.

The power we give users over the data model can also be damaging. Haystack does not offer users much protection to users as they perform operations that could destroy their data. Beyond the users' own data, since the entire interface is described as data, users can corrupt their interfaces in ways that make them impossible to use. For example, users can dissociate views from the data types they present, and suddenly find themselves unable to view information.

The proper solution to this problem is to develop effective access control (particularly write-control) methods on the data. We have not addressed this critical issue, and pose it as an open problem below.

## Other Applications

In this section, we speculate on some other roles for the architecture we have created: to let users consume the semistructured data being produced by the *Semantic Web* effort (Berners-Lee, Hendler, and Lasilla 2001), and to let individual users contribute to that effort by sharing or publishing some of their own semistructured information.

### The Semantic Web

Whether or not one accepts the need for a semantic network on each user's desktop, semantic networks seem destined to play a critical role in information dissemination as the so-called Semantic Web (Berners-Lee, Hendler, and Lasilla 2001) evolves. The web is an extremely rich source of information, but its HTML documents present that information in "human readable" form—that is, one in which the semantics of the documents are decoded by human beings based on their understanding of human language. Such documents cannot be easily digested by automated agents attempting to extract and exploit information on behalf of users. Thus, momentum is building behind an effort to present information on the web in RDF and XML, forms more amenable to automated use.

One might think that the richer semantics offered by the Semantic Web versus the traditional web could also increase human users' ability to retrieve information from it. But at present the opposite is true, since no good interfaces exist for the Semantic Web. On the Semantic Web, data and services are exposed in a semantics-rich machine-readable fashion, but user interfaces for examining that data, when they exist at all, are usually created from centralized assemblies of data and services. For example, with a semantic portal (e.g., SEAL, Stojanovic et al. 2001), or Semantic Search (Guha, McCool, and Miller 2003), database administrators aggregate semantically classified information together on a centralized server for dissemination to web users. This helps users access the Semantic Web through a traditional web browser.

But a web portal interface has the same drawbacks as traditional applications. It seems unlikely that one designer can create an interface that is "just right" for all the distinct individuals who will use it. Also, the design of any one portal has in mind a fixed ontology; arbitrary information arriving from other parts of the Semantic Web ("other applications") cannot be automatically incorporated into views generated by the portal. If some schema is augmented, no portal will be able to present information from the augmented schema until the portal developer modifies his or her display system. Thus, portals take us back to the balkanized information structures we tried to remove with a semantic network model.

On the other hand, if the user's client software could perform this data aggregation and user interface construction on a per-user basis, then we could restore a user's ability to freely navigate over information and services on the Semantic Web. Our view architecture offers just such an opportunity to integrate data at the client end (Quan and Karger 2004). Separate pieces of information about a single resource that used to require navigation through several different websites can be merged together onto one screen, and this merging can occur without specialized portal sites or coordination between websites/databases. Furthermore, services applicable to some piece of information need not be packaged into the web page containing that information, nor must information be copied and pasted across websites to access services; semantic matching of resources to services (operations) that can consume them can be done by the client and exposed in the form of menus. By crafting and distributing views and operations, users can create and publish new ways of looking at existing information without modifying the original information source.

## Collaboration and Content Creation

Our discussion so far has focused on one user's interaction with her own information (and then the Semantic Web). But we believe that our system can enhance the recording of knowledge by individuals for communal use, as well as the search for and use of that knowledge by broader communities.

One of the tremendous benefits of the World Wide Web is that it dramatically lowered the bar for individuals wishing to share their knowledge with a broader community. It became possible for any individual, without sophisticated tool support, to record information that could then be located and accessed by others. If the same were done on the Semantic Web, then information recorded by users can be much richer, making it more useful to other individuals (and automated agents) than plain HTML.

Unfortunately, the state-of-the-art tools for authoring Semantic Web information are graph editors that directly expose the information objects as nodes and properties as arcs connecting those nodes (Eriksson et al. 1999; Pietriga, n.d.). Such tools require a far more sophisticated user than do the simple HTML editors that let naive users publish their knowledge to the World Wide Web.

Haystack makes it easy for users to author structured information, which is already represented in the Semantic Web's native RDF format. This lowers the bar for a user who decides to expose some of his "internal use" information to the world at large. Traditionally, someone who read a document and annotated it for his own use would have to do substantial work to convert those annotations (and possibly the document) to HTML to be published on the web. With a semantic network representation, the document and annotations are already in the right form for publication on the Semantic Web, and the user only needs to decide who should have access to them.

Of course, the access-control problem is a difficult one, made more difficult by the fine granularity of the data model. We need a simple interface letting users specify which properties and relationships on which objects should be visible to which people.

On the opposite side, when information is being gathered from numerous sources, an individual must start making decisions of trust. Again, interfaces must be developed to let users specify which Semantic Web assertions they wish to incorporate as "truth" in their own semantic networks.

Another significant issue that must be tackled when users collaborate is the problem of divergent schemata. If each user is allowed to modify his information representation, then it is unlikely that these representations will align when data is exchanged. We hope that this problem can be ameliorated by sharing view prescriptions and operations along with data.

A piece of related work that we should mention here is the REVERE system, and in particular the MANGROVE project (Halevy et al. 2003). REVERE shares many of Haystack's goals and methods. Like Haystack, REVERE aims to colonize a useful point somewhere between structured and unstructured information. Haystack focuses on helping each individual manage their own information better. For REVERE, in contrast, collaboration is a primary goal. Thus, issues of schema alignment that can be pushed to the future for Haystack become primary drivers for the design of REVERE.

## Related Work

Much recent work has highlighted the problems created by application-centric data management and has proposed ways to stretch or coordinate applications to address the problem. Bellotti et al. (2003) observed that email applications were being used for task management, and showed how to augment an email application's "views" to support this additional task. Ravasio, Guttormsen-Schär, and Krueger (2004) have given evidence of the problems users run into when trying to perform tasks whose data spans multiple applications. In this volume, Kaptelinin and Boardman argue that one must instead take a "workspace-centric approach" that brings together the data needed for a task, instead of the data managed by one single application.

There have been several efforts in the past to center information management on the idea of relations. The Presto project (Dourish et al. 2000) proposed to do away with static directories as the key organizing framework documents, and to instead base location on queries against metadata that was recorded for each file. Lifestreams, discussed in this volume (Freeman and Gelernter), focused on one piece of metadata above all: the time of last use. These two systems continued to focus on the file as the basic unit of information, however, and emphasized queries rather than linking, display, and browsing.

The ObjectLens system (Lai and Malone 1988) is a clear forerunner of many of the ideas we explore in Haystack. ObjectLens emphasized the idea of arbitrary information objects drawn from a type hierarchy, with attributes and links to other objects. OVAL (Malone, Lai, and Fry 1995) was a tool for rapidly creating applications out of "objects, views, agents, and links" similar to the workspace design used in Haystack.

The WinCuts tool (Tan, Meyers, and Czerwinski 2004) demonstrates an alternative approach to freeing data from applications: it cuts out small windows into applications so that individual pieces of data from those applications can be viewed (near data from other applications) without the clutter of the rest of the application. Because WinCuts operates at the pixel level, it is extremely generic—it can snag information from near any application. But this is also its weakness. Since only the pixels of different applications are unified, and not the data, WinCuts creates no additional semantic linkage between the data in multiple applications. Dragging data from one WinCut to another works only if the two underlying applications are already set up to share data.

Several chapters in this volume propose interesting new relations that are worth recording between information objects, or interesting new visualizations of existing or new relationships (e.g., Fisher and Nardi, Freeman and Gelertner, Plaisant et al.). Under the current approach to application development, each of those tools must be developed from scratch, and extensive work invested in attaching to and remote-controlling existing applications for working with the given data objects. This kind of integration work must be repeated for each new approach. And the work would multiply even further if someone were ambitious enough to try to build an application that incorporated *all* the different approaches. This seems wasteful, given that in each case the core idea is simply to track some additional relations and to create some views that exploit those relations. An infrastructure such as Haystack would make it much simpler to incorporate such new relations and views in a single system as they arise, and invoke each of them at the times that are appropriate, as opposed to crafting new and distinct applications (and convincing users to migrate to them) for each new idea.

## Conclusion

The Haystack framework demonstrates some of the benefits of managing user information uniformly in a semistructured data model. Its separation of data from presentation lets us knock down the barriers to information manipulation imposed by the current application model. It will allow users to gather precisely the information they need to tackle a given task and visualize it with the views that best convey the information required.

## Notes

1. A direct observation of this phenomenon can be found in Nicolson Baker's (1994), in which he laments how the transfer of paper card catalogs to electronic databases lost fascinating information that had been penciled onto the cards by patrons.
2. Even though we are optimistic about the payoff, a quick perusal of colleagues' offices and desks suggests that many of us are too shortsighted to invest the organizational effort now that would pay off in better retrieval later.

## References

Adar, E., Karger, D., and Stein, A. L. (1999). Haystack: Per-user information environments. In *Proceedings of the 8th International Conference on Information and Knowledge Management,* pp. 413–422. Kansas City, Missouri, November 2–6.

Baker, N. (1994). Discards. *New Yorker* 68 (April): 81–83.

Bakshi, K. (2004). Tools for end-user creation and customization of interfaces for information management tasks. Master's thesis, MIT.

Bellotti, V., Ducheneaut, N., Howard, M., and Smith, I. (2003). Taking email to task: The design and evaluation of a task management centered email tool. In *Proceedings of the CHI 2003 Conference: Human Factors in Computing Systems,* pp. 345–352. Ft. Lauderdale, Florida, April 5–10.

Berners-Lee, T., Hendler, J., and Lasilla, O. (2001). The Semantic Web. *Scientific American* 284 (5): 34–43.

Bosc, P., Motro, A., and Pasi, G. (2001). Report on the fourth international conference on flexible query answering systems. *SIGMOD Record* 30 (1): 66–69.

Codd, E. F. (1970). A relational model of data for large shared data banks. *Communications of the ACM* 13 (6): 377–387.

Dourish, P., Edwards, W. K., LaMarca, A., Lamping , J., Petersen, K., Salisbury, M., Terry, D. B., and Thornton, J. (2000). Extending document management systems with user-specific active properties. *ACM Transactions on Information Systems* 18 (2): 140–170.

Eriksson, H., Fergerson, R., Shahar, Y., and Musen, M. (1999). Automatic generation of ontology editors. In *Proceedings of the 12th Banff Knowledge Acquisition Workshop, 1999*. Banff, Canada, October 16–22.

Guha, R., McCool, R., and Miller, E. (2003). Semantic search. In *Proceedings of the World Wide Web Conference, 2003*, pp. 700–709. Budapest, Hungary, May 20–24.

Halevy, A., Etzioni, O., Doan, A., Ives, Z., Madhavan, J., McDowell, L., and Tatarinov, I. (2003). Crossing the structure chasm. In *Proceedings of the First Biennial Conference on Innovative Data Systems Research (CIDR)*. Asilomar, California, January 5–8.

Hogue, A. (2004). Tree pattern inference and matching for wrapper induction on the World Wide Web. Master's thesis, MIT.

Hogue, A., and Karger, D. (2005). Thresher: Automating the unwrapping of semantic content from the World Wide Web. In *Proceedings of the 14th International World Wide Web Conference (WWW)*, pp. 86–95. Chiba, Japan, May 10–14.

Huynh, D., Karger, D., and Quan, D. (2002). Haystack: A platform for creating, organizing, and visualizing information using RDF. *Semantic Web Workshop at WWW2002*. Honolulu, Hawaii, May 7.

Karger, D. R., and Jones, W. (2006). Data unification in personal information management. *Communications of the ACM*, January 2006. 49 (1): 77–82.

Lai, K.-Y., and Malone, T. W. (1988). ObjectLens: A spreadsheet for cooperative work. *ACM Transactions on Office Information Systems* 6 (4): 332–353.

Malone, T. W., Lai, K.-Y., and Fry, C. (1995). Experiments with OVAL: A radically tailorable tool for cooperative work. *ACM Transactions on Information Systems* 13 (2): 177–205.

Manola, M., and Miller, E. (2003). RDF primer. Http://www.w3.org/TR/rdf-primer/.

McGuinness, D. L., and van Harmelen, F. (2003). Owl web ontology language overview. Http://www.w3.org/TR/owl-features/.

Muslea, I., Minton, S., and Knoblock, C. (1999). A hierarchical approach to wrapper induction. In *Proceedings of the Third International Conference on Autonomous Agents (Agents '99)*, pp. 190–197. Seattle, Washington, May 1–5.

Pietriga, E. (n.d.). *Isaviz*. Http://www.w3.org/2001/11/IsaViz/.

Quan, D., Bakshi, K., Huynh, D., and Karger, D. R. (2003). User interfaces for supporting multiple categorization. In *Proceedings of INTERACT: 9th IFIP International Conference on Human Computer Interaction*, pp. 228–235. Zurich, Switzerland, September 1–5.

Quan, D., Bakshi, K., and Karger, D. R. (2003). A unified abstraction for messaging on the semantic web. In *Proceedings of the 12th International World Wide Web Conference*, p. 231. Budapest, Hungary, May 20–24.

Quan, D., Huynh, D., Karger, D., and Miller, R. (2003). User interface continuations. In *Proceedings of UIST (User Interface Systems and Technologies)*, pp. 145–148. Vancouver, Canada, November 2–5.

Quan, D., and Karger, D. R. (2003). Haystack: A platform for authoring end-user Semantic Web applications. In *Proceedings of the International Semantic Web Conference, 2003*. Sanibel Island, Florida, October 20–23.

Quan, D., and Karger, D. R. (2004). How to make a semantic web browser. In *Proceedings of the 13th International World Wide Web Conference*, pp. 255–265. New York City, May 17–22.

Ravasio, P., Guttormsen-Schär, S., and Krueger, H. (2004). In pursuit of desktop evolution: User problems and practices with modern desktop systems. *ACM Transactions on Computer-Human Interaction (TOCHI)* 11 (2): 156–180.

Sinha, V. (2003). Dynamically exploiting available metadata for browsing and information retrieval. Master's thesis, MIT.

Sinha, V., and Karger, D. R. (2005). Magnet: Supporting navigation in semistructured data environments. In *SIGMOD '05: Proceedings of the 2005 ACM SIGMOD International Conference on Management of Data,* pp. 97–106. Baltimore, Maryland, June 13–16.

Stojanovic, N., Maedche, A., Staab, S., Studer, R., and Sure, Y. (2001). SEAL: A framework for developing SEmantic portALs. In *K-CAP '01: Proceedings of the 1st International Conference on Knowledge Capture,* pp. 155–162. Victoria, Canada, October 22–23.

Tan, D. S., Meyers, B., and Czerwinski, M. (2004). WinCuts: Manipulating arbitrary window regions for more effective use of screen space. In *Extended Abstracts of Proceedings of ACM Human Factors in Computing Systems CHI 2004,* pp. 1525–1528. Vienna, Austria, April 24–29.

Teevan, J., Alvarado, C., Ackerman, M., and Karger, D. R. (2004). The perfect search engine is not enough: A study of orienteering behavior in directed search. In *Proceedings of the ACM CHI Conference on Human Factors in Computing Systems, 2004,* pp. 415–422. Vienna, Austria, April 24–29.

Yee, P., Swearingen, K., Li, K., and Hearst, M. (2003). Faceted metadata for image search and browsing. In *Proceedings of ACM CHI Conference on Human Factors in Computing,* pp. 401–408. Ft. Lauderdale, Florida, April 5–10.

# 4

# Explorations in Task Management on the Desktop

George Robertson, Greg Smith, Brian Meyers, Patrick Baudisch, Mary Czerwinski, Eric Horvitz, Daniel Robbins, and Desney Tan

## Introduction

An increasing number of tasks require that users coordinate and operate on information from multiple sources. Each source of information is typically contained within a window, the fundamental unit at which users currently manipulate information. With continuing advances in computing and networking capabilities, users can open large numbers of windows, each containing different information. Often, users benefit from simultaneously viewing related information that exists within different windows. Additionally, the spatial layout of this information may be crucial to effective task performance as it helps users not only to establish spatial relationships but also to visually compare contents.

Subsequent chapters in this book describe various projects aimed at making users more efficient at managing and performing their tasks. Owing to the various interpretations of what constitutes a coherent activity, each project defines the meaning of a task differently. We have found through interviews that many end users loosely define a task by a group of windows and the actions that operate on them. Examples include working on finances, writing a paper, or managing correspondence, each of which may involve a continuously changing set of many windows and/or applications. Users today are faced with an increasingly difficult job of managing these windows and tasks. In this chapter we describe our work in building tools that allow users to effectively manipulate windows on their desktop in order to complete their tasks.

**Task Management Research**

When working on a task, users often need to see multiple windows simultaneously (Kandogan and Shneiderman 1997). Additionally, researchers have observed that information workers often switch between concurrent tasks, either because of multitasking activities (Bannon et al. 1983) or external interruptions (Cutrell, Czerwinski, and Horvitz 2001; Czerwinski, Cutrell, and Horvitz 2000; Czerwinski, Horvitz, and Wilhite 2004; Gillie and Broadbent 1989; Maglio and Campbell 2000). Thus, the two main problems that we focus on are (i) effectively managing multiple windows and tasks, and (ii) recovering from task switches and interruptions.

There exists a large body of research exploring window management systems, which allow users to manage multiple windows on the screen (for history and review, see Myers 1988). In the traditional desktop metaphor, managing tasks can involve dozens of operations, including opening, moving, and resizing windows, as well as scrolling content. This can be extremely tedious and adds considerably to cognitive load as users perform their main tasks. Additionally, the desktop metaphor has inadequate support for saving and switching between tasks, leading to wasted effort and frustration on the part of the user (Card, Robertson, and York 1996; Henderson and Card 1987; Kandogan and Shneiderman 1997; Robertson, Card, and Mackinlay 1993; Robertson et al. 1998).

Card and Henderson (1987) proposed a solution to these problems in their Rooms system. They observed that tasks can be supported by managing working sets of windows, in much the same way that operating systems manage working sets in memory. In this work, they identified several desirable properties of task management systems, including fast task switching, fast task resumption, and easy reacquisition of mental task context after interruptions. The Rooms system provided a mechanism for particular windows to be associated with particular tasks and for users to switch between these tasks easily.

As an extension to the desktop metaphor, several modern operating systems provide virtual desktop managers. These managers allow users to organize windows onto multiple virtual desktops, and to switch easily between them. Many of these systems are currently available, and are described in XDesk 2003. The virtual desktop metaphor treats the physical display as a viewport into a much larger virtual space. Hence, users with virtual desktop managers potentially have to keep track of how windows and tasks are laid out within a fairly large amount of space. Although users can treat each virtual desktop as a different task, most virtual desktops do not provide explicit task management features. Although virtual desktop managers have had some success, there has been little published on the usefulness or usability of these systems, especially as they relate to task management (cf. Ringel 2003).

In addition to virtual desktop managers, a number of alternative solutions for managing large numbers of windows have been proposed, including extending the user's desktop with additional low-resolution screen space (Baudisch, Good, and Stewart 2001), extending the desktop into 3D space (Wurnig 1998), into zoomable space as in Pad++ (Bederson and Hollan 1994), and into the time dimension (Rekimoto 1999). Also, systems that involve bumping other windows away (Bell and Feiner 2000; Hutchings and Stasko 2004; Kandogan and Shneiderman 1997) and tiled window managers (Bly and Rosenberg 1986; Morris et al. 1986; Teitelman 1986) address some of these issues. Elastic Windows uses a space-filling tiled layout and addresses the problem of simultaneous display of multiple windows by allowing the user to create containers into which multiple windows can be dragged (Kandogan and Shneiderman 1997).

3D Rooms (Robertson, Card, and Mackinlay 1993) extended the ideas of Rooms using a 3D virtual environment to represent the information workspace. This system was not strictly a window manager, since abstract information visualizations replaced windows. The basic motivation in this system was to engage human spatial cognition and perception in order to make task management easier. Web Forager (Card, Robertson, and York 1996) and Data Mountain (Robertson et al. 1998) each used a virtual environment to more fully engage human spatial cognition and memory while managing documents. Studies of Data Mountain (Czerwinski et al. 1999; Robertson et al. 1998) demonstrated that placing documents in space helps users remember where the documents are during later retrievals. Our work shares this approach. We provide tools to bring the advantages of human spatial cognition and perception to managing windows and tasks within our current set of computer applications.

## Our Approach

While working on their tasks, users need easy access to particular windows and applications that contain relevant information. Hence, we assert that an effective task management system should provide mechanisms for users to easily group relevant sets of windows, to organize the groups and windows within the groups, to switch between groups, and to lay out how the groups and windows are displayed on the screen.

In this chapter, we present three systems that explore different facets of task management: *GroupBar*, *Scalable Fabric,* and *Task Gallery.* GroupBar adds new semantics to the existing Microsoft Windows taskbar for organizing and managing tasks. Scalable Fabric uses scaling and a focus-in-context metaphor to visualize groups of related windows. In this system, all tasks are scaled and located in the periphery so that they are simultaneously visible. Finally, Task Gallery is a 3D environment in which organizing and managing tasks is grounded in the physical-world metaphor of a gallery. For each of these interfaces, we performed user studies that illustrate lessons learned through the design process that test the usability of our systems.

## GroupBar

GroupBar was designed with the goal of providing task management features by extending the current Windows taskbar metaphor. GroupBar preserves basic taskbar tile functionality, presenting one tile for each open window in the system, and showing the currently "active" window tile in a darker, depressed-button state. Any tile can be clicked on to activate the corresponding window or to minimize the window if it is already active. Going beyond current taskbar functionality to offer task management support, GroupBar allows users to drag and drop tiles that represent open windows into high-level tasks called "Groups," and to switch between these tasks with a single click of the mouse. Since no drag interaction is defined on the tiles of the original taskbar, users who choose not to use this grouping functionality can use GroupBar as if it were the regular taskbar. The similarity to the Windows taskbar not only allows leveraging familiarity in order to reduce learning time, but also provides us with a basis for a targeted comparison of the task-management features GroupBar provides.

## Task Formation in GroupBar

With GroupBar, users can group multiple windows into tasks simply by dragging a window tile onto another tile. During the drag, a white caret animates along the bar to track the pointer location and suggest the result of the drop operation (figure 4.1a). When a Group is formed, GroupBar visually unifies member tiles by surrounding them with a gray background and complementing the newly formed unit with a green "tab" at the top. Users can add windows to a Group by repeating this drag-and-drop action, and they can ungroup a tile by dragging it out of a Group. When a Group is reduced to a single tile, the remaining tile is automatically ungrouped and the Group tab disappears.

## Task Organization in GroupBar

The currently shipping Windows taskbar displays the window tiles in the order in which the underlying applications were started. However, we felt

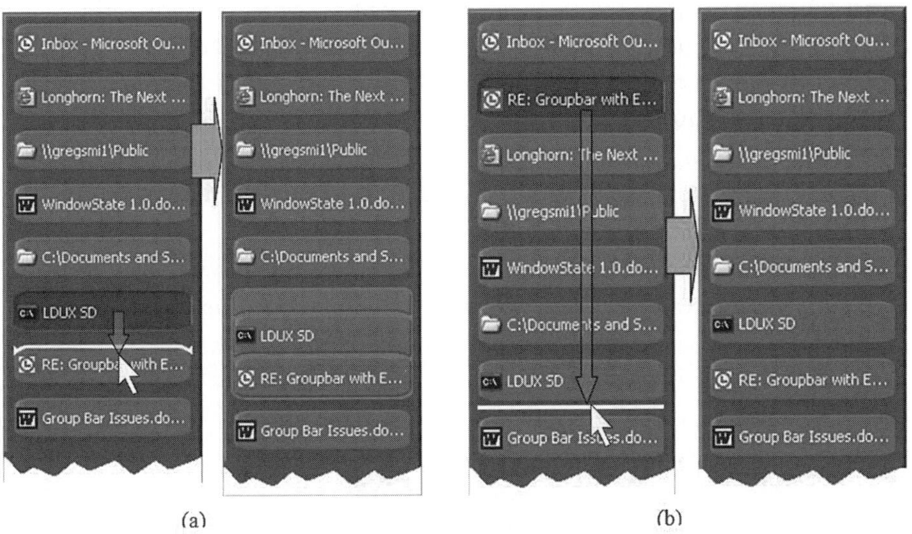


**Figure 4.1**
GroupBar's basic look and functionality: In (a), dragging a window on top of another tile combines both tiles into a Group. Grouping information is primarily conveyed via subtle changes in shape and surrounding coloration of grouped tiles, using the green Group tab as a high-contrast unifier and control surface. In (b), dragging a window tile or Group tab between other tiles rearranges the ordering of tiles to allow users to make better use of spatial memory.

that users could more easily locate their windows and tasks if they were allowed to explicitly order the tiles. Hence, we allow users to rearrange tasks as well as individual tiles to provide a more meaningful order within the GroupBar (figure 4.1b). This function is accomplished by dragging and dropping the items to the desired location on the bar between existing tiles or Groups. With this small improvement, we are building upon our philosophy of using spatial positioning as a memory and task-switching aid.

Providing simultaneous support for grouping and reordering semantics within the drag-and-drop operation required careful design. Grouping carets (see figure 4.2) are distinguished from rearrangement carets not just by position but also by curvature, which provides a much more definitive visual cue. In fact, this consideration was the motivation for choosing a curved window tile design instead of purely rectangular tile designs used by previous prototypes and by the taskbar itself.

As figure 4.2 shows, the screen space containing the straight-line caret is too small to allow users to actually acquire this space efficiently. GroupBar solves this problem by decoupling the target surfaces from the visual location of the caret symbols—distributing the screen space between tile centers evenly among the three adjacent targets, independent of where the caret symbols appear. Our experience so far with this assignment of target surfaces is positive, and the benefit of larger minimum drop areas seems to outweigh the lack of absolute positional precision.

As evident in the first two figures, GroupBar can be configured to either horizontal or vertical form at any time by dragging the bar to a different edge of the screen, just like the standard Windows taskbar.

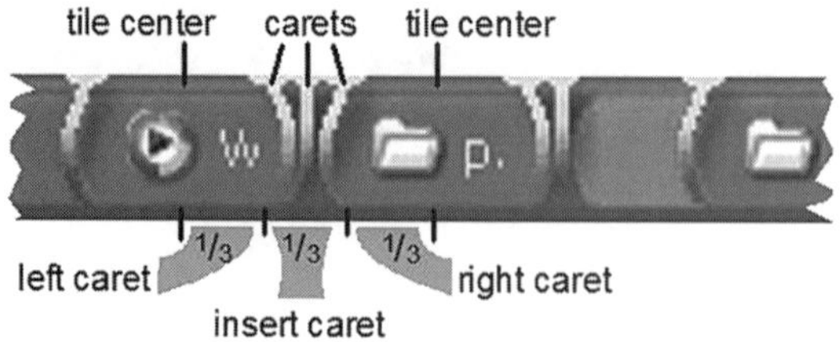


**Figure 4.2**
Bar fragment and all possible carets over it. In order to allow users to easily acquire the drop position for insertion, GroupBar distributes the activation surface evenly over the various possibilities.

**Switching between Tasks in GroupBar**

Users can quickly switch between tasks by clicking on a task's green Group tab. The Group-level operations in GroupBar are analogous to existing window-level operations for minimizing and restoring windows using the Windows taskbar. Clicking on an inactive Group tab activates the group. Clicking on an active Group tab toggles between minimizing all windows within the Group and restoring all those windows. With this simple extension, GroupBar becomes an efficient task-switching tool. Switching between multi-window tasks is done by clicking the GroupBar tile of the new task, much as switching between individual windows is done by clicking the corresponding tile of the new window.

Whereas virtual desktop managers tend to make a strict separation between tasks, GroupBar deliberately allows users to simultaneously display any subset of windows, even if they are assigned to different tasks, simply by clicking the individual tiles. For maximum flexibility, we included several options in the right-click (context) menu of the bar to control the experience of switching between various windows and tasks. For instance, the "Minimize Others on Group Click" binary option can be useful in reducing unnecessary screen clutter when switching to a new task.

**Task Layout in GroupBar**

Beyond task-switching, we added a number of window management features into the right-click (context) menu of the Group tab (see figure 4.3).

As noted before, repeatedly moving and sizing multiple windows individually to get just the right information displayed is tedious when managing one or more multi-window tasks. We saw an opportunity to address some of these window layout issues when extending the familiar window "Maximize" function to the Group level. The obvious translation, maximizing each window in the Group, would make all the Group's windows overlap one another, which is not likely to be useful. Instead, we extended the analogy by creating a "Layout Group" operation which serves to maximize the *collective* space taken up by the Group, rather than maximizing the space taken up by each individual window. By using the grouping information that the user has provided, the system can make much

**Figure 4.3**
Clicking the green Group tab restores all windows in that Group and brings them to the foreground. Right-clicking a Group tab offers other actions.

more intelligent choices about the most effective usage of overall screen space for a given task. The current implementation of GroupBar offers a submenu, shown in figure 4.4, which allows users to choose among several layout templates that take into account the screen configuration of the system.

This implementation is only a small step toward realizing what we believe to be the full potential value of such layout assistance. For one, we envision future Group layout choosers that fill in the stylized window representations with thumbnail previews of the actual windows in the Group. This would provide the user with the strongest sense of control and predictability about the effects of the operation. Also, the layouts should take into account the number of windows in the Group and their current sizes and positions in order to present the most specific, customized set of options for a given Group. Customization could be further

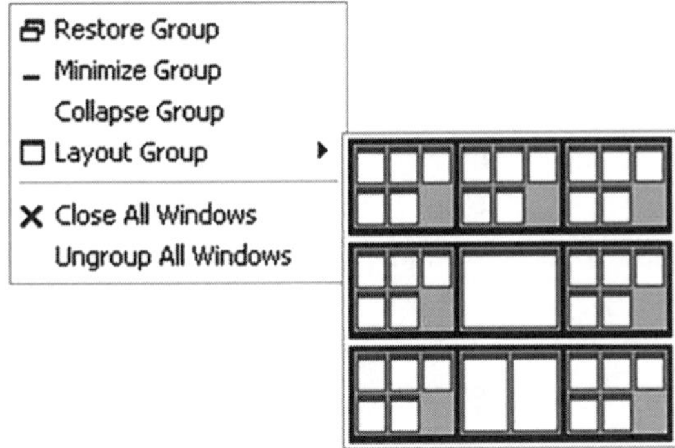


**Figure 4.4**
GroupBar context menu allows users to arrange all windows in that Group according to layout templates. Here the user uses a triple-monitor display in a horizontal configuration, thus every layout extends across three screens.

exploited by allowing users to design their own layout templates, or by using learning algorithms to develop auto-customized templates corresponding to individual usage patterns over time. Even further out, we imagine being able to use the semantic and visual content of the windows and tasks themselves to provide even more efficient and intelligent layout choices to the user.

## Scaling Up

Our research suggests that increasing display size is associated with larger numbers of open windows, leading to even more crowded desktops in the future. Hence, we must create designs that can smoothly scale to larger numbers of managed windows. As the number of displayed windows increases, any type of fixed bar interface will eventually run out of space. GroupBar extends the current mechanisms used by the taskbar and implements two ways of dealing with increasing numbers of windows and tasks.

On the standard Windows taskbar, the "Group Similar Taskbar Buttons" option is turned on by default. This option combines all window tiles belonging to the same application into a single taskbar tile that acts as a pop-up menu when clicked. Unfortunately, the taskbar "grouping" criteria (namely, the application) has no necessary correlation with the user's notion of the task at hand, and consequently no necessary correlation with the frequency and recency relationships inherent in a user-defined Group. So although the taskbar's grouping mechanism does serve to reclaim space, it actually hinders window and task switching by invalidating spatial memory and relegating a relatively arbitrary set of windows to hidden locations regardless of their importance to the task at hand.

Our approach to dealing with large numbers of windows leverages GroupBar's knowledge about Groups. Groups have a "collapse" ability that can be triggered explicitly via the "Collapse Group" command on the Group context menu or automatically under certain circumstances (for example, when running out of tile room on a particular bar). Groups collapse into a more space-efficient representation (as shown vertically in figure 4.5b and horizontally in figure 4.5c), which shows just the icon of each window inside the Group tab. The "Auto-Collapse Inactive Groups" option in GroupBar collapses any Group that does not have a currently active window. Even relying on a simple "least recently used" Group criterion to collapse only when strictly necessary, we believe the GroupBar's features to be an improvement over the existing taskbar.

When the "grouping" strategy is insufficient, the taskbar allows users to page through sets of tiles using small arrow handles (shown in figure 4.5a). This makes a large number of potentially relevant tiles difficult to access, and with no feedback as to the current tile "page" number, the search for an individual tile can be lengthy. Alternatively, the user can resize the taskbar such that more tiles are visible, but this subtracts directly from the space used for window content.

Rather than paging through multiple tilesets on the bar or increasing the individual bar's size, GroupBar allows multiple simultaneous bar instantiations on different edges of the same desktop. Additional bars, initially empty, are added using the "Add New Bar" command from the GroupBar context menu. The user can position the newly created bar on any external edge of any monitor, and then populate it using the same drag-and-drop mechanism as used within a bar. This allows GroupBar to handle a much larger number of windows and Groups effectively. Following our principle of trying to better exploit spatial memory, this also complements and expands upon the simple tile reordering feature by allowing a much wider range of 2D placement opportunities, either when moved explicitly by the user or automatically by the system.

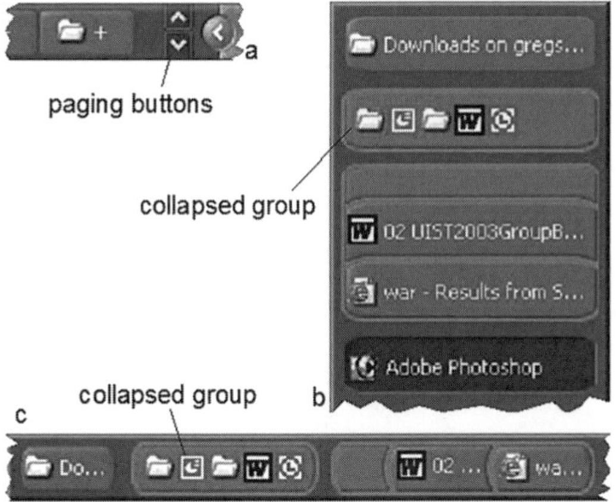


**Figure 4.5**
(a) Taskbar overflow vs. (b, c) Collapsed Groups in GroupBar.

**First Study Results**

We performed two studies involving GroupBar. The first study was a 7–10 day *in situ* study of five people using GroupBar on their own multiple-monitor systems with their own work. In this study, our goal was to determine whether our design of the GroupBar would contradict existing taskbar users' expectations, and to determine if the new grouping abilities would be easy to learn. To that end, we provided our participants with only the GroupBar executable and a very brief email tutorial on how to use its grouping features. As the GroupBar prototype was not integrated with the taskbar itself (which would have required modifications to the Windows operating system), users were instructed to hide the existing taskbar when running GroupBar. All participants fulfilled their commitment to use GroupBar as their primary taskbar for one week, and they did not report any problems with installing GroupBar or understanding its use. As we had hoped, users were able to easily integrate GroupBar into their existing work practices, as evidenced by their comments and grouping habits.

After using GroupBar for a week, four of the participants filled out a user satisfaction questionnaire about the perceived benefits of the system and areas in need of improvement. One user did not return his questionnaire. The user satisfaction findings were favorable, and two of the participants stated they would like to continue using GroupBar after the study, despite its rough edges and lack of integration with the real taskbar. GroupBar scored above average in response to such questions as:

- It is useful to be able to group the tiles on GroupBar by dragging them "on top" of each other.
- It is useful to be able to close/open a group of windows all at once.
- It is useful to have GroupBar remember a layout for a group of windows, so that they open in the same layout as when the user closed the group.
- GroupBar makes multiple monitors more useful.

On the other hand, users did not report finding utility in having non-group windows minimize on a group switch, or in running more than one GroupBar at a time.

We asked users what features of GroupBar most helped them manage their open windows, and what more we could do to design better windows/task management support into GroupBar, and found several commonalities in the responses. Three out of four users talked about their window groupings, implicitly confirming that they considered the "Group" concept to be something that was applicable to their work habits. And virtually all the comments concerning possible improvements were summed up in two suggestions. The first suggestion was simply that the GroupBar and taskbar needed to be unified, so that other features of the taskbar (system notification tray, Start Menu, etc.) were available with grouping semantics on a single bar. This, of course, represents our vision all along—the GroupBar prototype was designed to address only the tile behavior of the taskbar, and would certainly need to incorporate the rest of the non-tile features of the taskbar to be fully functional and viable as a taskbar replacement. The second suggested improvement was more complex. Users suggested that GroupBar perform "auto-grouping" in appropriate cases, so that the benefits of grouping were available without even the minimal drag-and-drop effort to create the Groups. It did not appear from the users' comments that they thought this would be a particularly difficult feature to provide, and this is in fact a feature we had considered during the design phase. We investigated several strategies ranging from simplistic (always adding new windows to the most recent group) to complex (using window title text similarity to perform grouping) but rejected each strategy as potentially more often wrong than right. We realized that to be consistently correct an auto-grouping strategy would have to involve detection and understanding of the user's intent, an extremely difficult problem.

**Second Study Results**

We decided to take the initial feedback from our small field study and get a more robust understanding of GroupBar's hypothesized ease of use over the taskbar. We conducted a comparative lab study with eighteen participants performing timed tasks using either the taskbar or the GroupBar. Each task required participants (all experienced Windows users) to switch between windows within the task in order to complete it; for example, to copy/paste or to reference another document. In addition, the experimenter systematically interrupted the user's work on one task to prompt a switch to a different task. We wanted to see whether we could get a measurable productivity improvement with GroupBar simply by alleviating some of the built-in task-switching overhead imposed by taskbar's constraint of performing task management at the single-window level. Users commented that the tasks and interruptions forcing the switches were similar to what they experienced in the real world, so we feel that the experiment successfully simulated an information worker's daily task switching.

We found a borderline significant task completion time advantage for GroupBar, as shown in figure 4.6. While the quantitative results certainly could have been stronger, we were very encouraged by the consideration that GroupBar was technically a "new" tool for task switching, and we were comparing it against an existing tool that all the participants had years of daily experience using. Even more encouraging were the results of the user satisfaction questionnaire. As shown in table 4.1, users significantly favored GroupBar over taskbar on every question (as determined by ANOVA with Bonferroni corrections for multiple tests, all significant at the $p<.05$ level).

Finally, GroupBar was unanimously preferred over the taskbar. Despite this, many participants suggested improvements to GroupBar. Most frequent requests were for color coding or labeling of the different tasks organized in the bar, and adding tooltips showing document names when a group is collapsed. These features could easily be added to GroupBar.

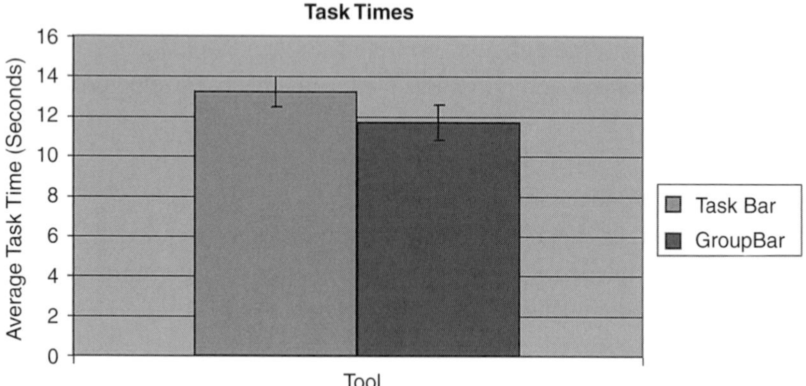


**Figure 4.6**
Average task times +/– one standard error of the mean for taskbar and GroupBar.

**Table 4.1**
Average Satisfaction Ratings for the Taskbar and GroupBar

| Survey Question (1 = Disagree, 5 = Agree) | Taskbar | GroupBar |
|---|---|---|
| Task switching was easy to perform using the . . . | 2.95 | 4.63 |
| It was hard to go back and forth between my various windows and applications using . . . | 3.32 | 1.42 |
| I was satisfied with the functionality of the . . . | 2.68 | 4.42 |
| The [Taskbar/GroupBar] is an attractive innovation for Windows. | 3.16 | 4.42 |

Note: All ratings were significantly in favor of GroupBar at the $p < .05$ level.

Several expert users wanted to see better keyboard accelerator support (like Alt-Tab for switching between Groups) enabled in GroupBar.

## Summary

With GroupBar we wanted to allow users to group and regroup windows easily and quickly, and then allow them to operate on groups of windows (or tasks) as though they were a single unit. We thought that by incorporating a wider array of spatial arrangement preferences, offering users a higher-level organizational structure (the Group), and extending existing window manipulation functions to the Group level, we could design an improved window management experience that is built on the existing taskbar metaphor. We feel that we have achieved these goals: the field study suggested to us that GroupBar was considered valuable by the participants, and the laboratory study allowed us to better verify these benefits in a more controlled setting against familiar, extant techniques. The studies further provide evidence that software tools like GroupBar can provide user assistance as users manage multiple, complex tasks. We find that the task management experience can indeed be improved simply by addressing the existing constraint that window management mechanisms operate only at what has increasingly become an unnaturally "low" level (the level of the individual window).

In the next section, we present Scalable Fabric, a task-management system designed specifically for future computing display surfaces, when large displays or wall projections will replace the smaller, more isolated display surfaces upon which most users interact today.

## Scalable Fabric

In designing our second prototype, Scalable Fabric, we moved beyond the one-dimensional taskbar metaphor dominating current operating systems. The goal in designing this prototype was to look further into the future where users would have larger screens containing many more windows. In an informal study at our corporation (Hutchings et al. 2004), we found that expert users on larger display surfaces leave more applications running and have more windows open. For example, we observed in sixteen users that single-display users tend to keep an average or four windows open at once, while dual-monitor users keep twelve and triple-monitor users keep an average of eighteen windows open.

Scalable Fabric is a system based on managing multi-window "tasks" on the Windows desktop, this time using a focus-plus-context display to allocate screen real estate in accordance with users' attention. Scalable Fabric allows users to leave windows and clusters of windows open and visible at all times via a process of scaling down and moving the windows to the periphery. Scalable Fabric is a focus-plus-context display in the sense that users focusing their attention on a primary task are provided with the context of other work (i.e., competing or potentially related tasks) displayed in the periphery. This use of the periphery leverages both the user's spatial memory and also the user's visual recognition memory for images in order to facilitate task recognition and location (Czerwinski et al. 1999). This mechanism was inspired by the scaling at the edges of the display in Flatland (Mynatt et al. 1999) and by ZoomScapes' location-based scaling mechanism (Guimbretiere, Stone, and Winograd 2001). While ZoomScapes is not a task-management system, its management of sheets and groups of sheets is similar to Scalable Fabric's management of windows and tasks.

To facilitate task switching, Scalable Fabric allows users to group collections of windows that are used together, much like GroupBar does, but in a manner that exploits spatial memory much more extensively. We know from user studies on Data Mountain (Robertson et al. 1998) that spatial memory works in a virtual environment similarly to the way it works in the physical world, and that user task performance is enhanced particularly when the task involves retrieving items placed spatially.

In the remainder of the section, we will first describe details of the Scalable Fabric methodology. We present the results of a comparative user study of Scalable Fabric and the Windows taskbar, as well as a longitudinal field study of Scalable Fabric. Finally, we discuss project directions and opportunities for future research.

**Layout in Scalable Fabric**

In Scalable Fabric, the user defines a central focus area on the display surface by moving periphery boundary markers to desired locations. In figure 4.7, these boundary markers are visible (defined by the thin blue rectangle), but users usually hide the boundary markers unless they are changing the size or shape of the focus area, in which case the markers serve as resize handles. The user's choice of location and size of focus area is typically influenced by the configuration and capabilities of the physical displays. For example, on a triple-monitor display, users may prefer to define the central monitor as the focus area having no upper or lower peripheral regions and use the side monitors as the only peripheral regions.

Within the focus area, windows behave as they normally do on the Windows desktop. The periphery contains windows and clusters of windows, or tasks, which are not currently in use, but may be put to use at any time. Windows in the periphery are smaller so that more tasks can be held there when the user is focusing on something else. With this metaphor, we believe users will rarely need to close or minimize windows in

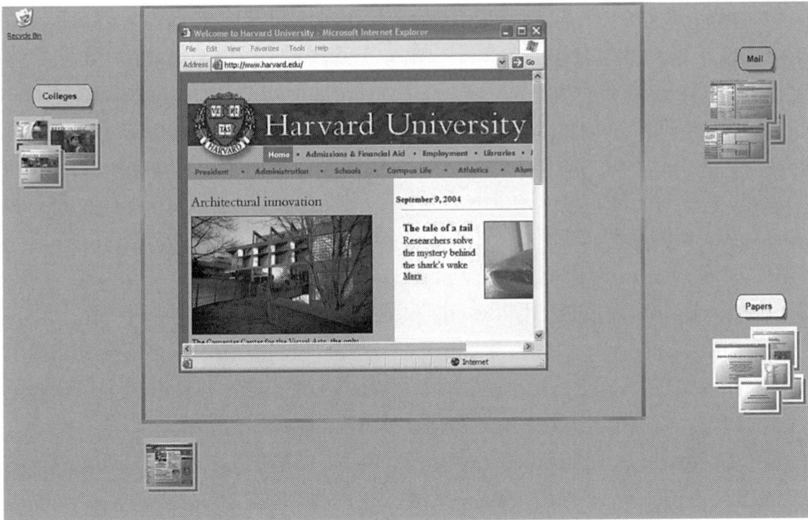


**Figure 4.7**
Scalable Fabric showing the representation of three tasks as clusters of windows, with one of the windows from the Colleges task shown in the focus area. In this case, an option to display the border of the central focus region is turned on.

the traditional sense. Users can take advantage of extra screen real estate, especially on larger displays, to allow the peripheral windows to always be visible.

When a user moves a window into the periphery, it shrinks monotonically with the distance from the focus-periphery boundary, getting smaller as it nears the edge of the screen. When the user clicks on a window in the periphery, it returns to its last focus position; this is the new "restore" behavior, and is accomplished with a one-second animation of the window moving from one location to the other. When the user "minimizes" a window in the focus area, for example, by clicking the window's "minimize" button, it returns to its last peripheral position.

## Task Formation in Scalable Fabric

Scalable Fabric uses natural metaphors and gestures that allow users to define, access, and switch between tasks. To define tasks, windows in the periphery are grouped into clusters enclosed with a colored banner (see figures 4.8 and 4.9). To create a new task, the user simply moves a window in the periphery near another that is not in a task. The user can then name the implicitly created task. Until the task is named, it is ephemeral. That is, if the number of items in the task is reduced to one then the task will be removed (i.e., the task marker will disappear). Moving a window near any task marker makes it part of that task. This behavior makes it easy for users to construct tasks by dragging and dropping windows onto existing windows or clusters of windows.

### Task Organization in Scalable Fabric

When a window is moved into the periphery, other windows temporarily move out of the way. This is similar to the occlusion avoidance behavior employed in Data Mountain (Robertson et al. 1998), and it makes it impossible to obscure one peripheral window with another.

When clusters are moved around, they avoid each other similarly to the way windows avoid one another, except that the stationary cluster remains in position, and the moving cluster moves around it. For moving and scaling windows and clusters in Scalable Fabric, we considered findings from ZoomScapes (Guimbretiere, Stone, and Winograd 2001). As windows are rectangles rather than points, it is important to identify the point about which scaling occurs. Like ZoomScapes, Scalable Fabric uses the cursor location (i.e., the drag point) as the scale point. We experimented with several alternatives and concur with the earlier work that the cursor position is the most useful scale point.

When moving a cluster, scaling the windows in the cluster is not sufficient. ZoomScapes scales the distance between the center of the sheets and the cursor dragging point. In Scalable Fabric, we achieve a more pleasing effect by scaling the distances from the window centers to the center of the cluster. That is, as the cluster gets smaller, the windows move closer together. When a window moves across the scaling boundary, an abrupt change in scale is disconcerting. ZoomScapes solves this by having a bridge zone where a sharp ramp in scaling is applied. Scalable Fabric uses a different approach, and applies a half-second transition animation to the new scale. This appears to be more graceful than the ramp-zone approach.

### Task Switching in Scalable Fabric

In Scalable Fabric, users can use natural gestures to access and toggle among tasks. When a user clicks on a task marker, the entire task is selected, restoring its windows to their focus positions. If the user clicks on a task marker when all of its windows are currently in the focus area, each window in the cluster returns to its peripheral position. If one task is selected and the user clicks on a different task marker, a task switch occurs, that is, all windows of the current task move to their peripheral positions, and the windows comprising the task being selected in the periphery move to their previous configuration in the focus area.

**Iterative Design**

We have pursued a process of iterative design for refining and testing versions of Scalable Fabric. To date, we have created three implementations of the system.

The first version of Scalable Fabric was a prototype that worked with images of windows, which allowed us to refine the visual design and interaction behaviors. Informal studies were conducted to collect usability issues to drive the second design iteration. While users understood the basic ideas, they had significant problems understanding the task marker, which was a 3D card holder.

The second design worked with real windows on the Windows Desktop. A user study comparing Scalable Fabric to the Windows XP taskbar suggested that Scalable Fabric was easily learned and considered valuable by the participants, but several usability issues were noted. The task marker was redesigned to be like a flagpole, but test participants still had problems identifying what it was. In addition, we found that the task occlusion avoidance behavior caused confusion. In this version, while a task was being moved, other tasks would move out of its way (similar to the way peripheral windows avoided each other to prevent occlusion of windows). A study showed no significant difference in task performance time between the two approaches.

The third version of Scalable Fabric (shown in the figures) was developed as a set of refinements on the second design. Figure 4.8 shows a close-up of the appearance of windows and task markers, with the cursor hovering over one window to show its title tooltip. Most of the time the task marker appears as displayed in figure 4.9. However, if the user hovers over the marker or moves a window into the task group, a box appears as rendered in figure 4.9. Based on feedback from the first two designs, the task marker is much simpler in the final design. Also, we redesigned task occlusion avoidance so that the moved task avoids other tasks, rather than

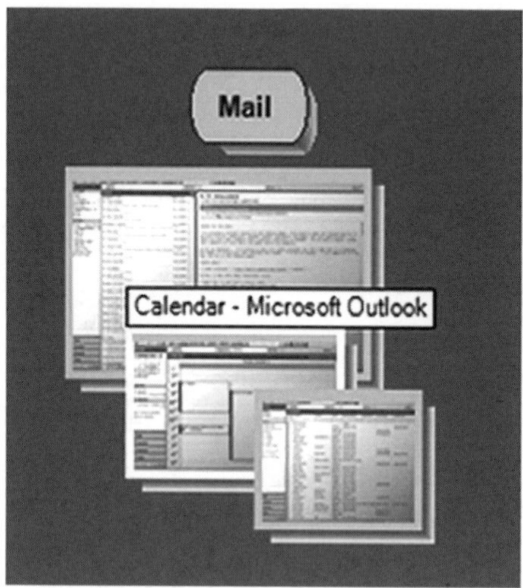


**Figure 4.8**
Close-up of task (third design).

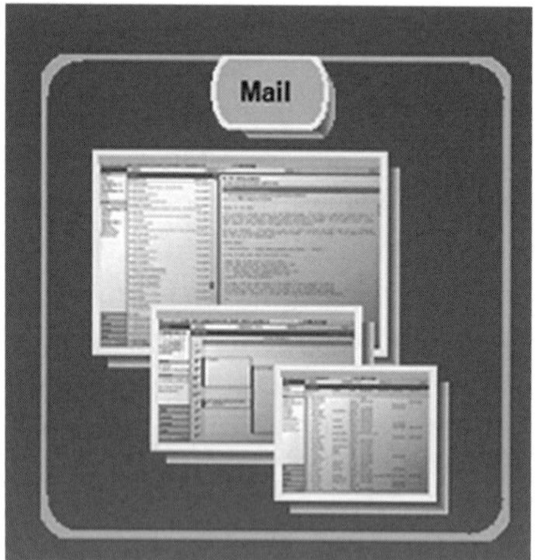


**Figure 4.9**
Task-highlighting during hover.

having the others tasks move out of the way. Test participants found this much more intuitive.

To gather further information about how people actually use virtual desktop managers, and to begin to understand in a more detailed manner how Scalable Fabric might be used in real situations, we conducted a longitudinal study with thirteen participants using their real systems and tasks. This study revealed new opportunities for design iteration. Specifically, as core issues with the design are addressed, system performance and bug fixes have become more important to our end users.

A version of Scalable Fabric was released for public use in 2005. During the four months following its release, approximately 11,300 people have downloaded and used it. The response has generally been favorable, with most users continuing to use it. However, several implementation-specific performance and behavior problems have led some people to stop using the prototype after an evaluation period. Some of these problems can be addressed with changes to the current implementation, but others will require rewriting Scalable Fabric as a replacement for the legacy window manager.

**Next Steps**

Scalable Fabric provides basic task management, using a focus-plus-context spatial metaphor. Windows in the central focus area behave as usual, while windows in the display periphery are scaled-down, "minimized" windows. By requiring less space, peripheral windows can remain open and live. Task switching is accomplished using a single mouse click. Two user studies have provided guidance for the iterative design of Scalable Fabric and suggest that users prefer this approach to the standard Windows taskbar, especially for multiple monitors or large displays. The studies have also identified problems that still need to be addressed. Many of these problems can be attributed to the decision to build Scalable Fabric on top of an existing window manager rather than building it within or replacing the window manager.

A future implementation of Scalable Fabric will address these issues. However, it is also interesting to explore what future desktop interactions might be possible now that powerful graphics cards and better rendering support are available, making virtual 3D desktops a viable alternative candidate to the typical desktop user interface. We address this in the next section with the Task Gallery.

## Task Gallery

Similar to Scalable Fabric, Task Gallery creates a visible representation of a task and allows users to switch easily between tasks. The Task Gallery also takes advantage of the user's spatial memory for task management. In the Task Gallery (figure 4.10), the current task is displayed on a stage at the end of a virtual art gallery. It contains opened windows for that task. Other tasks are placed on the walls, floor, and ceiling of the gallery. The user switches to a new task by clicking on it, which moves it to the stage. Viewing multiple windows simultaneously is done with a button click, and uses automatic layout and movement in the 3D space to provide uniform and intuitive scaling. Applications and frequently used documents are kept in a Start Palette carried in the user's virtual left hand. Studies

**Figure 4.10**
The Task Gallery.

suggest that users are enthusiastic about the Task Gallery, that it is easy to navigate the space, and that it is easy to find tasks and switch between them.

**Task Gallery Design**

The choice of a navigable spatial metaphor was motivated by a desire to leverage human spatial memory. An art gallery was chosen because of its familiarity. To increase ease of retrieval, the Task Gallery includes the images of documents and tasks in the space in addition to their spatial location and title cues. Classical mnemonic research has documented that mental cues in the form of visual images are an excellent way to enhance memory for items (Patton 1990). Our previous studies have shown the strong influence of snapshot/thumbnail cues to aid spatial memory during the storage and retrieval of web pages (Czerwinski et al. 1999).

The existing Windows desktop metaphor uses menus (especially the Start Menu) and toolbars to give the user access to commonly used tools and documents. To better fit the metaphor of moving through a hallway and using an adaptation of Glances and Toolspaces (Pierce et al. 1999), we designed the Task Gallery so that the user carries tools and documents associated with the virtual body. Glances are a lightweight, ephemeral way of looking around in a virtual environment without moving the virtual body. Toolspaces are placed around the user and hold various tools or objects, keeping them associated with the virtual body as it moves through the virtual environment.

The Task Gallery has toolspaces to the left, right, above, and below the user. Hands and feet are shown to make the scale of the objects in the toolspaces more obvious and to suggest that these tools stay with the user as he navigates the environment. In the Task Gallery, glances are initiated with the controls shown in figure 4.11. Glances remain in effect until the user selects something in a toolspace or glances elsewhere.

The left toolspace contains the "Start Palette," which is a Data Mountain (Robertson et al. 1998) with the appearance of an artist's palette (figure 4.12). The original Data Mountain was a tilted 3D plane in holding favorite web pages. The objects on the Start Palette are icons and snapshots for applications, favorite documents, or web pages. The behavior of the Start Palette is similar to a Data Mountain, including object movement and occlusion avoidance. The only difference is that selecting an object

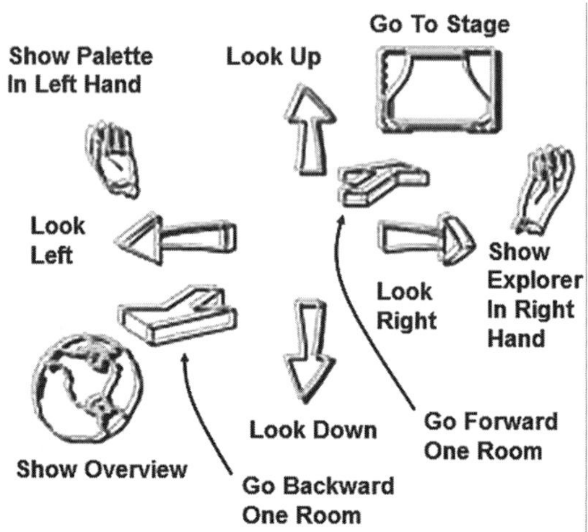


Figure 4.11
Onscreen 3D navigation controls appear in the lower left corner of the screen.

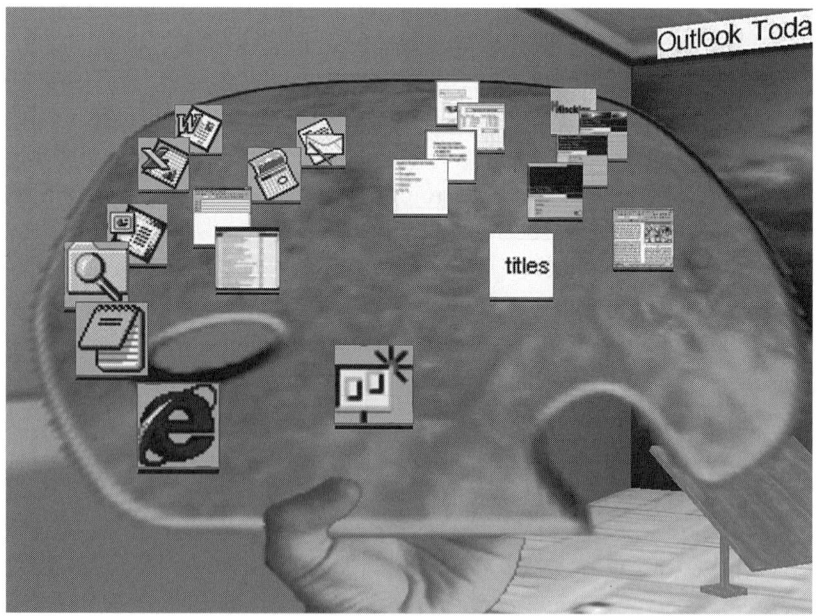


Figure 4.12
Start Palette—A Data Mountain, held in the user's left-hand toolspace.

from the Start Palette causes an application to launch with its window(s) in the current task. When an application is launched, the glance is terminated. Our user testing demonstrated that participants learned to add applications and documents to their tasks easily using the Start Palette. Earlier studies of Data Mountain (Robertson et al. 1996) suggest that users should be able to find icons on the Start Palette much faster than in the traditional Start Menu.

**Task Formation in Task Gallery**

New tasks can be created by picking the "new task" item on a menu or on the Start Palette. A background image is chosen by the system to distinguish the new task from existing tasks. The user's desired location of the new task is not yet known, so it is placed on the floor in front of the stage. Other tasks on the floor are moved back away from the stage to make room for the new task. This is done with a three-step animation: move the camera back to make the action visible, move the tasks on the floor back and place the new task on the floor, and finally do a task switch as described earlier. The three-step animation was implemented as a result of user testing, and greatly improved the usability of task creation. We assume that the user will move the task to a more appropriate location in the gallery later.

**Task Organization in Task Gallery**

The user can move tasks wherever desired with a dragging movement. Tasks are constrained to the walls, floor, or ceiling, but can be moved between these surfaces in a way inspired by Object Associations (Bukowski and Sequin 1995). The transition from wall to floor, for example, causes the task to shift to the appropriate orientation on the floor. Task frames are tilted outward so that they are more legible from a distance. Task frames on walls are mounted on a stand to make the metaphor more obvious and to ground them visually in depth. Segmentation of the gallery into separate rooms, grouping of task windows into mounted pieces of artwork, and using distinctive backgrounds all provide landmark and spatial cues that act as memory aids.

Users (especially non-gamers) tend to get lost in many 3D systems that require them to navigate. We avoid this problem by keeping the space simple (a linear hallway), by choosing a metaphor appropriate for the context (viewing art in a gallery), and by constraining the navigation. Thus, we provide a few simple controls rather than a general egocentric navigation mechanism. Figure 4.11 shows these on-screen controls, which allow the user to "jump" backward, forward, home (primary view), and to a bird's-eye view showing all the tasks in the Task Gallery. Each jump control starts a one-second camera animation from the current position to the desired target. Our studies showed that users did not become disoriented in the 3D space when using these controls, and that they could easily find their desired tasks.

**Switching Tasks in Task Gallery**

In the Task Gallery, switching between tasks and viewing multiple windows simultaneously are simple actions. In addition, the Task Gallery provides a strong spatial framework for encoding location information and front-to-back relationships, thereby engaging the user's spatial memory to help retrieve tasks and services. Task switching is accomplished by clicking on the frame in the gallery. A one-second animation is used to reenforce the spatial metaphor. The current task is closed by creating a snapshot which is moved back to the task's frame in the gallery. The newly selected task is then moved from its frame to the stage. When it arrives at the stage, it is transformed from artwork into live windows. A "ghosted" view of the task remains in the gallery, to mark the spot that it came from.

The initial and primary working view is a close-up of the stage (figure 4.14), showing the current task and its live windows. To view other tasks, the user backs up to see more of the gallery, as in figure 4.10. The gallery is composed of a sequence of rooms, with only one closed end; more rooms

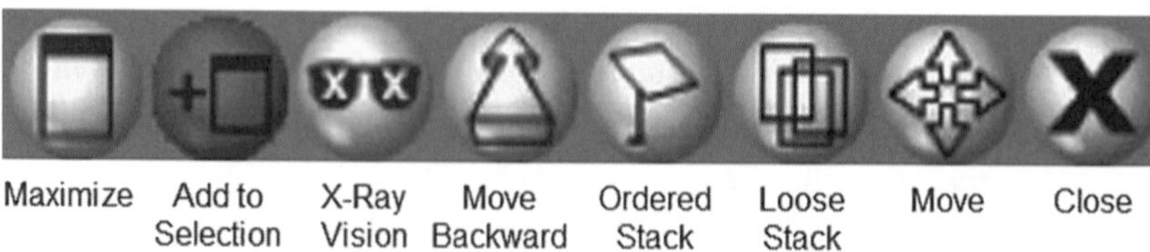


**Figure 4.13**

Window manipulation controls appear over a window banner when the user points to it.

are revealed without limit as the user moves back. This provides a simple way of managing the user's attention. As the user backs away, attention is widened. Moving to the stage focuses attention on the current task.

**Layout in Task Gallery**

The current task on the stage has several components, including a loose stack, an ordered stack, and a selected windows set. The loose stack is used for overlapped windows in much the same way as the current desktop metaphor. These windows are mounted on stands to visually ground them to the stage. Clicking on one of these windows will bring it forward to a selected window position, replacing the current selected window. The window manipulation controls shown in figure 4.13 are used for moving windows around and placing them on various stacks. These controls appear over the window banner when the user points to the banner. Windows in the loose stack can be directly moved anywhere on the stage. Using a technique similar to Point of Interest object movement (Mackinlay,

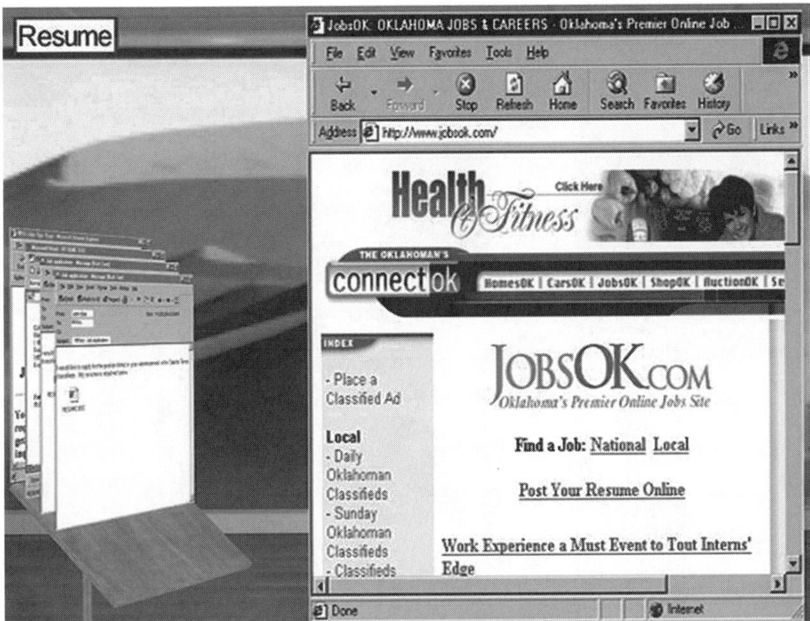


**Figure 4.14**
The stage with an ordered stack and one selected window.

Card, and Robertson 1990), the mouse controls movement in the plane perpendicular to the line of sight, and the shift and control keys control movement toward or away from the user.

The ordered stack appears to the left of the stage, as shown in figure 4.14. Users choose to place windows in the ordered stack to keep currently unused windows organized (e.g., open email messages). If one of the windows on the podium is moved, the stack is tidied to have a fixed distance between each window. Clicking on a page in the ordered stack moves it to the selected window region.

When windows are selected, the system moves them closer to the user for greater legibility. Multiple windows can be selected using the "Add to Selection" icon in figure 4.13. Each time a window is added, an automatic layout moves the windows so they are all visible side by side (figure 4.15). Unlike tiled window managers that crop windows and may force users to scroll, this operation does not affect what is visible in selected windows. Thus we use distance in 3D to provide uniform scaling in an intuitive way.

**Figure 4.15**
Multiple selected windows.

## Task Gallery User Studies

Our first three studies examined task management before and after various usability issues were resolved. The third study took place several months after the first two, and included evaluation of features added in response to the first two studies (e.g., icon identification). In addition, we were interested in how spatial cognition pertains to 3D environments like the Task Gallery, and whether or not aspects of real-world spatial location memory transfer to electronic environments.

We were interested specifically in how well users could create and modify tasks and arrange the overall task space. In addition, detailed information about organizing and retrieval strategies was collected to support those strategies in future designs. We wanted to know whether organizing strategies were based on frequency, size, type of content, or time. While the art gallery metaphor suggests use of the walls over the floor and ceiling, previous research suggests that certain bodily axes are considered primary in the real world (Bukowski and Sequin 1995; Feiner et al. 1993). We wanted to know if participants' organizing strategies and subsequent retrieval performance and representation of the space related to properties of the metaphor or to up–down, front–back, and left–right axes relative to the user's orientation in the space.

## User Study 1 and 2 Results

**Method** Eleven participants (five female) between the ages of 16 and 65 participated—five participants evaluated the first iteration prototype, and six participants evaluated the second iteration prototype. Two prototype versions of the Task Gallery, which used "snapshots" of documents, were fully interactive except that the applications were not live. During the experimental trials, users created tasks, organized the tasks in a way that was meaningful to them, retrieved eight tasks and their specific content items, and finally carried out various Windows operations. After the first experimental trial, we asked users to draw what the hallway looked like to them, and what location and orientation they had within the hallway. At the end of the session, users drew their information layout in the hallway in as detailed a manner as they were able. In addition, they filled out a user satisfaction questionnaire.

Between the first and second study, several changes were made to the prototype in response to observed user problems. We changed the manner in which tasks were created, named, and labeled when selected.

Participants placed significantly more tasks on the left and right walls of the gallery than the ceiling or floor. This tendency to conform to the way space is typically used in a real-world gallery suggests that participants were using the metaphor to guide interaction. Legibility was the same on walls, floor, and ceiling in these two studies.

Participants' organization of tasks involved spatially grouping related tasks. Tasks that "went together" were placed close together on the same surface. A variety of organizational strategies were observed including ordering by frequency of use, location of use (i.e., home versus work), semantic relations, and alphabetical. Furthermore, most participants used more than one organizing strategy.

Eighteen percent of the tasks were recalled but placed incorrectly. Analysis of those errors showed that it was more difficult to remember whether a task had been placed on the left or right wall than to remember its depth order (i.e., was it closest to the stage, next closest, and so on). Ninety-two percent of the placement errors were due to drawing tasks on the wrong wall. Only 8 percent of these errors were due to drawing tasks in the wrong relative depth order. This is consistent with the literature on memory for spatial arrays (Franklin and Tversky 1990; Siegel and White 1975), which finds that front–back relations are easier to remember than left–right relations. This supports our design by showing that users leverage the front–back relations afforded by the use of 3D to represent and recall task location.

Overall, user satisfaction ratings were positive, given that this is the first evaluation of the prototype. Average satisfaction ratings were 4.9 for both the first and second iterations, using a 7-point scale, with 7=positive.

### User Study 3 Results—Live Task Gallery

Nine participants (three female) between the ages of 16 and 52 participated in this iteration of testing with a version of the system including live Windows applications. For this study, eight tasks and their contents were identified and created prior to the study. Tasks typically contained between 5 and 11 documents (like Word documents, Excel spreadsheets, web pages, and email). Note that this iteration of testing included many more documents in tasks than the previous two iterations, as we were interested in how the Task Gallery might scale up to larger numbers of documents. Therefore, we did not attempt any quantitative comparisons to the previous two iterations.

On average, users identified the windows control icons (figure 4.13) 44 percent of the time and matched the icons correctly 48 percent of the time. Given the users had not seen the Task Gallery and did not know what could be done in the environment at the time of the icon evaluation, this is not a surprising result. After using the system for under ten minutes, all users understood how the novel 3D windows controls operated and what their unique functions were.

Satisfaction ratings were higher with this iteration. The overall average satisfaction ratings were 5.3 (standard deviation = 1.4) using a 7-point scale, with 7= positive. On average, users rated the Task Gallery as preferable to their current Windows software (average = 5.0, 7= prefer Task Gallery).

We asked participants where they had laid out their tasks at the end of the session, and why they chose those spatial locations. The majority of the participants felt that placing tasks on the ceiling or floor would violate the Task Gallery metaphor. Some participants simply did not like the idea of tasks lying on the floor. Two participants, however, mentioned that tasks on the ceiling and floor were more difficult to read, due to the angle at which they are placed. This was not true in the prototype tested in experiments 1 and 2. Legibility problems arose in the final version of the system as a result of addressing some serious texture management issues.

### Discussion

The Task Gallery is an exploration of the use of 3D virtual environments for window and task management. It is motivated by the desire to leverage human spatial cognition and perception and to take advantage of the coming ubiquity of 3D graphics hardware for more than computer games. User tests suggest that the Task Gallery does help with task management and is enjoyable to use. But we have only scratched the surface.

In our usability studies we observed users exhibiting many of the same principles of spatial cognition as are exhibited in the real world. Users had a strong sense of front-to-back ordering of their tasks, rarely confusing that ordering in memory. We will continue to explore metaphors leveraging users' real-world knowledge in our future 3D environments.

One of the key technical challenges in building a 3D window manager is to get existing applications to work in the 3D environment without changing or recompiling them. This requires both output and input redirection facilities in the operating system. Output redirection requires notification whenever an application has updated its visual display, so that the system can force applications to render to off-screen bitmaps for use as textures in the 3D environment. Input redirection causes mouse and keyboard events to be received by an application rather than the 3D environment's main window, but with mouse coordinates translated from 3D to 2D.

There are several improvements we plan to make to the Task Gallery. We have seen that better landmarks could make a significant difference in helping users remember on which wall they placed tasks. Also, the Data Mountain occlusion avoidance algorithm can be used to help avoid occlusion problems while moving task frames.

Our goal was to design a 3D window manager that solves two problems with the current desktop metaphor: task management and comparison of multiple windows. The Task Gallery is a first-generation system that addresses these issues and is built on a general-purpose application redirection technology which will allow us to explore alternative user interfaces for application environments.

## Task Persistence

Any task management system that loses all its accumulated task knowledge on reboot is ultimately of limited utility. Microsoft Windows, like most common operating systems today, does not offer any standardized mechanisms for encapsulating the state of a particular running window in a way that can be persisted or recreated—indeed, to be useful, any such mechanism would require the application developer's cooperation —so there is currently no ideal solution to the problem of task persistence. The three systems we describe in this chapter are all built on top of unmodified Windows systems, and hence are limited in the range of task persistence solutions they offer.

We designed GroupBar explicitly with quick, lightweight interaction mechanisms to keep the organizational effort low and hopefully thereby to encourage even transient Groups. However, some tasks are longer-term and require a persistence mechanism. We introduced the idea of the "Snapshot," which is a time-stamped, binary file containing a sequence of window titles, window positions, window thumbnails, window persistence strings, and Group membership information. We use a number of techniques to try to extract from a window the persistence strings necessary to re-create it. We attempt to save off both the name and path for the application that owns the window, as well as the "document" string representing the current content of the window. We also allow the user to write in custom persistence strings in cases where our techniques are insufficient. To surface Snapshots in the interface, we added a permanent, top-level button to GroupBar, displaying a camera icon that invokes a dialogue to allow the user to select individual windows, individual groups, or all windows and groups on the bar for Snapshot inclusion. A second, top-level button (labeled "**List . . .**") launches a Snapshot explorer that provides a list of existing Snapshots with their accompanying properties and graphical previews of the contained windows. The user can select the "Restore" command from this explorer to reposition or relaunch the windows for any selected Snapshot.

In Scalable Fabric, rather than attempting to solve the general persistence problem, we simply save window position, size, and title information for windows and tasks that are running. This information is updated whenever a window is created or moved, or when a task is selected or changed. When Scalable Fabric is restarted, if an open window of the same title is discovered, it will be restored to the last state it was rendered within Scalable Fabric. If the window is not present, Scalable Fabric does not try to start the application and restore its running state. This approach means that Scalable Fabric can be terminated and restarted, and all states will be restored. However, if the user logs off or reboots the machine, Scalable Fabric will not be able to restore the state, although the task markers will remain. Obviously, the Snapshot or window persistence strings used by GroupBar could also be used for Scalable Fabric in a future version.

Task Gallery takes an intermediate approach, recording and storing the information used to launch an application. This is similar to GroupBar's approach, except that no provision was made for modifying the persistence strings used for restarting applications.

These interim solutions are far from ideal. Some Windows applications allow inspection of their open documents through various COM interfaces. It is also possible that this can be done by tracking file opening and closing and window creations, but this approach is difficult without modifying existing applications. Additionally, applications often allow the user to change what files are open, and some even provide a sophisticated form of window management within the application with could conceivably be useful to persist. Without some standard way of getting at the state of open files and subwindows within an application, it is extremely difficult to solve the general problem. In the original Rooms system (Henderson and Card 1987), the operating system environment (a Lisp-based OS) provided the necessary application and document information to allow the system on relaunch to restore the Room state exactly as the user last saw it, providing a certain system-wide level of persistence support. However, at the individual window or task level, the persistence problem can be even more complex than that. Ideally, a robust task-management persistence model would need to allow subsets of working items to be flexibly named, persisted, modified, and recalled. It would also need to allow for different granularities of persistence: for example, when a user tries to persist a collection of open web-browser windows, the desired long-term information might be the current content of the windows' web pages, or it might be just the URLs that the windows point to, or it might even be just the physical layout of the multiple browser windows. Ultimately, we need operating system modifications that permit applications to reveal and restore their state, and for applications to be written so that their state is available for task-management systems to inspect and use.

## Conclusion

As display costs drop and processors and video cards continue to increase in power, the use of multiple-monitor systems or larger displays is likely to increase. It would be difficult to understand how (or, in fact, *whether*) to design for this coming change if one does not understand both how people generally interact with and manage windows, and how multiple monitor practices differ from those of the past. The overall value of the results we present in this chapter is in gaining starting points from which to further investigate these practices, similarities, and differences. We have also presented several ideas for how to begin novel user-interface designs that leverage how users interact with windows across variable display sizes.

In the three designs presented in this chapter, we have assumed that users manually identify tasks by grouping windows and perhaps naming the groups. Many users and test participants have requested tools that automatically do the grouping, or at least suggest groupings. We have begun research on monitoring user activity and semi-automatically deriving task groupings, for example, by observing clustering of window interactions over time. However, much research remains to be done to make this work effectively.

For each design (GroupBar, Scalable Fabric, and Task Gallery), we discussed how task-switching support was improved over existing tools, in addition to areas where each design could iteratively be improved. In combination, we have seen ample evidence that software support for rapid and repeated task switching is of great value to desktop PC information workers, and that the time has come to incorporate many of these research ideas into commercially available products.

## Acknowledgments

We gratefully acknowledge Maarten van Dantzich, Ken Hinckley, Kirsten Risden, David Thiel, and Vadim Gorokhovsky for contributions to the development of Task Gallery, and Dugald Hutching for contributions to the development of Scalable Fabric.

## References

Bannon, L., Cypher, A., Greenspan, S., and Monty, M. (1983). Evaluation and analysis of user's activity organization. In *Proceedings of CHI '83*, pp. 54–57. New York: ACM.

Baudisch, P., Good, N., and Stewart, P. (2001). Focus plus context screens: Combining display technology with visualization techniques. In *Proceedings of UIST'01*, pp. 31–40. New York: ACM.

Bederson, B., and Hollan, J. (1994). Pad++: A zooming graphical interface for exploring alternative interface physics. In *Proceedings of UIST '94*, pp. 17–26. New York: ACM.

Bell, B., and Feiner, S. (2000). Dynamic space management for user interfaces. In *Proceedings of UIST '00*, pp. 238–248. New York: ACM.

Bly, S., and Rosenberg, J. (1986). A comparison of tiled and overlapping windows. In *Proceedings of CHI '86*, pp. 101–106. New York: ACM.

Bukowski, R., and Sequin, C. (1995). Object associations: A simple and practical approach to virtual 3D manipulation. In *Proceedings of 1995 Symposium on Interactive 3D Graphics*, pp. 131–138. New York: ACM.

Card, S. K., and Henderson, A. H., Jr. (1987). A multiple, virtual-workspace interface to support user task switching. In *Proceedings of CHI+GI 1987*, pp. 53–59. New York: ACM.

Card, S., Robertson, G., and York, W. (1996). The WebBook and the Web Forager: An information workspace for the World-Wide Web. In *Proceedings of CHI '96*, pp. 111–117. New York: ACM.

Cutrell, E., Czerwinski, M., and Horvitz, E. (2001). Notification, disruption, and memory: Effects of messaging interruptions on memory and performance. In *Human-Computer Interaction—Interact '01*, pp. 263–269. IOS Press.

Czerwinski, M., Cutrell, E., and Horvitz, E. (2000). Instant messaging and interruption: Influence of task type on performance. In *Proceedings of OZCHI 2000*, Paris, C., Ozkan, N., Howard, S., and Lu, S. (eds.), pp. 356–361. Sydney, Australia, Dec. 4–8.

Czerwinski, M., and Horvitz, E. (2002). Memory for daily computing events. In *People and Computers XVI: Proceedings of HCI 2002*, Faulkner, X., Findlay, J., and Detienne, F. (eds.), pp. 230–245. September 2–6. London: Springer-Verlag.

Czerwinski, M., Horvitz, E., and Wilhite, S. (2004). A diary study of task switching and interruptions. In *Proceedings of CHI '04*, pp. 175–182. New York: ACM.

Czerwinski, M., van Dantzich, M., Robertson, G., and Hoffman, H. (1999). The contribution of thumbnail image, mouse-over text, and spatial location memory to web page retrieval in 3D. In *Proceedings Interact '99*, pp. 163–170, August 30–September 3. London: Springer-Verlag.

Feiner, S., MacIntyre, B., Haupt, M., and Solomon, E. (1993). Windows on the world: 2D windows for 3D augmented reality. In *Proceedings of UIST '93*, pp. 145–155. New York: ACM.

Franklin, N., and Tversky, B. (1990). Searching imagined environments. *Journal of Experimental Psychology: General* 199: 63–76.

Gillie, T., and Broadbent, D. (1989). What makes interruptions disruptive? A study of length, similarity, and complexity. *Psychological Research* 50: 243–250.

Guimbretiere, F., Stone, M., and Winograd, T. (2001). Fluid interaction with high-resolution wall-size displays. In *Proceedings of UIST'01*, pp. 21–30. New York: ACM.

Henderson, D. A., Jr., and Card, S. K. (1987). Rooms: The use of multiple virtual workspaces to reduce space contention in a window-based graphical user interface. *ACM Transactions on Graphics* 5 (3): 211–243.

Hutchings, D. R., and Stasko, J. (2004). Revisiting display space management: Understanding current practice to inform next-generation design. In *Proceedings of Graphics Interface 2004*, London, Ontario, Canadian Human Computer Communications Society, pp. 127–134, May 17–19.

Hutchings, D. G., Smith, G., Meyers, B., Czerwinski, M., and Robertson, G. (2004). Display space usage and window management operation comparisons between single monitor and multiple monitor users. In *Proceedings of AVI 2004*, Gallipoli, Italy. pp. 32–39, May 25–28.

Kandogan, E., and Shneiderman, B. (1997). Elastic Windows: Evaluation of multi-window operations. In *Proceedings of CHI '97*, pp. 250–257. New York: ACM.

Mackinlay, J., Card, S., and Robertson, G. (1990). Rapid controlled movement through a virtual 3D workspace. *SIGGRAPH '90*, pp. 171–176. New York: ACM.

Maglio, P. P., and Campbell, C. S. (2000). Tradeoffs in displaying peripheral information. In *Proceedings of CHI '00*, pp. 241–248. New York: ACM.

Morris, J., Satyanarayanan, M., Conner, M., Howard, J., Rosenthal, D., and Smith, F. (1986). Andrew: Distributed personal computing environment. *CACM* 29 (3): 184–201.

Myers, B. (1988). Window interfaces: A taxonomy of window manager user interfaces. *IEEE Computer Graphics and Applications* 8 (5): 65–84.

Mynatt, E., Igarashi, T., Edwards, W., and LaMarca, A. (1999). Flatland: New dimensions in office whiteboards. In *Proceedings of CHI '99*, pp. 346–353. New York: ACM.

Patton, B. M. (1990). The history of memory arts. *Neurology* 40: 346–352.

Pierce, J., Conway, M., van Dantzich, M., and Robertson, G. (1999). Toolspaces and glances: Storing, accessing, and retrieving objects in 3D desktop applications. In *Proceedings of Symposium on Interactive 3D Graphics*, April 1999, pp. 163–168. New York: ACM.

Rekimoto, J. (1999). Time-machine computing: A time-centric approach for the information environment. In *Proceedings of UIST '99*, pp. 45–54, New York: ACM.

Ringel, M. (2003). When one isn't enough: An analysis of virtual desktop usage strategies and their implications for design. In *CHI Extended Abstracts 2003*, pp. 762–763. New York: ACM.

Robertson, G., Card, S., and Mackinlay, J. (1993). Information visualization using 3D interactive animation. *CACM* 36 (4): 57–71.

Robertson, G., Czerwinski, M., Larson, K., Robbins, D., Thiel, D., and van Dantzich, M. (1998). Data Mountain: Using spatial memory for document management. In *Proceedings of UIST '98*, pp. 153–162. New York: ACM.

Robertson, G. van Dantzich, M., Robbins, D., Czerwinski, M., Hinckley, K., Risden, K., Thiel, D., and Gorokhovsky, V. (2000). The Task Gallery: A 3D window manager. In *Proceedings of CHI '00*, pp. 494–501. New York: ACM.

Siegel, A., and White, S. (1975). The development of spatial representations of large-scale environments. In H. Reese (ed.), *Advances in Child Development and Behavior*, vol. 10, pp. 9–55. New York: Academic Press.

Smith, G., Baudisch, P., Robertson, G., Czerwinski, M., Meyers, B., Robbins, D., and Andrews, D. (2003). GroupBar: The taskbar evolved. In *Proceedings of OZCHI '03*, Brisbane, Australia, Nov. 26–28.

Teitelman, W. (1986). Ten years of window system—A retrospective view. In Hopgood, F., Duce, D. Fielding, E. Robinson, K., and Williams, A. (eds.), *Methodology of Window Management*. Berlin: Springer-Verlag.

Wurnig, H. (1998). Design of a collaborative multi-user desktop system for augmented reality. In *Proceedings of the Central European Seminar on Computer Graphics*, Budmeric, Bratislava, April 21–22.

XDesk Software (2003). About virtual desktop managers. Http://www.virtual-desktop.info/.

# II

# The Social Dimension of Personal Environments

# Introduction to Part II

The main focus of the book is on personal work environments, not groupware. However, support of communication and collaboration is a major concern for most of the contributors. There is no contradiction here, since creating contexts for personal work is no less important for successful collaboration than creating shared work contexts. Much of collaboration takes place when the collaborating individuals are working in their personal environments. The chapters in part II describe novel design approaches to creating "collaboration-friendly" personal work environments.

It is widely recognized that our work habits and behaviors change based on the roles we take on as we carry out our information tasks. Owing to increased work hours, mobility, and pervasiveness of technology in our lives, our personal activities, hobbies, family-based communication, and formal work are becoming increasingly intertwined. The chapter on personal role management by Plaisant and Shneiderman, with Baker, Duarte, Haririnia, Klinesmith, Lee, Velikovich, Wanga, and Westhoff, attempts to design and study a system that supports this ever-increasingly important aspect of our digital lives. The idea of role-based task management is seen as a promising approach in the design of today's software environments and tools.

Fisher and Nardi's emphasis on people and communication is a refreshing take on information work. The systems discussed in their chapter—ContactMap and Soylent—take people to be "first-class citizens" in computing environments, a trend that is receiving worthy and long overdue attention.

There is a similarity between the chapters in that both employ representations of the social context of individual work. However, the proposed approaches embodied in the systems designed by the authors emphasize different poles of the social dimension of personal work environments. While ContactMap represents *other people (*contacts*)*, Personal Role Manager focuses on the various *roles of the user* in collaboration with other people. It appears that these perspectives can complement each other. This possibility is one of the many intriguing directions for further work on the social dimension of personal work environments, suggested by discussions in part II.

# 5

# Personal Role Management: Overview and a Design Study of Email for University Students

Catherine Plaisant and Ben Shneiderman
with H. Ross Baker, Nicolas B. Duarte, Aydin Haririnia, Dawn E. Klinesmith, Hannah Lee, Leonid A. Velikovich, Alfred O. Wanga, and Matthew J. Westhoff

## Introduction

Our daily activities are rich and complex as we switch among many roles at work, at home, and in our community. A professor may be a teacher of several courses, an advisor to students, a member of academic committees, a principal investigator of grants, a conference organizer, an editor of scientific journals, and a liaison to industry. Most job descriptions include multiple responsibilities: even a salesperson may deal with categories of clients, train new employees, manage the company car pool, and supervise website maintenance. Work needs to be juggled with personal roles, such as being a soccer player or volunteer fireman, and family roles, such as being a parent, a home remodeler, a Parent–Teacher Association member, or a remote caregiver for an older adult. We talk about wearing "different hats" and about the things we do in our "other lives." This language provides hints to the importance and the distinctiveness of those roles. Different roles require different states of mind, different levels of pressure, privacy, and professionalism. Those hats may also symbolize how we highlight different personality traits in different roles. Nevertheless, we conduct our activities using the same computer environment. Some applications may have ways to customize their appearance and behavior to fit users' needs and wishes, but the underlying environment remains unchanged as we switch between those often very disparate roles. The question for designers is: How can we design graphical user interfaces that provide more efficient actions by taking into account these various roles?

Some users attempt to create distinct roles by having separate email accounts or even separate computers for their work, household, hobbies, and so on. We define roles as enduring (from a month to many years) efforts of an individual, for which there are mostly distinct sets of people, events, and documents. A task is a short-term (from an hour to a week) effort for an individual, whereas a project is an enduring effort for a group of people. Organizations are typically concerned about project management, so they emphasize tools for coordination among individuals and critical path techniques to speed completion of the team effort. Since we are concerned with enabling a person to manage multiple roles inside and outside his or her organization, we emphasize document management, calendar support, communication needs, and attention switching among multiple roles.

Current graphical user interfaces are based on the physical desktop metaphor of documents, files, and folders and applications to manipulate them. To fulfill their obligations within a role, users have to think in terms of low-level actions such as launching applications, opening files, navigating directory structures, and searching for information. Then they have to save results as new documents and send them to others. Aside from the possibility of saving files in role-specific folders, today's graphical user interfaces do not take into consideration the need to handle separate roles in separate ways. Worse still, they do not allow for rapid role switching.

A typical scenario might go like this: John is the principal investigator of a large grant. He has been working for an hour on the project report. File explorers and email tools are focused on the correct project folder; word processors show the right set of documents; the web browser history is now full of the relevant web pages he just looked at. His windows have been resized and laid out in a convenient way. Work seems to be moving along nicely, but now John needs to switch to another task. One of his many roles is to be the chair of a symposium, for which a conference call is scheduled in five minutes with the representative from the printer's office. John starts by browsing the contact list to recognize the name of the printer, but he fails in this task because the list is too long. He switches to the word processor to open the planning document that might contain the printer's name. Unfortunately the list of the documents opened recently are all related to the principal investigator role of writing the report, so he patiently navigates the file hierarchy up from the recent report directory and then down to the symposium directory. After carrying out a search, he recognizes the file name that deals with the printer and gets the phone number to call. But before starting the call he switches to the calendar application and flips nervously through the weekly views to refresh his memory of the symposium's camera-ready deadline and the ship-to-printer deadline that were set earlier. Finally he opens a web browser and browses his long list of favorites to find the symposium webpage. After the conference call is over, he switches to setting up a doctor's appointment for his son and writes a letter to his son's teacher to request permission to take his son out of school during lunchtime. He also responds to a call requesting an immediate change in the web announcement for the holiday party he organized. Later on he returns to the project report, but he has to spend a few minutes to reopen windows, resize them, and renavigate each application to the right folder. He realizes that the list of recently opened documents is useless now and that default folders are mapped to the wrong place.

In contrast, a Personal Role Management environment would allow John to switch instantly from being a project manager to being a symposium organizer in one step. He would find his environment focused on the selected role: file browsers would be opened in the relevant home directory, recently opened files would be based on the tasks he performed last in that role, the contact list would appear filtered on the contacts relevant to that role (making it easy for users to recall relevant names), the calendar would highlight the relevant deadlines entered while that role was selected, and key applications and documents could be saved and opened at once.

We proposed the Personal Role Management strategy in 1994 as a guiding concept for the next generation of graphic user interfaces. The first generation was the command line interfaces, which required users to know about computer concepts and syntax. These were replaced by second-generation graphical user interfaces, using the desktop metaphor, icons, and folders. Next, the third generation emphasized a docu-centric approach, in which applications faded into the background while multimedia documents become the center of attention. Our proposed fourth-generation user-centered design emphasizes users' roles, collaborators, and tasks rather than documents. Each role involves coordination with groups of people and accomplishment of tasks within a schedule.

As interface environments have allowed multitasking, some users have managed to support roles by keeping multiple windows open simultaneously. By running window managers that allow multiple desktops, sometimes called Rooms (e.g., Henderson and Card 1986; Robertson et al. 2000), it is possible to simulate a Personal Role Management strategy. However, this approach does not address key issues of organizing documents, contacts, calendars, web favorites, and recent files. In such multiple desktop environments, focusing on a role corresponds to a change of location in the virtual space, but the behavior of the individual applications remains unchanged as they remain blind to the change in their context of use.

In contrast with the research on role theory (Sarbin and Allen 1968; Biddle and Thomas 1979; Roos and Starke 1981), or computer-supported collaborative work (Singh and Rein 1992), which focuses mainly on the coordination of individuals within an organization, Personal Role Management focuses on helping individuals manage their multiple roles. Newer frameworks, such as activity theory (Redmiles 2002), view work as an activity driven by various needs in which people seek to achieve goals. Activity theory proponents provide useful insights for accomplishing organizational goals, but they have not provided adequate frameworks for understanding how users view their multiple roles inside and outside the organization.

## Early Explorations

Our original work on Personal Role Management was based on an observational study of World Bank employees. The study looked at project lifecycle, document management, email practices, training, and availability of software tools, and it identified problems that World Bank employees regularly struggle with which seemed generic enough to be significant in other organizations. One of those problems was the juggling of many roles within the organization. Managers often supervised several projects at once and also had various roles within their business unit or group. For example, an employee could be in charge of two projects (a healthcare clinic in Algeria and the construction of a drinking water supply system in Mali), a member of three task forces, editor of the magazine, and organizer of the holiday party. A great deal of personal organization is required to manage such roles whose goals, collaborators, tools, and documents are mostly distinct.

Our exploration led to two main concepts: Personal Role Management and organizational overviews. Organizational overviews were proposed as a consistent background for presenting results of searches in databases but also as a way to map the multiple personal roles an individual has in an organization and serve as a resizable control panel used to switch roles (figures 5.1, 5.2, 5.3). The prototype showed Personal Role Management

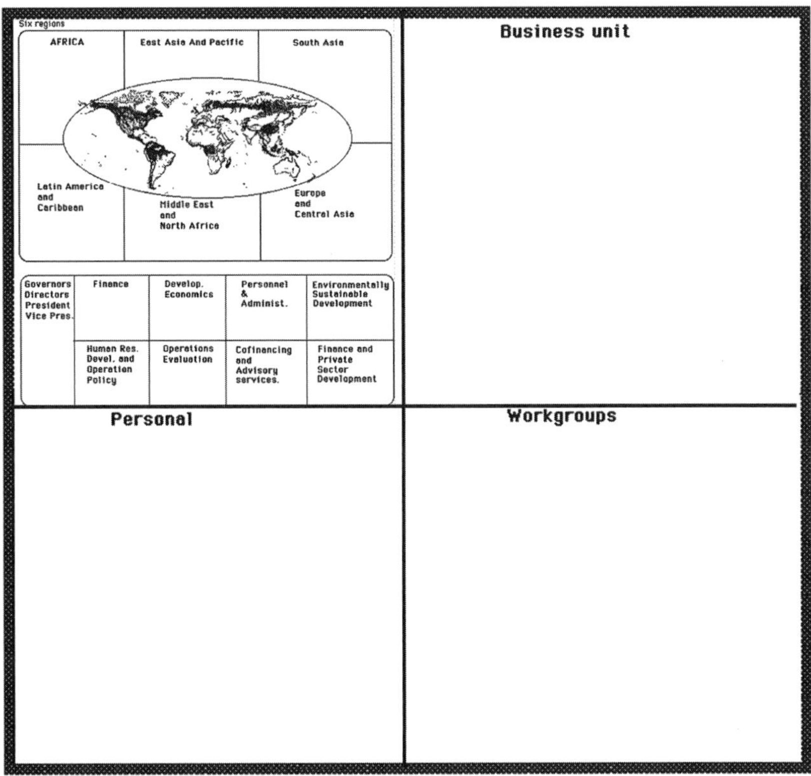


**Figure 5.1**

A new employee of the bank would see this role overview before he or she is assigned a new job. On the top left is the bank's main organization structure. And the three other boxes are to organize and cluster the roles related to the business unit, and user's workgroup personal roles.

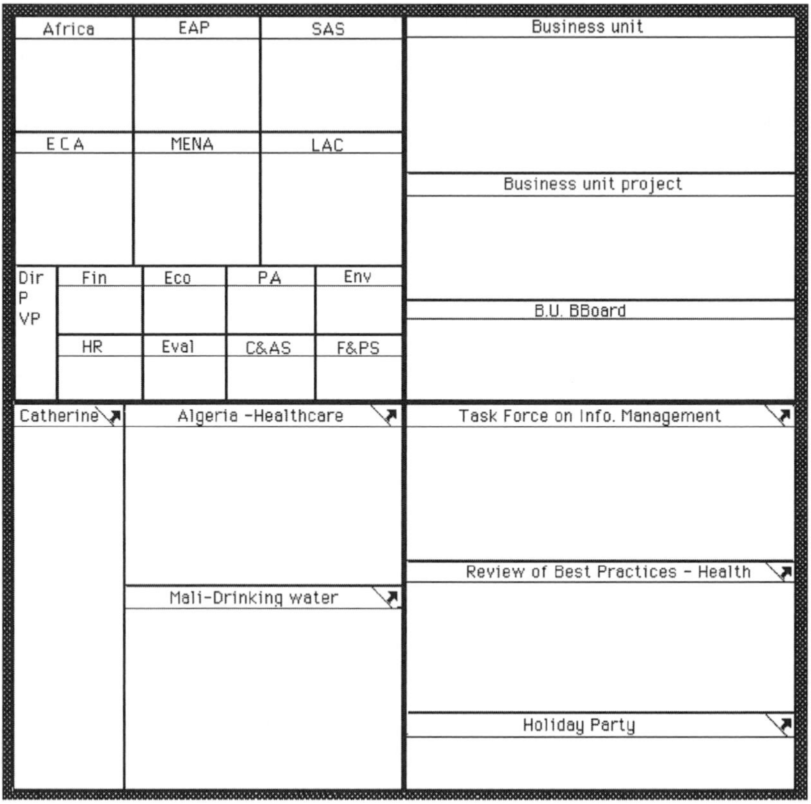

**Figure 5.2**
As roles are assigned to our new employee they can be organized on the overview and used by personal role managers. Such role overview can also be shrunk to the size of a large icon and displayed at all time to allow users to switch roles easily. Keyboard shortcuts can also speed role switching.

as a strategy that allowed knowledge workers to organize information according to their roles in the organization. The roles were defined as having a vision statement, a set of people, a schedule, and a task hierarchy. The vision statement is a document established by the individual or the superior. It may facilitate training or transfer of responsibility. The set of people is a contact list narrowed down to show only the most relevant contacts for this role. The schedule is focused on a specific role and the relevant files and tools are shown. Moving in and out of a specific role, or switching roles, is instantaneous and seamless (figure 5.4). A role over-

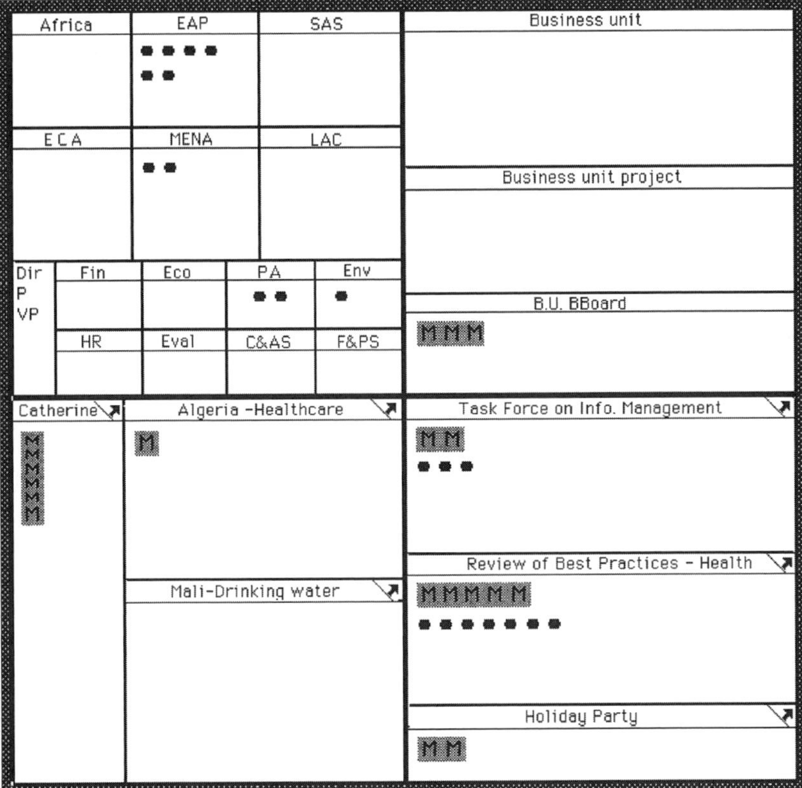


**Figure 5.3**
Here we see the same organization overview but simple visualization techniques summarize the amount of unread emails (M) and To-do items (*) for each role, alerting users of which roles may need more attention today.

view icon, even when very small, can be used to switch roles, and enlarged to reveal more details when needed. When John receives a call regarding a different role, shifting to that role is done with a single click on the overview, or using a keyboard shortcut.

A low-fidelity prototype was developed to illustrate the Personal Role Management strategy (Plaisant and Shneiderman 1995a). The strategy was first presented in a keynote talk by Ben Shneiderman at the British HCI conference on People and Computers in 1994 (Shneiderman and Plaisant 1994), and a longer description of the work appeared a year later (Plaisant and Shneiderman 1995b).

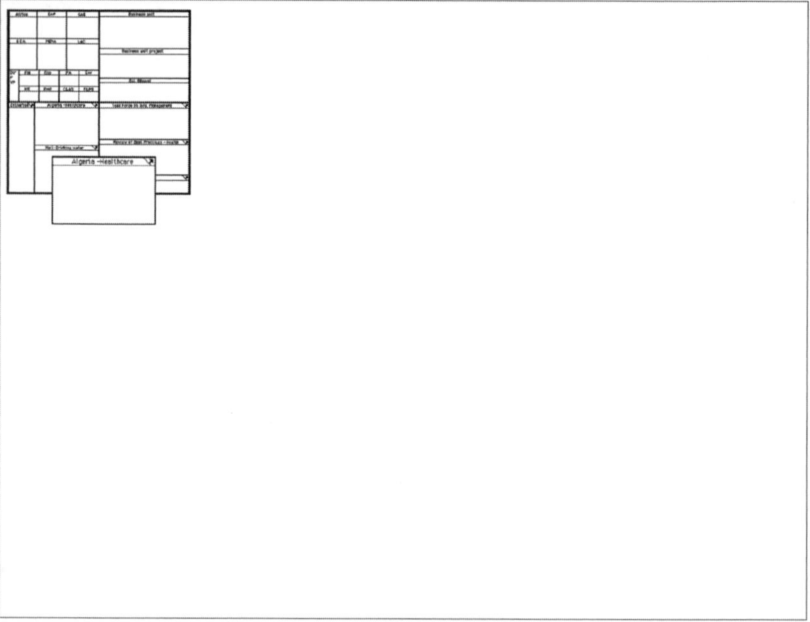


(a)

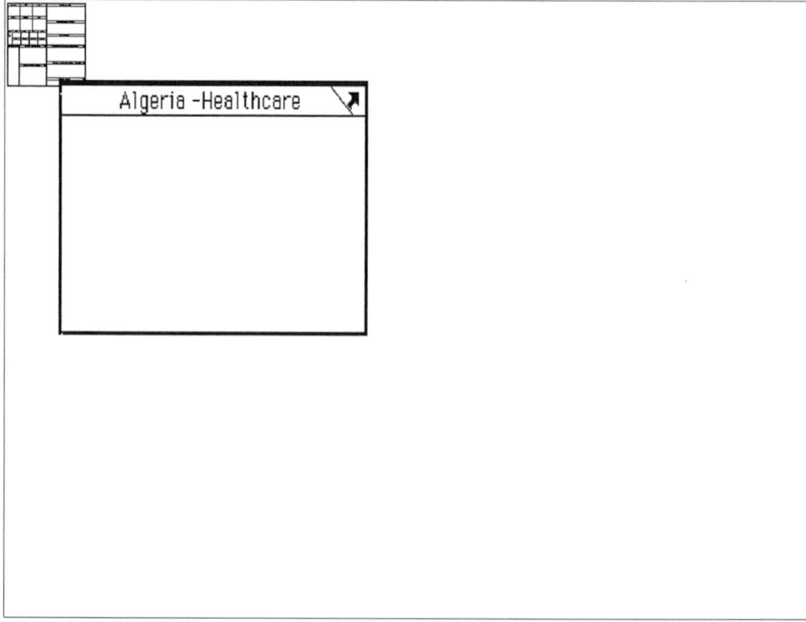


(b)

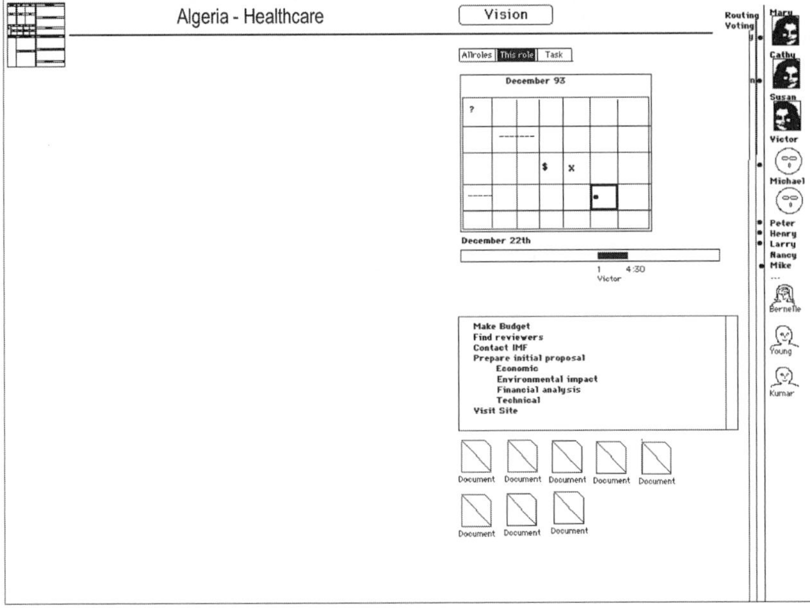


(c)

**Figure 5.4**
Three steps of the animation of a mockup prototype showing how (a) selecting a role in the role overview (which appears as a large icon on the top left) opens the selected role (b) which fills the screen (c), and reveals the calendar, contact list, and file hierarchy focused on the role. The role overview is still visible on the top left for rapid switching to another role.

Personal Role Management was also used to illustrate a window management environment called Elastic Windows (Kandogan and Shneiderman 1997). The hierarchical layout (figure 5.5) indicates the hierarchic relationship between the contents of the windows by the spatial cues in the organization of windows. It provides the users with an overview of all their roles, so that they can pick any role or parts of it and start working on it. Hierarchical grouping provides a role-based context for information organization. It also supports the ability to hide graphical information, as window hierarchies can be collapsed into a single icon (or other primitives), making the approach scalable. The collapsed hierarchy of windows can be saved and retrieved, which allows users to reuse a previous window organization.

While most discussants are sympathetic to Personal Role Management, a common critique is that roles are often interrelated and that it can be

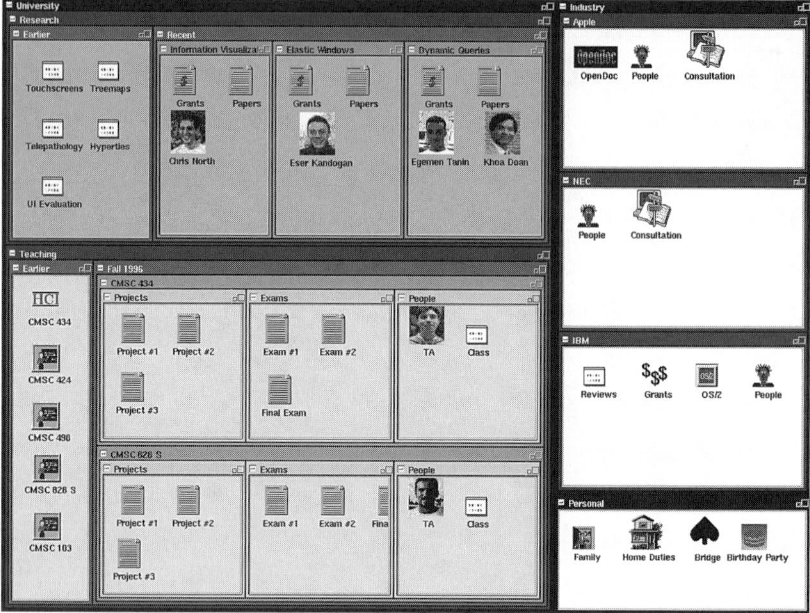


**Figure 5.5**
An illustration of the later implementation of a university professor role manager prototyped with Elastic Windows. This professor is advisor to a number of graduate students in a number of research projects (three recent ones and five earlier projects are represented here). He teaches two courses this semester at the university (CMSC 434 and 828S), is industry liaison to three companies, and has personal duties.

difficult to separate them. Sometimes users work with the same people on multiple projects and even organize social events or family vacations with them. Documents may be reused in different contexts, and calendars also need to show all events for all roles, especially when the user is scheduling a new event or just planning the day. There is a legitimate danger that managing roles may consume more time than it saves. We recognize that role management may not be useful to all users, but nevertheless, we believe that many users hold distinct and stable roles (i.e., with a mostly distinct set of collaborators, documents, and schedule for month, years, or longer). Therefore, there is a strong advantage in filtering the interface environment to reveal only the relevant information and allow users to focus their attention on that role. A short list of contact names might remind users of things to do—just as it happens when one see collaborators in the hallway. A focused view of the calendar will remind them of deadlines and plans, and a focused view of the file system can save some navigation steps. Of course, Personal Role Managers need to allow for user control of the amount of focusing that occurs when they switch roles, and in some cases they may not be able to filter or focus their environment at all when new tasks arise.

A pragmatic way to define roles in a role management environment is as a subset of real-life roles that are distinct enough to allow for beneficial automatic customizing of the environment. For example, a university faculty member's multiple roles as researcher may not be distinct enough to be seen as multiple roles in such a role-based environment (because colleagues may be involved in multiple projects and overlapping research topics). On the other hand, it is likely that being the chair of a conference, a member of the dean search committee for another college, or a member of an elementary school parent–teacher association will be very distinct roles that can be identified fairly easily.

The creation of new roles is also a challenging issue. Some roles may be inherited from other users, or provided by organizations. For example, a professor is given a teaching role that includes a schedule, a set of students, and preset documents. A new mother on maternity leave might pass a particular work role and all its components to a temporary replacement. Roles may also split as they become more complex, such as when a subcommittee is formed to concentrate on a specific issue. Or roles may be merged, such as when two sales teams reorganize under one manager. Finally new roles can be created on the fly by simply initiating a role and performing work in that role. For example, if a user creates a new role for himself as carpool coordinator that role will become more defined as he sends email, creates documents, or enters events in his calendar within that role. Switching roles must be easy and rapid, with clear feedback about the active role.

It is natural to consider the possibility of the automatic creation of roles from templates provided by organizational designers. It is easy to understand how professors could be sent roles from the registrar or department chair based on registration data, the assignment of teaching assistants, and the university calendar. Just as the creation of Excel or Word macros or templates has become a specialty in many organizations, the creation of role templates could greatly facilitate adoption of the Personal Role Management approach.

## Case Study of Role-Based Email for College Students

The Personal Role Management strategy was recently revisited by a team of University of Maryland undergraduates who investigated how it might improve email interfaces for university students. Although all users assume multiple roles, college students constitute an interesting example of users assuming fairly distinct and predictable roles, at least when they start as freshmen. Their school role—or *student role*—is structured by the rhythm and interactions of classes, projects, and exams. Their *family role* is usually disconnected from school; and they are often employed outside of campus, *work role*, interacting with yet another separate group of people. Our team of students conducted small surveys looking at email usage patterns and the subjective experiences of students on campus. These surveys suggest that email overload and feature intimidation are the main hindrances to email communication on campus.

We looked at how Personal Role Management in email can exploit the categorical nature of college students' email correspondence. The contacts, schedule, and many of the documents involved in class communication are typically well defined (e.g., students and professors in specific classes), which are known ahead of time and can be preset automatically. This knowledge permits an email program to automatically organize many of a student's messages and contacts by grouping them separately. Class directory listings and specialized views of calendars become possible with the requisite back-end support. We describe scenarios of use, an interface mockup, and user reactions. Our research suggests that using those roles as a driving component for designing an email interface for college students might address some of the problems identified in our surveys and interviews.

User groups in other settings may also benefit from role-based email interfaces as long as some of their roles are sufficiently distinct to allow some level of automatic role detection, and to benefit from customization of the interface for different roles.

### Related Work on Electronic Mail

In their study of email overload, Whittaker and Sidner (1996) observed that people were using email for task management and personal archiving. They describe the goals of task management as "[ensuring] that information relating to current tasks is readily available." The researchers conclude from a study of Lotus NotesMail users that keeping email organized presents a major problem for some email users, resulting in backlogs of unread and unanswered mail.

More recently, Ducheneaut and Bellotti (2001) described further how email is being widely used as a personal information manager (PIM). Through interviews, they examined how people at work sort their email messages and deal with clutter in a business environment. The researchers suggested that "to better support the use of email as a PIM tool, organization of folders should be more flexible. . . . the management of to-dos and reminders within email should be supported." The interview results indicated that available software did not adequately expose such features. They raise the following question based on their research: "Would it be possible to leverage a model of users' roles and organizational environment in the design of email clients? One possible way is to present a different interface, with different email management options, depending on a user's role."

Bellotti et al. (2003) developed a prototype of a task management-centric email client that received positive feedback from business users who tested it. Two other recent papers discuss the organization of email by task or activity (Kaptelinin 2003; Venolia and Neustaedter 2003). The choice of task management over role management may better suit some business usage patterns, where employees juggle many short-lived tasks—all within a single role (ESA&NTIA report, 2002). However, many users have multiple distinct roles, and often integrate non-work aspects of their personal lives in their email activities (Nippert-Eng 1996), introducing distinct social groups of people, events, and tasks which should be managed separately from work activities. Our informal surveys suggest that college students often assume a number of distinct roles; therefore a Personal Role Management strategy may be fitting for college students. Because our student team had first-hand experience with the life of college students and access to a large number of friends and classmates to interview they decided to focus on this particular user group. In another domain, Barreau and Nardi (1995) have argued for the importance of location-based saving and searching, and have shown that the user's perception of their information space and the location of information within that space serve a reminding function. This is contrast with researchers who suggest that users only need better tools to find their documents in archives that are organized only by temporal sequence (Fertig, Freeman, and Gelernter 1996a,b). Another key direction is to use computer-based tools that analyze frequency of email exchanges with particular individuals, as a starting point for user identification of distinct groups of collaborators (Nardi et al. 2002; Fisher and Dourish 2004; Fisher and Nardi, this volume). ContactMap and Soylent productively focus on people, while the role manager concept includes schedules and documents as parts of the role.

The U.S. Department of Commerce surveys show email use among the general U.S. population at 45.2 percent in 2002, up from 35.4 percent in 2000 (ESA&NTIA 2002). College students represent a continuation of this trend. A study by the Pew Internet and American Life Project in 2002 indicates that "college students are heavy users of the Internet compared to the general population . . . in part because they have grown up with computers. [The Internet] is integrated into their daily communication habits and has become a technology as ordinary as the telephone or television" (Jones 2002).

The rest of this section summarizes information gathered about the use of email by the student population and presents an interface mockup illustrating how a "student role" might be implemented in a role-centric email program. This work was conducted by an interdisciplinary "Gemstone team"[1] of undergraduate students at the University of Maryland (the last eight authors of this chapter).

**Understanding Students' Needs**

In order to learn about the concerns, preferences, attitudes, and needs of students, two on-campus surveys were conducted. The first survey, a small general one, was conducted in November 2001 with students at the University of Maryland, College Park. The survey was distributed outside one of the dormitory cafeterias during dinner hours. It showed that college students use email to communicate on a daily basis. Of 35 students surveyed, 86 percent check their email several times a day and 100 percent check their email at least once a day. In addition, 89 percent of students use more than one email address to send and receive email messages.

To assess the quality of current email software in meeting the needs of college students, students were asked to identify the email functions that they use regularly. Some functions (e.g., send attachment, forward message, delete messages) were used by nearly all students, while other functions (e.g., send signature file, send autoreply message) were used by only a few. While some of the features were simply not relevant to them, other features went unused apparently because of their complexity and lack of visibility in the email program. For example, 100 percent of respondents reported receiving junk email and 43 percent used filters to block the unwanted messages. At the same time, 6 percent of students were uncertain of what filters were, and 40 percent believed filtering should be improved, particularly its ease of use.

The topic of email organization was also addressed in the survey. Students were asked if they use folders to sort and store email messages. Eighty percent of students surveyed use folders; 75 percent of these students had fewer than 10 folders. The rest of the students surveyed had between 10 and 30 folders. Email organization is relevant to college students as evidenced by the 48 percent of students who saved more than half of all the emails that they receive. Only 21 percent of students saved less than one tenth of all the email that they received.

Students were also asked to identify the people that they email regularly. As expected, students use email to communicate with friends and family members. Sixty-three percent of students also use email to communicate with coworkers (figure 5.6).

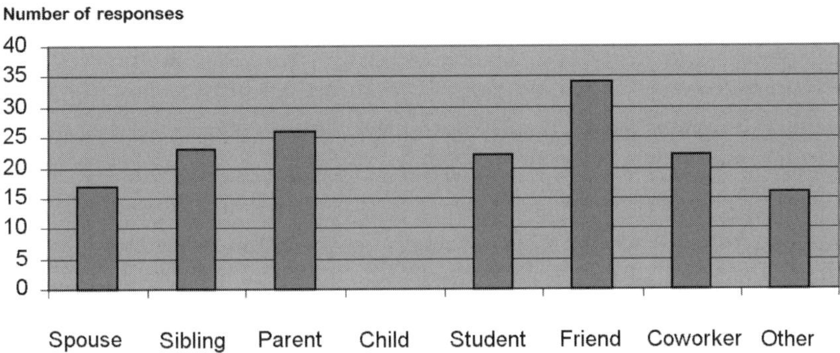


**Figure 5.6**
Persons to whom the thirty-five survey respondents sent emails to.

A section of the survey was devoted to the evaluation of current email software by students. Our sample of students used a wide variety of email tools. Students commented on email features that they like and dislike, naming the following positive features frequently:

- simplicity
- email notification
- address book
- folders
- support for multiple email addresses

Students also identified problems with current email programs. The following issues were acknowledged by students:

- difficulty changing how features work
- difficulty setting up
- lack of spell-checking (in some tools)
- feature overload

Despite its small sample size, the first survey provided some insight into student email use and helped us develop a second survey. In April 2002, the second survey was distributed to 47 students, most of whom again were students at the University of Maryland, College Park. Like the first survey, the second survey addressed problems that students encountered with current email software. In addition, the second survey considered students' attitudes toward potential changes to the user interface.

To investigate filtering, students were asked if they understand and know how to use filters. Nine percent of students confessed that they did not know how to use filters, and 32 percent had only a vague idea. In general, students were receptive to automation in email. Most students (72 percent) told us that they would like to have their emails automatically sorted for them. Also, 66 percent of the students were enthusiastic about an email program that changes to accommodate their personal preferences. Most students, however, were not comfortable using an email program that keeps track of their usage patterns and makes inferences about their intentions (even for the exclusive purpose of adjusting the user interface).

### System Mockup

Based on the feedback received, the student authors set out to independently design a user interface that addresses two major problems for college students per their observations: email overload and feature overload. They investigated how Personal Role Management may address these problems in two ways. First, organizing messages by role may manage email overload. Second, the ability to select a current role permits hiding functionality irrelevant to that role, alleviating some feature overload. A lighter feature set also leaves more room for special functionality in a given role, such as a customized class calendar organized by semester.

In designing a role management user interface, the students established criteria for simplicity. They believed that the interface ought to be sufficiently familiar to current email users. Ideally, novices could use the program exactly like existing email software while they explored the role management functionality. The additional overhead from using Personal Role Management ought to be minimal to reduce the switching penalty. Finally, the interface must degrade "gracefully" and be useful and usable when no information is available about the roles of the users or when the users were not willing to make use of the new features.

After several revisions of sketched paper mockups, screenshots were generated using computer graphics tools to better resemble an actual interface. Those screenshots were used to collect feedback from potential users. Finally, they implemented a Visual Basic prototype to illustrate some of the interactions. Figures 5.7 through 5.9 show sample screenshots of the prototype.

The most significant departure from standard email clients is the presence of role selection tabs. Each role has a separate view, defined by the user or preset by the university, where only messages, contacts, and functionality relevant to the role are visible. In the example of figure 5.7 two specific roles are available—school and work—with the school role currently selected. The General role corresponds to the "standard" entry to the email interface where no role is selected. Roles could include subroles; for example, each class (e.g., ANTH 240, ENEE 435) is a subrole that provides further filtering in the school role.[2]

Figure 5.8 shows the calendar view of the School role. The school calendar displays data in a manner convenient for school-related tasks,

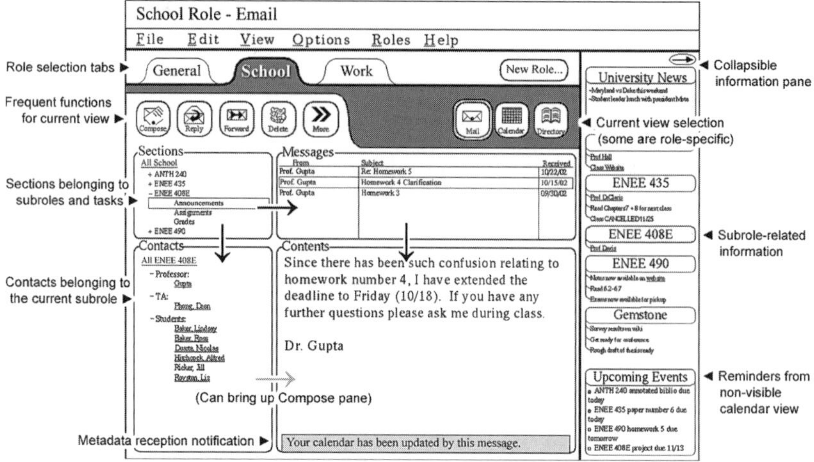


**Figure 5.7**

Role management email interface in school role under mail view. Arrows added to the screen shot indicate the linkage between parts of the display. Here the student has clicked on ENEE 408E to show only the mail related to the ENEE 408E class. The contact list was filtered as well to show only students enrolled and instructors teaching that class. Further filtering of the mail list can be done; here only announcements are shown. Once the ENEE 408E role is selected, a click on "calendar" will switch to the calendar for that particular class.

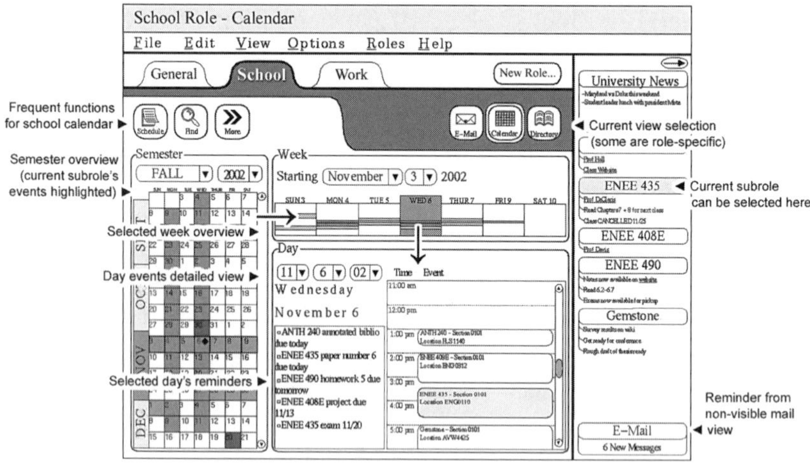


**Figure 5.8**

Role management email interface in school role under calendar view. Here the ENEE 435 class (or subrole) has been selected. A semester calendar corresponding to the class duration is shown, color coded to represent class meeting time, assignments and exams, on top of a black and white view of the complete school role calendar. Day events are listed for all classes as well but ENEE 435 events are highlighted.

such as using a semester layout, as opposed to a financial quarter layout for the work calendar. The calendar can use different colors to indicate class times, exams, assignment deadlines, and so on. The school role view shows all the events relevant to that role, while focusing on a particular class—by clicking on the right side of the information panel—focuses on the schedule of that class.

When a role is selected, the information panel located on the right side of the screen summarizes the information most relevant to the role. For the school role, it shows University Announcements and the list of classes. For the work role, it shows general announcements and two projects, "Circuit project" and "Reports" (figure 5.9). For contextual cues, a different visual theme or skin can distinguish each role; this was limited to color in our prototype but can includes fonts, icon style, sound effects, and so on, to indicate which role is currently being assumed. The subroles belonging to a role appear in the role information panel on the right side of the screen and are also shown as folders in a hierarchical browser. This view also allows users to create traditional folders if needed in the role. The bottom portion of the information panel can provide a summary of roles that are not currently visible. Figure 5.8 shows it reminding the user that new mail has arrived, which can be found in the Mail view (clicking

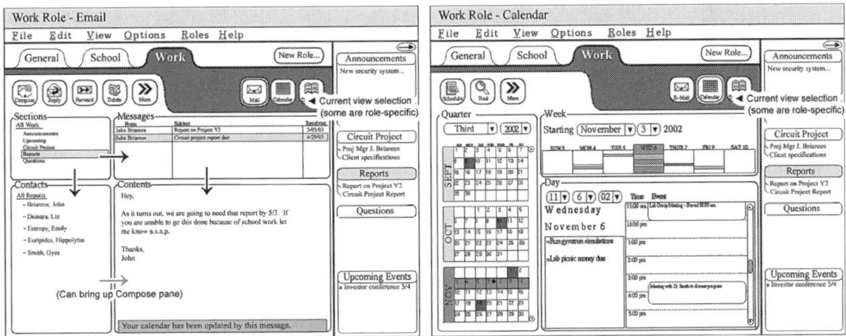


**Figure 5.9**
Role management email interfaces in the work role for mail (left) and calendar views (right). The work role is not as well defined as the school role. Still users can define customized calendars (here a quarter calendar), or different options—for example, a different signature file and automatic spell-checking. The contacts are limited and different from the school role, and play an important part in characterizing the role itself.

the reminder would switch to it). Each role allows several tabs as well, but with a larger screen all the information would be visible at once.

The general role is unique because it encompasses messages and contacts from all roles, acting like a regular email application, and allows users to transition from non-role-based email and back to it when needed. The other purpose of the general role is to hold correspondence that does not fit any defined role.

Several potential problems arise when considering Personal Role Management as a method of organization. Most importantly, roles are not always mutually exclusive. To deal with this, a given message or contact can be made visible in any role to which it is possibly related. In other words, a role acts as a filtered view to see messages, contacts, and events that can be relevant to that role. This allows for role overlap, such as an email from a friend requesting help on homework while commenting on recent social events. There is also the question of how the application determines what messages and contacts fit under which roles. A potential solution comes from the fact that many students in our surveys used several email addresses (they typically have a university address, an older personal address, and a work address). Those different addresses could easily be used to filter content in different roles. A less restrictive approach is to assume nothing about an unmarked message until the user assigns it to a role (e.g., by dragging it to the role tab or using a keyboard shortcut). The new contact is added to the role, and all subsequent correspondence with that person will be assigned to that role unless the thread is marked with another role. Alternatively, if the user initiates the communication from a given role, the recipient is automatically marked to that role. Adding a role selection option to the email header might prevent some mistakes, but it is more useful to provide rapid and seamless role-switching with shortcuts. Unassociated messages and contacts remain in the general role, which can alternatively show all emails, or "general-only" emails, as well as all people, and all events equally displayed in the calendar. Not everything can be sorted, but even if only 20 to 30 percent of items are sorted automatically it can represent a significant time savings and reduce the overhead of task switching. Benefits should increase with the number of unambiguously distinct roles.

Another issue is how to deliver useful role-specific functionality. Some functionality can be delivered automatically at the institutional level (e.g., using a semester-based calendar for the class role), and adequate user control can further customize the interface for each role. At the institutional level, a university might define and disseminate default roles to students. For example, signing up for a class would send the student a new role with the class syllabus, book information, exam dates, and lists of teachers and classmates; the newly elected president of the badminton club would receive a new role containing a calendar of deadlines, a specific list of contacts, and a budget viewer. Some of the automation could take place by embedding metadata in an email.

Using ideas promoted by Semantic Web researchers (Hendler, Berners-Lee, and Miller 2002), the email client could provide tools for embedding role associations, news items, event changes, or other meta-information into messages. Upon receiving such messages, the client could reliably read and act on the information (with requisite security considerations). Metadata-unaware email clients would simply ignore the data. Metadata encoding could be implemented as an icon toolbox allowing users to click and drag "forms" into their message. Once properly filled out, these forms could then offer the recipient to add dates, meetings, contact information, or other data to his or her role-based email program. Ideally, the past president of the badminton club could email his now ended role to the new president.

For advanced users, personal customization of the roles will increase the benefits of using roles. Roles could use a different signature (formal for work, informal for school, home address for friends and family). Automatic spell-checking might be enabled in the work role but not the friends role, where communication is less formal (students clearly indicated that spell-checking was annoying when talking to friends). Different skins could be chosen to match the mood of those different roles. Search could be automatically limited to the role information by default. Automatic copies could be turned off in the friends role and archiving turned on in the work role. The more roles that are differentiated the more time savings Peronal Role Management can generate.

### Scenario of Use

Consider the following scenario of use: Matt, a typical college student, has just arrived as a freshman at the University of Maryland. He has brought his computer to school and is encouraged to download and become familiar with a recommended (role-based) email program that has been tailored to University of Maryland students. When he installs the software, the school calendar is already populated with class registration deadlines, university holidays, events, and the last day of class. When Matt registers for classes he receives an automated acknowledgment message that includes metadata information about the class. This information is used by the email program to set up the school role for Matt. His calendar is updated (after he reviews the information and acknowledges the automatic loading of his calendar); the contact list includes information about the instructor and the teaching assistant; and the syllabus is saved in the class file folder. When class starts, a reminder email indicates a classroom change and loads the contact information of classmates.

When reading email Matt can now choose to read all his email at once (using the General role tab), or focus on his school role first, then review the other messages. While he is reading his school role email, he sees in the information panel that the ENEE 430 professor has highlighted the upcoming group project first deadline. In one click he can switch to that class subrole and review the class calendar, which is useful since—like most undergraduate students—he does not maintain a personal calendar. He switches to the email view, but can't quite remember the name of the fellow classmate he is supposed to work with so he scans the list of about twenty classmates. He recognizes the name and sends email to set up a meeting.

A few months later, Matt gets a part-time job in a local company. At first, all his work-related email appears in the General role. After a few weeks, Matt has received emails from many people in the company and he spends five minutes setting up his work role. He drags messages sent by work colleagues onto the work role to add their names in the work role contact list. A few months later he is already working on two projects so he creates two subroles within his work role. A month later the company adopts a role-based email system, but since Matt is graduating and quitting his job, he can pass his role to the fellow student taking his place by emailing him the role information (calendar, contacts, selected important emails, to-do lists, reports) all at once. Soon he will also archive his entire school role all together.

**Informal User Feedback**

We conducted scenario testing and interview sessions. Twenty students from the University of Maryland, College Park were interviewed during November–December of 2002. The testing procedure involved printed prototype mockups, and was designed to measure the subject's understanding of the interface and concept of role management. Before testing, initial impressions were recorded. Several scenarios calling for simple tasks were then presented. No prior training or demonstration was provided. The subjects were encouraged to verbalize their thought process, and their remarks were recorded. A follow-up interview was conducted afterward.

From the initial impressions, many of subjects considered the interface "busy." These subjects were asked what information they would eliminate, and how well the information was organized. Several subjects thought that the information panel was not always useful, and thought it should be collapsible. The calendar's weekly and daily views seemed too detailed, since many students seldom used calendars to record personal information. A simplified calendar was thought to be more helpful. Feedback on the organization of information was generally positive, and the hierarchical views in the calendar received praise. One student commented that it was easy to focus on short-term activities without losing sight of long-term goals. The majority of subjects recognized the purpose of role folders right away; a few initially mistook the work role tab for campus job searches (which in fact could be the default setup for students who do not have a job yet).

In the scenarios, the subjects had little trouble recognizing the needed interface features, including the view selection buttons, the information panel, and the contacts hierarchy. Asked to look up the dates of next semester's spring break, 75 percent correctly selected the calendar view and manipulated the pull-down semester menu. Starting from the calendar view, the subjects were asked to email their class instructor. Sixty percent took the shortest path by using the instructor email link in the information panel, while the rest preferred to switch to the mail view and use the contact list. To send a mass email to everyone in a class, 70 percent made the optimal choice by clicking the class's root node in the contacts hierarchy inside the mail view.

The follow-up interviews examined the interface's perceived viability as a personal information manager. This issue is relevant to the target audience, since 65 percent of the subjects reported using a date book or another kind of scheduler. Seventy percent said they would consider using a program like the one presented in place of their current planner; 65 percent said they would use the program to check their daily agenda. While such statements may not predict actual usage, they suggest a generally positive reaction. The remaining questions involved automation, and the students remained opposed to automatic changes: 75 percent wanted to be notified of changes to their schedule and to be asked for their approval.

Feedback from faculty and colleagues was less enthusiastic as more concerns were raised about the capability of the system to correctly sort emails by role. Faculty and staff typically have a large number of less distinct roles with overlapping sets of colleagues. Everyone had some roles for which the separation was sufficient to be detected correctly, and some where the separation would be difficult. For example, teaching roles or campus-wide committee member roles are more distinct, but research projects have a lot of overlap and may have to be grouped into a large role.

## Conclusions

Our research findings on campus email use have several implications for those designing future email clients: students use email in different ways than the average business user and would benefit from specially designed interfaces. Although school-related email use is heavy, functionality beyond simple messaging is sparsely used and students spend very limited amount of time organizing their emails.

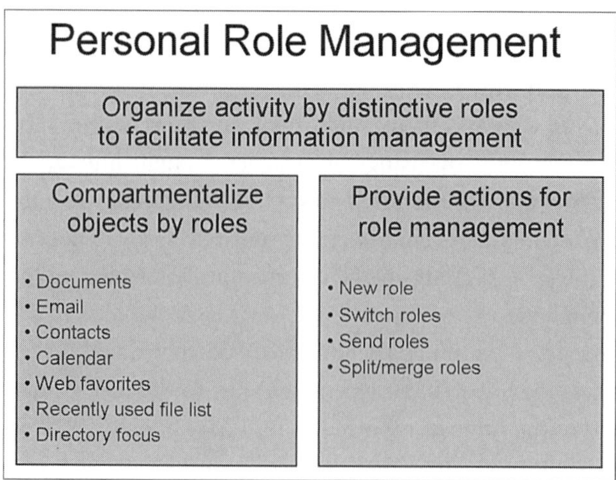


Figure 5.10

Freshmen come to campus ready to start a new life and are likely to adopt software that helps them get organized with their classes. Customizing the interface to their needs and providing personal information management features from the start by creating a program to gather and display university or class schedules is likely to increase use and streamline email and calendar management. Most students keep a significant portion of their incoming mail. Many would like to have the messages automatically sorted into folders, but don't seem to know how—or worry that messages will be misplaced. The Personal Role Management strategy may contribute to lessening those problems.

The proposed interface illustrates one way that Personal Role Management might be implemented, and initial reactions from students are positive. We hope others will continue developing the Personal Role Management strategy for email clients. Developing a fully functional prototype would be the next step in evaluating the practicality of this approach.

Other user groups may also benefit from role-based interfaces when their roles are sufficiently distinct to allow an adequate level of automatic role detection, or to benefit from customization of the interface for the different roles. Personal Role Management benefits will be greatest when users switch to focused and distinct roles, as it would allow them to focus rapidly on the information relevant to each role. Personal Role Management alone will not solve all the problems of information or email overload, but it has the potential to organize interface environment in a way that is meaningful to users and mirrors the many lives they live.[3]

## Acknowledgments

We appreciate partial support from National Science Foundation Grant for Information Technology Research no. 0086143, Understanding the Social Impact of the Internet: A Multifaceted Multidisciplinary Approach. Additional thanks to Harry Hochheiser and Rina Levy for helping us in the past to refine our understanding of Personal Role Management.

## Notes

1. The Gemstone Program at the University of Maryland focuses on the development of the students outside the standard classroom environment, and challenges the students in the development of research, teamwork, communication and

leadership skills. The team included students from Civil Engineering, Biochemistry, Electrical Engineering, Physiology and Neurobiology, German, and Computer Science. Working under the guidance of a mentor (Catherine Plaisant) they met once a week for three years. The students conducted their research mostly independently. They conducted surveys, designed prototypes, collected user feedback, and wrote a final thesis, which is summarized in this essay.

2. The idea of subroles was introduced by the students. The original Personal Role Management proposal specifically avoided subroles because of the added complexity.

3. About the student authors: H. Ross Baker is a computer scientist with an interest in linguistics; he is now a graduate student in the Department of Linguistics at Northwestern University. Nicolas Duarte is an electrical engineer with an interest in nanotechnology; he is now a graduate student seeking his Ph.D. in the Department of Electrical Engineering at Pennsylvania State University, researching thermal transport in nanowires. Aydin Haririnia is a biochemist with an interest in protein NMR and crystallography. He is now a graduate student in the Department of Chemistry and Biochemistry at the University of Maryland. Dawn Klinesmith is a civil engineer with an interest in structural engineering; she is a Ph.D. student in the Department of Civil and Environmental Engineering at the University of California, Berkeley. Hannah Lee is a recent graduate of the University of Maryland with an interest in physiology and neurobiology. Leonid Velikovich is a computer scientist with an interest in computer graphics; he is a recent graduate of the Department of Computer Science at the University of Maryland. Alfred Wanga is an electrical engineer with an interest in electronic materials and devices. He is now a graduate student at Penn State University. Matt Westhoff is a computer scientist with an interest in computer graphics. He recently graduated from the University of Maryland, College Park.

## References

Barreau, D. K. (1995). Context as a factor in personal information management systems. *Journal of the American Society for Information Science* 46 (5): 327–339.

Barreau, D. K., and Nardi, B. A. (1995). Finding and reminding: File organization from the desktop. *SIGCHI Bulletin* 27 (3): 39–43.

Bellotti, V., Ducheneaut, N., Howard, M., and Smith, I. (2003). Taking email to task: The design and evaluation of a task management centered email tool. In *Proceedings of CHI 2003 Conference: Human Factors in Computing Systems,* pp. 345–352. Ft. Lauderdale, Florida, April 5–10.

Biddle, B. J., and Thomas, E. J. (1979). *Role Theory: Concepts and Research.* New York: Krieger Publishing.

Ducheneaut, N., and Bellotti, V. (2001). E-mail as habitat: An exploration of embedded personal information management. *interactions* 8 (5): 30–38.

ESA&NTIA, U.S. Department of Commerce (2002). Economics and Statistics Administration, and National Telecommunications and Information Administration. *A Nation Online: How Americans Are Expanding Their Use of the Internet*. Washington, D.C. Http://www.esa.doc.gov/508/esa/ANationOnlineEXSFeb02.htm/.

Fertig, S., Freeman, E., and Gelernter, D. (1996a). "Finding and reminding" reconsidered. *ACM SIGCHI Bulletin* 28 (1): 66–69.

Fertig, S., Freeman, E., and Gelernter, D. (1996b). Lifestreams: An alternative to the desktop metaphor. In *Companion Proceedings of CHI 96 Conference: Human Factors in Computing Systems*, pp. 410–111. Vancouver, Canada, April 13–18.

Fisher, D., and Dourish, P. (2004). Social and temporal structures in everyday collaboration. In *Proceedings of CHI 2004 Human Factors in Computing Systems*. Vienna, Austria, April 24–29.

Henderson, D. A., and Card, S. (1986). Rooms: The use of multiple virtual workspaces to reduce space contention in a window-based graphical user interface. *ACM Transactions on Graphics* 5 (3): 211–243.

Hendler, J., Berners-Lee, T., and Miller, E. (2002). Integrating applications on the Semantic Web [English version]. *Journal of the Institute of Electrical Engineers of Japan* 122 (10): 676–680.

Jones, S. (2002). *The Internet Goes to College: How Students Are Living in the Future with Today's Technology*. Washington, D.C.: Pew Internet and American Life Project. Http://usinfo.state.gov/usa/t091602.htm/.

Kandogan, E., and Shneiderman, B. (1997). Elastic Windows: evaluation of multiwindow operations. In *Proceedings of CHI'97 Conference: Human Factors in Computing Systems*, pp. 250–257. Atlanta, Georgia, March 22–27.

Kaptelinin, V. (2003). UMEA: Translating interaction histories into project contexts. In *Proceedings of CHI 2003 Conference: Human Factors in Computing Systems*, pp. 353–360. Ft. Lauderdale, Florida, April 5–10.

Nardi, B., and Barreau, D. (1997). "Finding and reminding" revisited: Appropriate metaphors for file organization at the desktop. *SIGCHI Bulletin* 29 (1): 76–78.

Nardi, B., Whittaker, S., Isaacs, E., Creech, M., Johnson, J., Hainsworth, J. (2002). ContactMap: Integrating communication and information through visualizing personal social networks. *Communications of the ACM 49* 4 (April): 89–95.

Nippert-Eng, C. (1996). *Home and Work: Negotiating Boundaries through Everyday Life*. Chicago: University of Chicago Press.

Plaisant, C., and Shneiderman, B. (1995a). Organization overviews and role management: Inspiration for future desktop environments. In *Proceedings of IEEE 4th Workshop on Enabling Technologies: Infrastructure for Collaborative Enterprises*, pp. 14–22. Berkeley Springs, West Virginia, April 20–22.

Plaisant, C., and Shneiderman, B. (1995b). Organization overviews and role management: Inspiration for future desktop environments. In *Video Proceedings of CHI'95 Conference: Human Factors in Computing Systems*. Denver, Colorado, May 7–11. Also included in the 1994 HCIL Open House video, http://www.cs.umd.edu/hcil/pubs/video-reports.shtml/.

Redmiles, D. (2002). Introduction to the Special Issue on Activity Theory and the Practice of Design. *Computer Supported Cooperative Work* 11 (1–2): 1–11.

Robertson, G., van Dantzich, M., Robbins, D., Czerwinski, M., Hinckley, K., Risden, K., Thiel, D., and Gorokhovsky, V. (2000). The Task Gallery: A 3D window manager. In *Proceedings of the SIGCHI Conference on Human Factors in Computing Systems*, pp. 494–501. The Hague, The Netherlands, April 1–6.

Roos, L. L., Jr., and Starke, F. A. (1981). Organizational roles. In Nystrom, P. C., and Starbuck, W. H. (eds.), *Handbook of Organizational Design*, vol. 1: *Adapting Organizations to Their Environments.* Oxford: Oxford University Press.

Sarbin, T. R., and Allen, V. L. (1968). Role theory. In Lindzey, G., and Aronson, E. (eds.), *Handbook of Social Psychology,* 2nd ed. New York: Addison-Wesley.

Shneiderman, B., and Plaisant, C. (1994). The future of graphic user interfaces: Personal Role Managers. In *People and Computers IX*, pp. 3–8. Glasgow, Scotland, August 23–25.

Singh, B., and Rein, G. (1992). Role Interaction Nets (RINS): A process description formalism. Technical Report CT-083–92. Microelectronics and Computing Center, Austin, Texas.

Venolia, G. D., and Neustaedter, C. (2003). Understanding sequence and reply relationships within email conversations: A mixed-model visualization. In *Proceedings of CHI 2003 Conference: Human Factors in Computing Systems*, pp. 361–368. Ft. Lauderdale, Florida, April 5–10.

Whittaker, S., and Sidner, C. (1996). Email overload: Exploring personal information management of email. In *Proceedings of CHI 1996 Conference: Human Factors in Computing Systems*, pp. 276–283. Vancouver, Canada, April 13–18. New York: ACM Press.

# 6

# Soylent and ContactMap: Tools for Constructing the Social Workscape

Danyel Fisher and Bonnie Nardi

## Introduction: Exploring and Articulating the Social Workscape

Within computer systems, people can be anywhere, and should be everywhere. We believe that representations of meaningful social presence within computer systems will lead to more meaningful and more interesting interactions with both the computer and other people in our workday environments.

Little of what knowledge workers do is done alone. Nardi, Whittaker, and Schwarz (2002) interviewed workers about how they manage and interact with people at work. It was found that workers were careful managers of their personal social networks, perpetually aware of the ways in which they interacted with others. People managed three interpersonal tasks: building social networks, maintaining the networks, and activating nodes within the networks as needed.

While users manage these tasks with communication and contact-management tools, many of the tasks continue to be difficult. Three-pane mailers, for example, do a poor job of providing contextual information such as communication histories about message senders. Message attachments are frequently lost, or dissociated from the messages to which they are attached. Instant message (IM) transcripts, mail histories, and other forms of interaction are all stored and presented separately.

Users attempt to work around the problems of current tools. Research has shown that email is used not only for its intended purpose of asynchronous communication, but for *task management* and *personal archiving* (Whittaker and Sidner 1996; Ducheneaut and Bellotti 2001). For example, Ducheneaut and Bellotti found that users kept old messages as an address book. They used the inbox as a to-do list, a memo-pad, and a future calendar. They used email archives as version-control systems. They blurred the lines between personal and collaborative technologies, reappropriating the one application available to them that would associate persistent information with people into a people-oriented personal database and communications center.

In repurposing email, users found ways to place the work objects within their computer system—contacts, files, and information—into a social context. In other words, they constructed a social workscape. The email they archived and contacts they maintained built a context, allowing them to track and connect relationships between their contacts and their information.

However, such ad hoc unprincipled solutions are unsatisfying. Leaving attachments in mail means losing their file system aspects (such as sorting into folders and searching); storing dates within the inbox does not have a useful calendar-based interface. The social workscape is incompletely supported by current technology, no matter how many workarounds users devise.

In this paper, we explore the implications of supporting a social workscape within a computer system. We discuss the idea of representing people and relationships within the computer system as first-class entities: groupable, selectable objects linked to other resources, connected to underlying data sources. We envision a system that is designed around ubiquitous connections between *people, activities,* and *artifacts.*

That these ubiquitous connections are useful might be seen by a variety of frequent information and networking tasks. A user might:

- Look for files associated with a particular person.
- Get the current location or travel information for a person associated with a particular file or task, or find the most available person associated with the task.
- Find out who has sent them information or requests relating to a particular topic.
- Collect all correspondence and emailed files relating to a particular file.
- Find the history of communication by a person or group of people.

We refer to a system that assists with these tasks as person-centric; it is a system whose design is centered around the notion of the person.

Our vision of the workscape is similar to that of Plaisant et al. (this volume); their notion of "role management" places interactions with documents and systems within specific roles. In contrast, both of the systems we describe step away from the administrative task of specifying roles, and instead concentrate on understanding the social structure of our networks.

## Building the Workscape with Personal Social Networks

A crucial aspect of such a system is that of the relationships between people. Some systems track large amounts of archival information (Dumais et al. 2003), but do not attempt to track interconnections between people. We use the notion of "personal social network" to organize these interconnections. By tracking groups of contacts in a network, we can associate these groups with the social and technical contexts in which they are situated.

Personal social networks are different from the public social networks that have become popular recently, such as those supported by Friendster (boyd 2004). Public network systems attempt to connect people who do not know each other, by connecting friends of friends to each other. Personal social networks represent a single user's perspective on the connections between the people they contact. This chapter looks at two different systems that collect, track, and interpret personal social networks. *ContactMap* takes a top-down approach, starting from a user interface and working down to a system design. *Soylent* takes a bottom-up approach, building a generalized infrastructure for storing and displaying the social context around people. The chapter then discusses a series of philosophies that would direct the design of a future person-centric computer system.

## ContactMap: A Top-Down Approach

ContactMap began with the insight that personal social networks are critical resources in today's economy (Nardi, Whittaker, and Schwarz 2002). ContactMap organizes the computer desktop according to people in the user's personal social network (Nardi et al. 2002). It does this by displaying the contacts in the user's social network and providing functionality relevant to those contacts. A contact can be an individual or group whom the user is familiar with and wishes to make available to themselves. Each contact has an icon: a photo of the contact, or another mnemonic image.

Contacts may be clustered together into groups; each contact may belong to none, one, or more groups, as shown in figure 6.1.

ContactMap integrates communication and information management in a single user interface. Each contact can be clicked to access information associated with the contact or to communicate with the contact. Let's say Sally is our user and Sam one of the contacts in Sally's ContactMap. In a typical scenario, Sally clicks on Sam to get a list of the email messages he has sent her. Sam's contact information shows reminders and notifications of unread email messages associated with him. She reads the last couple messages from him, and then wants to call him. She clicks on his icon, and uses ContactMap's click-to-dial feature to make the call. After the call, Sally remembers something she forgot, and she clicks on Sam to send an email message. ContactMap opens a new message addressed to Sam. Sally's work has taken place with a minimum of fuss—no looking up phone numbers or email addresses, no launching of additional applications. Sally sees only the email from Sam and does not have to search through folders.

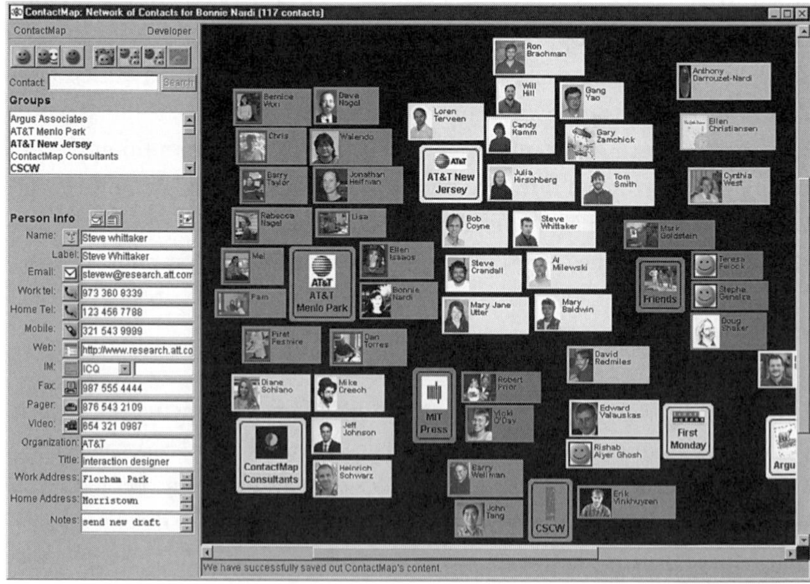


**Figure 6.1**
ContactMap.

ContactMap helps people manage the multitasking with different individuals and groups characteristic of work in the modern economy (Nardi, Whittaker, and Schwarz 2002).

Within the tool, Sally can find any documents Sam had sent her, as they are indexed by contact. Sally can start a videoconference with Sam, or an IM exchange; she can send him a fax or go to his website.

Any ContactMap functions can be performed on a group instead of an individual. A conference call can be initiated, a group email sent, a website linked to, and so forth. Individual contacts can be placed in multiple groups in ContactMap, as individuals in a social network often occupy more than one role in a user's life. Sam might be Sally's coworker and also a member of her gardening club.

Empirical research shows that most users have small social maps, with an average of 95 people (Whittaker et al. 2004). While maps certainly grow over time, people keep a small set of active contacts. This allowed us to step away from a multilayered hierarchical design: there are groups of people, but no groups of groups of people. An elaborate means of organizing contacts is unnecessary and would be confusing for many users. As active contacts come in and out of a user's life, the user can shrink down contacts to small icons, or place offscreen when not needed. The information about contacts is preserved, but does not need to be visible, cluttering the display.

ContactMap is a social workscape in which the most common actions of a user's daily work are reorganized to reflect the people with whom the user interacts. It does not replace operating system functionality but provides a different user interface to that functionality. Instead of privileging files and folders, ContactMap centers on people in the user's personal social network.

Setting up ContactMap begins with a numerical analysis of the user's email folders. Based on domain names, frequency of contact, and frequency of replies to messages, ContactMap presents a list of contacts to the user (Nardi et al. 2002). Users select the contacts to include in their map, and group them as they wish. Groups can be color coded. ContactMap supplies a default color scheme, or the user can choose any colors desired.

While not currently implemented, future versions could connect contact lists to address books, phone logs, and other digital sources. Web-based updates could handle the chore of keeping up with changes in contact information. Contacts could be shared selectively among work groups or "buddies" as in instant messaging.

ContactMap was tested with 15 users including researchers, managers, administrative assistants, and marketing staff (Whittaker et al. 2004). The tests showed that the mean number of contacts chosen was 95, with a range of 15 to 184. Even 184 contacts is an easily manageable number to display iconically on a full screen.

Users grouped their contacts, with a mean of 11 groups and a range of 2 to 23. Constructing automatic groups seemed like a good idea during the initial design of ContactMap, but after several failed experiments, it was decided to allow users to form their own groups. With the small number of contacts, the grouping task was easy and users even seemed to enjoy reflecting on their social networks as they grouped contacts. The average size of groups was 8, and nearly all contacts appeared in groups. Only 7 percent were "singletons." An individual contact can appear in multiple groups. The nature of the groups was surprisingly uniform across the test population: work groups, work projects, friends, family, and special interests, which in our sample included the PTA, a rock band, and a stock club.

Research on the importance of face-to-face interaction in everyday communication (Nardi and Whittaker 2002) suggested that making it easy to use a photo of a contact would be pleasing. Users simply need to locate a digital photo or image and ContactMap will size and place it properly in the map. This feature was popular with those in the user test.

Further testing would be needed to learn more about this issue and other aspects of the typical user of ContactMap. At this time, ContactMap exists as a prototype but is no longer under development.

## Soylent: A Bottom-Up Approach

Soylent forms the basis of an infrastructure which can be used to construct ContactMap-like applications. The name, a punning reference,[1] is a way of stating its goal: that computer systems be "made out of people." It consists of tools to create, store, and access personal networks, ways to visualize and interact with those networks, and preliminary tools that connect those networks to applications.

Soylent was developed in part to respond to issues raised in the NetWORK and ContactMap research (Nardi, Whittaker, and Schwarz 2002;

Nardi et al. 2002). While ContactMap starts by addressing current needs with a tool, Soylent was designed to more generally explore ways that social information infrastructures can be assembled and designed. It uses email correspondence information to build a social network, and tracks both the temporal extent of interactions and the groups that implicitly are parts of the interaction.

In this section, we discuss the construction of the Soylent system, and describe a prototype built over the Soylent infrastructure: a series of social extensions to an email program.

Soylent's data are collected from email archives and assembled into a history of interaction. The history stores and indexes messages by message sender, date and time, recipients, and attachments. These data are used as the basis of a network based on co-occurrence within message headers. The fact that a user has sent an email to a pair of people (either sharing a "to" line, carbon-copying both, or some combination) is evidence that the two people have something in common from that user's perspective. Therefore, by examining *outgoing* messages for clustering information, Soylent develops a notion of a user's workscape.

### Directing Design with Social Networks

Fisher and Dourish (2004) discussed some of the dominant features of this large personal archive of email messages when seen as a whole. Here, we look at ways of interpreting smaller subsets of the graph to understand personal interactions and the immediate contexts around people.

**Analyzing the network** Network visualizations of email (such as Eveland and Bikson 1988; Tyler, Wilkinson, and Huberman 2003) traditionally examine pairs of names, tied by who sends email to whom. These techniques provide a collective and global view of email records, and are analyzed using a "to-from" approach, drawing directed links between sender and receiver. Those social networks are used to connect a great many people together, and provide a broad view of how people are connected. In contrast, our system is intended to help understand a *single user's* workspace. Within Soylent, and as in boyd's (2002) work, a message co-addressed to two different persons, whether via a "to," "cc," or "bcc," is understood as implicitly tying those persons together; the sender believes that they share an interest in that message. The Soylent network diagram therefore ties these two people together. This mechanism is shown schematically in figure 6.2.

The diagrams are interpreted by focusing on a perspective that examines a *single correspondent*. Each of these diagrams will look at the social interactions between a *user*, a *correspondent*, and the cluster of people around the correspondent: that is, people to whom the user has sent messages along with the correspondent. These smaller, person-centered graphs give a social context around the recipient. In figure 6.2, for example, consider viewing "Z" as the correspondent. In this scenario, Z is connected to two groups: the one consisting of Y and Z, and the one consisting of V, W, and Z.

Soylent uses this network to provide a "personal radar" view around a single recipient. Given a specific name, this radar view can give an over-

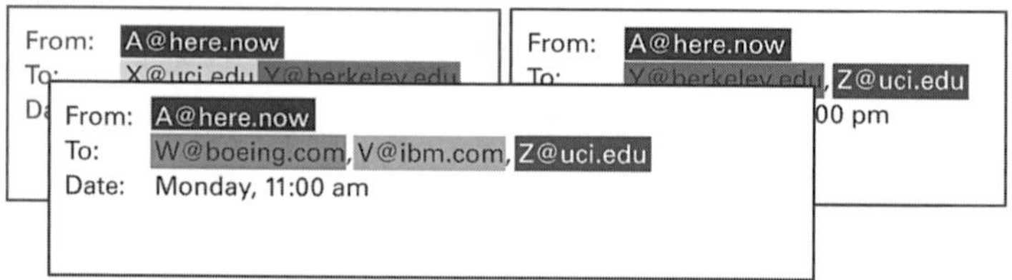


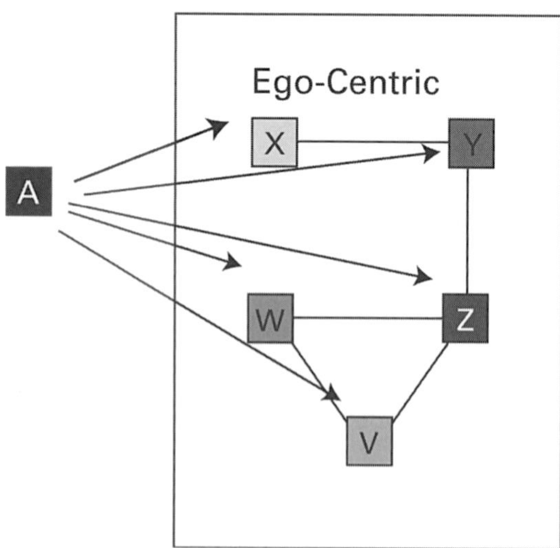


**Figure 6.2**
Schema for the Soylent "ego-centric" visualization.

view of the interaction history with the person: whom they are associated with, when those associations most recently happened, and what interactions took place.

To give a brief example, consider the display in figure 6.3. The user is a professor and the correspondent (center) is a former member of his research group (left). Edges are coded by recency; more recent communications are drawn in darker colors. The professor ran a workshop recently (right); the student joined that workshop. While the research group is now dissolved (gray), the workgroup continues onward. The student sits at the connection between these groups, and thus exists in two very different contexts.

A different example can be seen in figure 6.4, where the makeup of a social group changes over time. The user is a student; the correspondent is one of the user's friends, a social coordinator. Note the three clusters in the network diagram, separated by color; these are parts of a social group. As members of the group graduated, clusters of them fell out of touch.

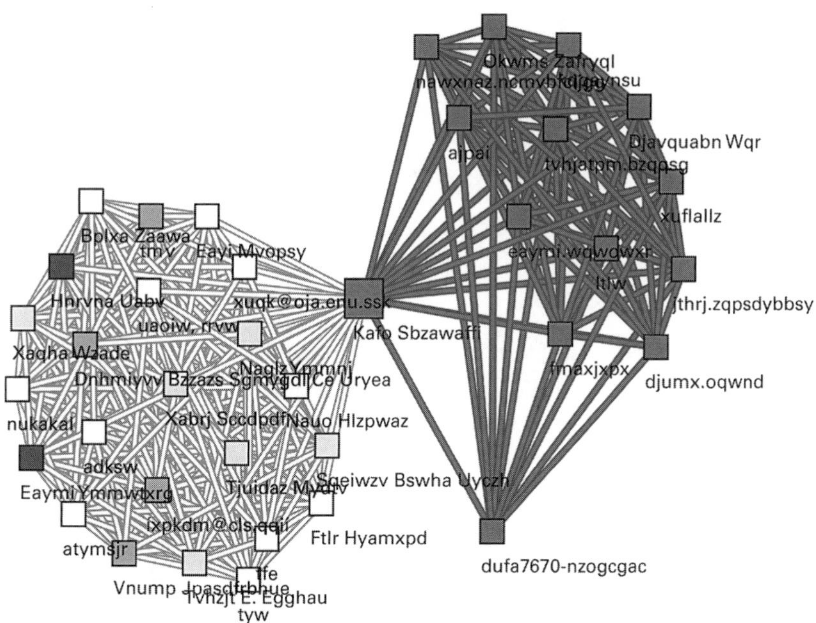


**Figure 6.3**
An ego-centric view centering on a professor. More recent communications are drawn in darker colors.

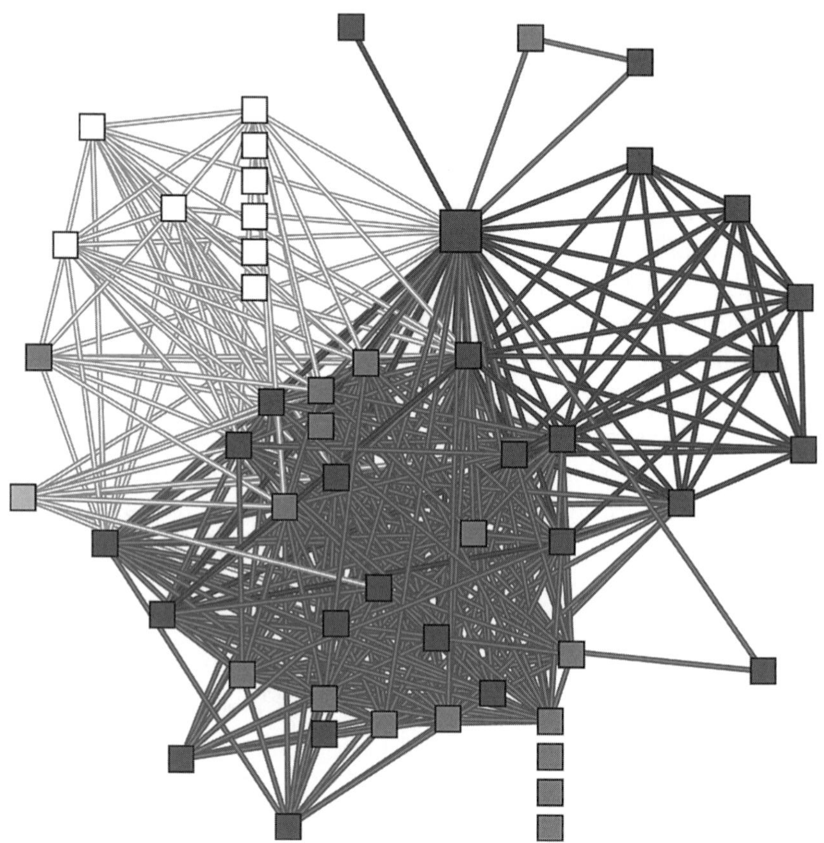

**Figure 6.4**
An ego-centric view showing a changing social group.

## Applying Awareness to Everyday Tasks with EE4P

Soylent can use parts of the social network of personal online interactions as features in an email client to produce context for email messages. A prototype email client, called "EE4P" ("Enhanced Email for People"), uses the network to help make information available to users and address some of the problems raised above. EE4P is an extension to a traditional, three-pane email client. Its code is based on ICEMail (Nourie 2001, http://icemail.org), an open-source project. EE4P currently exists in a proof-of-concept implementation.

EE4P uses the Soylent databases and API to provide the user with annotated information about both incoming and outgoing email. Every message and every person is tied to a series of other messages, people, and groups; as the user reads or writes a message, EE4P provides auxiliary information about current interactions with them. Thus, for example, while the user writes an email to a current group, the system makes available past emails both received and sent to members of the group, and a selection of past people who were associated with it, in a sidebar.

EE4P provides three major features: recipient prediction, an enhanced display with easy access to user histories, and an enhanced address book.

**Recipient prediction** Recipient prediction uses networks to suggest logical groups. Recipient prediction is triggered when the user types in a name on the "to" line of a message and presses the comma key, which suggests that more names are to come. The system then searches the immediate network of people around that name, and suggests them in a pull-down menu. It is easy to invoke an entire carbon-copy list at once (figure 6.5). The system is not constrained to historical combinations; it is able to suggest groupings that are logical expansions of the previous names. By using clustering algorithms, EE4P is able to suggest various granularities of groups. For example, when a message is sent to a team leader, it might suggest four distinct lists, based on different sections of the network:

- the core members of a team;
- the core members plus the developers;
- the core members plus the designers; and
- everyone involved in the team, including core members, developers, and designers.

Of course, these are only recommendations; the user is free to select names that the system does not suggest at all.

**User histories and the message display** When a user is reading or writing a message, EE4P uses the network around the name to allow easy access to other messages (based on similar audience and time) and other groups that may be relevant to the user. Each of these names, messages, and groups is selectable, and can reveal broad information about the user's history. In particular, the user has access to:

- address book entries for every person involved in the message;

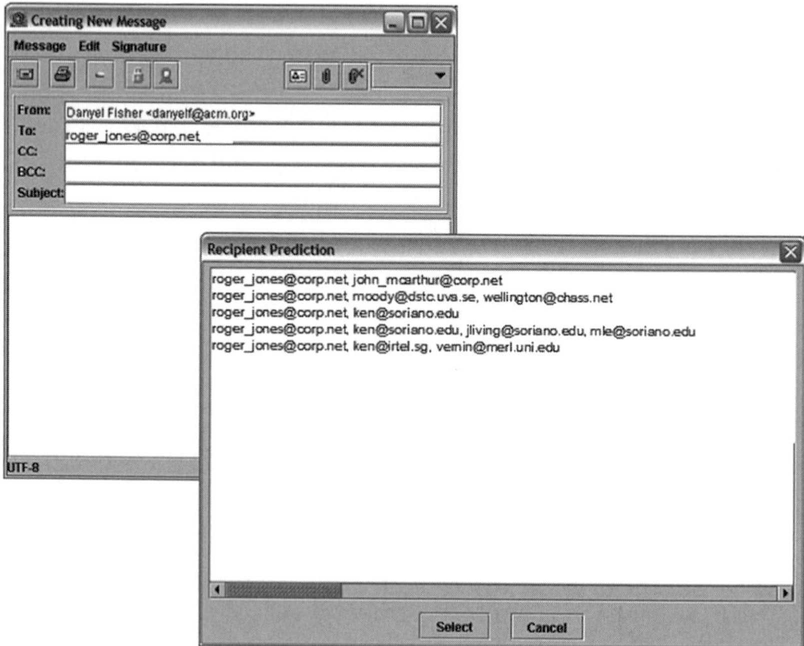


**Figure 6.5**
Filling in a carbon-copy list through EE4P.

- other people who may be closely linked to the people mentioned in the message;
- message histories for every person involved in the message, and other people who are closely involved; and
- a group "message history" that covers the participation of the whole group.

While the implementation does not currently take into account some potentially useful data, such as links to attachments or directly related messages, the mechanism is designed to be extensible enough to add those features.

**Enhanced address book** EE4P provides a standard address book that stores manually entered information about individuals. Entries, however, are annotated with additional information: one pane shows a social network view, while another pane gives a history of past messages to and

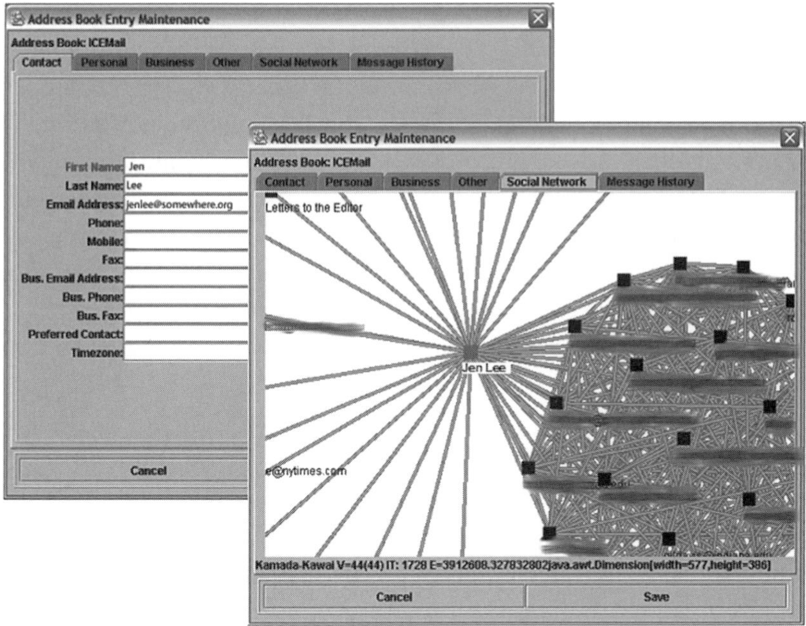


**Figure 6.6**
Viewing a social network through EE4P.

from that person. EE4P can also generate address book entries on the fly for groups of people (figure 6.6).

## Soylent as a Philosophy

The crucial insight from the Soylent work is that the implicit information generated through online interaction can give a meaningful (if incomplete) picture of the contexts in which people interact. These traces can be accumulated into a history that can be usefully processed and provided to the user. In this case, we have illustrated contact management possibilities with the tool.

In a more general case, however, Soylent suggests a more ubiquitous use of connections between people, artifacts, and times. ContactMap had a way of associating file information with personal data; so, too, Soylent suggests that connections between people and resources could be available within an operating system, providing social information as a service to system components.

While Soylent currently has a fixed notion of groups, imposed by the social network that it collects, the system can support other sorts of interconnection information. Future work calls for generalized access to groups that can be input by the user. In this way, Soylent could support hierarchy charts and organizational group membership sets—and could also support the explicit groupings that ContactMap supports. These dynamic groups could, in turn, be dynamically associated with artifacts based on their membership and their temporal extent: the system that calculated the groups would also track the files associated with the people in those groups.

Like ContactMap, Soylent currently exists as a working prototype; however, it is not under active development.

## Comparing Soylent and ContactMap

Soylent and ContactMap are both platforms for handling social network information. While ContactMap is an end-user tool, designed to model groups of people, Soylent is an infrastructure for developing and constructing social workspaces. ContactMap could be built as an end-user application with Soylent.

ContactMap visualizes networks explicitly for users to help them integrate communication and information tasks in a single user interface. In contrast, Soylent uses the networks as a form of background information on how users interact with each other.

Soylent gathers information from an email network, while ContactMap uses an automatically generated list of contacts from which the user manually assembles the network. Both, however, start from the user's communication history as a basis for understanding the set of contacts that should be modeled. There is a shared logic to how both Soylent and ContactMap view social networks. While traditional social network analysis tends to view the broad span of a network, and while tools like Friendster allow users to explore their networks at a distance, Soylent and ContactMap emphasize the user's personal social network. They look only at the people with whom the user has interacted. This information is a reflection of the user's perspective on the world.

Because both ContactMap and Soylent scan only the user's personal email folders (and the user can specify which particular folders to scan), conventional privacy issues do not arise. However, both sets of user tests observed a different privacy problem, which we might call "social privacy." ContactMap, with its photos and color-coded groups, makes the user's personal social network so instantly visible that it reveals quite a lot about how the user thinks about her social world to anyone glancing at the user's desktop. In our informal interactions with users of the prototype, they would sometimes be embarrassed, if, say, their manager was not centrally located on the map.

Similarly, the Soylent display also clearly marks how sets of people are connected. Users were sometimes concerned that connections that they considered important not be too visible to passers-by—or that people not appear to have status on their maps that they do not deserve.

**Differences between ContactMap and Soylent**

Soylent automatically collects personal information from archives and assembles networks. These automatically generated networks are incomplete. Farnham (2002), for example, has suggested that these networks may seem incomplete to some users, especially those who are in frequent face-to-face communication. ContactMap uses a hybrid approach: while it seeds the network with automatically collected names, it then allows the user to organize the entries into groups, and thus allows a person to assign importance even to unrecorded contacts.

ContactMap is structured in a nonhierarchical manner; it allows selection of a group or of its constituent members individually. The use of groups in ContactMap can be less flexible than in Soylent. For example, it would not be possible in ContactMap to specify "all the members of a group, less a few." This can be mitigated, to some extent, by creating several groups with overlapping membership. In contrast, while Soylent allows generalized access to groups as the clusters of people around a correspondent, these groups do not have a consistent identity within the system. As such, it is more difficult to index information to a specific group.

ContactMap has a strong notion of visualizing the personal social network. The ContactMap designers argue that viewing faces is something like bringing the spirit of face-to-face contact to computer-mediated communication. The presence of the contact nodes is also important for easy access to contacts and for a place to attach reminders and notifications, as well as a means of displaying groups.

Neither ContactMap nor the Soylent "EE4P" interface show the explicit box-and-line visualization traditionally associated with social networks. Instead, both store network information in the back end. ContactMap stores sets of names. Soylent's views repeatedly process parts of a large network in order to generate displays and recommendations. While the networks are a useful way to handle social information, they are not necessary—and, indeed, are likely to be confusing as a primary interface.

## The Integrated Workscape

We use these two prototype tools to discuss a more integrated image of the workscape. As we stated earlier, people *can be anywhere, and should be everywhere*, within computer systems. If the notion of "people" becomes a fundamentally available service within the computer, then applications can be adapted to use that information.

The file system, for example, can be extended to consider the people who are involved in it; calendar entries can be annotated with personal information. Files have several groups of people associated with them: those who created the file, who sent it, who edited it—as well as the future steps, those to whom it has been sent, or those who are the ultimate audience. Some of this information might be associated automatically, while other parts might have to be connected manually.

Similarly, word processors and other end-user applications might follow the cues of both EE4P and ContactMap: a document would be automatically connected with the resources and people that helped generate it. While Sally writes the next draft of her paper, for example, Sam's contact—as her teammate in writing the paper—is immediately available *within the word processor*, as both a history correspondence and as a live contact with an instant messaging status.

This calls for a consistent notion of personal identity throughout the operating system. The name for an editor of a file must be connected to his instant messaging identity and his email identity, all collected in one place.

### Existing Tools

A first step in this direction might be seen in both the Macintosh OS X "Mail" program and Microsoft's Outlook. Both programs connect instant messaging tools to email clients, so that messages from correspondents who use instant messaging are annotated with a symbol showing whether that correspondent is online or not. In deciding whether and how to respond to an email, a user can have quick access to an IM connection. This first step begins to connect different tools to share a unified notion of a workscape.

The "Stuff I've Seen" project (Dumais et al. 2003) creates a searchable archive of email messages, viewed web pages, and files; it allows users to search through personal archives to find documents indexed by both author and audience. Stuff I've Seen can be understood as a data source that, connected to social network and grouping tools, could form the core of a social workscape. Indeed, the recent release of desktop search tools from several major software vendors provides a new opportunity to begin to index this information to take advantage of its social information.

**Future Directions**

The following section discusses how to get from the current implementations into these more developed forms. We take our guidance from technologies such as "placeless documents" (Dourish et al. 1999) that suggest ways of broadly associating information within systems. In a "placeless system," the operating system supports arbitrary sets of tags to be associated with files, which can then be dynamically queried and displayed. When those tags are labeled with personal information, a placeless document system becomes person-centric.

It is not sufficient, however, to simply annotate each file, or even each piece of data, with a single name. Soylent's field research has reminded us that people and projects are closely associated with *temporal extents* and *social clusters*. Thus, the interconnections between people provide us with valuable information as to how to index their messages and information. To fully flesh out this notion of the social workscape, three layers of information are needed.

- First, there must be a layer of personal annotation associated with files and messages. Those annotations connect one or more names with computer resources, and can be associated at a variety of times: at creation time, when emailed, transferred, or received, and so on.
- Second, this information must be able to tie people to *each other*. Some form of data storage should be able to track interconnections between people as they are revealed in shared editing of files, sending and receiving communications, and so on.

- Third, there must a way to specify and learn groups. The results from ContactMap make it clear that allowing *both* automatic and manual interconnections between people is important and useful. Group information can, and should, come from a variety of sources: social network information, corporate hierarchy information, and manual choices.

**Limitations**

This section has emphasized information that can be derived automatically from message headers, file locations, and attachment connections. This view intentionally ignores the content of messages and artifacts. Instead, it illustrates how powerful an approach based strictly on interaction patterns can be. The computational power for full-text processing is not necessary to gain useful information about how sets of people interact; structural information is a powerful tool that provides much of what is needed.

That said, there are still many ambiguities in derived information. An isolated message sent from a new correspondent carries little structural information with it. Is it from a new member of a carpool, a new member of a work team, or perhaps junk mail? Modern text-analysis techniques are a potentially powerful way to resolve these ambiguities, as well as to bring together people working on related projects, but who have not been sent joint messages. These techniques could examine the texts of messages sent back and forth, and, by examining shared vocabulary and the presence of keywords, could collect other information about logical groups and connections between people.

**Summary**

In this essay, we have discussed the notion of the social workscape which ties objects into their social context. We discussed two systems that explore and articulate the workscape: ContactMap, an end-user application, and Soylent, an infrastructure for handling social information. Last, we used lessons from developing and using ContactMap and Soylent to help develop a vision of a unified workscape.

Designers may not, of course, be able to incorporate a person-centric perspective throughout all of new systems. However, there are some important lessons that can be incorporated into a variety of collaborative applications:

- *Interactions between people are meaningful.* Applications should remember the sets of people who have interacted, and make those groupings available.
- *Interactions are not only pairwise.* It is important to track the interactions of triads and larger groups, and to detect how those groups change over time.
- *Temporal aspects of interaction are important.* Most applications neglect historical information, preferring to give only the current status of a group or an interaction. This misses the fact that the changes in a group have important implications for tasks ranging from network maintenance to expertise location.
- *Information must remain associated with people.* Information that is exchanged between two people, or that is delivered via a social conduit, ought not to be divorced from that conduit: there should be ways to find the information a contact has sent, and vice versa. This principle can already be found today in version control systems, where an edit or a file is always associated with the person who changed the file, even if that information no longer seems relevant. Files are not divorced from their social context. With this set of design ideas, future users of digital environments will find representations of people anywhere and everywhere throughout the tools they use.

## Note

1. The 1973 movie *Soylent Green,* starring Charlton Heston and directed by Richard Fleischer, features the revelation that "Soylent Green is made out of people."

## References

boyd, d. (2002). Faceted Id/entity: Managing representation in a digital world. Unpublished master's thesis. Media Lab, School of Architecture and Planning, Massachusetts Institute of Technology.

boyd, d. (2004). Friendster and publicly articulated social networking. In *Proceedings of the 2004 Conference on Human Factors in Computing Systems (CHI 2004)*. Vienna, Austria, April 24–29.

Dourish, P., Edwards, W. K., LaMarca, A., and Salisbury, M. (1999). Presto: An experimental architecture for fluid interactive document spaces. *ACM Transactions on Computer Human Interaction* 6 (2): 133–161.

Ducheneaut, N., and V. Bellotti (2001). E-mail as habitat. *interactions.* 8: 30–38.

Dumais, S., Cutrell, E., Cadiz, J. J., Jancke, G., Sarin, R., and Robbins, D.C. (2003). Stuff I've Seen: A system for personal information retrieval and re-use. In *Proceedings of the 26th Annual Conference on Research and Development in Information Retrieval (SIGIR 2003),* pp. 72–79. Toronto, Canada, July 28–August 1.

Eveland, J. D., and Bikson, T. K. (1986). Evolving electronic communication networks: An empirical assessment. In *Proceedings of the 1986 ACM Conference on Computer Supported Cooperative Work,* pp. 91–101. Austin, Texas, December 3–5.

Farnham, S. (2002). Visualizing discourse architectures with automatically generated person-centric social networks. Presented at the 2002 Workshop in Discourse Architecture. In *Extended Proceedings of the 2002 Conference on Human Factors in Computing Systems (CHI 2002),* pp. 936–937. Minneapolis, Minnesota, April 20–25.

Fisher, D., and Dourish, P. (2004). Social and temporal structures in everyday collaboration. In *Proceedings of the 2004 Conference on Human Factors in Computing Systems (CHI 2004)*, pp. 551–558. Vienna, Austria, April 24–29.

Nardi, B., and Whittaker, S. (2002). The role of face-to-face communication in distributed work. In Hinds, P., and Kiesler, S. (eds.), *Distributed Work*, pp. 83–112. Cambridge, Mass.: MIT Press.

Nardi, B., Whittaker, S., and Schwarz, H. (2002). NetWORKers and their activity in intensional networks. *Journal of Computer-Supported Cooperative Work* 11: 205–242.

Nardi, B., Whittaker, S., Isaacs, E., Creech, M., Johnson, J., and Hainsworth, J. (2002). ContactMap: Integrating communication and information through visualizing personal social networks. *Communications of the ACM* (April): 89–95.

Tyler, J., Wilkinson, D. M., and Huberman, B. (2003). Email as spectroscopy: Automated discovery of community structure within organization. In Huysman, M., Wenger, E., and Wulf, V. (eds.), *Communities and Technologies,* pp. 81–96. Deventer, the Netherlands: Kluwer.

Whittaker, S., Jones, Q., Nardi, B., Creech, M., Terveen, L., Isaacs, E., and Hainsworth, J. (2004). ContactMap: Using personal social networks to organize communication in a social desktop. *ACM Transactions on Computer Human Interface* 11 (4): 445–471.

Whittaker, S., Jones, Q., and Terveen, L. (2002). Contact management: Identifying contacts to support long term communication. In *Proceedings of Conference on Computer Supported Cooperative Work,* pp. 216–225. New Orleans, Louisianna, November 16–20.

Whittaker, S., and Sidner, C. (1996). Email overload: Exploring personal information management of email. In *Proceedings of the 1996 ACM SIGCHI Conference on Human Factors in Computing Systems (CHI'96),* pp. 276–283. Vancouver, British Columbia, Canada, April 13–18.

# III

# From Tasks to Activities

# Introduction to Part III

Part III includes two chapters that make the case for *activity* as a fundamental concept in the design of digital work environments. Again, the authors describe the novel systems they designed. The Kimura system, described in the chapter by Voida, Mynatt, and MacIntyre, goes beyond the desktop metaphor by integrating regular computer monitors with a different type of information-displaying surface, namely, the wall space of an office. Automatically created visualizations of user projects are shown on the walls to help the user keep track of and switch between the projects.

Bardram's chapter presents the ABC (activity-based computing) framework as a way to support pervasive computing in hospitals. While most of the chapters in the book deal with work environments for individual users—even though the design of concrete systems is often explicitly intended to support communication and collaboration—Bardram's chapter describes an integrated work environment that can be used by groups of people working toward a common goal. Activities, which may be distributed between several people, are first-class objects in the system architecture, which makes it possible for the system to recognize and support individual contributions to an activity as a whole.

Even though both chapters deal with concrete designs, their intentions are not limited to presenting particular technologies. Neither do they place their sole emphasis on design ideas exemplified by the systems. Both chapters make a more general point, namely, they emphasize the need for designers to expand their perspective on how technology should support people. Both chapters claim that technologies should support attaining meaningful goals, in collaboration with other people and through the use of multiple computer devices. In other words, technologies should support activities rather than low-level, technologically specific tasks.

There are a number of similarities between the chapters. First, they both deal with ubiquitous computing. Not only does ubiquitous computing challenge the desktop metaphor, it also makes it necessary to extend the focus of analysis and technological support. Designers cannot confine their efforts to one particular technology, as often happened in the past. Ubiquitous computing requires that designers be concerned with how people integrate the use of various technologies to attain a meaningful goal. Second, the theoretical foundation of both chapters is activity theory. This framework originating from Russian psychology, became a popular approach in human–computer interaction (Nardi 1996).

Despite their apparent similarities, the perspectives presented in the chapters are also substantially different. In one respect they can even be considered opposite to each other. While Voida et al. mostly deal with "activity" in a traditional sense, as meaningful, social, and mediated interaction between a human subject and the world, Bardram's suggestion to make activity a first-class object in the computing architecture indicates an emphasis on activity as a computational concept. Given that both "human" and "computational" meanings of activity are relevant to design of technological support of people in everyday life, how are these two meanings related to each other? Both chapters in part 3 take initial steps in addressing this question, which is likely to stimulate further discussion in HCI research.

## References

Nardi, B. (ed.) (1996). *Context and Consciousness: Activity Theory and Human–Computer Interaction.* Cambridge, Mass.: MIT Press.

# 7

# Supporting Activity in Desktop and Ubiquitous Computing

Stephen Voida, Elizabeth D. Mynatt, and Blair MacIntyre

The emergence of the ubiquitous computing paradigm in the early 1990s marked the beginning of a new era of computation in the workplace. Weiser envisioned a world in which we would no longer focus our attention on a single box while working with information; rather, the proliferation of small, powerful, connected computing devices would allow computation to "vanish into the background" (Weiser 1991).

Although Weiser's vision of "ubicomp" is not yet commonplace, mainstream computing technology has begun to evolve in many of the ways that Weiser predicted over a decade ago. Computation has become an integral part of many personal information appliances such as PDAs, cell phones, and digital music players that users carry with them throughout the day. A recent surge in interest in the tablet computer form factor has led some business professionals and students to abandon the use of pen and paper for electronic ink while taking notes and annotating documents. The desktop computer itself is spreading beyond its traditional beige-case-and-monitor boundaries—information that was once stored primarily on the PC hard drive is making its way onto websites and web services; multiple monitor use is now becoming quite commonplace, and in many domains, such as financial trading, virtual walls of tiled monitors are entirely replacing traditional displays; and experiments in wearable computing and augmented reality are evolving into commercial enterprises seeking to bring the functionality of a desktop computer to users at any place and at any time.

At the intersection of all these developments, *ubicomp environments* have themselves become a recurring fixture in the research community. Tangible workbenches for designers (e.g., Ishii and Ullmer 1997; Leibe et al. 2000), smart kitchens (see, e.g., Tran and Mynatt 2002), context-aware classrooms (see, e.g., Abowd 1999), and reconfigurable meeting spaces (see, e.g., Johanson, Fox, and Winograd 2002; Streitz et al. 1999) all demonstrate the advanced interaction techniques and social collaboration that become possible when small, inexpensive computation permeates a space, coupled with sensors, cameras, projectors, and various networking technologies.

Although the ubicomp paradigm shift is having a dramatic impact on the design and deployment of new devices and applications, it is also affecting the study of technology and work practice. In general, the migration of the computer off the desktop and into the world has drawn greater attention from interrogating *users' dialogue with the computer* to the *contexts in which computers are used.* Field studies of how users carry out their work, from the ways in which they organize the information around them (e.g., Kidd 1994; Malone 1983; Mander, Salomon, and Wong 1992), to the ways in which they use existing office technologies such as whiteboards (Mynatt 1999), to the ways in which they juggle multiple simultaneous tasks and handle interruptions (e.g., González and Mark 2004), are becoming even more of a prerequisite for the design of new ubicomp technologies than they were during the PC era. The ubicomp vision breaks with the previous tradition of creating application designs based on a single, universal metaphor such as the graphical user interface's "desktop"; instead, ubiquitous computing technologies can only achieve their goal of becoming "invisible" when their design is informed by and well matched to the context in which they are used.

In this chapter, we outline our agenda and approach for supporting the concept of "activity" from a user's perspective in an integrated digital and physical workplace. This perspective encompasses the context in which computers are used, the multitude of work artifacts that make up an activity, and the historical trajectory of an activity over time. We describe five challenges for matching computation to activity. These are:

- *activities are multifaceted,* involving a heterogeneous collection of work artifacts;
- *activities are dynamic,* emphasizing the continuation and evolution of work artifacts in contrast to closure and archiving;
- *activities are collaborative,* in the creation, communication, and dissemination of work artifacts;

- *activities exist at different levels of granularity,* owing to varying durations, complexity and ownership; and
- *activities exist across places,* including physical boundaries, virtual boundaries of information security and access, and fixed and mobile settings.

We examine ubiquitous computing support for activities in the workplace from two complementary angles. In the first, we describe our experiences designing the Kimura system, an integrated desktop and interactive whiteboard environment that supports individual knowledge workers in managing and shifting among multiple work activities. Following a description of Kimura, we critique its design with respect to the five challenges. We then examine support for activities from the theoretical perspective of activity theory. In particular, we note how recent extensions to activity theory have addressed theoretical shortcomings similar to our five challenges and suggest directions for bridging the gap between everyday practice and systems support. We conclude by considering ways in which a combination of theoretical and pragmatic perspectives can provide solutions to the five challenges for future system designs.

## Kimura: An Activity-Centered Work Environment

Our research seeks to design an office that better supports knowledge workers—business professionals who interpret and transform information (Drucker 1973). Successful knowledge workers manage multiple tasks, collaborate effectively with several colleagues and clients, and manipulate information that is most relevant to their current task by leveraging the spatial organization of their work area (Kidd 1994; Malone 1983; Mynatt 1999; Grudin 2001). The diversity of these work practices and the complexity of implementing flexible computing tools make it difficult to meet all of these workers' needs.

We have spent several years developing technologies that support knowledge workers. Our work on the Kimura system has allowed us to begin exploring different notions of activity both on and off the desktop (MacIntyre et al. 2001; Voida et al. 2002). Our experiences suggest that activity may be a useful, unifying framework for ubiquitous computing environments, but also foregrounds several challenges for future research in ubicomp environments.

In order to explain the fundamental concepts underlying the design of the Kimura system, we begin with a brief scenario highlighting unique aspects of an imagined interaction with the system on a typical workday. Scenarios like this one have served to focus our designs and define key user interactions in an activity-centered digital work environment.

**Kimura in Practice: A Scenario**

Wendy, a knowledge worker, walks into her office Monday morning following a week's vacation. She scans the piles of paper on her desk and the contents of her whiteboard, recalling the work that has been waiting for her.

After quickly surveying the various whiteboard montages that represent ongoing activities, she annotates the budget plan with "Work on Wed., Due Friday" and throws it to the whiteboard's far side.

The calendar image in the Acme design project montage reminds her of a design briefing later that day.

She studies the montage for a moment, trying to remember how far into the design briefing activity she was before she left on vacation. She sees opaque images of the documents she worked with most recently: her calendar, an illustration, a presentation file, and a web search page. The montage also includes several translucent images of past documents—two important email messages from her group's client and the original project proposal. She taps on the montage to load it onto her desktop. The design briefing documents reappear on her desktop computer, just as she left them.

After a quick perusal, she resumes her web search for details on an interesting technology and fine-tunes one of her sketches. After sending the new sketch to the printer, she decides to spend some time catching up on the theme ideas for the upcoming open house. Using the desktop controls to switch activities (and virtual desktops), the montage for the Acme design activity reappears on her whiteboard, now annotated with a printer icon, to indicate that a print job is in progress.

As Wendy contemplates her reply to an interesting theme idea from one of her colleagues, she notices that his face has appeared on her whiteboard. Ah, Joe must be in the coffee room. Deciding that a face-to-face discussion would be more useful than sending another message, she goes to join Joe for coffee and brainstorming.

Later that day, she decides to go ahead and start working on some budget numbers. From the corner of her eye, she notices the softly changing calendar in the Acme design montage. It is time for the meeting. As she runs out of the office, she sees the icon for the completed print job. Grateful that someone—or something—is on top of things, she heads to the printer on the way to the meeting.

### System Design and Implementation

Kimura separates the user's "desktop" into two regions: the focal region, on the desktop monitor; and peripheral displays, projected on the office walls. Each work activity is associated with a unique virtual desktop that is displayed on the monitor while the user is engaged in the activity. Background activities are projected as visual montages on the peripheral display, as shown in figure 7.1.

From Kimura's point of view, a work activity—such as managing a project, participating in a conference, or teaching a class—is modeled as a cluster of documents and a collection of cues representing ongoing interactions with people and objects related to that activity. We refer to this cluster as the

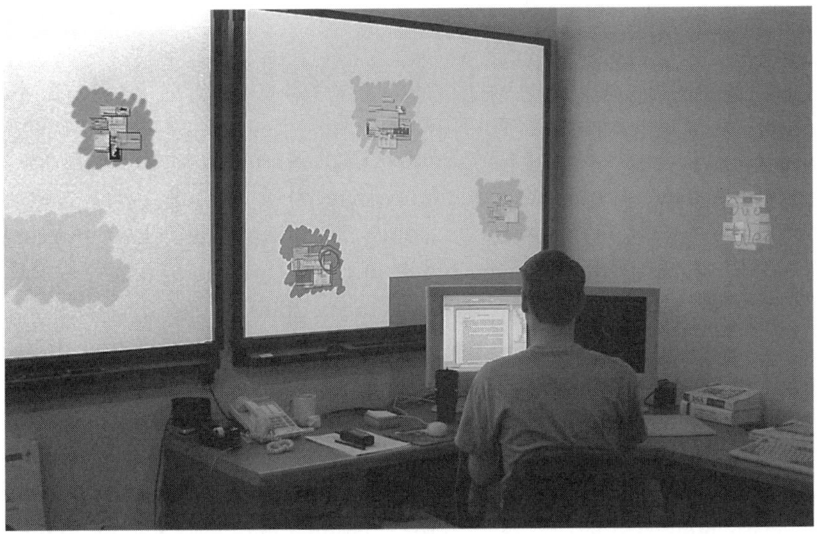

**Figure 7.1**
The Kimura system in an office environment, including the monitor and peripheral displays.

activity's *working context*. Each working context may have numerous documents, including text files, web pages, and other application files. A working context may also have iconic indications of ongoing activity, including email messages without replies and outstanding print jobs. Kimura automatically tracks the contents of each working context and tags documents based on their relative importance. As in previous systems, such as Rooms (Henderson and Card 1986), users define the boundaries of working contexts manually—in our case, by creating virtual desktops. We chose this strategy because these operations are easy for the user to perform and can be easily monitored to detect working-context changes, and because this strategy avoids relying on the system to infer these transitions.

Each working context is displayed as a *montage* of images garnered from system activity logs (see figure 7.2). These montages are analogous to the "room overviews" provided by other multicontext window managers. But where these systems show the exact layout of the windows in each room, our goal is to provide visualizations of past activity in context. These visualizations help remind the user of past actions; the arrangement and transparency of the component images automatically create an icon for the working context. Additionally, montages can serve as anchors for background awareness information that is gleaned from a context-aware infrastructure.

The electronic whiteboard—the primary display surface for the montage visualizations—supports common whiteboard practices (Mynatt 1999). Whiteboards feature an intuitive user interface and are well suited to supporting informal information management activities. Our system implementation incorporates existing electronic whiteboard interaction techniques with montages and notification cues (Igrashi et al. 2000; Mynatt et al. 1999, 2000; Hong and Landay 2000). This allows the user to annotate montages with informal reminders and to reposition montages to indicate the respective priority of background activities. Additionally, the whiteboard's large display area is an ideal, unobtrusive location to show contextually relevant information about the user's work activities and the context information sensed from around the office.

The whiteboard lets users monitor each ongoing work activity, transition smoothly between activities, access a wide variety of contextual information designed to facilitate collaboration, and maintain awareness about relevant activity changes. Additionally, the interactivity provided by the

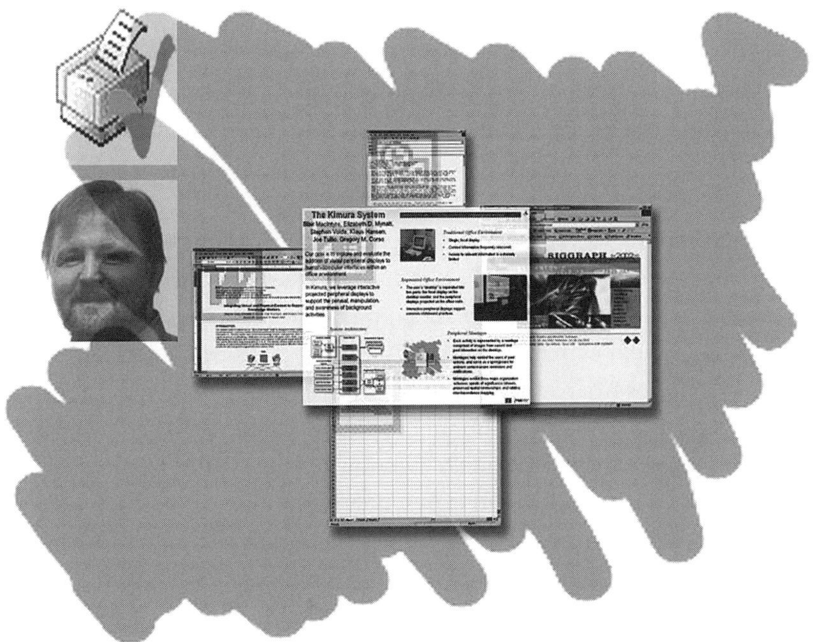


Figure 7.2
A montage of a working context, including a number of application windows and two external context notification cues, representing both virtual (completion of a print job) and physical context information (the availability of a colleague).

electronic whiteboard allows the user to informally annotate and spatially organize the montages.

The montage design relieves the user of burdens associated with maintaining a large amount of information—information about each work activity and its related contextual information—and with synthesizing that information on the fly from a potentially overwhelming number of sources. The montages are designed to present this information without intruding on the user's focal activity and in a manner that supports the needs of knowledge workers.

## Activity and Context-Awareness in Kimura

The Kimura system allows its users to continue using whatever tools and practices they would normally use in the course of their work while providing activity-level support by sensing and responding to the virtual and physical context surrounding the user's activities. Unlike the majority of context-aware systems that have generally focused solely on the acquisition and interpretation of physical context—primarily location—to adapt an application to a user's social and physical surroundings, Kimura leverages virtual context—the processes and resources involved in manipulating digital information—as well.

Our system uses several monitoring components and proxies to acquire virtual context about the users' ongoing activities. Our focus is on capturing the users' interactions with the application and document windows that are associated with each activity. We have developed a desktop monitoring system for Microsoft Windows using the Win32 system hooks API. When the Kimura system is running, Windows sends notification of low-level user actions (e.g., opening a window, changing the window focus, pressing a key, clicking the mouse) to a desktop-monitoring process. The monitoring process encodes the event and forwards it to a distributed activity log. Additionally, the desktop monitor creates a screenshot of each window each time the window system's input focus changes. The context interpreter integrates these screenshots into the montages so that the visual representations of the user's activity can include actual images of the user's work. The images, similar to thumbnails, provide more relevant visual reminders than generic icons or labels. We use metrics, such as the amount of time a particular window has been in focus and the number of focus switches between open windows, to determine the size and placement of the screenshot images in the montage visualizations displayed on the electronic whiteboard.

Kimura also acquires virtual context through an email-monitoring system, tracking the user's interaction with colleagues during work activities. A small process running on the user's mail server monitors changes in each of the user's mailboxes. It monitors all email messages that the user sends and associates each mail recipient with the active working context. The process also adds the recipient to a list of individuals with whom the Kimura user might be trying to connect, and instructs the location-monitoring component to actively monitor the availability of that individual by watching for their presence in public areas of the office.

In addition, Kimura observes the user's interactions with distributed peripheral devices over the course of a work activity. We have implemented a printer proxy that records the ID and status of pending print jobs in a working context. As the status of each print job changes (for example, a print job is sent to the spooler, prints after being buried in a long queue, or stalls because the printer is out of paper), the context interpreter adds a notification cue to the appropriate montage.

Kimura also helps the user reconstruct the environmental circumstances surrounding a working context and provides cues about the user's colleagues' location and availability using physical context. In our current prototype, we simulate a pervasive, location-aware infrastructure (e.g., Dey, Abowd, and Salber 2001) with a series of Dallas Semiconductor i-Button docks distributed throughout the office environment. We designed our sensor network to detect the arrival and departure of known individuals in our augmented office environment, in public areas of the office, and near peripheral devices (that is, next to the printer). This functionality lets the system determine the general location of the Kimura user and her colleagues, and allows the system to infer when those colleagues might be available for collaboration or when they have joined the user in the augmented office for an informal meeting.

## The Challenges of Supporting Activity in Ubicomp Environments

The design of the Kimura system was based on our understanding of *activity*, supplanting the traditional "desktop," application-and-document metaphor, and allowing users to manage their ongoing activities in the same way that they conceive of and manage their tasks in the real world. It was also built upon the findings of previous studies of knowledge work, allowing users to organize their work spatially and without needing to explicitly name or label information in order to work with it. We developed our designs with the belief that even though ubiquitous computing is changing how, where, and when we work, the desktop computer will still play a key role in office computing for the foreseeable future.

However, we made several explicit design decisions to limit the scope, and therefore the complexity, of our design space for the Kimura project. For example, we opted to design a system that would be used in one worker's personal office, and primarily by that single user. We also represented activities as "flat" collections of documents, as opposed to hierarchical representations or representations with variable perspectives, so that we would be able to more readily evaluate the montage visualizations for each activity.

As we continue to work on the next-generation version of the Kimura system, we are looking to extend the system in ways that emphasize the *mediating* role of the digital work environment. Our informal experiences in using the system suggest that having a mechanism for organizing and managing one's own short-term activities is useful, but Kimura would be even more useful if it could allow users to manage substantially more numerous and complex activities over the course of months or years and enable users to coordinate activities among members of a project team.

We are confident that many of the design decisions we initially made will continue to prove useful as we move forward with the project. For example, the explosion of recent work on multiple displays in the workplace (Grudin 2001; Tan and Czerwinski 2003) and large-display groupware (Fass, Forlizzi, and Pausch 2002; Huang, Russell, and Sue 2004; Johanson, Fox, and Winograd 2002; Moran et al. 1996; Streitz et al. 1999) indicate that our intuitions about leveraging the electronic whiteboard as an organizing space will continue to prove fruitful. However, the side effects of our limited design space, such as our system's relatively simple representation of activities, the lifecycle of those activities, and the current means of populating and managing those activity representations over time may need drastic reconsideration if we are to be successful.

We have identified five challenges for representing and supporting activity in integrated digital work environments, based on our experiences with the Kimura system and our attempts to extend its capabilities. The challenges exist owing in large part to the inherent complexity of human activity, the technical affordances of the computing tools used in work practice, and the nature of (and culture surrounding) knowledge work.

**Activities are multifaceted** One of the primary departures of activity-centered computing from the traditional "desktop" metaphor is the recognition that one activity often spans several applications, and includes many types of documents and information resources. Although the "desktop" metaphor provided users with interface-level support for multitasking, application software has become so specialized and information sources so diverse that a typical desktop window layout, organized to support a single activity, might consist of dozens of windows spanning multiple applications—in addition to any real-world artifacts that are referenced over the course of the activity.

The Kimura system allowed users to organize and manage their work at the level of activities, as opposed to manually manipulating applications and documents. Our design was intended to lower the overhead of activity switching by allowing the user to switch easily between relevant groups of applications and documents as needed—much the same motivation as in systems like Rooms (Henderson and Card 1986), Task Gallery, and GroupBar (Robertson et al., this volume; Robertson et al. 2000; Smith et al. 2003). Kimura initially associated activities with individual virtual desktops on the primary desktop computer; the number and contents of a user's virtual desktops were used to identify the user's current activities and associate applications, documents, and external resources with those activities.

Supporting the multifaceted aspects of activity in a ubicomp environment becomes a much more complex proposition. If activity is to be used as a unifying organizational structure across a wide variety of devices such as traditional desktop and laptop computers, PDAs, mobile telephones, personal-server style devices (Want et al. 2002), shared public displays, and so on, then those devices must all be able to share a common set of activity representations and use those representations as the organizational cornerstone for the user experience they provide. Additionally, the activity representations must be versatile enough to encompass the kinds of work for which each of these kinds of devices is used. Although this may sound like an unattainable vision, we have already demonstrated that support for activity can be added to a platform without dramatically changing the fundamental nature of its operating system or application software.

**Activities are dynamic** User studies and intuition both suggest that the activities that a knowledge worker engages in change—sometimes dramatically—over time. Projects and milestones come and go, and the tools and information resources used within an activity often change over time as well. Furthermore, activities completed in the past and their outcomes often impact activities in the present, and ongoing activities will, in turn, affect activities that will be undertaken in the future. Capturing activity over the course of time has long been a problem for desktop computing. For example, saved files frequently contain only the most recent state of a document and users must often adopt unusual work practices to capture and access the document's history, such as tracking changes using an auxiliary change-management system such as CVS.1 Another often-cited observation is that hierarchical filing systems do not readily reflect the fact that a single resource might be used in different contexts (see, e.g., Dourish et al. 2000).

One of our central design decisions in the Kimura system was to base our representations and visualizations of activity on users' actual, ongoing work. As users created new virtual desktops, opened and closed applications, referenced documents, and interacted with colleagues electronically, Kimura's model of the user's activity would automatically reflect these changes. Our approach in representing the history of activities was to provide visualizations that reflected the state of an activity throughout the entire course of its existence, rather than simply providing a snapshot of its current state. The document thumbnails within each montage are sampled both from the most current *and* the most significant components of each activity, even if the most significant components are documents that are no longer open and therefore no longer immediately accessible. Additionally, the integration of external context notification cues allowed our visualizations to reflect the dynamic nature of activities as affected by changes sensed from the "real world." We felt that in order to provide an accurate representation of the activity, this holistic view of the activity's contents would be invaluable, particularly for resumption of an activity that had not been active for an extended period of time.

However, some of our implementation decisions also made it difficult to work with many long-lived activities. In order to maximize compatibility with all desktop applications and not force users to adopt a small set of custom-built, "Kimura-aware" applications, we initially opted to track and manage activity using only window handles, application types, and window captions. Unfortunately, this imposed the limitation that activities could be resumed only if their windows were still open and available (albeit hidden) on the desktop computer. A design decision that was originally intended to enable more realistic evaluation—system users would be able to use whatever applications with Kimura that they already used in the course of their work—actually undermined long-term study of the system since even powerful, modern computers have practical limitations about the number of applications and documents that can be open at a given time.

There are a number of other systems that have been quite successful at capturing user activity as a function of time and exposing this record to the user. Although these systems have provided different means for navigating through the temporal record—Designers' Outpost via a "global timeline" at the bottom of the display (Klemmer et al. 2002), Flatland through snappable, per- "segment" time sliders (Mynatt et al. 1999), and TimeScape by presenting several interactive desktop visualizations (Rekimoto 1999)—all indirectly support the notion of activity in the interface by allowing users to restore the interaction state to that of a previous point in time. Regardless of the specific user-interface technique or techniques used to expose the interaction history to the user, this general approach is successful in allowing users to immerse themselves in the context of an activity from the past *and* have access to the content that they were using to accomplish that activity.

**Activities are collaborative** Most knowledge work is inherently collaborative. If activities aren't centered around synchronous interactions between multiple members of a project team or the user and some number of individuals external to his or her immediate workgroup, they almost certainly draw upon information that was created by others at some earlier point in time. Recognizing the mediating role of the digital work environment in enabling users to collaborate meaningfully is a critical step to ensuring the success of these systems.

However, as the large, diverse body of literature in the computer-supported collaborative work (CSCW) community suggests, supporting effective collaboration is rarely a trivial undertaking. Technical issues involving the exchange of information, preservation of state, and graceful operation in the face of network failures, coupled with social issues regarding awareness, negotiation about the roles that collaborators will play, and privacy—to name just a few—abound.

We initially limited the scope of Kimura to one user in order to simplify our design space and allow us to iterate on our infrastructure implementation and montage designs with fewer CSCW-related constraints. However, Kimura was able to detect certain patterns of electronic communication and associate individuals with ongoing tasks. We also provided a visualization technique that presented colleague availability as a component of the montages on the electronic whiteboard, based on information gleaned from the context-aware infrastructure. This appeared to be a useful initial step during our informal evaluations of the system.

Looking beyond our single-user implementation of the Kimura system, there are several design considerations that will be critical in enabling more robust collaboration support for work activities. First and foremost, other individuals must be represented as first-class objects in computational models of activity. One potentially useful way to incorporate colleagues into activity representations is to leverage and visualize the relationships between ongoing work activities and naturally occurring virtual and real-world social networks (see, e.g., Nardi, Whittaker, and Schwarz 2002; Fisher and Nardi, this volume). Additionally, activities need to be represented in such a way that their contents can be shared, with the caveats that individual participants in an activity may have very different perceptions of the activity, they may bring different resources to play over the course of the activity, and, particularly for large activities in which many individual users participate, users themselves may come and go over the life of the activity.

Moreover, such systems must be designed with the social context of the workplace in mind; providing support for collaboration requires somewhat more subtlety than simply exposing all participants' activity representations and constituent resources to one another. Participants may wish to exercise varying degrees of control over how and when their resources and work processes are shared with their colleagues. They may also wish to specify how their availability is shared with different colleagues. Finally, the organizational structure of the workplace may cause each collaborator to play different roles in the activity; as a result, each may need access to different activity representations or meta-information about the activity and contributions of its participants (Shen and Dewan 1992; Sikkel 1997).

**Activities exist at different levels of granularity** At any given point in time, a single user may report being involved in several different activities, each specified at a slightly different level of granularity. For example, she might be in the midst of writing a conference paper review, compiling a list of references for a proposal submission, and working toward a promotion. The paper review activity lasts only a short time and requires a unique set of resources—namely, the paper under review. It also might resemble other activities, for example, a conference paper review at about the same time last year, and it might take advantage of some resources affiliated with other activities, such as a repository of research papers often used for project literature reviews. The proposal submission might be a substantially longer task involving a broader spectrum of resources and, often, the input of several colleagues. Striving for the promotion might require years of work and encompass many other, subordinate activities.

The idea that activities may exist at different levels of granularity is not a new one. Boer, van Baalen, and Kumar (2002) provide a model explaining how an *activity* at one level of analysis may be modeled as an *action*—a component of an activity—at another. This holds true for individual users, as in the example provided above, but is even more pronounced when a single activity is viewed from multiple participants' perspectives. For example, a manager and a principal investigator might both be involved in the activity of completing a research project, but their perceptions of the importance of the activity, the tools, the actors involved, and specific goals might be quite different.

The Kimura system represented activities based on the contents of a single virtual desktop on a primary desktop computer, placing few limitations on the contents or lifespan of a tracked activity. Our montage visualizations were also designed to apply across activities specified at different levels of granularity. The visualization algorithm simply displayed the longest-used and most recently used window thumbnails associated with each activity; regardless how long- or short-lived the activity or the level of granularity at which the user conceptualized it, the documents with which they would most likely associate the activity were displayed on the whiteboard.

Of course, supporting activities shared among two or more users complicates the situation. Suppose one user manages her tasks at a high, project-oriented level, for example, *annual project review* and *teaching*, and another user participating in the same activities manages his tasks at a much finer granularity, for example, *project review demonstration debugging* and *preparing computer graphics guest lecture*. This scenario is particularly likely when colleagues with different roles (such as a team member and a manager) collaborate on a single activity. Although it would be relatively straightforward to provide activity-level support for either of these users on their own, maintaining a shared representation of each of the users' collaborative activities at their preferred granularity, providing each user with appropriate views of the activities, generating notifications to each user for relevant changes in the activities, and coordinating changes in the structure of the activities over time become very complex.

**Activities exist across places** Activities also span place; that is, it is common for work to take place outside of the immediate office environment. However, current office technologies sometimes present a very different view of information across different physical and virtual settings. For example, resources affiliated with a work activity may not be visible to users who are physically located outside of the workplace, owing to the presence of a corporate firewall. Even when physically located within the workplace, collaboration on an activity might not be possible between colleagues whose computers are connected on different network subnets, that is, when one is plugged into a wired network and the other is connected wirelessly.

Furthermore, portable devices currently operate with very different interfaces and hierarchies from those of their office environment counterparts. Where a desktop computer might store complex, detailed representations of user activities and the resources affiliated with them (and even more so when augmented with activity-aware applications), PDAs and mobile phones often store very simple, flat collections of information and require explicit user action to maintain information synchronization among devices.

We implemented the Kimura system using the Java programming language and enabled distributed computing using common TCP/IP networking protocols so that it would be easy to implement visualization clients and context-awareness providers on a wide variety of devices. Although we have not yet created information managers for use on PDAs and cell phones, it would be easy to do so using J2ME virtual machines or by creating WAP-based web interfaces to the Kimura system using our existing servers.

Network connectivity-related problems, although beyond the scope of our current research agenda, constitute a challenge for many ubiquitous computing efforts. Technologies like virtual private networks (VPNs), which allow users outside of a corporate domain to pass traffic through a secure tunnel to their company's internal network; zero configuration networking protocols such as Apple's Bonjour,[2] which allow users to see and use nearby resources without incurring network setup cost for the user; and research platforms like Speakeasy, which fosters service interoperability and enables ad hoc network bridging (Edwards et al. 2002) are all helping to lessen the impact of network topology on the visibility and availability of networked resources for mobile users.

## Understanding the Challenges: A Theoretical Framework

In order to address the challenges that we identified for the design of activity-centered ubicomp work environments, we are conducting more in-depth field studies to understand the subtleties of users' conceptualization of activity in their day-to-day work practices. However, we are also looking to theoretical frameworks to understand the role of activity in these types of environments.

We have already noted that the emergence of ubicomp and integrated digital work environments has had a dramatic impact on the way that researchers in human-computer interaction (HCI) and related fields think about the design of computing environments. Historically, HCI adopted and adapted knowledge, processes, and techniques from artificial intelligence (AI), cognitive science, and cognitive psychology in the service of understanding and modeling user behavior, and applied those findings to the creation of new interfaces and technologies through design practice. As a result of this lineage, many of the theories and techniques used in HCI to model users have exhibited a markedly cognitive, "agents as information processors" flavor; much of the research literature on user modeling in HCI has been based on the Model Human Processor (Card, Moran, and Newell 1983), which has its roots in the physical symbol system hypothesis. Other important user models, such as Norman's Seven Stages of Action model (Norman 1990), can trace their heritage back to Gibson's systems school of perception (Gibson 1979).

Over the last decade, the focus of the HCI community began to shift away from the quantitative evaluation of user interfaces based on cognitive models and toward more ecologically informed techniques, including contextual and participatory design (Beyer and Holtzblatt 1998; Kyng 1994). This "user-centered design" movement foregrounded the social context of technology use and incorporated user feedback and participation throughout the design process. While this transition has been invaluable in producing traditional computer systems that exhibit both *usability* and *usefulness*, ubiquitous computing is providing its own set of challenges for HCI practitioners. In particular, the fact that most users are only now beginning to experience the ubicomp vision and integrate this new, unique class of technology into their work practices suggests that another change in focus may be on the horizon: "[T]he shift from user-centered design to context-based design corresponds with recent developments in pervasive, ubiquitous computing networks and in the appliances that connect with them, which are radically changing our relationships with personal computing devices" (Gay and Hembrooke 2003).

The changes in how HCI researchers and practitioners are examining the relationships between users and their devices are not limited to cutting-edge tangible media computing or immersive environments, however. Throughout the field, much more work is being done in understanding users' existing work practices, often involving traditional desktop computer systems, and in developing better models of users' interactions with a variety of computing devices.

One of the frameworks for asking these kinds of questions that has garnered a great deal of attention in recent years is activity theory. Activity theory places a strong focus on the mediating role of tools and social practices in the service of accomplishing goals. Because this seems to echo the sentiment of the challenges we uncovered in developing activity-based computing tools, we believe that activity theory can serve as a useful framework to inform the design of activity-centered digital work environments.

## Activity Theory and Activity-Centered Design

The origins of activity theory can be traced back to the former Soviet Union as part of the cultural-historical school of psychology founded by Vygotsky, Leont'ev, and Luria. Rather than focusing on *action* as a unit of analysis, activity theory focuses at the broader level of an *activity* and incorporates the social and cultural context of cognition (Halverson 2001; Leont'ev 1978; Vygotsky 1978).

In their well-known "activity checklist," Kaptelinin, Nardi, and Macaulay (1999) identified five basic principles of activity theory:

1. Hierarchical structure of activity In activity theory, the unit of analysis is an *activity* which is directed at an *object* that motivates the activity. Activities are composed of conscious, goal-directed *actions*; different actions may be taken to complete any given goal. Actions are implemented through automatic *operations*, which do not have goals of their own. This hierarchical structure is dynamic and can change throughout the life of an activity.
2. Object-orientedness Activity theory holds that humans exist in a broadly defined objective reality, that is, the things around us have properties that are objective both to the natural sciences and society and culture.
3. Internalization/externalization Activity theory considers both *internal* and *external* actions and holds that the two are tightly interrelated. *Internalization* is the process of transforming an external process into an internal one for the purposes of planning or simulating an action without affecting the world. *Externalization* transforms internal actions into external ones and is often used to resolve failures of internal actions and to coordinate actions among independent agents.
4. Mediation A central tenet of activity theory is that activity is *mediated* by tools, and that these tools are created and transformed over the course of the activity so that the culture and history of the activity becomes embedded in the tools. Vygotsky's definition of tool is very broad; one of the tools he was most interested in was language.
5. Development Activity theory relies upon development as one of its primary research methodologies; that is, "experiments" often consist of a subject's participation in an activity and observation of developmental changes in the subject over the course of the activity. Ethnographic methods that identify the cultural and historical roots of activity are also frequently used.

Engeström (1987) provides a classic visualization summarizing the structure of an activity (figure 7.3). This model is based on three mutual relationships: that between the actor (*subject*) and the community (other *actors involved*), that between subject and the object (in the sense of *objective*) of the activity, and that between the object and the community.

These mutual relationships are *mediated* by the other components of activity. For example, the relationship between subject and object is mediated by tools (*mediating artifacts*); because of this, the subject's experience of the object is constrained by the tools used, and the tools that are created as a by-product of the activity are directly shaped by the subject and the object. The tools also embed the culture and history of the other components of the activity, such as the social rules governing the community, the community itself, and the organization of that community (e.g., the roles of its members), sometimes referred to as the *division of labor*.

However, Gay and Hembrooke (2003) point out a weakness in the original formulation of activity theory: "The model of activity theory . . . has traditionally been understood as a synchronic, point-in-time depiction of an activity. It does not depict the transformational and developmental processes that provide the focus of much recent activity theory research."

Boer, van Baalen, and Kumar (2002) provide an interesting suggestion for how the scope of activity theory can be expanded across time and the levels of an organization to explain connections between different activities as well as the influence that an activity may exert upon itself:

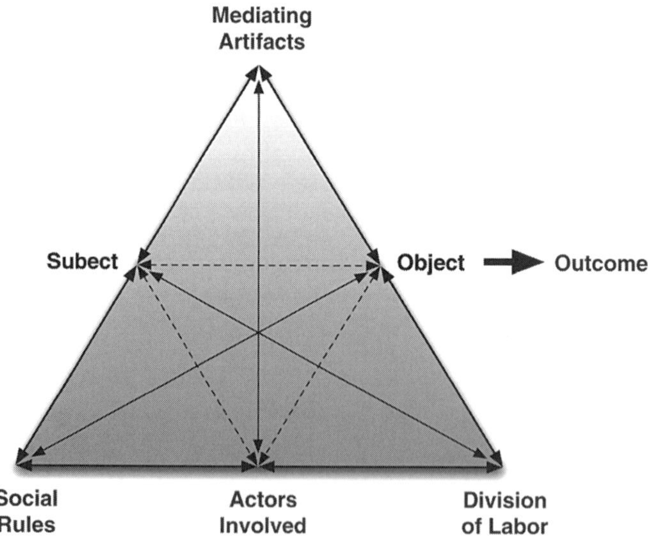


Figure 7.3
An adaptation of Engeström's analysis of activity and mediating relationships.

> Besides the fact that an activity is situated in a network of influencing activity systems, it is also situated in time. . . . In order to understand the activity system under investigation, one therefore has to reveal its *temporal interconnectedness*. . . . Rather than analyzing an activity system as a static picture of reality, the developments and tensions within the activity system need to be described and analyzed. . . . When analyzing an activity system at a particular contextual level, one should also take into account its relations with activity systems at other contextual levels (e.g., economic system, industry, supply chain, organization, department or production process). . . . The activity system under investigation is not only affected by activity systems at other contextual levels, it also exerts influence on them itself (bi-directional twisted arrows in figure [7.4]). This is in line with Giddens' theory of structuration which assumes that on the one hand human action is restricted by institutional properties of social systems, while on the other hand these institutional properties are the product of human action. (Boer, van Baalen, and Kumar 2002, authors' emphasis)

Boer et al. also consider the role that an activity may play in other activities at different levels of analysis. They suggest that the components of one activity system may play different roles in more broadly or narrowly scoped activities that exist in different cultural contexts, for example, on a project team, in a department, or in an entire corporation (see figure 7.4).

These extensions increase the complexity of the activity theory model but also help to explain tensions present in real-world systems such as when one agent plays different roles in two systems that have divergent goals. Furthermore, this approach provides activity theory with a similar degree of agility in representing complex, distributed cognition as competing theoretical approaches, such as distributed cognition (Hutchins 1995).

Nardi (1996) argues that one of the inherent strengths of activity theory is in its ability to capture the idea of *context* in user models for HCI, a notion that is gaining momentum particularly with respect to the ubiquitous computing paradigm and as its own design movement, so-called *activity-centered design* (Gay and Hembrooke 2003). The world that Gay and Hembrooke envision relies upon design that is not user-centered (which is currently the dominant view in the HCI community) but activity-centered, since activity theory provides the right "orientation" for future classes of interactions mediated by ubiquitous computing devices.

## The Intersection of the Pragmatic and the Theoretic

Activity theory is described both as a guiding framework for analyzing observations of work practice and as a language for communicating those

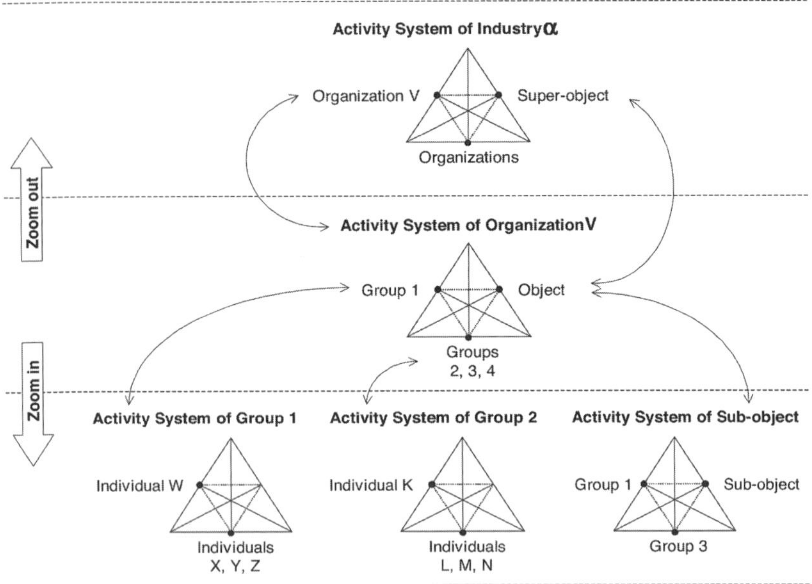


Figure 7.4
Relationships between different levels of analysis. (From Boer et al. 2002. Reprinted with permission. 2002 IEEE.)

findings within the community of practitioners (Halverson 2001). In the case of designing activity-centered ubicomp environments, activity theory can help to shape the definition of *activity* that such systems seek to support. It can help to focus and organize field observations of work practices and smooth the transition from those observations into design specifications. It can also suggest solutions to some of the most difficult challenges in supporting activity in these integrated digital work environments.

At its core, activity theory provides a useful model of a single user's perspective on the process of completing some objective. This model reflects many of the same underlying assumptions that we made going into our work with the Kimura system, most notably the idea of *object-orientedness*—that users mentally organize their work around activities (and their constituent actions) and that they use a variety of tools in the service of achieving the objects of those activities. This perspective contrasts with traditional principles held by the HCI community, which emphasize the dialogue between the user and the system rather than the system's role as one of many mediating tools in the context of an activity. Kimura reflected this change in

perspective by playing down the application-document metaphor, which presumes that the user will be able to complete a task within a single application. Instead, Kimura presented the user with clusters of applications and documents augmented with contextual cues sensed from the other virtual and physical aspects of the work activity. These clusters became the user's central point of interaction for managing activity, allowing them to interact at a level of abstraction above applications and documents but without requiring adoption of new and unfamiliar tools.

The activity theory framework also helps to expand the ways in which we study work practices *in situ* and seek to understand the roles that new technologies might play as part of users' activities. Although it is certainly useful to investigate how tools are being used and the aspects of collaboration that are critical in the workplace, activity theory encourages researchers to examine activity from the perspectives of each participant and to understand the role of social rules and participant roles, in addition to the use of artifacts and information resources.

But perhaps most compelling are the ways in which activity theory models interact with the challenges that we identified in our experiences with Kimura and our survey of other activity-centered ubicomp environments. Activity theory casts a wide but well-defined net around the multifaceted nature of activity, suggesting that the user's colleagues and the object of the activity are of the utmost importance, but that the tools, social rules, and roles of collaborators within the community must also be reflected back to the user as critical components of that activity. The idea that components of activity reflect their history of use through time suggests several ways for activity-centered systems to support a dynamic working landscape; for example, they might capture past activities in an archive for quick—and potentially automated—reference during related tasks in the future, and the tools used in previous and ongoing activities (e.g., documents and information resources) might need to both be available at all times and tagged with meta-information about how they have been used in the past. The hierarchical structure of the Boer et al. adaptation of the activity theory model can help to reconcile the differences in granularity and the difficulties of supporting collaboration identified in our work; future activity-centered user interfaces might take advantage of the zoomable user interface paradigm or feature control over the level of detail (LOD) represented in the interface to more accurately reflect the depth at which a given user conceptualizes his own tasks or the tasks of his colleagues.

While activity theory provides a useful lens for understanding users' work practices and a language for communicating models of users' behavior, there are some aspects of work practice that have been shown to be critical to knowledge work but are not captured in the activity theory framework. For example, knowledge workers have been shown to rely on the organization of information used in ongoing activities to accomplish their work, particularly when the value or role of that information has not yet been fully determined (Kidd 1994; Malone 1983; Mynatt 1999). Activity theory does allude to the fact that tools reflect the history of their use, but it does not place a strong emphasis on this critical component of knowledge work. This observation implies that supporting activity well in ubicomp environments will likely require us to draw upon a variety of activity models and inquiry techniques for understanding how work is accomplished in the real world.

However, theoretical frameworks provide only one perspective on understanding the role of activity in ubicomp environments. Another invaluable resource is the growing body of research literature describing design decisions related to and practical experience resulting from integrating activity into other kinds of computational tools. Activity is increasingly being used to organize and manage overloaded communication channels like email (see, e.g., Bellotti et al. 2003; Gwizdka 2002), as an index into personal information management on desktop computers (see, e.g., Kaptelinin 2003; Kaptelinin and Boardman, this volume), and as a means for coordinating actions among groups of users (see, e.g., Bardram 2005, this volume). The results of these experiments will further help to clarify the issues and challenges related to representing activity in the user interface and provide the community with a more diverse portfolio of approaches for modeling activity and exposing those models to system users.

As designers are faced with creating the next generation of integrated digital work environments, theoretical frameworks such as activity theory and pragmatic perspectives like those gained from our work on the Kimura system will both play a key role in informing the design of these systems and overcoming the challenges presented by supporting real-world work practices.

## Notes

1. Http://www.cvshome.org/.
2. Http://developer.apple.com/networking/bonjour/.

## References

Abowd, G. D. (1999). Classroom 2000: An experiment with the instrumentation of a living educational environment. *IBM Systems Journal: Special Issue on Pervasive Computing* 38 (4): 508–530.

Bardram, J. E. (2005). Activity-based computing: Support for mobility and collaboration in ubiquitous computing. *Personal and Ubiquitous Computing* 9 (5): 312–322.

Bellotti, V., Ducheneaut, N., Howard, M., and Smith, I. (2003). Taking email to task: The design and evaluation of a task management centered email tool. In *Proceedings of the ACM Conference on Human Factors in Computing Systems (CHI 2003),* pp. 345–352. Ft. Lauderdale, Florida, April 5–10.

Beyer, H., and Holtzblatt, K. (1998). *Contextual Design: Defining Customer-Centered Systems.* San Francisco: Morgan Kaufmann.

Boer, N., van Baalen, P. J. and Kumar, K. (2002). An activity theory approach for studying the situatedness of knowledge sharing. In *Proceedings of the 35th Annual Hawaii International Conference on System Sciences (HICSS-35 '02).* Big Island, Hawaii, January 7–10.

Card, S. K., Moran, T. P., and Newell, A. (1983). *The Psychology of Human–Computer Interaction.* Hillsdale, N. J.: Lawrence Erlbaum.

Dey, A. K., Abowd, G. D., and Salber, D. (2001). A conceptual framework and a toolkit for supporting the rapid prototyping of context-aware applications. *Human-Computer Interaction Journal* 16 (2–4): 97–166.

Dourish, P., Edwards, W. K., LaMarca, A., Lamping, J., Petersen, K., Salisbury, M., Terry, D. B., and Thornton, J. (2000). Extending document management systems with user-specific active properties. *ACM Transactions on Information Systems* 18 (2): 140–170.

Drucker, P. F. (1973). *Management Tasks, Responsibilities, and Practices.* New York: Harper and Row.

Edwards, W. K., Newman, M. W., Sedivy, J. Z., Smith, T. F., Balfanz, D., Smetters, D. K., Wong, H. C., and Izadi, S. (2002). Using Speakeasy for ad hoc peer-to-peer collaboration. In *Proceedings of the ACM 2002 Conference on Computer Supported Cooperative Work (CSCW 2002),* pp. 256–265. Minneapolis, Minnesota, April 20–25.

Engeström, Y. (1987). *Learning by Expanding.* Helsinki: Orienta-konsultit.

Fass, A. M., Forlizzi, J., and Pausch, R. (2002). MessyDesk and MessyBoard: Two designs inspired by the goal of improving human memory. In *Proceedings of the Conference on Designing Interactive Systems: Processes, Practices, Methods, and Techniques (DIS 2002),* pp. 303–311. London, England, June 25–28.

Gay, G., and Hembrooke, H. (2003). *Activity-Centered Design: An Ecological Approach to Designing Smart Tools and Usable Systems.* Cambridge, Mass.: MIT Press.

Gibson, J. J. (1979). *The Ecological Approach to Visual Perception.* Boston: Houghton Mifflin.

González, V. M., and Mark, G. (2004). "Constant, constant multi-tasking craziness": Managing multiple working spheres. In *Proceedings of the ACM Conference on Human Factors in Computing Systems (CHI 2004)*. Vienna, Austria, April 24–29.

Grudin, J. (2001). Partitioning digital worlds: Focal and peripheral awareness in multiple monitor use. In *Proceedings of the ACM Conference on Human Factors in Computing Systems (CHI 2001)*, pp. 458–465. Seattle, Washington, March 31–April 5.

Gwizdka, J. (2002). TaskView: Design and evaluation of a task-based email interface. In *Proceedings of the IBM Centers for Advanced Studies Conference (CASCON 2002)*, pp. 136-145. Toronto, Canada, September 30–October 3.

Halverson, C. A. (2001). Activity theory and distributed cognition: Or, What does CSCW need to do with theories? *Computer-Supported Cooperative Work (CSCW)* 11 (1–2): 243-267.

Henderson, J. D. A., and Card, S. K. (1986). Rooms: The use of multiple virtual workspaces to reduce space contention in window-based graphical user interfaces. *ACM Transactions on Graphics* 5 (3): 211–241.

Hong, J. I., and Landay, J. A. (2000). SATIN: A toolkit for informal ink-based applications. In *Proceedings of the ACM Symposium on User Interface Software and Technology (UIST '00)*, pp. 63–72. San Diego, California, November 6–8.

Huang, E. M., Russell, D. M., and Sue, A. E. (2004). IM Here: Public instant messaging on large, shared displays for workgroup interactions. In *Proceedings of the ACM Conference on Human Factors in Computing Systems (CHI 2004)*, pp. 279–286. Vienna, Austria, April 24–29.

Hutchins, E. (1995). *Cognition in the Wild.* Cambridge, Mass.: MIT Press.

Igrashi, T., Edwards, W. K., LaMarca, A., and Mynatt, E. D. (2000). An architecture for pen-based interaction on electronic whiteboards. In *Proceedings of the Working Conference on Advanced Visual Interfaces,* pp. 68–75. Palermo, Italy, May 23–26.

Ishii, H., and Ullmer, B. (1997). Tangible bits: Towards seamless interfaces between people, bits, and atoms. In *Proceedings of the SIGCHI Conference on Human Factors in Computing Systems (CHI '97)*, pp. 234–241. Atlanta, Georgia, March 22–27.

Johanson, B., Fox, A., and Winograd, T. (2002). The Interactive Workspaces project: Experiences with ubiquitous computing rooms. *IEEE Pervasive Computing* 1 (2): 67–74.

Kaptelinin, V. (2003). UMEA: Translating interacting histories into project contexts. In *Proceedings of the ACM Conference on Human Factors in Computing Systems (CHI 2003)*, pp. 353–360. Ft. Lauderdale, Florida, April 5–10.

Kaptelinin, V., Nardi, B. A., and Macaulay, C. (1999). The activity checklist: A tool for representing the "space" of context. *interactions* 6 (4): 27–39.

Kidd, A. (1994). The marks are on the knowledge worker. In *Proceedings of the ACM Conference on Human Factors in Computing Systems (CHI '94)*, pp. 186–191. Boston, Massachusetts, April 24–28.

Klemmer, S. R., Thomsen, M., Phelps-Goodman, E., Lee, R., and Landay, J. A. (2002). Where do web sites come from? Capturing and interacting with design history. In *Proceedings of the ACM Conference on Human Factors in Computing Systems (CHI 2002)*, pp. 1–10. Minneapolis, Minnesota, April 20–25.

Kyng, M. (1994). Scandinavian design: Users in product development. In *Proceedings of the ACM Conference on Human Factors in Computing Systems (CHI '94)*, pp. 3–9. Boston, Massachusetts, April 24–28.

Leont'ev, A. N. (1978). *Activity, Consciousness, and Personality.* Englewood Cliffs, N. J.: Prentice Hall.

Leibe, B., Starner, T., Ribarsky, W., Wartell, Z., Krum, D., Weeks, J., Singletary, B., and Hodges, L. (2000). Toward spontaneous interaction with the Perceptive Workbench. *IEEE Computer Graphics and Applications* 20 (6): 54–65.

MacIntyre, B., Mynatt, E. D., Voida, S., Hansen, K. M., Tullio, J., and Corso, G. M. (2001). Support for multitasking and background awareness using interactive peripheral displays. In *Proceedings of the 14th Annual ACM Symposium on User Interface Software and Technology (UIST '01)*, pp. 41–50. Orlando, Florida, November 11–14.

Malone, T. W. (1983). How do people organize their desks? Implications for the design of office information systems. *ACM Transactions on Office Information Systems* 1 (1): 99–112.

Mander, R., Salomon, G., and Wong, Y. Y. (1992). A "pile" metaphor for supporting casual organization of information. In *Proceedings of the SIGCHI Conference on Human Factors in Computing Systems (CHI '92)*, pp. 627–634. Monterey, California, May 3–7.

Moran, T. P., Chiu, P., Harrison, S., Kurtenbach, G., Minneman, S., and van Melle, W. (1996). Evolutionary engagement in an ongoing collaborative work process: A case study. In *Proceedings of the 1996 ACM Conference on Computer Supported Cooperative Work*, pp. 150–159. Vancouver, Canada, April 13–18.

Mynatt, E. D. (1999). The writing on the wall. In *Proceedings of INTERACT '99*, pp. 196–204. Edinburgh, Scotland, August 30–September 3.

Mynatt, E. D., Igrashi, T., Edwards, W. K., and LaMarca, A. (1999). Flatland: New dimensions in office whiteboards. In *Proceedings of the ACM Conference on Human Factors in Computing Systems (CHI '99)*, pp. 346–353. Pittsburg, Pennsylvania, May 15–20.

Mynatt, E. D., Igrashi, T., Edwards, W. K., and LaMarca, A. (2000). Designing an augmented writing surface. *IEEE Computer Graphics and Applications* 20 (4): 55–61.

Nardi, B. A. (1996). Studying context: A comparison of activity theory, situated action models, and distributed cognition. In Nardi, B. A. (ed.), *Context and Consciousness: Activity Theory and Human–Computer Interaction*, pp. 69–102. Cambridge, Mass.: MIT Press.

Nardi, B. A., Whittaker, S., and Schwarz, H. (2002). NetWORKers and their activity in intensional networks. *Computer-Supported Cooperative Work* 11: 205–242.

Norman, D. A. (1990). *The Design of Everyday Things.* New York: Doubleday.

Rekimoto, J. (1999). Time-machine computing: A time-centric approach for the information environment. In *Proceedings of the ACM Symposium on User Interface Software and Technology (UIST '99),* pp. 45–54. Asheville, North Carolina, November 7–10.

Robertson, G., van Dantzich, M., Robbins, D., Czerwinski, M., Hinckley, K., Risden, K., Thiel, D., and Gorokhovsky, V. (2000). The Task Gallery: A 3D window manager. In *Proceedings of the ACM Conference on Human Factors in Computing Systems (CHI 2000),* pp. 494–501. The Hague, The Netherlands, April 1–6.

Shen, H., and Dewan, P. (1992). Access control for collaborative environments. In *Proceedings of the 1992 ACM Conference on Computer Supported Cooperative Work (CSCW 1992),* pp. 51–58. Toronto, Canada, November 1–4.

Sikkel, K. (1997). A group-based authorization model for cooperative systems. In *Proceedings of the Fifth European Conference on Computer Supported Cooperative Work (ECSCW '97),* pp. 345–360. Lancaster, England, September 7–11.

Smith, G., Baudisch, P., Robertson, G., Czerwinski, M., Meyers, B., Robbins, D., and Andrews, D. (2003). GroupBar: The taskbar evolved. In *Proceedings of OZCHI '03 (Australian Computer Human Interaction Conference)*, pp. 34–43. Brisbane, Australia, November 26–28.

Streitz, N. A., Geißler, J., Holmer, T., Konomi, S., Müller-Tomfelde, C., Reischl, W., Rexroth, P., Seitz, P., and Steinmetz, R. (1999). i-LAND: An interactive landscape for creativity and innovation. In *Proceedings of the SIGCHI Conference on Human Factors in Computing Systems (CHI '99),* pp. 120–127. Pittsburgh, Pennsylvania, May 15–20.

Tan, D. S., and Czerwinski, M. (2003). Effects of visual separation and physical continuities when distributing information across multiple displays. In *Proceedings of INTERACT 2003,* pp. 252–265. Zurich, Switzerland, September 1–5.

Tran, Q., and Mynatt, E. D. (2002). Cook's Collage: Two exploratory designs. Position paper for "New Technologies for Families" Workshop, ACM Conference on Human Factors in Computing Systems (CHI 2002), Minneapolis, Minnesota.

Voida, S., Mynatt, E. D., MacIntyre, B., and Corso, G. M. (2002). Integrating virtual and physical context to support knowledge workers. *IEEE Pervasive Computing* 1 (3): 73–79.

Vygotsky, L. S. (1978). *Mind in Society: The Development of Higher Psychological Processes.* Cambridge, Mass.: Harvard University Press.

Want, R., Pering, T., Danneels, G., Kumar, M., Sundar, M., and Light, J. (2002). The Personal Server: Changing the way we think about ubiquitous computing. In *Proceedings of the Fourth International Conference on Ubiquitous Computing (UbiComp 2002),* pp. 194–209. Gothenburg, Sweden, September 29–October 1.

Weiser, M. (1991). The computer for the 21st century. *Scientific American* 265 (3): 94–104.

8

# From Desktop Task Management to Ubiquitous Activity-Based Computing

Jakob E. Bardram

## Introduction

Conventional computer technology is designed according to an application- and document-centered model, partially as a response to users' needs for specific, targeted applications that support specific tasks and manipulate particular kinds of information, like writing a letter or making a budget. This application-centered computing model is deeply embedded in the hardware, operating systems software, user-interface software, and the development frameworks available today. It has proven well suited for office work situated at a desktop, but the personal and task-oriented approach provides little support for the aggregation of resources and tools required by higher-level activities. It is left to the user to aggregate such resources and tools in meaningful bundles according to the activity at hand, and manual reconfiguration of this aggregation is often required when multitasking between parallel activities. For example, when writing a business memo, one would be using a whole set of applications (word processor, spreadsheet, graphical tools, statistical packages, ERP systems, etc.), each using a specific set of data and documents. When shifting to another activity, like reading emails and/or browsing the web, a completely new configuration of applications, documents, and files are needed. Even though research has been addressing this challenge and has suggested systems like Rooms (Henderson and Card 1986), Task Gallery (Robertson et al. 2000), Kimura (MacIntyre et al. 2001), GroupBar (Schmidt et al. 2003), and Topos (Grønbæk et al. 2001), there is little or no support for alternating between such activities in most operating systems of today.

Mobile and nomadic work amplify the reconfiguration overhead when users move from one work context to another, potentially using different computers and different types of devices. Thus, users are often "tied" to their personal computer which creates a *one-to-one relationship* between such a (personal) computer and the user.

The world of computing is gradually moving into a world of pervasive and ubiquitous computing where users on the one hand are using a wide range of heterogeneous devices, like a car, the home entertainment computer, an automatic refrigerator, a mobile phone, and different kinds of small and large computers. On the other hand, a wide range of publicly available devices are used by many users, like the refrigerator, a public display, the TV, and so on. Hence, there is now a *many-to-many relationship* between users and computers.

In this chapter I will describe a novel concept for pervasive computing systems that I call *activity-based computing* (ABC) (Christensen and Bardram 2002; Bardram 2005b, 2004). In activity-based computing, the basic computational unit is no longer the file (e.g., a document) or the application (e.g., MS Word) but the *activity* of the user. The end users are directly supported by computational activities: computational activities can be initiated, suspended, stored, resumed on any computing device in the infrastructure at any point in time, handed over to other persons, or shared among several persons. Furthermore, the execution of activities is adapted to the usage context of the users, that is, activities are made context-aware. One of our goals is to enable developers of clinical applications to incorporate support for mobility, interruptions, parallel activities, cooperation, and context-awareness by designing and deploying their programs in such a pervasive computing infrastructure running in a hospital. The ABC framework provides a runtime infrastructure with services supporting these core challenges in medical work as well as a programming model for developing ABC services and applications.

## Prior Work

The concept of activity-based computing is mentioned briefly in Norman's book *The Invisible Computer* (2000). Based on observations of office users using PCs (Macintosh computers), Norman motivates the need for collecting applications or components into logical bundles based on the current activity, for activity resumption, and for sharing of activity spaces. These ideas were developed at Apple in the early 1990s, and the core technological idea was to base such an approach on the OpenDoc standard. OpenDoc was Apple's approach to component-based software on the desktop, like the OLE/COM component approach on the Windows platform. Unfortunately, the project did not get managerial support at Apple and hence was never realized. Inspiration for this activity-based computing approach at Apple originated in the Rooms system (Henderson and Card 1986), the grandfather of all virtual desktop programs. Rooms provided the mechanisms for arranging the application windows on a desktop in logical bundles (i.e., "rooms") and for easy alternating between these. Compared to the activity-based computing idea presented in our approach, the Apple ABC and the Rooms principles were still targeted for nonmobile, personal computing for office workers at a desktop. The approach of using the OpenDoc component technology inherently ties the bundling of components to one physical device, and there is no support for moving an "activity" from one device to another, or for sharing it, or parts of it, among collaborating users.[1]

The concept of activity-based computing has similarities with the task-driven computing concept in Aura (Sousa and Garlan 2002), including the focus on support for human tasks, user mobility across heterogeneous devices, support for context-aware adaptation, and local resource discovery. Activity-based computing has, however, a greater focus on *local mobility* within a work setting and not remote mobility as discussed in Aura. Furthermore, the ABC framework is inherently designed to support collaboration—asynchronous as well as synchronous—both of which are absent in the Aura project. In addition, Aura focuses on software architectures for ubiquitous computing middleware and the project has not done research into the design of user interfaces or the use of such computing environments. From a user-interface perspective, systems like Task Gallery for Windows (Robertson et al. 2000), GroupBar (Schmidt et al. 2003), and Kimura (MacIntyre et al. 2001) have designed ways of handling multitasking in window-based user interfaces. These "virtual desktop" approaches treat tasks as a cohesive collection of applications. When a user refers to a particular task, the system automatically brings up all the applications and documents associated with that task. This relieves the users from launching and arranging applications and documents individually. In our work, we extend this notion by modeling an activity as a collection of abstract services decoupled from applications that can handle such services. This decoupling of activities from specific applications allows an activity to be handed over to and instantiated in different environments using different supporting applications running on different hosts. This also means that different users, who participate in the activity, can use their own favorite application while working on an activity.

From a theoretical and conceptual level, support for "tools and materials" has been the dominant design ideal for the human–computer interaction for many years. This design ideal goes back to the early work on the Alto at PARC and the Utopia project (Bødker et al. 1987) and has been conceptually conceived as the "direct manipulation" approach to user-interface design (Norman and Draper 1986). This design ideal advocates direct support for what users are doing with their tools (i.e., artifacts) and the material they are working on (the object of the activity). This design ideal fits very nicely with the traditional reading of activity theory (Leont'ev 1978) as referring to the work of carpenters, blacksmiths, and other craftsmen. This approach was the starting point in design approaches for human–computer interaction based on activity theory, as suggested by Bødker (1991). Moreover, this design ideal and conceptualization of human activity also incorporates a fundamental skepticism toward workflow systems, because such systems incorporate (or materialize, in terms of activity theory) a conceptualization of human activity as a mental construct (and in the case of a workflow system a computational construct) that controls human work. This is in direct opposition to activity theory, which emphasizes that mental constructs (motives and goals) give direction to the activity, but the execution of an activity is adapted to the material conditions of the concrete situation at hand—a principle that Suchman (1987) has termed "situated action."[2] Therefore, the design ideal coming out of the traditional reading of activity theory advocates support for tools and materials, which allows users to adapt the execution of an activity (i.e., the operational level) to the situation in which it is taking place. In this way, an activity retains its dialectical relationship to the world as something that on one hand is guided by human cognition (the objective) but on the other is shaped according to the material conditions of its execution.

Our proposal for activity-based computing (ABC) might sound like a workflow system that tries to model human activities, including the actions making up the activity. We even talk about (and are currently working on) representing the human intent, that is, the objective of the activity as part of our computational support. However, ABC should not be seen as an approach to workflow systems. In activity-based computing, a "computational activity" is a digital counterpart to a "human activity," the former being merely a representation of the latter, which is the activity as defined by activity theory. Hence, ABC does not attempt to model activities in order to control the execution of human activities—on the contrary. In a workflow system computational activity controls and hence defines human activity. In ABC the human activity defines the computational activity.

Looking closer at the design ideal of creating support for tools and materials—the mediators and objects of an activity—this is actually also the case in ABC. Translating the tools and material support into low-level support for the basic operational-level artifact and objects like icons, documents, scroll-bars, and so on is not the only option. According to activity theory, especially the writings of Vygotsky (see Wertsch 1985) and Engeström (1987), mediators and objects are also higher-level aspects of human activity. For example, the language and its concepts, production and work plans, the division of work between people in an organization, and the rules and laws of a society are all examples of mediators in a complex modern society. Hence, representations of human activities that help people coordinate and execute their activities are primary mediators as well. Similarly, the object of work is not necessarily something physical like the carpenter's wooden house, the blacksmith's horseshoes, or the hunter's prey. Objects of modern human activity also include the treatment and care of a patient, creating manufacturing plans for the production of cars, and doing scientific research.

As computer technology continues to play an increasing role in our professional and personal lives, such objects are often digitally represented and some of them might only have a digital existence, like a computer-aided design/computer-aided manufacturing (CAD/CAM) system with its production plans or software programs. Hence, there is a need for computational support for handling this increasing level of complexity and the sheer amount of digital objects and mediators. The goal of ABC is to provide higher-level tools and material (mediators and objects) for the handling of human activities, which deals with a large amount of digital objects. The basic tenets of activity theory, however, still apply when moving the focus from operational support for tools and material to higher-level activity and action support. The execution of an activity still takes place in a specific material world, and its operations are hence adapted to the concrete opportunities and conditions of the situation at hand. This adaptation of the execution of an activity to the concrete material conditions of a specific situation is maintained in ABC. Furthermore, a distinct feature of human activities—as opposed to animal activity—is their collaborative nature. Hence, humans cooperate by distributing the actions of an activity among each other, and using mediating artifacts, including plans, schedules, and rules to coordinate such distributed activities. Thus, another core aspect of ABC is to support this cooperative nature of human activity by creating *computer-based collaboration artifacts* that mediate collaborative work activities (Bardram 1998).

## Empirical Background

The empirical background for the principles in activity-based computing is extensive field studies of work in Danish hospitals since 1995. When analyzing clinical work and patient treatment in a hospital—and as part of this study the use of computer technology—it becomes obvious that contemporary computers, operating systems, and applications do not fit well with the interrupted, distributed, nomadic, hectic work found in many parallel activities in a clinician's daily work. Personal computers, laptops, PDAs, and tablet PCs are mostly suited for office workers, who work relatively uninterrupted on personal tasks for a long period of time at a fixed location, and often at a desktop. Hence, there is a range of challenges for contemporary computer technology to be discovered in a hospital, which makes hospitals a well-suited application and research area when trying to research and design ubiquitous computing technology that moves "beyond the desktop." In this section we will look into some of these challenges in more details.

### Application- and Data-Orientation

The clinicians view their work as consisting of a large set of activities, some of which are interrelated. Such activities include "Treating Mrs. Pedersen" and "Educating the intern Mr. Hansen." The activities are carried out as a series of actions, which again are realized through a set of concrete physical operations. For example, the activity of treating Mrs. Pedersen involves a wide range of actions, like viewing X-ray images, viewing blood test results, ordering new blood tests, analyzing blood tests, monitoring the temperature and pulse of the patient, and prescribing and giving medicine. Clinicians, however, do not think much about such actions. When interviewing them, these actions are not a primary focus—when describing their work, they talk about the "treatment of Mrs. Pedersen," not about viewing blood test results.

When looking at how clinicians are using computers—in particular electronic patient records (EPRs)—it is often the case that different actions in an activity are supported by different computer applications. Hence, the application for viewing X-ray images is supported by a picture, archiving, and communication system (PACS), the medicine schema is shown as part of an EPR, and ordering blood tests is part of a booking and scheduling system. Even though all of these applications are used to support the same activity—for example, treating a patient—there is little support for aggregating related sets of applications and services into logic bundles corresponding to this activity. In essence, most contemporary computer technology is *application- and data-centered.*

As a consequence, there is little support for alternating between activities. Clinicians in a hospital are involved in many concurrent activities and they constantly switch from one activity to another. Hence, during a ward round a nurse might be engaged in the care of three patients, while also supervising an intern and helping some relatives locate their father. In addition, *interruptions* are a substantial part of working in a hospital where the nurses and physicians constantly interrupt each other to talk about a case, are called on the phone, or must rush to an emergency. It is important to notice here, that in contrast to many studies of interruptions in office work (Conaill and Frohlich 1995; Rouncefield et al. 1995), not all interruptions in a hospital are considered a nuisance, but rather are an essential part of the tight cooperation taking place in a hectic working environment.

### Stationary Work

Most contemporary computer technology is designed for *stationary* use at a desktop. However, clinicians working in a hospital are extremely mobile and most of them do not even have a desk or a chair (Bardram and Bossen 2005). Furthermore, computers in hospitals are often located in small offices in the ward, which implies that clinicians have to walk from work at the patient's bedside to this office in order to access a computer.

Therefore, the use of computers and EPRs increases mobility at a hospital (cf. also Bellotti and Bly 1996). On a more professional level, clinicians—physicians as well as nurses—do not consider "using a computer in a special room" to be a part of their job. Their job has to do with the treatment and care of patients and the education of students. We have observed how the introduction of an electronic patient record system had forced nurses to sit and use personal computers at a desktop (figure 8.1) (Bardram 2005c), which is not a typical work situation for them. They disapproved of no longer being able to finish their job at the bedside of the patient and now having to walk to a computer, log in, start the EPR system, find the patient, find the record or medicine schema, and make notes about the treatment of the patient.

Clearly, mobile devices like laptops, tablet PCs, and PDAs connected via wireless LAN are increasingly being used in hospitals (see, e.g., Bardram, Kjær, and Nielsen 2003a; Munoz et al. 2003). However, in many cases we have seen problems with the use of such technology. First of all, laptops

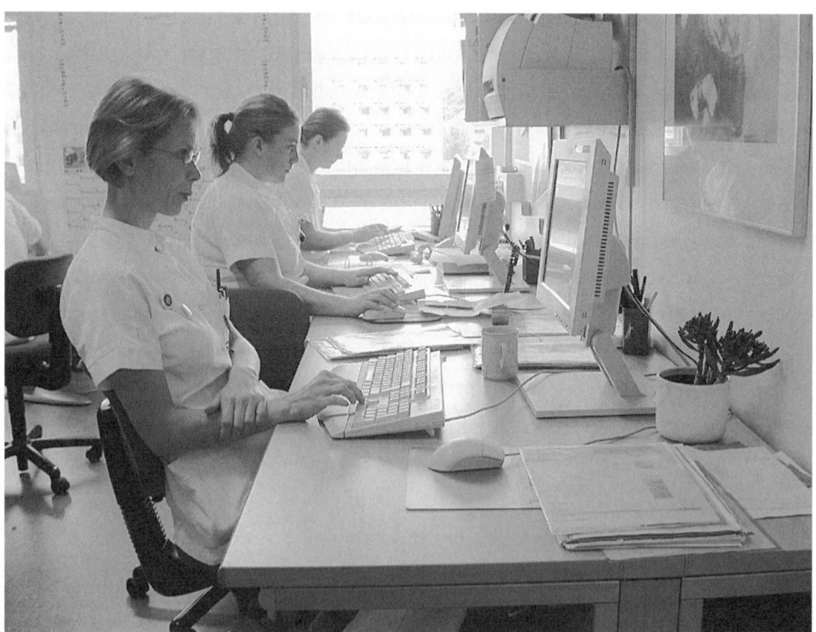

**Figure 8.1**
Nurses working at a desk in an office.

and tablet PCs are actually difficult to use without placing them on some stable horizontal surface. Hence, in most hospitals that have adopted the use of laptops they are mounted on trolleys and then wheeled around, and tablet PCs are often placed in the bed with the patient. Second, most mobile devices available today are not designed for a rugged environment like a hospital and are too fragile to survive being dropped on the floor. For example, when a clinician washes his hands and places a tablet PC on the edge of the sink, it might fall down and break, or the equipment often becomes wet with all kinds of liquid material, some of which needs to be extensively washed off and sterilized with alcohol. And finally, clinicians cannot use mobile equipment during all parts of carrying out an activity and hence need support for using different devices in the flow of work.

### Isolated on Homogeneous Devices

Clinicians roam around using many different computers and devices as part of carrying out an activity. For example, when a nurse in the office shown in figure 8.1 gets up to give some medication to a patient, her seat is typically taken by someone else. Hence, when returning from the patient she will need to locate another vacant computer, log in, start the EPR application, find the patient, find the medicine schema, scroll to the medication in question, and mark that it has been given to the patient. For her this is quite annoying and time consuming, because she had just spent the time and effort of establishing this view on the first computer, which now unfortunately is taken by someone else. In most computer applications and underlying middleware or operating systems there is little or no support for transferring user sessions between different computers, so the computational context for performing an activity must continuously and manually be reestablished during a work day.

The problem is that applications run *isolated on homogeneous devices*. It is difficult to move a set of applications or services from one computer to another, and even more difficult to move it between different kinds of devices, for example, from a PDA to a large desktop computer.

### Single-User Tasks

The "personal computer" with its operating system is made for *single-user tasks*. However, a core aspect of everyday activities is their collaborative nature—especially in a workplace like a hospital. Owing to the specialized nature of medical work, treatment and care are inherently collaborative activities between specialized medical doctors, nurses, care assistants, and so on. In the example of treating Mrs. Pedersen, the radiographer takes the X-ray image, the radiologist describes it, and the physician makes conclusions for further treatment based on the images, the description, blood test results, and previous medical history. The nurse is then responsible for carrying out the treatment, including preparing and giving medicine to the patient and documenting it in the medical record. Hence, the component actions of an activity are often distributed among cooperating clinicians (Bardram 1998). When analyzing the use of paper-based records, we often find the physician and the nurse looking at and writing on the same document simultaneously. For example, the medicine schema is used by the physician to prescribe medicine and by the nurse for documenting the administration of the medicine to the patient while they are standing shoulder to shoulder. When using EPRs this collocated collaboration is often difficult to obtain, resulting in the need for e.g. using two PCs. And when not working collocated and at the same time, there is no support for a nurse to relate her "document medicine" action to the "prescribe medicine" action of the physician. They do not share the application.

Collaboration is thus an inherent quality of clinical work and there is often little support for distributing and congregating the actions of an activity among the people who are involved in it. Currently, collaboration is supported by specialized applications "outside" of the applications that can be used for communication or application sharing.

**Insensitive to the Work Context**

Computers are inherently *insensitive to the working context* of their users. Hence, there is no way in which a computer can take contextual information into consideration in the human–computer interaction. This is why the nurse has to constantly look up the patient in the case illustrated in figure 8.1—the computer or the EPR simply do not have any information about her working context, including which patient she is caring for at the moment. This lack of contextual awareness becomes even more challenging when mobile equipment is being used in a hospital because the working context for an application like the EPR is constantly changing and manual reconfiguration is hence required by the user.

## Activity-Based Computing

To mitigate the challenges to modern computing outlined above, we have introduced the concept of activity-based computing (ABC). Activity-based computing is an approach to ubiquitous computing that focuses on computational support for mobile, collaborative, and distributed human activities. We argue that support for whole activities, rather than individual tasks, is in the roots of ubiquitous and pervasive computing—when users are dealing with a multitude of heterogeneous computing devices, the need for supporting the users at the activity level becomes essential. It will become impossible to get by in a ubiquitous computing world, if one has to consider rearranging applications and services whenever shifting to a new computational device and/or activity. Furthermore, the ubiquitous computing concept of merging computational devices at hand necessitates the need for these devices to adjust themselves to the users according to some sense of the users' context and what he or she is currently doing—that is, his or her activity.

Activity-based computing has the following core principles, each of which addresses the challenges identified above.

*Activity-centered* A "computational activity" collects in a coherent set a range of services needed to support a user carrying out a certain "human activity." For example, the collaborative activity of treating a patient in a hospital can be modeled in ABC as a computational activity, which includes services for displaying and manipulating the patient's medicine schema, blood test results, recent X-ray images, and so on. This principle is illustrated in figure 8.2, which shows how a computational activity embraces a set of services, each of which handles a specific set of data, like files, documents, or remote data in servers. This principle addresses the challenge of *application-centered* computing and supports interruptions in work by enabling the user to alternate easily between the activities he or she is involved in.

*Activity suspend and resume* A user participates in several activities and he or she can alternate between these by suspending one activity and resuming another. Resuming an activity will bring forth all the services and data that are part of the user's activity. This principle addresses the lack of support for interruptions.

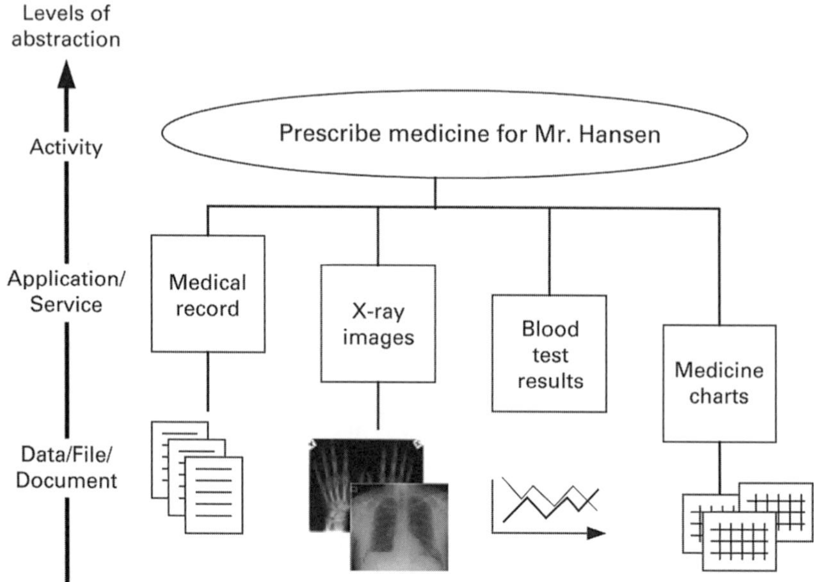


**Figure 8.2**
A single activity involves many services and applications, which again access a wide range of data.

*Activity roaming* An activity is stored in a distributed infrastructure. An activity can be suspended on one workstation and resumed on another in another place. This principle addresses the challenge of *mobility.*

*Activity adaptation* An activity adapts to the resources available on the device that it is being resumed on. This includes network bandwidth, CPU power, and display size. Consequently, an activity might look quite different whether it is resumed on a wall-sized display or on a PDA. This principle addresses the challenge of *isolated and homogeneous devices.*

*Activity sharing* An activity is shared among collaborating users by having a list of participants who can access and resume the activity. Two users, like the nurse and the physician above, can both be working on the activity and thereby cooperating on the treatment of a patient. Users can take turns working on an activity by letting one user take over where another user left the activity; or they can work together at the same time, collocated or remotely. This principle addresses the challenge of *personal computers* and their lack of support for collaboration.

*Context-awareness* An activity is context aware, that is, it is able to adapt and adjust itself according to its usage context. Context-awareness can be used for adapting the user interface to the user's current work situation—for example, by showing medical data for the patient currently being treated—or it can be used in a more technical sense, where the execution of an activity, and its discovery of services, is adjusted to the resources available in its proximity. This principle addresses the challenge of *context-insensitivity.*

**A Scenario**

Let us consider a list of scenarios that illustrates how activity-based computing might support a physician during a typical day.

The group of physicians at department A are gathered in the large conference room for the morning conference. The purpose of this conference is to discuss particular severe cases in common—partly to get second opinions and partly for educational purposes. The conference room is equipped with two large wall-based displays and there is a display built into the table. Some of the physicians have PDAs but the use of tablet PCs has been abandoned because they didn't fit into a whitecoat pocket. However, most of the physicians prefer to use public displays scattered around the hospital and not to carry around computational devices.

Dr. Christensen starts to present a cancer patient—Mrs. Jensen—in a critical condition. He has prepared the presentation as a "Presentation of Mrs. Jensen" activity containing relevant medical data, like a historical view of blood test results, X-ray images of a whole body scan, the medical record, and the medicine history. He walks up to one of the wall-based displays, gets automatically logged in, and the activity is resumed, thereby immediately displaying all the medical views prepared earlier. While presenting the case, one of the senior physicians starts using the display on the table. Because he is a participant of the activity, he can resume it on the table. This enables a collaborative session where changes on one display are reflected on the other. The senior physician highlights a certain blood test result and asks about this while his highlighting is reflected on the wall display. Because the participants are in the same room, a voice link between the two displays is not established.

After the conference, Dr. Christensen walks to the ward to make his rounds. While walking he is interrupted by a nurse asking about another patient. He picks up his PDA and selects from the list of activities the activity concerning this patient. The activity is resumed on the PDA but because of the limited screen size and processing power of the PDA, only part of the services in the activity is resumed. He cannot, for example, see the X-ray images. Therefore, he moves to a public display in the hallway, and by approaching this display he is logged in and his current activity is resumed. Here he can watch the X-ray images and help the nurse to get on. During the ward rounds Dr. Christensen and a nurse are visiting patients at their bedside. He uses the built-in display on the bed to look up medical data about each patient. When he is approaching a patient and is being logged in, the computer always suggests resuming the activity that concerns the patient in the bed. It also displays a subtle warning if Dr. Christensen resumes an activity for another patient than the one he is visiting right now.

Later during the rounds he gets an invitation to participate in an activity from the radiologist. He is notified via his PDA. From the description he can see that the radiologist has analyzed some urgent picture he ordered this morning on Mrs. Jensen and he rushes to the ward's conference room and resumes this activity on the wall display. He enters a real-time activity sharing session with the radiologist, who provides the answers for Dr. Christensen.

The next section describes how these scenarios are supported by the ABC framework.

## The ABC Framework

The ABC framework is the current implementation of the principles of activity-based computing. The main goal of the ABC framework is to provide a technical platform for the development and deployment of computer applications that can be used in our activity-based computing concept.

The components of the ABC framework can be segmented into three categories: *runtime infrastructure*, *user interface*, and *programming model*. The runtime infrastructure is the set of components that handles the computational complexities of managing distributed and collaborative activities by adapting to the available services or resources in a specific environment. The user interface enables the users to access and manipulate activities and to use ABC-aware applications in mobile and collaborative working situations. The programming model is a set of interfaces that enable the construction of new ABC components, which can be deployed in the runtime infrastructure.

### ABC Runtime Infrastructure

This section describes the actual runtime infrastructure that underlies the ABC framework. Its responsibilities regarding activities are to manage, store, activate, and distribute activities, manage and distribute shared state information, ensure synchronization methods on collaborative activities, and manage collaborative sessions. Figure 8.3 illustrates the ABC runtime infrastructure. It consists of a range of server processes running on one or more servers and a range of client processes supporting the execution of the ABC applications.

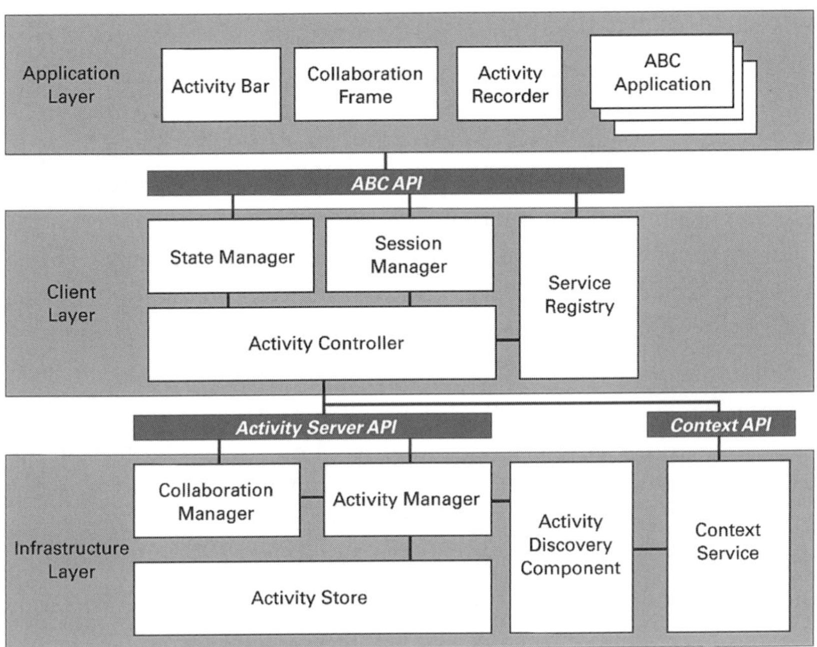


**Figure 8.3**
The ABC runtime infrastructure illustrating both server-side and client-side processes.

The server part of the ABC infrastructure is built in a scalable manner and the different processes making up the activity server can thus be deployed on different hosts. The ABC infrastructure consists of the following key processes.

*Activity Store* This handles the persistence of activities by providing an interface to create, delete, and assess activities and templates for new activities by reference or query. The store keeps track of which activity the user is currently engaged in and the usage history for a user, enabling the user to step forward and backward in the list of activities.

*Activity Manager* This manages the runtime behavior of an activity by enabling activities to be created, initialized, paused, resumed, and finalized by clients. The manager keeps track of ABC clients who register with the manager, and it provides a subscribe-publish-notify interface which can be used to notify clients about relevant changes to activities running of a specific client.

*Collaboration Manager* This handles the real-time requirements for synchronous collaboration among active participants within an activity. To do this it manages a *session* object for each ongoing collaborative activity currently activated by one or more users at different host machines, including the same user on several hosts. Basically, a session notifies its active participants if the session or its associated activity changes. Typical changes are entrance, movement, and departing of users in a session and changes to the state of an activity. Parties interested in listening to changes to a session can add a *Session Listener* to the session. A central listener on session objects is the client-side *Session Manager* described below.

*Context Service* This acquires, stores, and manages context information in the infrastructure. The context service acquires context information via *context monitors* (not illustrated) and provides both a request-response and an event-based publish-subscribed mechanism for clients to access such context information. This context-awareness infrastructure builds on the Java Context-Awareness Framework (JCAF) (Bardram 2005a).

*Activity Discovery Component* (ADC) This tries to discover relevant activities on behalf of the users. The ADC constantly monitors changes in the context service and based on a set of first-order logic rules it is capable of creating new activities, which are sent to the activity manager (Christensen 2002).

*Activity Controller* This is the link between the client and the server. A client's Activity Controller registers at one or more Activity Managers and maintains a link to the *Activity Bar*, the user interface to the ABC infrastructure (see figure 8.5), which via the controller gets a list of activities for a user. The Activity Controller can also be remotely controlled by the Activity Manager, which can force the client to change user, for example. The Activity Controller is also notified about relevant events from the server processes. For example, if the current user is invited to participate in another activity, the Activity Controller is notified and an appropriate signal can be made to the user via the bar. When an Activity Controller activates an activity, the local *State Manager* is notified, which in turn uses the *Registry* to look up appropriate *ABC application*, which can handle the services collected in the activity.

In the scenarios above, there is a server cluster running the activity server processes of activity store, manager, and collaboration manager, and a central context service. Each client deployed in the hospital, including all the public displays and the PDAs, run the client part of the infrastructure, including the activity controller, state manager, session manager, and service registry. Applications that are able to handle different service requests are registered in the service registry. Each user is registered in the context service, which works as a directory service.[3] When an ABC client is idle, it shows a blank screen. When the user logs in on a machine using name and password or proximity-based user authentication (Bardram, Kjær, and Pedersen 2003b) the activity controller on this computer loads a list of the user's activities and shows them in the activity bar (see the next section on the GUI of ABC). It also requests from the activity manager the user's current activity and resumes this on the client. When an activity is resumed, the activity controller iterates through the activity's set of services, and for each service description the controller asks the local service registry if there is a local application that can handle this service description. If a matching service application is found, the state manager is given a handle to this application and the state manger spawns a separate thread launching the application and hands over the state information part of the service description to the application. The application is then responsible for restoring the correct state of the service. For example, a medicine schema application should show the medicine data for the correct patient and scroll to the correct place in the schema.

When the user selects another activity or logs out, the activity controller asks the state manager for the activity state. The state manager iterates through all the running applications and for each asks for state information and returns this state information to the controller. This state information is saved in the activity, which is handed over to the activity manger. The manager stores the activity in the activity store and updates the history.

This basic state management mechanism also supports real-time activity sharing. If two or more participants of an activity are online on different hosts simultaneously, then state changes on one client are saved to the server, which then via the collaboration manager broadcasts this state change to the other online participants. On each client, state is then managed as described above. Collaborative widgets like the voice link and the tele-pointers are initialized, managed, and finalized by the client's session managers. For example, tele-pointers are set up in a peer-to-peer fashion between clients in the same session, and are not replicated as state information to the server (see Bardram 2005b for details).

### The ABC User Interface

The ABC user interface for desktop PCs, tablet PCs, and wall-based computers is illustrated in figure 8.4. This screen shoot shows how a radiology conference activity would look like. The main user interface components are the *activity bar*, the *collaboration frame*, examples of *ABC applications*, and the *tele-pointers*.

The activity bar is the central user-interface component representing access to the ABC framework. Figure 8.5 shows the bar in details. From the left, the bar has the following groups of buttons: (i) a "Start" button[4] for launching ABC-aware applications (those registered in the service registry); (ii) two buttons for creating and finalizing activities; (iii) two buttons for inviting participants to this activity and for showing the collaboration frame (no. 2 in figure 8.4); (iv) two buttons for moving forward and backward in the history of activities, and a dropdown box to select an activity from the list of active activities; (v) the "lamp" icon, which is used to notify the user about new activities added to his list or changes to existing ones; (vi) one button to start the activity recorder, and buttons for enabling and disabling sound and microphone; and (vii) the login button, which shows the current user's name and can be used to log users in and out.

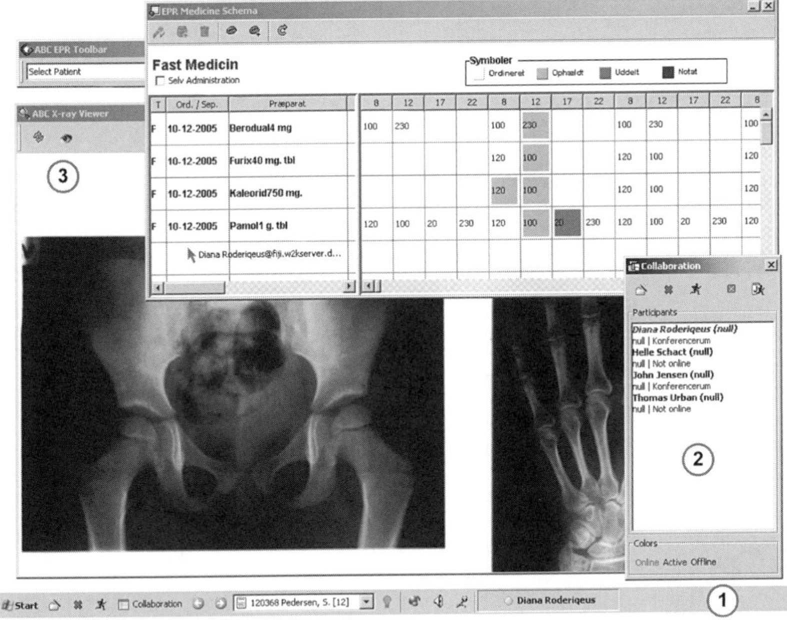


**Figure 8.4**
The user interface of the ABC framework containing the activity bar at the bottom; the collaboration frame on the right hand side; two ABC applications, one showing radiology images and the other the patient's medicine chart; and a tele-pointer from a remote user. The name of the activity is shown in the selection box in the activity bar, showing that this activity is about a patient of the name Mrs. Pedersen.

Let us investigate how the ABC user interface supports the core principles of activity-based computing as presented earlier.

**Activity centered** As illustrated in figure 8.2, an activity is made up of a set of services that again manipulates a set of data. In the user interface, activities are immediately accessible from the activity list or by moving forward or backward in the activity history using the forward and backward buttons. A user is always working within an activity, that is, there is always an activity resumed. We call this the "active activity." When the user logs in, the last used activity is resumed and restored to the exact same state as it was suspended previously—potentially on another device. A service is mapped to an application. In figure 8.4, the "Radiology image viewer" service is mapped to the "ABC X-ray viewer" application (no. 3

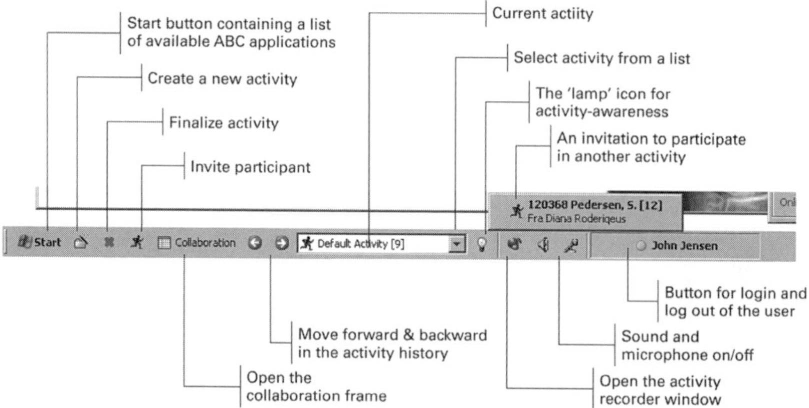


**Figure 8.5**
The Activity Bar.

in figure 8.4). An application that supports a specific service is able to pass on state information concerning this service and reestablish its state accordingly. This includes getting access to the data elements, whether they are stored in the activity or accessible on a distributed file system or a server. In the X-ray viewer case, the X-ray images are stored on a hospital image server and the activity holds state information about where and how to access these. State information for most applications also includes size and position of the window.

Services are added to an activity by launching them from the Start menu and are removed by closing the window. When the activity is suspended, all state information, including data references, is stored in the activity, which is sent to the activity manager in the underlying infrastructure.

**Activity roaming** Because activities are persistently stored in the underlying infrastructure via the activity store, the activity can be distributed across different ABC-enabled devices. Activity roaming is governed through a set of lifecycle events:

*Registry*—when the ABC client starts up, this client is registered in the activity manager.

*Login*—when a user logs in, the client requests a list of this user's activities from the activity manager.

*Resume*—when the user resumes an activity by, for example, selecting it from the activity list, the activity is fetched from the activity manager and its services are mapped to locally available applications, which are started and restored according to the state information in the activity.

*Suspend*—when an activity is suspended, all services return to their current state, which is stored in the activity and handed back to the activity manager.

*Logout*—when the user logs out, the active activity is suspended and the user's activities are removed from the activity list.

*Unregistry*—when the ABC client is stopped, it is unregistered at the activity manager.

If the user is roaming between two identical devices—for example, between two desktop PCs—then activities are restored to look exactly the same, including window size and position. This feature was considered essential by all the involved clinicians because it enabled them to move around inside the hospital while maintaining the exact look and feel of their workspace. One of the major complaints about the existing client-server systems was a significant overhead associated with restoring the user session when moving between computers because only clinical data were stored on servers, not the user sessions. The primary drawback of restoring the exact size and position of all windows is that desktop PCs (and similar devices like a tablet PC) may have different display resolutions, ranging from 1024 × 768 to 1600 × 1200. Thus, you could have situations where parts or whole windows are not visible when you move from a large to a small screen. In reality, however, the clinicians did not consider this a problem since all machines and screens in a hospital were often of the same kind. Nevertheless, this is a problem that we are addressing in our current work.

**Activity adaptation** From a user-interface perspective, activity adaptation is handled by the applications running locally and implements the different services. If a local application maps to a service type, then this application is given the service state information, and by parsing this state information it decides how to restore the service on this specific device. On some devices, window size and position may be used or adapted (e.g., adjusted to fit the screen resolution); on other devices, this information may be ignored (e.g., on a PDA that shows all services full screen); some services simply cannot be supported, like the X-ray viewer application shown in figure 8.4 which is not available on PDAs.

**Activity sharing** Activity sharing is supported by having several participants associated with the same activity. The collaboration frame (no. 2 in figure 8.4) lists the current activity's participants. Collaboration between these participants is supported in three ways. *Asynchronous collaboration* is supported by allowing participants to resume an activity in turn, that is, participants can take turns working on an activity. Because state is saved in an activity, one participant takes over the activity exactly as another participant left it when suspending it. Furthermore, by using the activity-roaming mechanisms, different users can resume activities in different places. To allow simple communication between participants, an activity chat exists (not shown in figure 8.4). The chat is specific to the activity and saves a conversation between participants. This chat is saved persistently as a part of the activity's state information.

*Synchronous collaboration* takes place if two or more participants resume the same activity on different devices at the same time. In this case, the active participants engage in a synchronous conference session handled by the collaboration manager on the server side and the session manager on the clients' side. The collaboration mechanisms ensure that the activity, including its state information, is synchronized between all participating users. From the user-interface perspective, this means that user-interface state information is synchronized, including window position, size, and the state of the individual services. In addition to synchronizing user-interface state information between participating peers, the collaboration mechanisms also include a voice link between the participating peers, as well as tele-pointers.

The user-interface support for synchronous collaborative activity sharing is illustrated in figure 8.6, which shows the top frame of an ABC application and two tele-pointers. Because we want to support users who are active in the same activity at the same time but who focus on different parts of the activity, the ABC framework does not enforce strict What-You-See-Is-What-I-See (WYSIWIS). Hence, two different users can have focus in two overlapping windows without disturbing each other. The top frame of each window just reveals which window each user has focus in

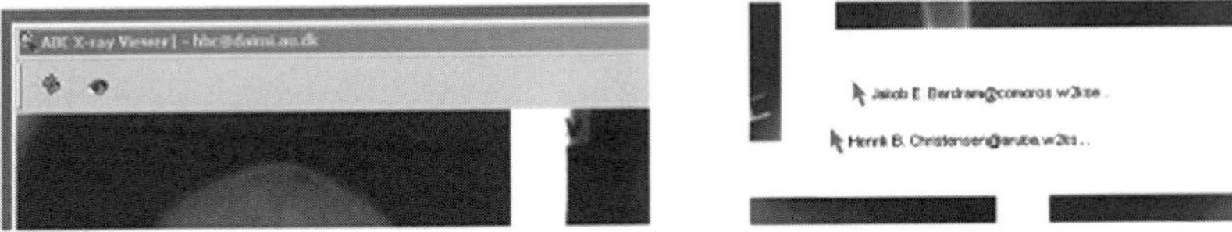

**Figure 8.6**
Collaboration widgets in the ABC user interface. On the left, the top frame of a window is decorated with the color and username of the user(s) currently having focus in this window. On the right, two tele-pointers are shown.

by showing the user's name and decorating the frame with a user-specific color. This enables one user to say things like "have a look at this," and the other user will know which window is being referred to and can bring this window into focus. The tele-pointers reveal the name of the user and the hostname of his or her machine. We attach the hostname because the same user can be active in the same activity on different clients at the same time—a feature that turned out to be used quite often during our evaluation sessions.

Synchronous collaboration is often evident in a hospital, typically in conference situations. The ABC framework allows for clinical desktop conferences across several computers. This may take place collocated, as in the scenario above where the group of physicians are participating in the conference using different devices. Or it may take place where participants are separated from each other, as in the scenario where medical doctors who cannot attend the "real" radiology conference can listen in remotely by participating in the "radiology conference" activity running in the radiology conference room. In the ABC framework this would imply that the remote medical doctors can see the X-ray images being shown on the large display in the radiology conference room, can see the radiologist's gestures with the mouse via the tele-pointers, and can listen using the voice link. The medical doctors are, however, also active participants in the conference and may ask questions, use their tele-pointers to indicate areas of an X-ray image, and may rearrange or bring up new medical data from the EPR.

The third type of collaboration supported by the ABC framework is *temporal collaboration*. Temporal collaboration is a mixture of synchronous and asynchronous collaboration, which allows participants to collaborate across time almost as if they were together at the same time. In the user interface, temporal collaboration is supported by the ABC memoplayer, shown in figure 8.7. This memoplayer is an activity recorder that is able to record the unfolding of an activity in time and captures activity state information, mouse events, and sound. Technically, the activity recorder is using the same mechanisms as those used in the synchronous desktop conference, but instead of streaming state events, mouse events, and sound to another computer, these data are streamed to a persistent data object stored in the activity store. The activity recorder can hence be used for recording a multimedia message for other participants in the activity, which later can be fetched from the activity manager and replayed on the same or another computer. Other participants can then reply by recording their continued use of the activity, while thinking aloud. In the example shown in figure 8.7, the first user (Jakob E. Bardram) initiated a discussion which was then responded to by two other users (John Jensen and Diana Roderiqeus) and is now back with the first user.

Temporal collaboration is essential in most medical work. It is often difficult to ensure that two or more clinicians can meet at the same time, and a wide range of mechanisms for leaving messages is used in hospitals. These mechanisms involve voice recorders, post-it notes, and answering machines. Activity recording is designed to support this kind of messaging within the activity, thereby ensuring that the message is recorded and replayed in the correct activity context. In this way, clinicians can leave multimedia messages that are directly related to a specific task they collaborate on.

**Figure 8.7**
The Activity Recorder, used for recording and replaying the unfolding of activities.

**Activity and context awareness** Once we support the work in a hospital by modeling activities, providing awareness about the unfolding of activities becomes essential. Keeping a peripheral awareness on how an activity is progressing, what other participants are doing, and whether there are issues that require attention become important in an activity-based computing environment. The current user interface supports this kind of activity awareness through two mechanisms; one is the lamp icon illustrated in figure 8.5 and the other is the ability to send messages to the user's activity-enabled mobile phone. The lamp icon is used to notify the user about changes to activities other than the one he or she is engaged in right now. The lamp icon will light up and play a sound if the current user receives a new activity, is invited to participate in another activity, or if a new recording has been added to an activity. These events are also sent to the user's mobile phone which provides him with simple activity-awareness while not using a computer. The mobile phone, however, supports only the display of basic activity information and is hence used merely to take a look at an activity that has been changed. The user may then decide to resume this activity on a nearby computer to have a closer look or to participate in an activity-sharing session. This support for activity awareness is admittedly rather limited and we are currently working on extending it.

As illustrated in figure 8.3, a context service is a core component in the ABC infrastructure. Context information is added to this context service from various sources, including the ABC clients which hand over information about who is logged in at the different computers and which activity is currently active. Other context information, such as location and status, comes from other sources. This kind of context information is shown in the collaboration frame in figure 8.4.

The most interesting use of context information is, however, for activity discovery (Christensen 2002). The activity-discovery component (ADC) in figure 8.3 stores a set of first-order logic rules that is constantly evaluated against the context information available in the context service. The ADC is able to recognize different typical activities based on changes in context. For example, if a nurse picks up a medicine container for a specific patient in the pharmacy, then the ADC reasons that an activity containing medical information for this patient is useful for the nurse. Using an activity factory, the ADC then creates the appropriate activity for the user's current context and pushes it to the activity manager. If the nurse is online, the activity manager then notifies her ABC client, and in the user interface, the nurse will now see the notification lamp light up in the activity bar and will hear a small sound. This notifies her about the new activity, and by clicking on the lamp icon she can see and resume the proposed activity. To support contingent situations—for example, where the nurse is holding two medicine containers for two patients—more activities can be created and are listed when pressing the lamp icon. In this way the nurse can choose which activity is most relevant to her current context, or choose not to use any of the suggestions but stay in the current one. Hence, we have tried to make activity discovery as nondisruptive as possible while still notifying the user. We call this designing for *nonintrusive context-awareness.*

### The ABC Programming Model

The runtime infrastructure both supports the programming model and makes use of it. The programming model is intended for programmers to extend the ABC framework by adding new types of activities, components, applications, or collaborative widgets. The programming model consists of a range of interfaces that the programmer can implement and add to the runtime infrastructure. Together, these interfaces make up the distributed extension of the standard ABC functionality included in the ABC framework. Among the interfaces that make up the ABC programming model are the following:

- The Activity interface, which defines a way of creating custom types of activities. For example, in our ABC-based implementation of an electronic patient record there is an EPRActivity, which is able to handle EPR specific activities, including being related to a specific patient.
- The Activity Store, Activity Manager, and Collaboration Manager interfaces, which make up the interfaces of the Activity Server. Normally, application programmers would access these interfaces using the client layer's Activity Controller, but these interfaces are available for the programmers to make their own client layer functionality or new user interfaces.
- The Stateful Application interface, which enables the programmer to create client-side applications that can participate in the ABC runtime infrastructure.

- The event and notification interfaces, which are used to subscribe to changes to certain components. The most used ones are the Activity Listener interface for listening to changes to activities, the Session Listener interface for listening to changes to collaborative real-time sessions, and the Entity-Listener interface used for listening to changes in context information.
- The Session Manager and the Session interfaces, which can be customized for special purposes in the real-time collaboration support in the infrastructure.

A key design invariant in the ABC framework is that applications are stateful, which implies that they can hand over and restore their own state. The runtime infrastructure collects, manages, distributes, and synchronizes this state information across the movement of users between physical machines and in the participation in synchronous collaborative sessions. The collection of state information from all applications running in an environment is saved in the activity, and hence the activity can be assumed to always contain the shared state. The State Manager guarantees this invariant: it is a singleton process running on the client-side and it creates the link between the Activity Controller (and hence the Activity Managers running as server processes) and the applications running on the client machine.

The programming model provides interfaces and a default implementation of stateful applications and UI components. In order to help application programmers to build ABC-aware applications that can handle state information, the programming model contains stateful user-interface components. In the Java-based version of the ABC framework, these stateful user-interface components are wrappers to Swing components (Bardram 2005b). For example, we have extended core Swing components such as JFrame, JScrollPane, and JComboBox to set and get state information. These user-interface components are intended to make state management easy to implement for application programmers. By using these ABC Swing components, the programmer needs not worry about user-interface state, but merely has to manage application-specific state information.

**Implementation Status**

The ABC framework described above is version 3, which has been implemented in the Java 2 Standard Edition version 1.4 (J2SE), using Java RMI as its distribution mechanism and the Java Media Framework (JMF) for audio-broadcast between devices; all ABC-aware applications are written in the Java Swing user-interface framework. We have created a special ABC Swing library that enables programmers to create ABC-aware applications (Bardram 2005b). Version 3 runs on both Microsoft Windows and Linux owing to the platform independence provided by Java. The ABC client interface illustrated in figure 8.4 is designed to run on wall-sized displays, tablet PCs, and desktop computers.

Version 3 does not fully support small devices (the Java 2 Micro Edition, J2ME), such as PDAs or mobile phones. However, the scaled-down client can run on a PDA and a mobile phone, which show only the basic details of an activity (its name, participants, and involved services). A user can activate an activity on the small devices, which has the effect that this activity is resumed when approaching a full-scale ABC client, like the wall-based display. Version 3 does not support native applications such as Word, Emacs, or PowerPoint, and all ABC-aware applications need to be developed using the ABC programming API (see Bardram 2005b for details)—or at least wrappers for native application need to be made in the ABC API.

Currently, we are implementing version 4 of the ABC framework based on the .NET framework. This version is integrated into the Windows operating system. We are, for example, replacing the Windows taskbar with our own "Activity Bar" and are providing support for native Windows applications to be part of the ABC framework. In addition, the tight synchronous communication paradigm in Java RMI has been replaced with a loosely coupled, asynchronously publish-subscribe infrastructure, which makes it more robust to general failures and exceptions. We are also working on implementing ABC clients for PDAs and mobile phones, which can participate in activity roaming and activity sharing.

## Discussion

It is difficult to directly evaluate a runtime infrastructure with a corresponding programming framework—especially when we are researching completely new types of ubiquitous computing technology (Abowd and Mynatt 2000). Nevertheless, in order to evaluate whether the conceptual principles of activity-based computing and their technical incarnation really help users manage a complex ubiquitous computing environment, we have implemented an electronic patient record on top of the ABC framework and have been using this in a number of design and evaluation sessions with clinicians from the University Hospital of Aarhus. We have conducted eleven such workshops where for a whole day clinicians were asked to co-design, use, evaluate, and test the framework. A common method in our design workshops was to let the clinicians role-play a number of clinical scenarios (Bødker and Christiansen 1997), trying out different design alternatives. In the design of real-time activity sharing, we applied walkthrough methods very similar to the method of Groupware Walkthrough (Pinelle and Gutwin 2002). In addition, we conducted four whole-day evaluation workshops with clinicians who had never before seen the ABC framework or been introduced to the concepts of activity-based computing. All workshops were video-recorded and the tapes were later analyzed by categorizing "interesting" conceptual and usability issues.

The general impression from our series of evaluation workshops was that the clinicians gave very positive feedback on the basic concepts of activity-based computing. With its support for mobility, interruption, parallel work, collaboration, and user-interface adaptation based on context-awareness, the computing platform deliberately addresses some of the core challenges they face in their daily clinical work (Bardram 2004). Many comments and suggestions for improvement have been incorporated in the framework along the way, and the present version of the ABC framework hence materializes a considerable amount of design knowledge obtained in close cooperation with many clinicians. Limitations in the current design and implementation of activity-based computing support, however, also surfaced during these evaluation sessions. We want to discuss some of the limitations here in greater details because they point to our current work on improving support for activity-based computing.

Difficulties of separating one activity from another were a recurrent issue during our evaluation sessions: When does a "Prescribe medicine for Mrs. Hansen" stop being a prescription activity and become a "Document medicine given for Mrs. Hansen"? In several cases, we observed that one activity just transformed into another without the user selecting or creating a new activity. Hence, the "Prescribe medicine for Mrs. Hansen" activity sometimes also evolved into a "Check medicine for Mr. Pedersen" activity, because a nurse would just select Mr. Pedersen as the current patient in the

EPR, even though she was working in the activity devoted to Mrs. Hansen. Several suggestions for accommodating these "activity-separation" problems have been designed (Bardram 2004). These include the use of activity templates, to create the activity post hoc instead of before beginning to use an activity, to bookmark an activity as it unfolds (this could be done automatically, e.g., when the user switches between patients), and to use the programming model to model an EPR activity. Such an activity would ensure a tight connection between an activity and a patient, thereby helping users to avoid switching patients in the middle of an activity—an issue that was deemed rather critical during the evaluations.

From a theoretical point of view, the problem of separating one activity from another is closely tied to the matter of identifying real-world activities in activity theory. One central concern within activity theory is to be able to analytically distinguish one activity from another. This is basically done by looking at the motive or objective of the activity. Hence, asking "why" people are doing something can reveal the identity of individual activities. In a clinical setting, the objective is often tied to the treatment and care of a specific patient, and the technical proposal of creating computational activities that are tied to a patient therefore seems appropriate. Seen from this perspective, it is questionable whether the "prescription" and "documentation" of medicine for Mrs. Hansen actually belong to two different activities or are instead two actions within the same. If the latter is the case—and we believe it is—then what we call "activities" in the ABC framework might from an activity-theoretical point of view rightly be called actions. This also corresponds to the notion of distributing actions within an activity among collaborating people, where the physician is responsible for prescribing medicine and the nurse for the documentation.

The problem of separating activities from one another is also tied to the scalability problem (Bardram 2004). In a real-world setting a clinician may be involved in dozens if not hundreds of activities. The current implementation of the activity-based computing principles in the ABC framework does not scale in its user interface. For example, the list of activities in the activity bar quickly gets too long to be practical. The present linear ordering of activities does not scale in a conceptual manner, either. How would users conceive of so many activities with no way of relating them to each other or to some contextual information? There is a potential danger that we are just moving the burden of navigating and managing large amounts of digital data from more traditional tools, such as an electronic patient record, to the activity-based computing framework.

These empirical and theoretical challenges in separating activities, the relations between activities and actions, and the scalability of activities have made us consider how activity-based computing might be improved. Our current suggestions focus on three design ideas: (i) to represent human intent in activity-based computing support, (ii) to support relationships and viewpoints in an activity space, and (iii) to support native applications.

In the same line as we have represented human activity, we believe that it would be worthwhile to represent the human activity's objective as part of the computational representation of an activity. Clearly, this would only be a weak representation of an activity's human motivation, but it would be an externalization that would help users manage activities. Furthermore, sharing (i.e., externalizing and internalizing) the common objective of an activity is essential in cooperative work, where collaborating people align their individual actions according to a common objective (Leont'ev 1978; Bardram 1998). But the most promising use of representing the objective of an activity lies in the support for *pro-activity*—to have computers be active instead of reactive in their relation to users. Pro-activity and adaptation are essential but challenging aspects of ubiquitous computing. Going beyond the current support for context-awareness and base pro-active adaptation on a representation of the intent or objective of an activity seems a promising step to take in activity-based computing. We are, for example, working on extending the context-aware functionality of showing a default patient activity when a certain patient is approached to show a whole range of interrelated activities, which are all related to the treatment of this patient.

The support for sharing an activity space is intended to help users organize, manage, and relate a large amount of interrelated activities (of which some may be actions, i.e., subsumed under other activities). In our current work we are designing a hypermedia structure with a network of activities and related actions—that is, a large web of interrelated activities and actions upon which users can apply different viewpoints. Currently the ABC framework only supports a user-specific viewpoint into available activities—that is, a user can get a list of his activities. This viewpoint can be extended to support other viewpoints related to, for example, time, location, context, patient, colleague, or type of disease. We are, furthermore, creating support for copying, cloning, merging, splitting, and linking activities.

Finally, the support for native applications seems like a natural step to take for several empirical and theoretical reasons. Empirically the evaluations showed that users had problems with adjusting or using an unfamiliar electronic patient record (i.e., the one we implemented on top of the ABC framework) (Bardram 2004). Even though the ABC framework and its programming model can be seen as a new set of foundation classes for programming user applications on a certain platform (i.e., the operating system), it is still important to consider how existing applications and systems may be integrated as part of the activity-based computing platform. Hence, support for native applications is quite essential from an empirical-practical viewpoint. This argument is also backed up from a theoretical viewpoint since keeping with familiar applications helps users to realize activities as being routines on the operational level of an activity. From a more technical point of view, however, dealing with existing applications that are not built to support activity-based computing can be rather cumbersome. It is, for example, rather difficult to get and set state information in many applications; it is difficult to migrate one application across heterogeneous devices; and it is difficult to use applications made for desktop use in an activity-based ubiquitous computing environment. As a result, our current work is devoted to a double strategy of both trying to make technological fixes for legacy applications and designing a programming model and a set of foundation classes for building native activity-based applications.

## Conclusion

In this chapter we have presented our work on activity-based computing. The notion of activity-based computing aims at moving computing technology for everyday use beyond the desktop in a double sense—both physically away from the desktop on which most computers are placed today, and conceptually away from the desktop user-interface metaphor of supporting individual applications. Many suggestions for what we call activity-based computing have been proposed and researched and this approach embodies many intriguing suggestions for addressing most of the core shortcomings in contemporary personal computing. Activity-based computing thus seems to be a good candidate as a new design ideal in the creation of future computing infrastructures and operating systems that move beyond the desktop. Based on our experience in designing, implementing, and evaluating such an activity-based computing infrastructure, we have suggested the six principles of activity-based computing, which are to support: (i) *activity-centered* collection of applications, services, and data; (ii) *suspension and resumption* of activities, (iii) *activity roaming* between distributed computing devices; (iv) *activity adaptation* to the available resources on heterogeneous computing devices; (v) *activity sharing* among several participants within the same activity; and (vi) *context-awareness* by enabling activities to adapt to the their execution context.

Based on our experience in having a large number of clinicians evaluate our ABC framework, we believe that addressing the challenges of separating activities and handling large amounts of them are essential in the further development of activity-based approaches to ubiquitous computing. As discussed in the early work on the Rooms system (Henderson and Card 1986) these challenges also emerged in the use of virtual desktops, where it was not uncommon for a user to have difficulties setting up which applications actually belonged to which room. It may also apply, for example, to the task-based approaches in Kimura (MacIntyre et al. 2001) and Aura (Sousa and Garlan 2002), where the notion of "intent" is mentioned but does not seem to play any role in the computer technology. Similarly, workflow systems are often criticized for their strict separation of one activity from another. This does not resemble real-world activities, which often are highly interrelated, with no strict boundaries, and which often serve several purposes (i.e., activities are poly-motivated according to activity theory; see Kaptelinin 1996). Therefore, researching how support for activities can incorporate support for such interlinked activities with fuzzy boundaries is a core challenge in activity-based approaches to ubiquitous computing.

The concepts and technologies for activity-based computing have emerged from our experimental research into devising ubiquitous computing infrastructures for clinical work in large hospitals. As argued in the introduction, this is a particularly challenging environment for computing technology and is therefore ideal for researching ubiquitous computing architectures and platforms. Clinical work is characterized by the necessity of handling a huge amount of medical data in the treatment of just one patient, of which there are thousands; a high degree of mobility; many parallel and interrupted work activities; a high degree of cooperation; the use of many medical applications and digital material; and the use of many heterogeneous devices. Electronic patient records are built on top of existing computer technology (operating systems and middleware layers) and are thus typically designed according to the desktop model of computing, which these contemporary technologies embody. Present-day clinical systems therefore do not support the above-mentioned core aspects of clinical work, and hence they are often inadequate in daily use. We do believe, however, that activity-based computing is a viable computing principle outside the medical setting of a hospital. Many work situations are characterized by handling large amounts of digital data, mobility, parallel and interrupted work, and cooperation. Even in an office environment, activity-based computing support might be very useful, and we believe that it also would be beneficial as a programming environment, even though mobility is not always as prevalent here.

Theoretically, we have argued that despite its name activity-based computing is not another workflow system—on the contrary. The "computational activity" in activity-based computing is a means for collecting, managing, distributing, and sharing material and tools that are related to each other within a specific activity. As human activities increasingly involve the manipulation of digital material, there is a profound need for computational tools that can help users to manage this large amount of digital material in a manner that reflects the activity itself. A fundamental part of this need includes support for the distribution and integration of actions among collaborating people. Hence, support for activity-based cooperation is essential in such a ubiquitous computing platform that goes beyond today's personal desktop model of computing.

## Acknowledgments

We would like to thank all the clinicians who have given us their valuable time. Henrik B. Christensen was involved in outlining some of the initial thoughts on activity-based computing (at that time called activity-centered computing) and Claus Bossen was part of the field studies of hospital work. This work was financially supported by the Danish Centre for Information Technology Research (CIT) and the Competence Centre ISIS Katrinebjerg. Currently the ABC project is supported by the Danish Research council under the NABIIT program.

## Notes

1. Norman mentions support for "sharing activity spaces." However, since none of these concepts was ever realized it is difficult to judge what is exactly meant by this. The Rooms system does not support the movement of rooms between devices or any kind of collaboration.

2. A detailed discussion of the relationships between activity theory, plans, situated actions, and workflow systems can be found in Bardram 1997.

3. This is done in our prototype solution. In a real-world deployment scenario we would clearly have to cooperate with a real directory server and use, e.g., the LDAP interface for interoperability.

4. We borrowed the "Start" icon from the Windows taskbar to help users recognize its purpose.

## References

Abowd, G. D., and Mynatt, E. D. (2000). Charting past, present, and future research in ubiquitous computing. *ACM Transactions on Computer–Human Interaction (ToCHI)* 7 (1): 29–58.

Bardram, J. E. (1997). Plans as situated action: An activity theory approach to workflow systems. In *Proceedings of the Fifth European Conference on Computer Supported Cooperative Work*, pp. 17–32. Lancaster, U. K, September 7–11.

Bardram, J. E. (1998). Collaboration, coordination, and computer support—An activity theoretical approach to the design of computer supported cooperative work. Ph.D. dissertation, Department of Computer Science, Aarhus University, Aarhus. Daimi PB-533.

Bardram, J. E. (2004). Activity-based computing—Principles, implementation, and evaluation. Technical report, University of Aarhus, Centre for Pervasive Healthcare. Submitted to ToCHI, April 2004.

Bardram, J. E. (2005a). The Java context awareness framework (JCAF)—A service infrastructure and programming framework for context-aware applications. In *Proceedings Pervasive Computing: Third International Conference, PERVASIVE 2005*, pp. 98–115. Munich, Germany, May 8–13.

Bardram, J. E. (2005b). Activity-based computing: Support for mobility and collaboration. *Ubiquitous Computing—Personal and Ubiquitous Computing* 9 (5): 312–322.

Bardram, J. E. (2005c). The trouble with login: On usability and computer security. *Ubiquitous Computing—Personal and Ubiquitous Computing* 9 (6): 357–367.

Bardram, J. E., and Bossen, C. (2005). Mobility work: The spatial dimension of collaboration at a hospital. *Computer Supported Cooperative Work* 14 (2): 131–160.

Bardram, J. E., Kjær, T. K., and Nielsen, C. (2003). Supporting local mobility in healthcare by application roaming among heterogeneous devices. In *Proceedings of the Fifth International Conference on Human Computer Interaction with Mobile Devices and Services*, pp. 161–176. Udine, Italy, September 8–11.

Bardram, J. E., Kjær, R. E., and Pedersen, M. Ø. (2003). Context-aware user authentication—Supporting proximity-based login in pervasive computing. In *Proceedings of Ubicomp 2003: Ubiquitous Computing*, pp. 107–123. Seattle, Washington, October 12–15.

Bellotti, V., and Bly, S. (1996). Walking away from the desktop computer: Distributed collaboration and mobility in a product design team. In *Proceedings of the 1996 ACM Conference on Computer Supported Cooperative Work,* pp. 209–218. Boston, Massachusetts, November 16–20.

Bødker, S. (1991). *Through the Interface: A Human Activity Approach to User Interface Design.* Hillsdale, N. J.: Lawrence Erlbaum.

Bødker, S., and Christiansen, E. (1997). Scenarios as springboards in design. In Bowker, G., Gasser, L., Star, L., and Turner, W. (eds.), *Social Science Research, Technical Systems, and Cooperative Work,* pp. 217–234. Hillsdale, N. J.: Lawrence Erlbaum.

Bødker, S., Ehn, P., Kammersgaard, J., Kyng, M., and Sundblad, Y. (1987). A UTOPIAN experience: On design of powerful computer-based tools for skilled graphical workers. In Bjerknes, G., Ehn, P., and Kyng, M. (eds.), *Computers and Democracy: A Scandinavian Challenge,* pp. 251–278. Aldershot: Averbury.

Christensen, H. B. (2002). Using logic programming to detect activities in pervasive healthcare. In *Proceedings of International Conference on Logic Programming.* Copenhagen, Denmark, July 29–August 1.

Christensen, H. B., and Bardram, J. E. (2002). Supporting human activities—Exploring activity-centered computing. In *Proceedings of Ubicomp 2002: Ubiquitous Computing*, pp. 107–116. Göteborg, Sweden, September 29–October 1.

Carroll, J. (ed.) (1995). *Scenario-Based Design: Envisioning Work and Technology in System Development.* New York: John Wiley and Sons.

Engeström, Y. (1987). *Learning by Expanding: An Activity-Theoretical Approach to Developmental Research.* Helsinki: Orienta-Konsultit Oy.

Grønbæk, K., Gundersen, K., Mogensen, P., and Ørbæk, P. (2001). Interactive Room support for complex and distributed design projects. In *Proceedings of the Interact '01*, pp. 407–414. Tokyo, Japan, September 1–5.

Henderson, J. A., and Card, S. (1986). Rooms: The use of multiple virtual workspaces to reduce space contention in a window-based graphical user interface. *ACM Transactions on Graphics (TOG)* 5 (3): 211–243.

Kaptelinin, V. (1996). Computer-mediated activity: Functional organs in social and developmental contexts. In Nardi, B. (ed.), *Context and Consciousness: Activ-*

*ity Theory and Human–Computer Interaction,* pp. 45–68. Cambridge, Mass.: MIT Press.

Leont'ev, A. N. (1978). *Activity, Consciousness, and Personality.* Englewood Cliffs, N. J.: Prentice-Hall.

MacIntyre, B., Mynatt, E. D., Voida, S., Hansen, K. M., Tullio, J., and Corso, G. M. (2001). Support for multitasking and background awareness using interactive peripheral displays. In *Proceeding of ACM User Interface Software and Technology 2001 (UIST01),* pp. 11–14. Orlando, Florida, November 11–14.

Munoz, M., Rodriguez, M., Favela, J., Gonzalez, V., and Martinez-Garcia, A. (2003). Context-aware mobile communication in hospitals. *IEEE Computer* 36 (8): 60–67.

Norman, D. A. (2000). *The Invisible Computer: Why Good Products Can Fail, the Personal Computer Is So Complex, and Information Appliances Are the Solution.* Cambridge, Mass.: MIT Press.

Norman, D. A., and Draper, S. (eds.) (1986). *User-Centered System Design.* Hillsdale, N.J.: Lawrence Erlbaum.

O'Conaill, B., and Frohlich, D. (1995). Timespace in the workplace: Dealing with interruptions. In *Proceedings of the SIGCHI Conference on Human Factors in Computing Systems*, pp. 262–263. Denver, Colorado, May 7–11.

Pinelle, D., and Gutwin, C. (2002). Groupware walkthrough: Adding context to groupware usability evaluation. In *Proceedings of the SIGCHI Conference on Human Factors in Computing Systems*, pp. 455–462. Minneapolis, Minnesota, April 20–25.

Robertson, G., Dantzich, M. van, Robbins, D., Czerwinski, M., Hinckley, K., Risden, K., Thiel, D., and Gorokhovsky, V. (2000). The Task Gallery: A 3D window manager. In *Proceedings of the SIGCHI Conference on Human Factors in Computing Systems (CHI '00)*, pp. 494–501. The Hague, The Netherlands, April 1–6.

Rouncefield, M., Viller, S., Hughes, J., and Rodden, T. (1995). Working with constant interruption: CSCW and the small office. *Information Society* 11 (4): 173–188.

Smith, G., Baudisch, P., Robertson, G. G., Czerwinski, M., Meyers, B., Robbins, D., Horvitz, E., and Andrews, D. (2003). Groupbar: The taskbar evolved. In *Proceedings of OZCHI 2003*. Brisbane, Australia, November 26–28.

Sousa, J. P., and Garlan, D. (2002). Aura: An architectural framework for user mobility in ubiquitous computing environments. In *Proceeding of the 3rd Working IEEE/IFIP Conference on Software Architecture.* Montreal, Canada, August 25–30.

Suchman, L. (1987). *Plans and Situated Actions: The Problem of Human-Machine Communication.* Cambridge: Cambridge University Press.

Wertsch, J. (1985). *Vygotsky and the Social Formation of Mind.* Cambridge, Mass.: Harvard University Press.

# IV

# Reflections on the Desktop Metaphor and Integration

# Introduction to Part IV

Part IV, the last part of the book, focuses on two general issues related to the desktop metaphor and the design of integrated digital work environments. One of these issues, discussed in the chapter by Ravasio and Tscherter, is how users understand and interpret the desktop metaphor. The metaphor is oriented toward different categories of people involved in the analysis, design, and use of computer systems, including researchers, designers, and users. Of all these categories users are arguably the most important target audience for the metaphor, but surprisingly little is known about how they, as opposed to the other categories, understand and employ the metaphor. Another issue considered in part IV is that of general approaches to the integration of work environments. Can integration be accomplished by extending one particular application until it allows users to carry out all types of tasks? This question is discussed in the chapter by Kaptelinin and Boardman.

The discussion in the chapter by Ravasio and Tscherter is based on empirical studies conducted by the authors. The aim of the studies was to understand the "theories" users develop in their everyday work in environments based on the desktop metaphor. Through observations and interviews the researchers discovered a number of conceptual problems emerging in the everyday use of modern computer technologies and their integration in physical office environments. The origins of the problems can be traced to difficulties with understanding very basic things about how desktop systems work. The authors provide numerous examples of how the desktop metaphor breaks down and prevents people from using some of the available functionality of computer technologies. In particular, it was found that less experienced users were often not aware that the desktop was a part of the file system and can be used to store files and folders.

The chapter illustrates the importance of combining design-based research with empirical studies on the use of existing technologies. Empirical analysis of actual problems and work practices of people who use these technologies can reveal problems located in the blind spots of studies conducted with novel technologies and advanced users. For instance, as presented in the chapter, the perspective of "common users" (who are not necessarily technology experts) on critical system features can be quite different from that of researchers or designers. Therefore, it is important to check novel design ideas against the concerns of the target end users.

In the second chapter of part IV, Kaptelinin and Boardman differentiate between two approaches to integrating work environments: (a) application-centric integration, that is, creating a "mega-application" that allows users to work with different types of information objects; and (b) workspace-level integration, which supports the coordinated use of multiple applications within a unified workspace. An example of an application-centric integration is adding functionality to email to transform it into a general-purpose task-management environment. The chapter discusses strengths and weaknesses of such a development for email and provides arguments in favor of an alternative to application-centric integration, a workspace-level support for integration of several tools. Two systems developed by the authors, UMEA and WorkspaceMirror, are presented to illustrate the notion of workspace-level integration.

# 9

# Users' Theories of the Desktop Metaphor, or Why We Should Seek Metaphor-Free Interfaces

Pamela Ravasio and Vincent Tscherter

## The Desktop's Ups and Downs

Thirty years after its invention, the desktop metaphor—the metaphor par excellence to facilitate access to an integrated digital work environment—still represents the standard portal to current mainstream systems. At least commercially, alternatives are virtually nonexistent—perhaps with exception of PalmOS for PDAs. At its start, the desktop metaphor was intended to simplify poorly structured but common tasks and operations practiced by office workers (Johnson et al. 1989). Over the years, however, personal computers were introduced into areas with no relation to traditional office work, and with even less obvious routines to be supported. The desktop was adapted accordingly in order to keep pace with these developments. Consequently, many problems encountered today by users of commercial digital work environments stem from an overly concrete metaphor that no longer complies (and possibly never did) with the rules of the real world from which it originated. Despite or maybe because of updated desktop versions, personal computers nowadays still do not live up to the flexibility, powerfulness, and seamlessly integrated working procedures once formulated for the Dynabook (Kay and Goldberg 1977) that are claimed to have become reality.[1]

### Motivation and Aims of This Chapter

While a solid base of knowledge dealing with users' requirements for desktop-like systems exists, important issues still remain to be addressed. For example, outstanding issues include that (1) little is known about the use of the screen real estate; (2) so far, work environments have been regarded as a collection of individual components and not as an integrated whole whose aim is to support work activities; and (3) consequently, only selected issues have been addressed in the design and development of novel systems, which, again, have been pursued in almost complete exclusion from one another. Accordingly, our aims for this chapter are the following:

*First*—to provide knowledge on the use of the actual desktop, that is, the screen real estate, in the context of work practices. As the screen real estate is the entry portal to current systems, it is the most visible representative facility of a system and, notably, a decidedly user-owned area. However, thus far little information is known about this area, which, from our point of view, makes it necessary to fill this gap.

*Second*—to provide insights on how user experiences in the physical work environment "office" and the electronic work environment "desktop system" relate to and depend on one another.

The two environments have often been looked at as two sides of the same coin in that they complement and support each other in users' efforts to work with and organize information and together they comprise a whole. Nonetheless, unlike a typical coin, one of the environments is weighted more heavily than the other. Normally the physical office still serves as the primary environment as it is more heavily relied on and is therefore seen as the reference base for the other. After all, a large part of the goal for desktop computers was to become a fullfledged electronic version of the physical office. While this position might have been useful at the start of "desktop" computers, current computers can do more than merely reproduce the goals of the physical office, and can open new doorways to work with information and to the tools needed to manage it. Accordingly, it seems relevant to identify how the two environments compare and influence one another. For instance, with the emergence of reliable indexing mechanisms, some users started to store their information in a "pool" rather than hierarchically. Additionally, a significant portion of users have followed a "keep everything—you never know" strategy when collecting and storing information. These approaches were unthinkable in the past in the physical office environment.

These two approaches necessarily lead to the question of why research achievements thus far have had little or no impact on commercial systems. Although this is a question without any definite answer, we will try to analyze aspects of the issue that may be part of the answer. Therefore, this chapter revolves around the following central questions:

- What can we learn in general from users' work with present commercial systems? How can this knowledge influence the development of novel future systems? (Section entitled "Practices, Problems, and Desktop Systems")
- Given that from the users' perspective, integrated digital work environments are the electronic counterparts to physical offices, does this relationship lead to possibly unwanted mutual influences between the physical and the electronic "office"? (Section entitled "The Cohabitation of the Physical and the Electronic Office")
- What can be said generally that is relevant with respect to design issues for future developments of integrated digital work environments? (Section entitled "Design Approaches")

We address these questions by reporting on results from two different studies of ours (Ravasio, Guttormsen-Schär, and Krueger 2004; Ravasio 2004) and by discussing and concluding on the subsequent implications for ongoing work on future desktop systems.

**Background: A Brief History of the Use of Desktop Systems**

In an attempt to determine relevant requirements for electronic office information systems, Malone (1983) investigated physical, paper-based offices. He indicated that in addition to the commonly known files and folders, "piles" existed as a manner of organizing information quickly and informally. Malone also pointed out four problematic issues that were addressed repeatedly in systems in the subsequent decades, such as those represented in this book:

*Users prefer spatial over logical classification* Vicente, Hayes, and Williges (1987) proved that people with low spatial ability suffer from orientation problems in hierarchical file systems. The value of spatial layout (and therefore also classification) for knowledge work, that is, the development and acquisition of knowledge, was discussed by Kidd (1994).

*Access to information occurs normally by several attributes* Kwasnik (1991) showed that (physical) document classification depended not only on document attributes (i.e., the author, the title, etc.), but more importantly, on situational factors (context). As a result of her study, she also compiled a list of context-dependent categories along which her subjects classified personal documents. Barreau (1995) repeated the study for the personal computer (instead of the physical office) and found that ordering strategies were similar in electronic and physical offices. The amount of results dealing with searching the local system has turned out to be rather limited. The topic has so far only been touched by Barreau and Nardi (Barreau and Nardi 1995; Nardi and Barreau 1997), while the remaining work has concentrated on the traditional type of information retrieval (e.g., Bates 1979; Sutcliffe, Ennis, and Watkinson 2000).

*Information can rarely be classified unambiguously into a single category* Kaptelinin (1996) examined organization strategies that users applied within file systems in more detail, particularly those in place for project work. He noted the following problematic issues: (1) the lack of user support to track down and plan personal activities; (2) the lack of a facility for the support of temporary file configurations; and (3) the inability of the system's file information to recreate its context. Once personal computers had finally become widespread and the Internet accessible to untrained, "average" users, a total of 22 users were interviewed by Barreau (1995) and Nardi, Anderson, and Erickson (1995) in a study that addressed computer working practices. They concluded that (Barreau and Nardi 1995; Nardi and Barreau 1997) there were three generic types of information: ephemeral, working, and archived. Not only in physical offices, but also in electronic offices, file placement had an important reminder function. Information collections were in general not well maintained; and manual search procedures were favored over reluctantly used built-in search tools. They were also able to show that the hierarchical file system and its naming mechanisms were used to engrave reminders for later "orientation."

*Classification is a hard task* The acts of information acquisition and classification, respectively, are to some extent the beginning and the end of many activities in personal information spaces (Landsdale 1988). Nevertheless, they have so far been investigated only to a limited extent. In the same context, Abrahams et al. (Abrahams and Baecker 1997; Abrahams, Baecker, and Chignell 1998) analyzed the use of bookmarks. Their results correlate with Malone's in that they noticed the problems involved when labeling or managing the semantic organization, and that bookmarks also served as mnemonic devices to remember sequences of browsing sessions. Furthermore, they stated that most users thought of the information available on the web as divided into "my bookmarks" and "the cloud of unmapped sources."

Through dedicated research on email, Pliskin (1989), Whittaker and Sidner (1996), and Bälter (1997) managed to define a range of different email user categories: prioritizers, archivers, no-filers, spring-cleaners, frequent-filters, and folderless cleaners. More recently, Ducheneaut and Bellotti (2001) showed that email was a so-called habitat, that is, a facility used to accomplish and organize a wide range of professional and private activities.

In our own investigations, we studied the use of the desktop itself (i.e., the screen real estate) and tried to identify the range of problems users encountered in their daily work with computers (Ravasio, Guttormsen-Schär, and Krueger 2004). The insights gained were incorporated into the development of an interface prototype (Ravasio et al. 2003) and into a study that analyzed the mutual influences of the physical and the electronic office on one another during the acts of document classification and retrieval (Ravasio 2004). The following sections present a selection of insights, experiences, and reflections drawn from these studies.

Together, the information allows us to observe that computers have indeed changed office-based working processes in a variety of ways. Nevertheless, offices still remain "paper-based" (Whittaker and Hirschberg 2001).

## Practices, Problems, and Desktop Systems

Desktop systems support activities ranging from information acquisition to its classification, the usage and thereby compilation of new information, and finally, the information's classification. While support for the actual working tasks is left to individual applications, there are basic activities that need to be supported by the environment itself, that is, *not* by third-party software. Among these activities are the organization and retrieval of locally stored pieces of information, annotating and commenting, reviewing, and also versioning. We investigated the following two related questions within this context (Ravasio, Guttormsen-Schär, and Krueger 2004): (1) How is the so-called electronic desktop actually perceived, and for what is it used? and (2) Why do *users* consider the classification and retrieval of their own information to be difficult?

To answer these questions, we conducted 16 semi-structured interviews following guidelines. All of the interviews took place at the interviewees' work spaces in their familiar working environments. Interview questions were asked while the interviewees sat in front of their computers, with a video camera positioned to an interviewee's right, in order to capture the voices of both the interviewee and interviewer. The group of interview candidates comprised 12 Windows and 4 Macintosh computer users: 5 researchers (from the fields of health at work, visual perception, electrical engineering, and augmented reality), 2 research managers who also had lecturing duties, 2 business managers, 2 secretaries, 2 students, 1 full-time lecturer, 1 teacher, 1 programmer; the group consisted of 7 males and 9 females. The subsequent sections discuss the answers we found to the two aforementioned questions.

**The Screen Real Estate's Use**

As originally conceived, the actual desktop represents a user-owned area par excellence. Technically, though, it is just another folder within the file system that has some special properties, including its display in the screen real estate using spatial arrangements. The use of such a strong metaphor as a desktop not only offers the opportunity to adapt it to the users' needs and tastes, but more importantly, it allows for low- and medium-skilled users to progress quickly with their own system. However, this original intention does not correspond with the present situation as we observed that the use of the screen real estate depended strongly on the users' skills. Low-skilled users were not aware that the screen plane could be used as location for data storage and that it eventually would form part of the file system. Medium- and high-skilled users, on the other hand, employed the desktop consciously and quite extensively for their purposes and adjusted it according to their working needs. Therefore, skill remains an important criterion in handling this interface well and efficiently.

Nonexpert users also felt repeatedly irritated by the similarities in functionality between their folder hierarchy and the desktop, and they were surprised that simple actions had different effects from what they had expected. One medium-skilled user, for example, dragged his whole "My Documents" folder hierarchy (left side of the Windows Explorer) to the desktop, thinking this would allow him to gain an overview of the tree's *hierarchical structure only*. However, as he dragged the hierarchical tree to the desktop he eventually noticed, of course, that this action resulted in *moving* the *entire* hierarchy, including its content, to the desktop. A fact that contributed to this irritation is the system's misuse of the screen real estate for its own purposes—be it the storage of shortcuts to newly installed programs or the display of reminders of system activities (e.g., the tray) without an explicit requirement by the user. Typically, users did not dare to interfere and throw an unwanted item away, thinking that otherwise needed resources (such as the application to which there is a referring shortcut) would "magically" disappear from the computer.

Both medium- and high-skilled users employed the screen real estate first and foremost as *temporary* storage location. To serve this goal, the screen real estate was organized by each individual user in patterns that were intended to support his or her fast visual orientation (figures 9.1 and 9.2). The patterns themselves took the shape of simple geometric forms such as squares, circles, and so forth, and were organized by document

**Figure 9.1**
On this expert PC user's screen, different kinds of geometric shapes are distinguishable, as are groups sorted by file format and use. For instance, a square of program shortcuts is visible in the lower left corner and in the lower right corner is a collection of batch file shortcuts. The Windows taskbar is located to the left, since the (right hand) mouse can then be "thrown" at it, and causes less physical effort to complete a task.

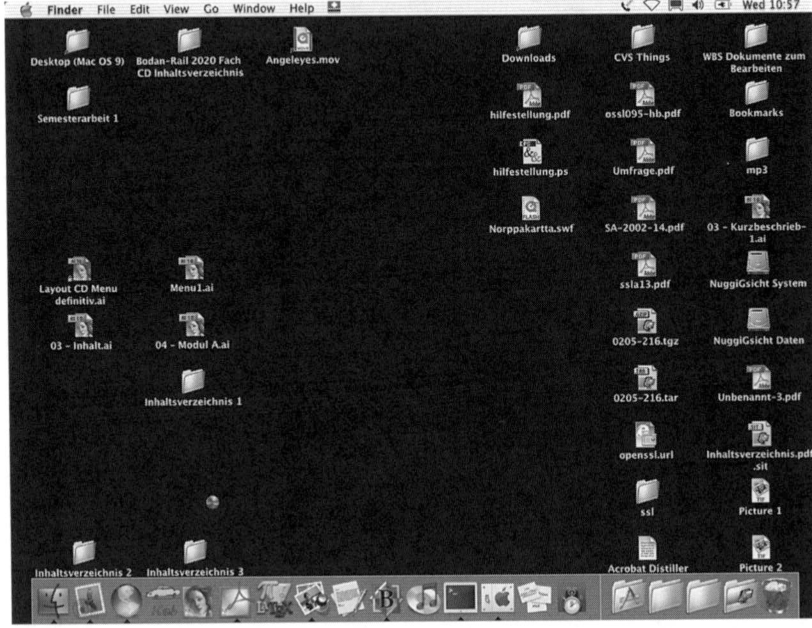


**Figure 9.2**
This expert Mac user has customized the "Dock" by adding folder shortcuts to it. He also uses a spatial arrangement of documents and folders that provides efficient access to frequently used resources.

type, topic, and so on. Proximity represented a topic-wise or type-wise relationship. Since the desktop served as temporary storage, it also became crowded over time and needed to be cleaned up or reorganized occasionally. Once a desktop was reorganized, its content was sorted out along the following three criteria: (1) temporary information remained on it; (2) information useful in the long run was filed away to "archive" folders; and (3) working information was either filed into folders containing ongoing work or reorganized on the desktop at a special location. Again, these criteria comply with the three generic types of information already found by Barreau and Nardi (1995).

Spatial arrangement was sometimes relied upon even within the hierarchically structured folders of the file system. In particular, it was relied upon as long as the total amount of stored information and the amount stored in each individual folder did not seem too large from the individual's point of view. For instance, some users knew that a particular folder within an opened Explorer window would be the second from the top or the third from the left in the second row from the bottom.

Overall, we agree with the critique articulated by Halasz and Moran (1982) that concrete metaphors—in this case the desktop—do not help novices to come to terms with computers. Still, we think the critique extends to all but expert users of computer systems. The mental model induced by a metaphor—the desktop—can hardly compare to its real-world counterpart of the physical office. Average users are not in a situation to judge how technical and other requirements affect the metaphor's correspondence with its counterpart. As a result, it is at least as hard for novices to learn the conventions of this mixture of conforming and non-conforming features in addition to the functionality of the computer itself. More advanced users have memorized these differences, but this fact does not help them to actually "understand" the system on which they are working. For them, learning is coupled with continuing to memorize even more conventions.

## Classification and Retrieval

While a physical office allows for a variety of ways to achieve tasks of classification and retrieval of information, the hierarchical folder structure and the possibility of naming files and folders reduce this variety to an indispensable minimum. This lack of flexibility makes it very difficult for the user to leave his or her marks of acquired and tacit knowledge that will serve to allow for tracking down specific pieces of information in the future. Therefore, users necessarily invest a fair amount of effort in order to define, organize, and maintain these hierarchies, and to transfer as much knowledge as possible. Hence, they invest their efforts into the one place where, in *their* opinion, the knowledge cannot be lost and will be retrievable: the folder hierarchy and its naming schema.

Nonetheless, the problematic issues with respect to organization start even before a physical office space or a computer comes into play. These issues are prominent in the educational setting; for example, for teachers introducing novices to the use of computers, one of the most difficult hurdles (Reichmuth 2004) is that for some, neither offices nor computers assist in organization. These users think about information or documents so differently that the kind of structured organization required in either of these environments does not mean anything to them.

Organizational efforts go hand in hand with efforts to archive important resources. Here, the aim is to guarantee the "constant" access to relevant sources (web pages, articles, reports, but also picture, sound, and video material, etc.) even when the web service in question may be down. Therefore, users try to make their information accessible for themselves by storing it locally. Likewise, their archive embodies a library role for them: It is seen as a collection of results and products that in turn can be reused directly without amendments, or alternatively, serve as reference material.

However, archives are useful only if they contain pure essentials and are not scattered with outdated, obsolete, or irrelevant material. For this reason, maintenance turned out to be a serious activity performed regularly by medium and advanced users. Maintenance guarantees that only valuable reminders and pieces of information that have not lost their relevance are kept while the rest is sorted out as soon as it becomes obsolete. Typically, maintenance was performed at project "milestones," when useful and important resources (e.g., the actual results and the relevant documentation) were kept while the rest was discarded. The ages of archived (i.e., nonworking) files were found to range roughly from six months to eight years, with diminishing quantities in older parts of the archives. The latter fact supports the finding that maintenance is not only performed, but that older parts of the archive are cleaned up repeatedly over the years, until they were found to consist of "pure essentials." Occasionally, we saw that older or very voluminous parts of an archive were outsourced to external storage media such as DVD, and subsequently "stored" on physical shelf space.

While the aim of *classification* is to engrave knowledge on the file system in order to create and leave hints so that information is findable again, its counterpart *retrieval* consists of the development of strategies that try to decipher these hints in order to reacquire the information previously stored away. It is important to note that retrieval within the local system is always an attempt to find information that is known to be there because it was handled at some point in the past; this is in contrast to web search tools or database retrieval tools that aim at retrieving a closest, previously unknown, match to information, given some specific criteria. This contrast could be one plausible explanation as to why built-in search tools are used only reluctantly—it is not a "closest match" that users are seeking, but rather a 100 percent hit.

Additionally, it seems that the use of search tools is cognitively demanding because the search criteria ("fields") employed are not those that people habitually use as they think, act on, and remember pieces of information during working activities. Consequently, search tool results tend to be poor. Based on these experiences, users end up favoring manual search. At the same time, this is to them a way to brush up their knowledge of their personally engraved organization, with no more (cognitive) effort than using the tool.

The following is the final question to be answered in this context: What do information-access procedures look like from different users' perspectives? In our study, all interviewees searched by accessing their categories directly as a first choice. As a next step, the interviewees reviewed all of their folders one by one, in a logical order, giving priority to folders that may contain the file in question, though without consulting each individual file contained therein. If at this point the specific piece of information had not yet been found, the interviewees finally proceeded to check all files in the folders in question, manually and individually. If the search was not successful up to this point, the procedure was restarted at the first step.

**Problematic issues** Classification and retrieval of information require tremendous cognitive effort. While an immediate solution to this problem is not within sight (though there are some promising developments; see, e.g., Copernic Technologies 2004), it is clear that efforts are needed to reduce this load. One cause that intensifies the cognitive load is the system-sided separation of the various information classes, such as bookmarks, emails, and files. Users think of their data as one single body of information. The existent separation increases the difficulty of filing pieces of information and finding them again. It is necessary to reunite *all* user-owned data at a single storage location within the environment with a simple storage mechanism that allows and supports the user creating and engraving relationships between pieces of information in accordance with his or her thought process. However, such a linkage mechanism must not consist simply of "hyper-linking" information (which would mean potentially linking everything with everything else—an approach known to have a devastating effect on a person's orientation capabilities [Conklin 1987]), but would rather aim at joining items that belong together *from the user's point of view.*

There is even less support for automatically compacting or summarizing personal information collections and archives, let alone for sharing information resources or working with them collaboratively. However, this fact results in the central advantage that maintenance activities, typically relocating and discarding pieces of information, are extremely easy tasks to perform, with hardly any inherent problems. If information were related to other information within the system (or even worse, at remote locations) through sharing or collaboration, "deleting" would no longer be a trivial issue. The situation would be even worse if different versions of a document were taken into account for the definition of the relations between various pieces of information.

While present commercial systems are primarily content-oriented (i.e., focusing on the actual information encapsulated in a specific document), working with a PC can also be task-oriented (focused on the task to be accomplished) or context-oriented (focused on various documents, programs, and tasks at hand concurrently). Since a user switches continuously between working modes, equal support must be provided for each mode. However, regardless of whether the activities on a PC system are looked at from a task-, context-, or content-oriented point of view, they can be assigned to one of three alternating phases, namely: (1) information acquisition from either local or remote sources; (2) actual work consisting of handling and transforming information previously acquired; and finally (3) the reclassification of both the original resources as well as the work's product (Landsdale 1988). While the act of information classification is supported by the environment itself, support for information acquisition as well as ongoing ("transforming") work is primarily outsourced to application programs. As a consequence, the system side and the application side need to be looked at in almost sheer exclusivity from one another.

Because of the desktop's focus on document management, support for ongoing work activities is almost nonexistent. For instance, the environment offers hardly any commenting, annotation, versioning, or global user-friendly search facility. Built-in search tools are typically based on metadata and, until today, have remained hardly appreciated by the average user. Since there is technically no way around working with metadata in retrieval tools, we would need to know how "user-friendly" metadata would look and its makeup in order to truly advance in the direction of system-sided support for automatic searching as well as for linkage or classification.

The work users complete within their systems is normally directly related to situational aspects (context) of immediate filing or accessing a piece of information. It is at this point that, no matter how well designed strategies for system-sided support for content- or task-oriented work may be, they are seriously challenged as soon as contextual issues enter the field. Context is something that can be foreseen or structured only with much difficulty, if at all. Therefore, the goal must be to design handy, easy-to-use, "on-the-fly" procedures that enable and support actual users to "reveal" their perception of context.

**Practices and Problems: Conclusion**

By original design, the desktop is a user-owned area. It should be a place where users, and *only* users, are able to engrave personal preferences and tastes, and the system should by no means misuse the area—including by way of installer routines that store shortcuts on it! The implications of how medium- and high-skilled users may *own* the screen real estate is apparent in figure 9.1. The particular user depicted in figure 9.1 not only ordered icons and documents according to criteria best suited for the work at hand, but also included a personal photograph to decorate the desktop's background.

Current commercial desktop systems are still designed primarily for document management. Support for the *act of thinking*, the compilation or generation of new information, is not its aim. Consequently, support for this act within the core system itself is rudimentary, and normally delegated to application programs. It is up to each user to get something out of a collection of individual documents and the range of third-party applications that he or she uses. While this may make sense from a *task-oriented* point of view, it barely helps the fact that without suitable comprehensive support available independent of specific applications, individual pieces of information eventually remain just that: isolated isles of knowledge. Specifically, this in turn means that a truly context-oriented view of a user's information is a "mission impossible."

It is important to keep in mind that users are aware that the value of a collection of pieces of information is larger than the sum of the values of each individual piece. However, they are also aware that the additional benefit in the form of implicit relations and *tacit knowledge* exists solely "in their brain," that is, that it is not contained either in the individual piece of information, within the collection in its entirety, or in the system. Experience tells them that at some point the system is not of much help to *get* informed in order to produce results.

The ultimate goal is to bring information-handling "closer" to the user. For instance, instead of separating pieces of user information into different parts of the whole system, they should become integrated, both with respect to their storage location as well as with respect to the representation of their overall value. Nevertheless, the resources manipulated by the system and those manipulated by the user must be separated from one another in such a way that the former does not interfere with the latter (and also vice versa for average users).

Finally, any kind of support that will help to engrave tacit and acquired knowledge into the permanent structures of the user's information organization, which may be reusable by both applications and services when needed, is useful and appreciated. Small, useful facilities have the potential for high impact: Annotations, versioning, format conversion, easy-to-use search, and so on are examples that we have mentioned. Many more could be conceived, especially if collaborative issues are also taken into account, which we have left out entirely throughout this chapter. Still, what can be learned from existing facilities is that as long as their use implies as much cognitive or physical effort as doing the same task by hand, these facilities will simply not be used.

## The Cohabitation of the Physical and the Electronic Office: Results of a Qualitative Experiment

Since the use of computers has become increasingly widespread, more paper than ever before is being consumed in printouts, books, reports, and so forth (Sellen and Harper 2002). This raises the question of whether the physical office *still* serves above all as the primary reference for orientation on how to handle its virtual counterpart, the desktop computer, and whether as a consequence the physical and the virtual offices influence each other mutually.

In a qualitative experiment (Ravasio 2004),[2] we investigated the basic procedures of "office" work after having filtered out the individual's personal context. Two groups of ten participants each were presented with either an unfamiliar office (i.e., a real office belonging to somebody else) or with an unfamiliar computer organization (i.e., an image copy of a computer really in use). The participants were of the following backgrounds: 4 computer scientists, 1 PC supporter, 7 students (2 business, 1 linguistics, 1 psychology, 3 environmental science), 1 electrical engineer, 1 physiotherapist, 1 chemist, 1 manager, 1 psychologist, 1 lawyer, 2 secretaries.

Two sets of documents had previously been extracted from each of the environments. During the experiment, the participants were then initially asked to search for the first set of documents, and later to classify the second set within the environment to which they had been assigned.

Our aim was to extract the average user's principles (document descriptors, tactics, and rules) applied in information orientation and handling, and to see if these showed a dependence or influence from one office environment onto the other respective environment. Each user session was videotaped, the tapes transcribed and subsequently evaluated, and were manually counterchecked by two individuals based on a previously generated codebook.

The next section provides a closer look at the issue of mutual influences of the two office environments on each other in light of the results we obtained in this qualitative experimental study.

## The Art of Office Organization

In a physical office that belongs to another person, users are apparently able to orient themselves almost at "first sight" and locate needed documents quickly—a phenomenon on which our participants each commented independently during our experiment. As matter of fact, in the setting of the unfamiliar (physical) office, we were able to observe that the participants indeed appeared to have an understanding of its organization after merely a few minutes. There seemed to exist conventions, or a "quiet understanding," about typical storage locations specific to a range of different types of information and documents.

The same "quiet understanding" did not seem to exist in the electronic world—either with respect to the organization of the file system nor to the screen plane. Here, a continuous effort to infer and draw conclusions about the logical whereabouts of a piece of information was noticeable. Widely understandable clues or conventions were either entirely absent or represented unsatisfactorily, so that the users' needs, expectations, and goals were not met. Occasionally, clues and hints drawn from the physical office were used, such as number-coding or color-coding folders. Still, these approaches failed in their intended purpose to engrave or "externalize" one's own organizational structure and to make it comprehensible to other persons as well as to a "future self."

Therefore, to some extent, users tried to use similar, sometimes even identical, conventions, structures, and procedures to organize both of their working environments (i.e., the physical office and the electronic file system). In our experiment, this became apparent when comparing the tactics and rules the participants applied in each of the environments while classifying or retrieving documents, and in crosschecking them with the users' own comments on their proceedings. However, the users' intents often did not work out as expected, which caused them visible confusion in that they could not identify a reason for the failure; it was therefore neither clear to them how the confusion could have been avoided nor what alternative approaches might have been. It is here that a range of fundamental conceptual differences between the two environments manifested in the way the participants proceeded and organized themselves. We were able to prove this fact by comparing the transcripts of actions and statements from the two environments.

Our experimental comparison revealed that many organizational concepts and ideas have been mutually absorbed from one of the environments into the other. We conclude that owing to its physical nature, in the real-life office environment the limitations and drawbacks, but also the benefits, of these "adoptions" became apparent to computer novices and experts alike. In the electronic environment of a computer, however, only experts were able to judge the implications. The lack of conceptual knowledge led novices and medium-skilled users rapidly to accept incorrect assumptions, which in turn caused them to have fundamental problems in their organizational habits and procedures with their computers.

Organization in a physical office is eventually a middle course in usefulness between searching and filing activities and the particular individuals needs. Mainstream computer systems implicitly assume that their users store documents and pieces of information according to the same concepts and ideas (criteria) as they apply to retrieve them. This assumption, however, is incorrect. The differences we found between the act of classification and retrieval were decidedly more distinct than the differences found between the two "office" environments. Furthermore, the weak but existing support for user work within mainstream system cores is restricted to the area of information organization and inherently leads a user to focus on optimal filing. Indeed, searching on a computer is a far more demanding task than filing, extremely error-prone and cognitively very difficult. Consequently, existing personal, but probably also collaborative, document- and information-management systems belong entirely to the group of systems that are intended for "good" classification; this has a devastating effect on individual productivity owing to failed retrieval attempts. This also raises the fundamental question of whether, for instance, existing information- and document-management systems (both personal and collaborative) are as suitable and productivity enhancing as they were expected to be when designed, implemented, and rolled out to consumers.

**Mutual Influences: A Meta-Reflection**

A metaphor is "a figure [of speech] in which a word or phrase is applied to an object or action that it does not literally denote in order to imply a resemblance" (Collins and Co. Ltd. 1998). Therefore, it is not surprising that the individual understanding of the metaphoric figure and its real-life counterpart manifest a mutual influence. Although the metaphor and its real-life counterpart do not resemble each other in depth, the relationship between the two may have only few inherent problems. Nevertheless, if the metaphor is used to explain the details of its real-life counterpart, the belief in an intuitive "natural" approach that completely relies on previous experiences and knowledge necessarily leads to misunderstandings. A metaphor by definition represents only a *part* of a whole, not the full details.

A somewhat similar mechanism applies if the electronic organization of information is the focus of attention. Users try to reuse the same strategies that are valid in the physical office in the context of the electronic world, regardless of whether or not they are actually suitable and applicable. Therefore, an influence of the physical organization of an office on the electronic organization of the hierarchical file system at this point seems only plausible.

On the other hand, the younger generation of users in particular also has extensive experiences in the electronic environment, and has developed strategies that serve well in this context. In this scenario a practice transfer to the physical office also seems to be plausible.

It certainly can be said that the organization of the physical office also suffers from drawbacks and is not itself the ultimate solution to the issue of information organization. That is why, for instance, libraries do not function according to these approaches, but require specialized personnel and procedures. Moreover, the understanding of clues embedded in a personal environment changes over time since the immediate working situation (context) of a person evolves. Clues embedded in the physical office are generally coarser (i.e., less precise) than those embedded in the electronic office and thereby less affected by changes in the office owner's (working) situation. As a result, they retain their meaning over longer periods of time. On the other hand, clues that are embedded in the hierarchical file organization because they are precise, fine-grained, and closely related to the state of a user's ongoing work lose much of their message over time. This phenomenon *could* mean that given the users' habits and long-term experiences, the physical office may well serve as a point of departure from which to learn better organization by looking at both its advantages and drawbacks.

Admittedly, the impact of the extensive use of a real-life metaphor is hardly foreseeable. The extent to which users may be able to perceive parallels from the metaphor to its real-life counterpart cannot be controlled in its entirety. This gives rise to a potentially huge range of inherent problems founded in this resemblance or dissemblance. Therefore, we think that the application of metaphors is justified only where their use and range of allusions is limited and can be controlled well (such as was the case with the Dynabook, whose designers said that it should be as responsive "as an instrument" [Kay and Goldberg 1977]). Abstract approaches, such as graphs, seem a better option in the long run, since they do not have any inherent significance or thereby predefined functional schemes—at least not to the average user.

Existing mainstream systems represent their original designers' focus; this aim was to facilitate the way information was organized while keeping the fundamental concepts unchanged, without considering what would best serve users other than themselves. Going forward, a different approach is needed: (1) It must be known *what* concept should be supported before identifying *how* to support it; and (2) more effort has to be invested in teaching users how to beneficially use these concepts.

**Design Approaches**

The essence of a personal integrated digital work environment is formed by the user's pieces of information encapsulated within files or records. A user works with his pieces following a wide range of possible working "policies," such as those already identified in research and subsequently listed in this section. The "policies" share the commonality that each supports a particular perspective on the data while the user is organizing working tasks, processes, and procedures, which, again, are driven by his or her basic need to (re-)acquire, process, organize, and (re-)distribute information. Therefore, the success or failure of future systems will depend on how well the different views are integrated with one another. If even a single common goal or task can be accomplished only in a complicated and awkward manner, the system will not be accepted and widely used unless no alternative options (as is presently the case) exist. The integrated digital work environments developed in the past decades represent four different, but complementary policies, or views (figure 9.3):

*Content-centered view* These systems focus on optimizing the user-related system behavior with respect to content, that is, documents and other pieces of information. Examples are the MIT Semantic File System (Gifford et al. 1991), Haystack (Adar, Karger, and Stein 1999), Presto (Dourish et al. 1999), Stuff I've Seen (Dumais et al. 2003), and Microsoft's WinFS system (Microsoft, Inc. 2004).

*Task-centered view* These systems' focus lies on the activities performed in order to achieve work goals. Documents are just one of several tools and resources required in order to achieve the task. Systems that fall into this category include Task Gallery (Robertson et al. 2000), UMEA (Kaptelinin 2003), Soylent (Fisher and Dourish 2004), and Contact Map (Nardi et al. 2001).

*Context-centered view* In such a system, the influence of situational issues and past actions on the present goals and activities of an individual user are addressed by the concept of personal role management

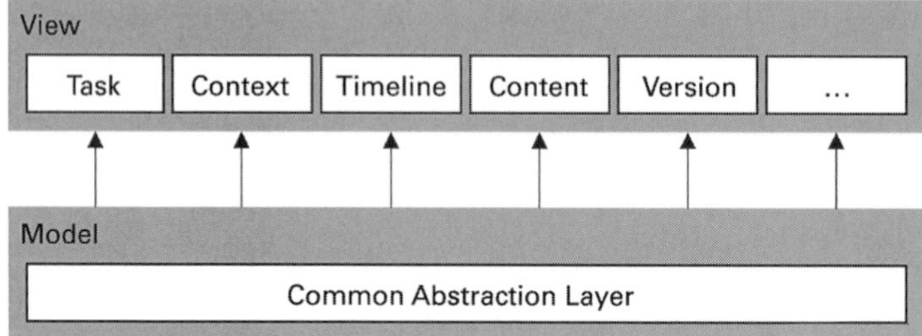


**Figure 9.3**
Known approaches represent one of several possible views of basically the same system. However, missing so far is a common understanding and the definition of what the underlying abstract model of the various views must be.

(Plaisant and Shneiderman 1994) or the Kimura system (Voida, Mynatt, and MacIntyre 2002).

*Time-centered view* In this system, ongoing as well as past and future work can also be naturally represented in a time-lined manner. Lifestreams (Freeman and Fertig 1995) is a state-less concept (i.e., time is used in first place to "line" documents up), while Timescape (Rekimoto 1999) presented us with a stateful approach (i.e., the visual file configurations depend on the point in time of viewing).

Other views could be thought of, such as "collaboration-centered" or "version-centered." While all of these views have in common that they tried to come up with new conceptual ideas for the system's handling and user interface, a common abstract model is so far lacking. Each implementation implicitly defined its respective, proprietary model in sole accordance with the individual view to be realized. This means that one of the central system design questions that remains to be answered is: "Is there such a thing as a common abstract model that can underlie all conceptually possible views? And what would it look like?"

In the past, most if not all developments have tied their user-interaction designs in one way or another to the structures predominant in the technical and physical base of their system core. The desktop metaphor is, while probably the most infamous example, certainly not the only one. However, from a software-engineering point of view, user experience and system core are independent from one another. The core system offers all the desirable power and options needed to design the user experience, but it leaves entirely unaffected the ways in which this happens. In other words: the structures and paradigms inherent in the core system are independent of what the user sees, or is made to experience. Nelson (1990) simply called this the *virtuality* of a computer system.

Several "on-board" tools that will necessarily come along with any future system have been mentioned throughout this book. Many more are currently being developed "out there." In the rest of this chapter, we would like to revisit two of the first-hour "on-board" tools—annotations on the one hand, and desktop search on the other—in order to find out what they already offer and in what direction they will evolve as a consequence of their deficiencies.

**Annotations**

An annotation is "a note added in explanation, etc., of some (esp. literary) work" (Collins and Co. Ltd. 1998). Annotations and comments are tools for work with documents and serve, among other things, as "reminders," highlighting mechanisms, emphasis, and for text correction and review remarks. In principle, one should be able to annotate "everything" within a system (to some extent even recursively, which means annotation can be annotated). They are a user-definable, technically spoken unstructured category of document metadata. Currently, annotations are coupled with a given document or application, usually with both. This implies that annotations are encapsuled within documents and are not generally accessible or useful unless they belong to the document on which work is being done. More particularly, application-specific support for annotations and commenting varies largely and only coincides at a very basic level.

In the foreseeable future, the range of basic annotation and comment types available to the user will not differ greatly from those already in use today; commenting, text highlighting, text underlining and crossing-out, support for "handwritten" remarks and reviewing will remain prevalent. The main difference, however, will be that annotations and comments will be administrated centrally and uniformly from within the environment itself and will be linked to the resource that they describe. Consequently, they will always be handled in the same or at least very similar manner throughout the whole system, independent of the specific application used. This demonstrates how not only "normal" documents can be annotated, but also "special" ones, such as emails, to-do lists, diaries, and even web pages for exclusively personal use. Annotations and comments that exist within a system will be dynamically filterable according to criteria that are understandable and useful to the individual user (i.e., other than is often the case in today's search tools).

In the long run, the user will need to be able to embed his or her tacit knowledge, as well as acquired insights, into the comments and annotations. Decades back, Luhman's file-card box was a tool invented to organize this type of knowledge. How would an electronic counterpart of such a file-card box need to be designed in order to preserve its simplicity and efficiency while still using the advantages computers offer? At this stage, the system would still take care of the most basic services in order to leave them independent of application. However, small tools may exist (and they always will!) to help otherwise repetitive tasks, such as "refactoring" one particular type of comment into finer-grained entities across the whole collection of annotations.

Yet at this point it is important to note that there is a "thin red line" that must not be crossed: Annotations and comments, and their respective handling, must not become yet another inherent metaphor embedded within a larger environment, appearing to be like its real-life counterpart, while still being sufficiently different so as to confuse its users. Therefore, re-creating the physical annotation facility identically and in every detail in an electronic environment is not the goal. The goal must be to offer basic, useful, and valuable *electronic* annotation and commenting facilities that address the users' requirements well.

### Desktop Search

In the past decades, the information collected by each individual person has grown exponentially (Sweeney 2001) and at least at a similar rate as the price for storage per entity has fallen (following Moore's Law [Moore 1965]; Grimm 1998). However, today we are still using the same concept (hierarchies of directories and files) and the same metaphor to organize as well as access both the countless pieces of information stored to our increasingly capacious hard drives and the virtually limitless information accessible on the web. Finding information on the web is not a challenge anymore. Will desktop search solve the problem of retrieving local information and simultaneously make the user's task of classification obsolete?

While classification serves to organize pieces of information and emboss tacit and acquired knowledge on this organization, information access aims to (re-)use existing information in order to pursue specific goals, such as writing reports, by compiling existing information and generating new information. Problems habitually confronted in such situations sound as follows: "I need to write an email to all people who formed part of the project team X back in 1994." Access procedures, as used and enforced by the systems facilities today, do not support a straightforward approach to access the relevant information efficiently.

It is only common sense that any kind of filing will support "overview, context and detail on demand" (Shneiderman 1996). That is, pieces of information and the relationships between them should initially be viewable or perceivable *at a distance*, stressing their embeddedness within the entire collection. Second, a *close-up perspective* should also be viewable that shows all details of the individual piece under exclusion of most contextual aspects and relationships; the exception would be the most fundamental ones that continue to be important for efficient work (such as the reference documents used to compile a report). While this description might sound at first like the description of yet another metaphor—it is not! It merely describes how a user should be able to work with and view his or her data, and what basic facilities would (and should) be available.

However, the questions that arise at this point are: According to what criteria and categories are the relationships between pieces of information built? To what extent and in what way can they be made independent from the preferences of the individual? How can "context" be defined in a way that it is useful to the individual without being either too limited or too broad? If, for instance, relationships are defined through metadata, as is often the case, it is important to know what the "metadata" of a document are from a user's perspective, that is, according to which criteria users create the relationships with which they later work.

Although older information is generally less useful, we think that archives will not entirely disappear because of both personal preferences and the fact that some businesses are legally required to keep them. Particularly for the latter case, if a system is going to be used in a specific application domain such as accounting, it needs to be determined where and to what extent support can happen automatically. Many of the classification and access procedures happen, for instance, through largely standardized routines. Therefore, while organization of personal information is a tricky issue owing to its lack of "obvious" structure, in industry and business applications domain-inherent characteristics may determine organizational procedures. This in turn makes it easier for designers to set up a "useful" system.

Yet another issue will be raised as soon as "versioning" is commonly available. While versioning solves a range of problematic issues inherent in the organization of archived or temporary information, it is questionable whether the partition of user information into the three kinds of information (temporary, working, archived) will be subject to a fundamental change. It is possible that the archive as such will no longer exist explicitly and the physical act of file deletion to maintain an archive will disappear as well (versioning would resolve the problem of potential "dead" links in this context). Still, as in the physical office, temporary and working information will always be actively compiled, while archives will just turn out to be "collections not used for a longer period."

### Design Approaches: Conclusion

A sizable portion of people who use computers out there are low- or medium-skilled users. They have different needs and ideas from those of power users as to what a system should be able to do and how work should be accomplished. In the world of reading and writing, such users would be considered *semiliterates*—they have never truly been taught how to use computers efficiently, but they use them extensively nonetheless. Alan Kay said that:

> One of the problems with the way computers are used in education is that they are most often just an extension of this idea that learning means just learning accepted facts. But what really interests me is using computers to transmit ideas, points of view, ways of thinking. You don't need a computer for this, but just as with a musical instrument, once you get onto this way of using them, then the computer is a great amplifier for learning. (Kay 2003)

We think that the same idea can be applied to the use of computers at work. The computer has been introduced in order to make work, and in particular *office* work, more efficient. However, its use and benefits to fundamentally expand—or change—previously existing possibilities have never become a reality, and the user's "return on investment" efforts will continue to be limited as long as there is a basic lack of knowledge on how to use computers. Using computers is a literacy that has to be taught properly in order to be beneficial. So far, it is clear that efforts to spread this new "literacy" among a wider public have failed.

The pursuit of a "new" metaphor—though of course, we would actually like to get away from metaphors entirely!—has so far followed two directions: (1) Research has explored a range of occasionally radical approaches to come up with novel designs of integrated digital work environments; (2) commercial systems have again followed what can be characterized best as "the way of small enhancements," which unfortunately often resulted in packing even more desirable features into an already overloaded system.

Although the route of small enhancement might not lead to the fundamental paradigm shift needed and aimed at in this context, the idea to start system optimization by improving individual aspects that are perceived as nerve-wracking by average users is not half-bad. In the beginning, such small improvements certainly seem like they are not directly related to problems caused by the desktop metaphor. However, small enhancements offer the opportunity to study users in their working environment, that is, to view their working logic while they are focused on the work to be accomplished. For most people, a computer is still a black box that they handle based on an action-reaction principle without actually knowing or even understanding what exactly is happening behind the curtains. These users, though, are a source of insight and knowledge that has the potential to lead to novel approaches, for it is here that inconsistent (but according to experts and semi-experts, already totally absorbed) inherent conventions manifest their problematic results most clearly. Collaboration with such users will lead to discarding the basic concepts related to the desktop metaphor and to conceiving something that may initially be abstract, but eventually would become more consistent and closer to the users' needs.

The systems described in this book show that a range of well-founded approaches exists. However, the critical point that remains is the often inherent coupling to a real-world metaphor, which will eventually face the same problems as the desktop does owing to encountered inconsistencies with the real office, its physical counterpart. As it is, if the presented concepts and achievements were to be teamed up in an effort to integrate them, one would necessarily have to come up with novel representational ideas, as it is unlikely for one to find them in the real world.

## Concluding Remarks

The desktop metaphor's invention was a result of the idea that computer systems as such are too complicated in nature to be understood by non-expert users, and that therefore something simpler was needed to explain them. This in turn resulted in the following situation: while workstations remained efficient for expert users who are happy only if provided with a command line, the workstations' principles which are not always consistent to an outsider's eye remained unchanged and obscure to average users. Moreover, further inconsistencies were introduced owing to the differences between the real-life counterpart of the interface metaphor and the environment it was intended to explain. The metaphor was an attempt to circumvent the necessity of teaching computer novices the concepts and fundamentals of computing that are required for at least some basic idea of the black box's (that is, the computer's) internal procedures. We would argue that it takes beginners as much or less effort to learn how to handle computers without metaphors, provided that the system itself behaves consistently. The desktop metaphor, in particular, has made assumptions on how we would use computers that have never corresponded with either the system's or the user's realities.

Therefore, the fundamental issue is not to come up with a more clever metaphor in order to better disguise inconvenient system-sided concepts, but to change the concepts themselves. Accordingly, the goal must be to develop an environment that is itself consistent while considering users' ways of working in each individual aspect. Separating the questions of technical concepts and feasibility entirely from considerations as to how working with the system should occur is the first step. Each of these aspects is, at this point, still a challenge in its own rights. This notion is even more enhanced if the consequent collaboration of interface and system designers, software engineers, and actual end-users is taken into account. After all, users' requirements are often inherently or explicitly much more demanding than those with which we ourselves would be content.

## Notes

1. During the work on this chapter Pamela Ravasio and Vincent Tscherter were post-doctoral researchers at the Swiss Federal Institute of Technology, Zurich, Switzerland.

2. Similar research settings were discussed in McDonald and Schvaneveldt 1988 and have been used in a range of studies, such as Hayhoe 1990; Lohse et al. 1994; and Carlyle 1999. The qualitative experiment was defined for the social sciences in Kleining 1986. A methodical transfer to HCI is discussed in Ravasio, Guttormsen-Schär, and Tscherter 2006.

## References


Abrahams, D., and Baecker, R. (1997). How people use WWW bookmarks. Paper presented at the ACM Conference on Computer–Human Interaction (CHI) 1997.

Abrahams, D., Baecker, R., and Chignell, M. 1998. Information archiving with bookmarks: Personal web space construction and organisation. Paper presented at the ACM Conference on Computer–Human Interaction (CHI) 1998.

Adar, E., Karger, D. R., and Stein, L. (1999). Haystack: Per-user information environment. Paper presented at the 8th International Conference on Information and Knowledge Management (CIKM '99), Kansas City, Missouri.

Bälter, O. (1997). Strategies for organising email messages. Paper presented at the HCI 1997, London.

Barreau, D. K. (1995). Context as a factor in personal information management systems. *Journal of the American Society for Information Science* 46 (5): 327–339.

Barreau, D. K., and Nardi, B. A. (1995). Finding and reminding: File organization from the desktop. *SIGCHI Bulletin* 27 (3):39–43.

Bates, M. J. (1979). Information search tactics. *Journal of the American Society for Information Science* 30 (4): 205–214.

Carlyle, A. 1999. User categorisation of works: Toward improved organisation of online catalogue displays. *Journal of Documentation* 55 (2): 184–208.

Collins and Co. Ltd. (ed.) (1998). *Collins English Dictionary: Millennium Edition* (fourth edition). Glasgow: Harper Collins.

Conklin, J. (1987). Hypertext: An introduction and survey. *IEEE Computer* 20 (9): 17–41.

Copernic Technologies. (2004). Copernic: Software to search, find, and manage information. Retrieved from http://www.copernic.com/en/products/desktop-search/index.html/.

Dourish, P., Edwards, W. K., LaMarca, A., and Salisbury, M. (1999). Presto: An experimental architecture for fluid interactive document space. *ACM Transactions on Computer–Human Interaction* 6 (2): 133–161.

Ducheneaut, N., and Bellotti, V. (2001). Email as a habitat: An exploration of embedded personal information management. *ACM Interactions* 8 (5): 30–38.

Dumais, S., Cutrell, E., Cadiz, J. J., Jancke, G., Sarin, R., and Robbins, D.C. (2003). Stuff I've Seen: A system for personal information retrieval and re-use. Paper presented at the SIGIR 2003, Toronto, Canada.

Fisher, D., and Dourish, P. (2004). Social and temporal structures in everyday collaboration. Paper presented at the Conference on Human Factors and Computing Systems (CHI) 2004, Vienna, Austria.

Freeman, E., and Fertig, S. (1995). Lifestreams: Organizing your electronic life. Paper presented at the AAAI Fall Symposium: AI Applications in Knowledge and Retrieval, Cambridge, Mass.

Gifford, D. K., Jouvelot, P., Sheldon, M. A., and O'Toole, J. W. (1991). Semantic file systems. Paper presented at the 13th ACM Symposium on Operating Systems Principles.

Grimm, B. T. (1998). Price indexes for selected semiconductors, 1974–1996. *Survey of Current Business* 78 (February): 8–24.

Halasz, F., and Moran, T. P. (1982). Analogy considered harmful. Paper presented at the ACM Conference on Computer-Human Interaction (CHI) 1982, Gaithersburg, Maryland.

Hayhoe, D. (1990). Sorting-based menu categories. *International Journal of Man–Machine Studies* 33: 677–705.

Johnson, J., Roberts, T. L., Verplank, W., Smith, D.C., Irby, C. H., Beard, M., and Mackey, K. (1989). The Xerox Star: A retrospective. *IEEE Computer* 22 (9): 11–26.

Kaptelinin, V. (1996). Creating computer-based work environments: An empirical study of Macintosh users. Paper presented at the ACM SIGCPR/SIGMIS '96, Denver, Colorado.

Kaptelinin, V. (2003). UMEA: Translating interaction histories into project context. Paper presented at the ACM Conference on Computer–Human Interaction (CHI) 2003, Ft. Lauderdale, Florida.

Kay, A. (2003). The Dynabook revisited—A conversation with Alan Kay. Online Symposium. The Book & The Computer. Retrieved from http://www.honco.net/os/kay.html/.

Kay, A., and Goldberg, A. (1977). Personal dynamic media. *IEEE Computer* 10 (3): 31–41.

Kidd, A. (1994). The marks are on the knowledge worker. Paper presented at the ACM Conference on Computer–Human Interaction (CHI) 1994, Boston, Mass.

Kleining, G. 1986. Das Qualitative Experiment [The qualitative experiment]. *Kölner Zeitschrift für Soziologie und Sozialpsychologie* 38 (4): 724–750.

Kwasnik, B. H. (1991). The importance of factors that are not document attributes in the organisation of personal documents. *Journal of Documentation* 47 (4): 389–398.

Landsdale, M. (1988). The psychology of personal information management. *Applied Ergonomics* 19 (1): 55–66.

Lohse, G. L., Biolsi, K., Walker, N., and Rueter, H. H. 1994. A classification of visual representation. *Communications of the ACM* 37 (12): 36–49.

Malone, T. W. (1983). How do people organize their desks? Implications for the design of office information systems. *ACM Transactions on Office Information Systems* 1 (1): 99–112.

McDonald, J. E., and Schvaneveldt, R. W. (1988). The application of user knowledge to interface design. In Guindon, R. (ed.), *Cognitive Science and Its Application for Human–Computer Interaction,* pp. 289–338. Hillsdale, N. J.: Lawrence Erlbaum.

Microsoft, Inc. (2004). The Windows File System. Microsoft. Retrieved from http://msdn.microsoft.com/Longhorn/understanding/pillars/winfs.htm/.

Moore, G. E. (1965). Cramming more components onto integrated circuits. *Electronics* 38 (8): 114–117.

Nardi, B., Anderson, K., and Erickson, T. (1995). Filing and finding computer files. Paper presented at the East-West Conference on Human–Computer Interaction, Moscow, Russia.

Nardi, B. A., and Barreau, D. (1997). "Finding and reminding" revisited: Appropriate metaphors for file organisation on the desktop. *SIGCHI Bulletin* 29 (1).

Nardi, B. A., Whittaker, S., Isaacs, E., Creech, M., Johnson, J., and Hainsworth, J. (2001). ContactMap: Integrating communication and information through visualizing personal social networks. *Communications of the ACM* 49(4):89–95.

Nelson, T. (1990). The right way to think about software design In Laurel, B. (ed.), *The Art of Human–Computer Interface Design.* Addison-Wesley.

Plaisant, C., and Shneiderman, B. (1994). The future of graphic user interfaces: Personal role managers. Paper presented at the People and Computers IX.

Pliskin, N. (1989). Interacting with electronic mail can be a dream or a nightmare: A user's point of view. *Interacting with Computers* 1 (3): 259–272.

Ravasio, P. (2004). *Personal Information Organisation: Studies on User-Appropriate Classification and Retrieval Strategies and Their Implications for Information Management Systems Design.* Aachen, Germany: Shaker Verlag. (Also doctoral dissertation 15579, Swiss Federal Institute of Technology, Zürich, Switzerland.)

Ravasio, P., Guttormsen-Schär, S., and Krueger, H. (2004). In pursuit of desktop evolution: User problems and practices with modern desktop systems. *ACM Transactions on Computer–Human Interaction (TOCHI)* 11 (2): 156–180.

Ravasio, P., Guttormsen-Schär S., and Tscherter, V. (2006). The qualitative experiment in HCI: Definition, occurrance, value, and use. Submitted.

Ravasio, P., Vukelja, L., Rivera, G., and Norrie, M. C. (2003). Project InfoSpace: From information managing to information representation. Paper presented at the Interact 2003—Ninth IFIP TC13 International Conference on Human–Computer Interaction, Zürich, Switzerland.

Reichmuth, A. (2004). Difficulties in teaching computer use to novices [personal communication]. Zurich, Switzerland. August 21, 2004.

Rekimoto, J. (1999). TimeScape: A time machine for the desktop environment. Paper presented at the ACM Conference on Computer–Human Interaction (CHI) 1999.

Robertson, G., Dantzich, M. v., Robbins, D., Czerwinski, M., Hinckley, K., Risden, K., Thiel, D., and Gorokhovsky, V. (2000). The Task Gallery: A 3D window manager. Paper presented at the ACM Conference on Computer–Human Interaction (CHI) 2000.

Sellen, A. J., and Harper, R. H. R. (2002). Introduction to *The Myth of the Paperless Office*. Cambridge, Mass.: MIT Press.

Shneiderman, B. (1996). The eyes have it: A task by data type taxonomy for information visualizations. Paper presented at the IEEE Visual Languages, Boulder, Colorado.

Sutcliffe, A. G., Ennis, M., and Watkinson, S. J. (2000). Empirical studies of end-user information searching. *Journal of the American Society for Information Science* 51 (13): 1211–1231.

Sweeney, L. (2001). Information explosion. In Zayatz, L., Doyle, P., Theeuwes, J., Lane, J. (eds.), *Confidentiality, Disclosure, and Data Access: Theory and Practical Applications for Statistical Agencies*. Washington, D.C.: Urban Institute.

Vicente, K. J., Hayes, B. C., and Williges, R. C. (1987). Assaying and isolating individual differences in searching a hierarchical file system. *Human Factors* 29 (3): 349–359.

Voida, S., Mynatt, E. D., and MacIntyre, B. (2002). Supporting collaboration in a context-aware office computing environment. Paper presented at the 4th International Conference on Ubiquitous Computing (UbiComp 2002), Gothenburg, Sweden.

Whittaker, S., and Hirschberg, J. (2001). The character, value, and management of personal paper archives. *ACM Transactions on Computer–Human Interaction* 8 (2): 150–170.

Whittaker S., and Sidner, C. (1996). Email overload: Exploring personal information management of email. In *Proceedings of the 1996 ACM SIGCHI Conference on Human Factors in Computing Systems (CHI '96)*, pp. 276–283. Vancouver, British Columbia, Canada, April 13–18.

# 10

# Toward Integrated Work Environments: Application-Centric versus Workspace-Level Design

Victor Kaptelinin and Richard Boardman

## Introduction

This chapter emerged from the authors' participation in a computer-supported cooperative work (CSCW) conference workshop that discussed possibilities for redesigning email (Gwizdka and Whittaker 2002). Each of us presented position papers asserting that a key priority in redesigning email should be to improve integration between email and other applications (i.e., "workspace-level integration") rather than transforming email itself (Boardman, Sasse, and Spence 2002; Kaptelinin 2002). To our surprise, we found ourselves to be the only champions of a workspace-level approach. The other participants advocated that expanding email, making it more sophisticated and powerful by adding advanced features and functionalities (i.e., an "application-centric" approach), was the way to face current challenges. As the authors' views were highly compatible, we decided to develop our arguments further and present them more systematically. This resolution eventually resulted in this chapter.[1]

In this chapter, we contrast two design perspectives for improving support for personal information management: (1) application-centric and (2) workspace-level. Our point of departure is to use recent email research as an example of the application-centric design perspective.

Email research is motivated by two main arguments. First, although there have been some low-level changes to the email user interface, today's email applications have remained broadly unchanged over the past two decades (Bälter 2000; Ducheneaut and Bellotti 2001; Neustaedter, Brush, and Smith 2005). Second, empirical studies have shown that email users experience a number of serious problems, which build up over time.

Many users experience *email overload* (Whittaker and Sidner 1996). This term describes the difficulties users encounter in monitoring the endless stream of incoming mail, as well as prioritizing, filing, and finding messages. Relevant messages are often difficult to find, which means that important information may be missed. In addition, the above problems are complicated by security concerns, such as spam and viruses. Despite these problems, email has been remarkably successful and has become a *habitat* for many users, that is, an environment where they spend much of their work and leisure time (Ducheneaut and Bellotti 2001). However, current email applications do not provide adequate support for the range of tasks that users now carry out in email, that is, they do not support task management (Whittaker and Sidner 1996; Whittaker 2005).

The above arguments are often interpreted as an indication that email needs to be redesigned (e.g., Bälter 2000; Ducheneaut and Bellotti 2001; Bellotti et al. 2003). Many designers have argued that email, created for another era of computer use, is out of sync with the needs of today's users, and that its antiquated design is in need of massive revision. One possible, and currently the most popular, approach to deal with user problems is to embed extra functionality within email applications, such as support for task management (Bellotti et al. 2003). This is an *"email-centric"* approach; it focuses primarily on email and aims to make email a workspace of its own.

Our position, presented in this chapter, is based on a different interpretation of the same arguments. The arguments per se are difficult to disagree with, but they do not necessarily point to an application-centric design focus. In this chapter we present and discuss an alternative approach, which emphasizes the need to improve the integration of email with the other applications that make up the larger-scale personal digital workspace. In contrast to the email-centric perspective, this approach is concerned with improving support for user activities *across the workspace as a whole*. In the following discussion we will refer to this approach as "workspace-level integration." Such a perspective, as witnessed by this book, is gaining ground in human–computer interaction (HCI) research (see also, e.g., Henderson and Card 1986; Robertson et al. 2000; Dragunov et al. 2005).

Empirical studies (e.g., Bälter 1998) do show that current email applications are not powerful enough to provide support for many activities such as task management. However, this does not necessarily mean that new features should be added to email. In some cases, appropriate support may already exist in other applications. For instance, a user composing a letter may not be satisfied with the basic formatting features provided by the email program she uses, while another user might like to edit a digital photograph, which he wants to attach to an email. In these cases an obvious solution would be to employ another application, such as a word processor or an image editor. Ideally those would be conveniently integrated with the email application. We highlight such an integrating design perspective as an alternative to the predominant route of embedding more functionality into email.

At this point, we would like to emphasize that we do not question the need and value of innovative designs promoting the evolution of email. Undoubtedly, numerous ideas that are being developed in current email research are likely to make email more usable and useful. What we do question is the fruitfulness of focusing purely at such an application-centric level, that is, separating the design of applications from the design of the (digital) workspace as a whole. A recurrent topic in this chapter is the need to combine or at least coordinate these two perspectives. We mostly focus here on potential advantages of one of these perspectives, namely, workspace-level integration. However, this emphasis partly reflects an intentional bias: it aims to counter the prevalence of the application-centric approach in current email research. Ideally, in our view, application-centric design and workspace-level design should both be employed as complementary approaches.

The rest of the chapter is organized into five sections. The second section deals with the email-centric approach, describing its underlying ideas, providing examples of recent work, and highlighting its limitations. In the third section, we present the contrasting workspace-level approach, its rationale and implications for email research. Again email is used as an example of the application-centric approach to contextualize our theoretical discussion. We present email as one component of the wider virtual workspace, and discuss the need for coordination between email and other applications to provide better support for higher-level user activities. The next two sections describe two research projects that are aimed at providing workspace-level support for user activities: (1) the UMEA system based on the creation of project contexts through interaction history, and (2) the WorkspaceMirror system that allows a user to share organizational categories between email and other applications involved in personal information management (PIM). Finally, we summarize the key points from each section, and then discuss the relationship between the application-centric and workspace-level design perspectives.

## The Application-Centric Approach

In this section we highlight the limitations of the application-centric perspective, centered on the example of email. First, we summarize research aimed at adding new functionality to email and developing it into a full-scale work environment. In our view, this research runs the risk of transforming email beyond recognition, obtaining new benefits at the expense of its core advantages. Furthermore, we argue that such email-centric research is based on an inherently piecemeal view. Not only does it increase the already high complexity of email interfaces, but it also ignores the wider context of user needs beyond the boundaries of email.

### The Email-Centric Approach to Task Management

Email is the most successful CSCW application to date, and millions rely on it in their daily communications. As mentioned above, it has been observed that email is not simply a tool, but rather a habitat where individuals spend much of their work and personal lives (Ducheneaut and Bellotti 2001). The key reasons why email has become an attractive alternative to other communication media are its high speed, low cost, and asynchronous nature.

Since email is ubiquitous, it is hardly surprising that much research has been conducted on email (e.g., Mackay 1988; Whittaker and Sidner 1996; Bälter 1998; Ducheneaut and Bellotti 2001; Bälter and Sidner 2002; Gwizdka 2002; Bellotti et al. 2003; Neustaedter, Brush, and Smith 2005; Neustaedter et al. 2005). The main findings from this body of research can be summarized as follows. First, researchers have discovered a diversity of individual *strategies* employed by email users, in particular, in filing processed messages. Second, they have identified a number of common user *problems*, such as difficulties in processing, organizing, and filing messages. Third, many studies have clearly showed that email has outgrown its original raison d'être and is now used for many "noncore" tasks, that is, tasks beyond communication. For instance, Whittaker and Sidner (1996, p. 276) observe that:

> email has evolved to a point where it is now used for multiple purposes: document delivery and archiving, work task delegation, and task tracking. It is also used for storing personal names and addresses, for sending reminders, asking for assistance, scheduling appointments, and for handling technical support queries.

In particular, Whittaker and Sidner (1996) highlight two primary functions for which email has been adopted: (1) task management and (2) personal archiving.

Observations of diverse strategies, problems, and unanticipated uses are generally interpreted as an indication that users require extra functionality to be added to email. Mackay (1988, p. 352) claims "it is important to look for powerful primitives that support the flexible extension of mail to support different kinds of individual and group work." Whittaker and Sidner (1996) also emphasize the need to redesign email to support filing and task management. They outline three directions for potential development, each of which exploits the organizing of messages into conversational threads: (a) allowing the user to view and manipulate entire threads associated with a selected message, (b) clustering semantically related documents to assist in filing incoming messages, and (c) message threading and clustering to better support task management by grouping messages related to current tasks. In their view, organizing messages into conversational threads and allowing the user to directly manipulate the threads opens up a range of new possibilities for integrating email and task management. Formally, conversational threads are structured clusters of email messages, which share a particular subject line. At the same time, threads are collections of thematically related information resources—not just messages but also embedded URLs and attached files—typically utilized in carrying out a certain task. Therefore, a message thread is a formally identifiable representation of a task that can be used for accessing the body of resources related to that task (e.g., meeting details in a reminder message), or checking the task status (e.g., whether a pending message has been received).

The directions indicated by Whittaker and Sidner (1996) have had a significant influence on subsequent email research. For example, the displaying of conversational threads has been explored through empirical studies of both traditional and innovative visualization techniques (Smith, Cadiz, and Burkhalter, 2000; Venolia and Neustaedter, 2003) However, the area of greatest interest has been that of providing efficient task management support within email.

The general idea of using email for task management is not new. It was clearly articulated, for instance, by Mackay (1988). Moreover, it has been implemented in familiar software products, such as Microsoft Outlook, which combines an email client with a suite of PIM tools: calendar, address book, tasks, notes, and journal. The new contribution made by Whittaker and Sidner (1996) was their analysis of design implications following from the observation that individuals typically develop ad hoc procedures for using messages in the inbox as implicit reminders rather than using a dedicated tool. Whittaker and Sidner noted that much of a user's inbox reflects ongoing projects and includes information items critical for task management. In a sense, the inbox is an analogue of the working memory. Users do not make use of dedicated task management software—but instead adopt email for this purpose (see, e.g., Bellotti and Smith 2000).

Bellotti et al. (2003) have investigated the potential of threads for task management. They describe a hybrid email/task management tool called *TaskMaster,* centered on the concept of a "thrask"—a cross between "thread" and "task"—defined as a threaded task-centric collection of resources. The user interface features three panes: (a) a list of thrasks, resembling a regular inbox with the exception that whole thrasks are represented as folder icons (cf. Whittaker and Sidner 1996); (b) a list of objects that make up a thrask, which includes not only messages but also attached files and embedded URLs; and (c) the content of the selected object. Each object can be assigned a PIM attribute, such as a deadline, reminder, or action. One advantage of using threads as task-related collections is that collections can be created automatically using the metadata already contained in messages, such as subject lines and reply sequences. A similar strategy was employed in the design of the *TimeStore* system (Yiu et al. 1997; Gwizdka 2002), where messages were organized along two dimensions—subject and time—to facilitate the monitoring of individual tasks.

The potential of using other email message attributes for task management has been investigated within the *ContactMap* system (Nardi et al.

2002; Fisher and Nardi, this volume). ContactMap organizes information resources around the user's contacts (thus employing email's "sender" attribute). Pictorial representations of contacts on the desktop allow users to create a spatial map of their social world which can be employed as an organizing principle for their entire workspace.

Although not proposed as a task management tool, the *Bifrost* system (Bälter and Sidner 2002) implements certain features that make it relevant here. The rationale behind this design is to reduce information and communication overload by automatically classifying incoming email into prioritized groups (see also Neustaedter et al. 2005). By default, Bifrost highlights two groups of high priority messages: (a) those that include fragments of text from the user's current calendar entries, and (b) those received from prespecified senders. These two classification strategies attempt to yield messages that are related to ongoing user tasks.

Currently the HCI/CSCW research community appears to be predominantly optimistic regarding the integration of task management functionality within email. The potential limitations of this approach seldom become an object of discussion. However, we argue that these limitations are significant.

### Problems with the Application-Centric Approach

In this section we discuss the limitations of the application-centric approach. Again, we focus on efforts to integrate task management with email. Some of the problems we discuss are related specifically to email, such as the issue of preserving the core advantages of the application. Other problems are more general, such as those related to the increased complexity of the user interface, resulting from the bloating of email. In addition, we point out that such an application-centric (more specifically, email-centric) approach may have a detrimental effect on the coherence of the digital workspace as a whole. In particular we discuss how the email-centric approach does not consider how email is coordinated with other applications. We argue that such considerations are crucial for the design of digital work environments.

**Diluting the key strengths of email** Email has several key features that may be lost as new functionality is added. Many email-centric designs involve dividing the single flow of incoming messages, typical of current email applications, into groups or threads. This feature can help the user cope with email overload by hiding the detail of individual messages, many of which are often closely related. However, such separation makes it harder to obtain an overview of the entire incoming flow. This in turn may lead to the user missing important information.

Let us consider the TaskMaster user interface. In the "Thrasks" pane the items are organized in a quasi-chronological order. If a new message does not belong to any of the existing thrasks, it is added to the list as the first (or the last) item, much like in existing email applications; but if the new message is recognized as belonging to an existing thrask the message is placed in the appropriate thrask folder instead. The thrask folder in that case changes its appearance to indicate that a new message has been received. However, if the thrask folder is not currently visible the message may remain unnoticed, unless the user scrolls down.

Of course, automatic distribution of messages in folders can play an important positive role, for instance filtering spam. However, several empirical studies have found that email users dislike filters (Whittaker and Sidner 1996; Bälter 1998), and prefer single-track views of communication to threaded views (Smith, Cadiz, and Burkhalter 2000). Furthermore, much of the appeal of the email-centric approach to task management lies in automatic linking of resources to tasks on the basis of information that can be extracted from messages, such as "sender" or "subject" attributes. However, there is no one-to-one correspondence between the formal attributes of a message and its relation to a specific task. For instance, a particular contact may be involved in a number of projects. In addition, people do not always make sure the subject corresponds exactly to the content of a message. For instance, a person may use the "reply" function to send a new message to a colleague without bothering to change the subject line. Also, a single message can be related to a number of tasks.

The above arguments do not imply that accurate automatic classification of task-related resources is not desirable. However, the issue of the practical usefulness of the classification needs to be further explored through empirical studies of real-life use patterns. Arguably, there is scope for design solutions that can cope with problems created by inaccurate classification.

**Bloating of email** Another downside of adding task management functionality to email is the resulting increase in the complexity of the user interface. We argue that such an increase is likely to create problems for users. Current email applications, like many other computer applications, are already overloaded with unused functionality. A study of the use of email in an academic laboratory, conducted by Bälter (1998), highlighted a variety of problems caused by increased tool complexity. It was found that even users with a background in computer science experienced difficulties with moving messages between mailbox folders, and distributing the use of email between work and home.

Redesigning email by radically extending it with sophisticated features not directly related to the basic functionality of the tool will only compound the problem. We argue that increased complexity will have a particular impact on less technical users.[2] Advanced functionality, although appreciated by power users, may pose a challenge for many others.

**Cross-application integration** Email is not the only digital environment "inhabited" by users during their work and leisure time. People may spend hours at a time in the contexts of other applications, such as word processors, programming environments, or chat rooms. Understanding how people use a multiplicity of habitats requires understanding how technologies support higher-level tasks—tasks that can be meaningfully defined independently of the applications with which they are carried out. An example of a higher-level task is canceling a scheduled meeting. To define the task one needs to describe the group of people to be informed, the reason for cancellation, and so forth. The task can be accomplished in a variety of ways, such as sending an email, using an instant messaging system, making phone calls, physically meeting other persons, or "meeting" them in a chat room. Which tool is to be used, if any, is of secondary importance. Higher-level tasks are contrasted with lower-level tasks, which are specific to particular technologies. Lower-level tasks, such as creating a new mailbox, only make sense in relation to a particular tool.

Higher-level tasks often involve the use of many types of information resources managed across a range of applications. The resources relevant to a particular task may be received via email (e.g., messages, attachment files, and embedded links) or may be created by the user herself. A key aspect of performing higher-level tasks is therefore the *coordination* of multiple applications, such as email and the file system explorer. When carrying higher-level tasks people need to switch between their digital subhabitats.

The need for cross-application coordination is recognized within the email-centric approach. However, this need is addressed in an application-centric manner. For instance, in the TaskMaster system users can manually add resources from other applications to email. The usefulness of the system depends, therefore, on how many additional resources the user needs to add manually. If most resources are included automatically, the overhead may be insignificant. In contrast, if the user needs to spend substantial time manually adding resources to thrasks, the system may become unusable. The amount of manually added resources will depend on the applications people use outside email. In an empirical study conducted by Czerwinski, Horvitz, and Wilhite (2004) it was found that tasks, which can be described as "email," constitute 23 percent of all tasks in the group of knowledge workers taking part in the study. The large proportion of "non-email" tasks (i.e., tasks that were not explicitly described as "email") can be interpreted as an indication that subjects carried out most of their task outside email. Therefore, a hybrid "email—task management" system may be a help or a hindrance depending on the use of other applications.

**The need to explore alternative approaches** This section has discussed some potential limitations of the application-centric approach using email as an example. Since email research is still in its infancy (Gwizdka and Whittaker 2002), it is too early to tell whether or not these potential limitations can be successfully overcome. Similar arguments can also be made in other application contexts. What can be claimed with certainty, however, is the need to explore a variety of possible approaches. In the long run, it might be a combination of approaches that will prove to be the most promising.

## Toward Workspace-Level Integration

### Application-Centric versus Workspace-Level Design Perspectives

Is email, in its current form, a dinosaur or a timeless classic? In lieu of the previous discussion, it is clear that email is neither. On the one hand, email in its traditional form appears to serve its core functions well enough to continue to be one of the most commonly used computer applications. On the other hand, email has been a victim of its own success. Apparent problems and unexplored potential associated with the current use of email indicate the need to explore new directions for design. The application-centric approach, discussed in the previous section, is an attempt to deal with these challenges by making email more advanced and powerful.

Here we advocate a contrasting perspective, based on the analysis of user needs at a higher level, that of the digital workspace as a whole. From this workspace-level perspective, the designer's key aim is to provide support for better integration between email and other applications (see figure 10.1). These two perspectives can thus be differentiated by the designer's scope of concern:

*Application-centric:* The designer's primary aim is the optimization of an independent application. The main design concern is what features and functions should be added to the application to make it more powerful.

*Workspace-level:* The designer's aim is to optimize how well the distinct applications work together within a workspace as a whole. A workspace can be defined as a spatial, temporal, and logical organization of resources that support higher-level tasks.

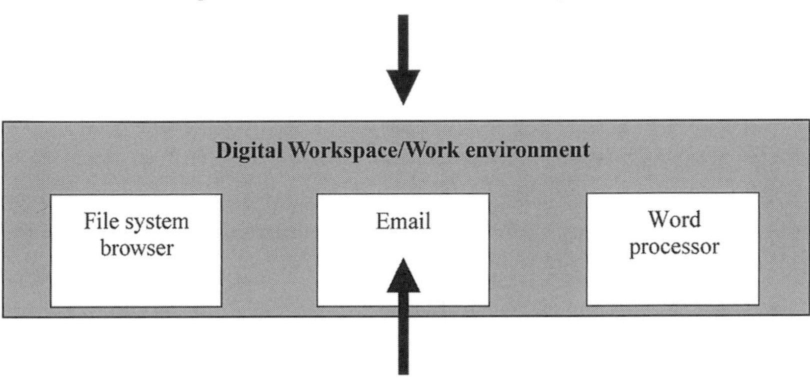


**Figure 10.1**
A comparison of the application-centric and workspace-level design perspectives.

The workplace-level perspective underlies many systems described in this book. However, in research and development related to specific applications—for instance, in email research—the application-centric perspective currently appears to be dominant. Digital workspaces contain information objects such as documents, messages, images, and music, and applications that support the production and consumption of information objects during communication, writing, and reading. Activities taking place in digital environments are integral parts of larger-scale activities that span the physical and digital domains. Accordingly, digital workspaces are integral parts of larger-scale physical-virtual environments. If the workspace-level perspective is adopted, the designers' key questions include: What are the unique core functions served by each application that distinguish them from other applications? How can such functions be preserved and enhanced when designing new systems? Conversely, how can a particular application contribute to the increased utility and usability of other applications? How should the workspace as a whole be designed to facilitate the integrated use of distinct applications and to provide optimal synergy between them?

In this section we address some of the issues identified earlier from a workspace-level perspective. We use email as a context for our discussion. We analyze email and its role in the workspace from three different perspectives: (1) support of higher-level user tasks, (2) collaboration, and (3) information processing.

## Roles and Functions of Email within the Workspace as a Whole

**Support for higher-level tasks** When people use email in support of higher-level tasks, for example, creating a digital photo album or working on a course assignment, the employment of multiple applications is the rule rather than an exception. Information resources received via email may need to be transferred to other applications. A phone number in a message may be stored in an address book, a digital picture may be edited with an image processing program, and so forth. The emphasis on supporting high-level activities, involving a variety of applications, gives priority to flexible solutions based on dynamic constellations of tools. Such tool constellations should be available under diverse conditions but yet provide consistent support for users' activities.

**Collaboration support** Early empirical studies on the use of email for task management focused on the division of labor within a group, rather than management of an individual user's tasks (Mackay 1988). Email is a prototypical example of a CSCW application, and therefore appears to be ideally suited for supporting collaborative task management. A possibility to integrate task management and collaboration support is one of the main arguments behind the email-centric approach (Mackay 1988; Bälter 1998). Although a highly successful tool for asynchronous and primarily textual communication, email does not provide support for other aspects of collaboration. Much collaboration takes place in collocated teams, where the emphasis is on face-to-face formal and informal meetings, phone calls, and so forth, rather than email communication. Collaborators often need to combine email with other technologies that provide additional functionality, such as access to shared archives, joint editing of objects in a shared workspace, or synchronous communication. A significant part of remote collaboration is currently carried out over the phone, in collaborative web environments, via videoconferences, and so forth. Essential as it is, email is often just one of the diverse technologies used to support collaboration.

**Digital work environments as information-processing systems** One useful analogy that can help identify the main advantages of email is portraying the workspace as an abstract information-processing system. General architectures of information processing systems typically include the following components: (1) input–output processes, such as perceptual and motor systems; (2) long-term memory; and (3) working memory (Newell, Rosenbloom, and Laird 1989). Information received through sensory inputs is processed, that is, perceived, recognized, and classified. It may be stored in long-term memory for later use, translated into working memory, transformed into motor responses, and hence used to solve the problem at hand.

Here, the information-processing system model is used to describe the notion of the workspace (see figure 10.2). Information enters the workspace through different "inputs" and is processed in a variety of ways to produce "outputs," which are eventually sent out to the world. For a traditional office worker it was typical to have "in" and "pending" trays for incoming documents and documents currently being processed

(Malone 1983). As well as information authored by a user, digital workspaces receive information from the world through sensors, networks, and portable memory devices such as digital cameras. They also distribute information through the same channels. The files and cabinet folders of a physical office, as well as files and folders typical of digital workspaces, often function as long-term memory, even though they can be used for temporary storage of information related to work in progress. The physical and digital desktops are analogous to working memory, where information needed to solve a problem is activated and ready at hand.

Despite the obvious limitations of the above analogy, it is useful when specifying the role and function of email in a digital workspace. First of all, it illustrates how email supports all three components of the system, to varying degrees.

**Input–output** Email is a key tool supporting this component of the model. However, it is not the only one. Other ways to exchange informa-

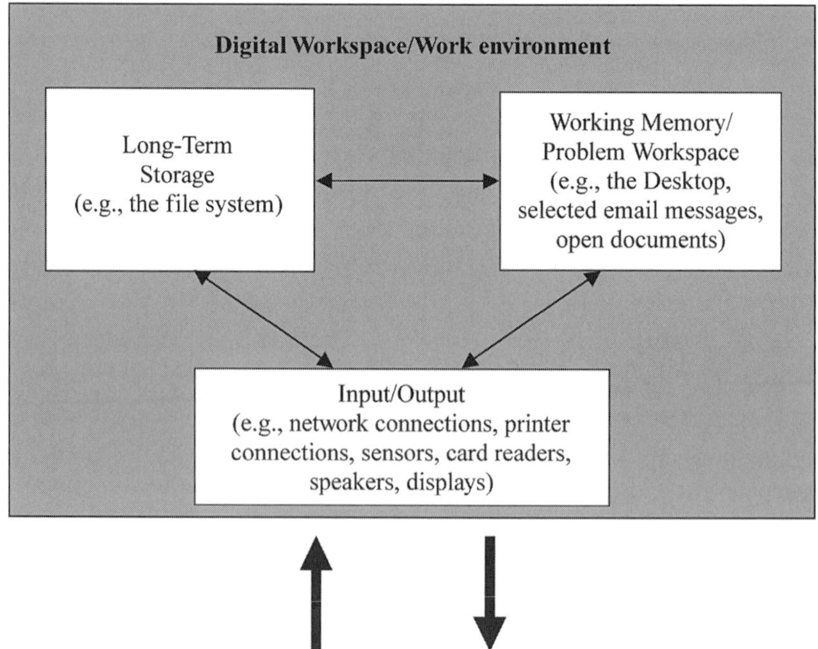


**Figure 10.2**
Abstraction of the digital workspace as an information-processing system.

tion with the world include downloading files from the web, filling in web forms, using IM systems, copying information to or from servers, exchanging files via FTP, and so forth. It is difficult to compare, in terms of both volume and importance, information sent or received via email with information sent or received via other channels. Perhaps it would be safe to say that at least in some cases the most important information is exchanged with the use of tools other than email. Especially notable is the ever-increasing share of the web in supplying information for current digital workspaces. Indeed, email itself may also be fragmented across multiple desktop and web-based clients.

Paradoxically, however, heavy information traffic beyond email does not undermine the key role of this tool. Quite the opposite: the more intensive and diverse information exchange is at the workspace, the more important email becomes for the exchange. Many user actions performed outside email, such as making a travel arrangement via Internet, result in notifications or confirmations sent to the user's email address. This is because email has become the de facto tool supporting a *single attention focus* of the user, which helps the user to keep track of the most important interactions and events taking place in the world.

**Long-term storage** Email has its own storage system consisting of mailboxes and messages. The mailbox hierarchy can be used as an archive of email messages and attachment files. Therefore, email contributes to a long-term storage component of digital workspaces. However, many other tools contribute to this functionality as well. The file system, to-do lists, URLs (favorites), as well as other application-specific information hierarchies and archives constitute other parts of long-term storage.

**Working memory/problem workspace** Workspaces can be set up to solve specific problems, containing the necessary resources, organized so that the user can easily access them when needed. Workspaces are often spatially organized in 2D (Henderson and Card 1986) or 3D (Robinson et al. 2000) environments. Workspaces typically contain ephemeral objects, which have a lifetime measured in hours or days. The meaning of an ephemeral object is determined by a temporary need, and so such objects quickly become obsolete (Barreau and Nardi, 1995). Even though "Working memory/problem workspace" is indicated in figure 10.2 as one component of the model, there are in fact a number of task-specific workspaces corresponding to the various interleaved tasks the user is working on. Therefore, to effectively accomplish their tasks, the users must maintain several foci of attention and switch between them when necessary.

Problem workspaces do not have a uniform structure. Their organization depends on a number of factors including the nature of the problem, the preferences of the user, and the time required to manage the workspaces. For example, to create a letter the user may just need to open a word processor. To carry out a more advanced task the user may need to open several word processor windows, a browser window for searching information on the web, an image-processing tool, and so on. Also, if the user can only work on a problem for a limited time, he can decide to focus on a specific subproblem, which may require a very basic workspace compared to the workspace needed to work on the problem as a whole. For instance, when creating a web photo album a user may decide to rename picture files first to give them meaningful names. To carry out this subtask the user only needs a viewing program. To accomplish other phases of the higher-level task the user may need to put together an advanced workspace including a variety of tools and information objects.

Moreover, the user may work on the task in different physical contexts, such as at the office, at home, or on a trip. These partial contributions to a particular task must be coordinated in order to complete the work.

Problem-specific workspaces, corresponding to the "Working memory" component of the above model, need to be highly flexible. The user may have to maintain several foci of attention, dividing her time and effort between several tasks and the corresponding workspaces. Thus it is important that the user should be allowed to focus on a specific problem while temporarily ignoring other problems. The structure and content of problem-specific workspaces is not predetermined but rather emerging and situated. To support the selective and flexible organization of resources, digital work environments allow for spatial organization. Placing objects in certain locations serves as a way to create ad hoc configurations providing an easy access to necessary resources (e.g., Robertson et al., this volume). The above analysis indicates that email may not be an effective tool for this purpose. Traditionally, email is based on a linear organization of messages, which makes it especially suitable for maintaining a single focus of attention and thus supporting the "input–output" processes.[4] For those users who do not delete messages email can also serve as a rather useful long-term storage. However, the tool is not especially good at providing the user with selective and flexible configurations of resources, unless their requirements conveniently map onto message threads.

**Implications for Email Redesign Strategy: Coordination versus Expansion**

To account for the success of email, one has to consider not only the tool—its functionality, interface, and technical implementation—but external factors as well. One can claim that it is likely email has become so attractive to billions of people because it is fast, ubiquitous, and often free, and that its design has always been of secondary importance. However, external factors do not explain why the specific implementation of email as a single-thread list of messages—the design that is currently often considered problematic—has become so popular. We already discussed two aspects of the classic email design, which constitute its key advantages: the asynchronicity of email as a communication tool and its support of a single focus of attention. In this section we will argue that the "classic" email design also provides (1) accessibility and (2) compatibility with other tools and tasks.

Perhaps, the most remarkable characteristic of email is its support for an enormous range of users and activities. The same tool is used by people of different ages, socioeconomic status, and occupations for all imaginable purposes: shopping, dating, keeping in touch with friends and family, telemarketing, job announcements and applications, project management, collaborative writing, customer service, political actions, and so forth. The purposes and patterns of electronic communication can be very different for different groups of people, but all of them invariantly find email useful and reasonably well integrated into their everyday practices.

Another remarkable aspect of email is that this "habitat" coexists with other applications and environments, some of which are likely to be "habitats" too, such as web browsers, IM systems, and programming environments. Email is used to send links to web pages, itineraries produced by ticket reservation systems, or documents created with a word processor. Interestingly enough, email does not seem to compete with other communication tools. While other types of programs, such as a web browser or a word processor, tend to become "the" tool for web browsing or creating documents, email in many cases supports and complements rather than substitutes other communication tools. For instance, email is used on a regular basis by the authors of this essay to get notifications of received voice messages, initiate a conversation with an IM program, or send login details for a website.

Therefore, the role of email in the wider digital work environment is threefold. First, email is a communication tool that supports user awareness of important events, of what is going on in the world, and enables the user to respond to these events. Such awareness helps users decide on the priority of their tasks and assures that critically important information is not overlooked. For a successful functioning of a digital work environment it is important that a balance is struck between concentrating on a task and monitoring the world. Second, when the user works on a certain task, or problem, email serves as a tool that provides access to some of the resources necessary to carry out the task (messages and attachment files) and thereby contributes to management of task-related resources. Third, email contributes to the long-term storage of information in a work environment.

In this chapter we claim that developing email into a task management tool, in other words taking steps toward making it a general-purpose work environment, is associated with two problems. The first is the *coordination* with the other tools and information objects that may be needed when working on a task. In some cases, such as collaborative writing (cf. Ducheneaut and Bellotti 2001), coordination with non-email resources may not be a major obstacle. However, as discussed above, many problem-specific workspaces involve a diverse range of resources. For instance, a travel agent using a ticket reservation system can use email extensively in addition to the system. The ticket reservation system may constitute a work environment featuring advanced task management tools. It would be hard to replicate such specific functionality in email. Therefore, transferring email into a task management system may require more than simply extending its functionality. Successful integration of email and task management within one system may mean a transformation of a general tool into a specialized tool suitable for a limited range of activities and a limited group of users.

The second potential problem is the *impact on the core strengths of email*—employing email as a task-management tool may make it a less effective communication tool. As shown in the previous section, problem workspaces and communication ("input–output") components of digital work environments are associated with different, even opposite, requirements. Elaborate spatially organized workspaces, supporting multiple foci of attention, may be effective for task management but less effective for communication than traditional single-focus linear email systems.

In our view a redesign strategy for email should aim at preserving the key features of email that make it such a remarkably successful communication tool, namely: (1) single attention focus, (2) a simple to follow linear structure, and (3) the possibility to check email from virtually any connected computer device. The most important problems to be addressed in future email research include, in our view: (1) filtering out or hiding irrelevant (or less relevant) information, (2) providing flexible visualizations, and (3) improving security.

However, we would argue that rather than focusing on email alone, designers should capitalize on its core advantages by maximizing the integration of email with other applications within virtual work environments. However, the consideration of integration often plays a minor part in standard HCI methodology. In the next two sections we describe two ongoing research projects intended as examples of concrete design explorations based on the notion of integration. We begin with describing the *UMEA* system based on the creation of project contexts through interaction history. After that we present the *WorkspaceMirror* system that allows a user to share organizational categories between email and other tools involved in personal information management.

Each system aims to provide workspace-level support for user activities. Empirical and theoretical motivation for each design is presented as well as findings from their evaluation, focusing on how they influence PIM practices across multiple applications. Both systems represent a shift in the design approach from embedding extra functionality in specific tools to providing integration across tools.

## Example System A: UMEA

### Background

The UMEA (user-monitoring environment for activities) system aims to provide low-overhead support for a user's higher-level tasks, or *projects*. Carrying out a project typically involves setting up and maintaining a project context, that is, arranging necessary resources so they are readily available when working on the project. Computer users often spend considerable time and effort finding and opening documents, web pages, email messages, contact details, and so on, to be able to carry out their work. As repeatedly emphasized throughout this book, conventional virtual work environments provide little support for managing project contexts, especially when projects span several applications and require multiple types of information objects (e.g., Plaisant et al., this volume; Voida, Mynatt, and MacIntyre, this volume). Since users often switch between different activities and work contexts (Czerwinski, Horvitz, and Wilhite 2004), this lack of support can cause substantial work disruptions.

The UMEA system addresses this problem by automatically creating project contexts as by-products of a user's work on respective projects. Project contexts are understood here as configurations of resources, associated with a project, which can be accessed by the user without undue effort. The UMEA system identifies information objects related to a project and conveniently organizes them to minimize time and effort needed to switch between projects or to continue working on a project after a break. More specifically, the underlying aims of the system are as follows: (a) make it possible for the user to directly indicate a higher-level task, that is, a project; (b) monitor user activities and track resources employed when carrying out the project; and (c) automatically organize and update these resources to make them easily available to the user when he or she resumes working on the project.

The design approach behind the system is based on both theoretical considerations and empirical studies. The theoretical perspective informing the system is activity theory (e.g., Kaptelinin and Nardi 2006). Activity theory maintains that technologies need to be designed to mediate meaningful human activities, rather than merely support low-level application-specific tasks. Empirical studies of how people use desktop work environments have reported numerous phenomena of everyday use that cannot be easily accounted for by underlying assumptions of the design of the environments (Barreau and Nardi 1995; Kaptelinin 1996). In particular, it was found that system features intended to support management of project-related resources, provided by a popular operating system, were not actually used for that purpose (Kaptelinin 1996).

**System Overview**

The UMEA system is an application running on Microsoft Windows. The most important feature of the system is the creation of interaction histories and their conversion into project contexts (see figure 10.3). Project histories comprise various interaction events, such as opening a folder, updating a document, or sending an email message. Each event is tagged to a project that was active at the time the event took place. Project-tagged interaction history thus identifies the set of resources that were employed by the user when working on a project. These resources are divided into

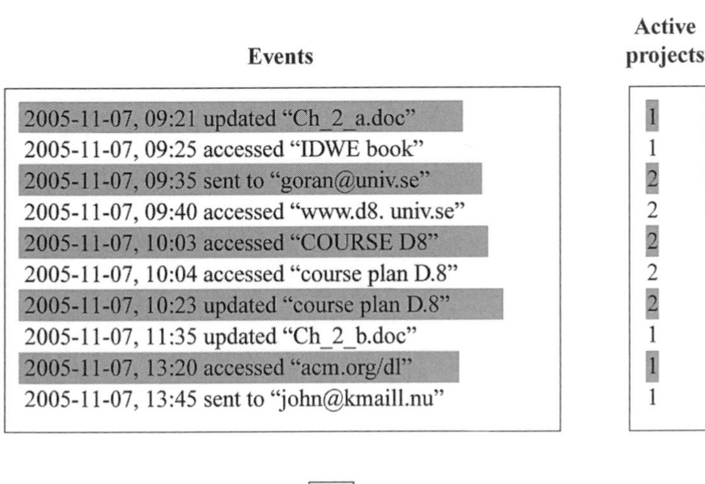


**Project 1**

| Documents | Folders | URLs | Contacts |
|---|---|---|---|
| Ch_2_a.doc<br>Ch_2_b.doc | IDWE book | acm.org/dl | john@kmaill.nu |

**Figure 10.3**
Translating an example interaction history into a project context.

four groups: documents, folders, URLs, and contacts (email addresses). Resources of each group are compiled into project-specific lists. The lists are organized sets of pointers that can be used to access a resource by selecting it from a pop-up menu. Selecting a document or a folder opens the corresponding information object, selecting a URL opens a web page, and selecting a contact opens a new email "compose" window with the contact's email address inserted.

The system can run in either the foreground or background. In the foreground mode the system presents users with an overview of their projects. The user can set up a new project or make one of the projects active by selecting it on a menu. After that the user can open a project-related resource by choosing it on a pop-up menu. The system also provides the user with a number of PIM tools: a calendar, notes, and to-do lists. The to-do lists, notes, and entries to the calendar are automatically linked to specific projects. In the background mode the system passively monitors interaction events. The events are stored in the interaction history with projects tags. If an event is associated with a new resource, that is, a resource that has not yet been used within the currently active project, this resource is added to the appropriate list. Adding a resource to a list does not change the resource itself, so the same resource can be used in multiple projects.

### First Experiences with the System

Empirical evidence about actual system use was gathered from two sources: the experience of its author, who used the system on an everyday basis for several months, and an empirical study, in which a group of eight users evaluated the system over a period of two to six weeks. The user group consisted of eight native Swedish speakers, from 21 to 51 years old, and included undergraduate and graduate students, university teachers, a programmer, and a secretary.

Most participants positively evaluated both the underlying approach and the current version of the system. The advantages of the system, mentioned by the participants, included: (a) access to various types of resources related to a project "from within one place;" (b) the provision of an overview of ongoing projects; (c) the ability to switch back and forth between projects; and (d) the help provided by the system in recalling the context of a project, which made it easier to resume working on the project after an interruption.

Two main problems with the system were reported. First, there was a need to manually clean up resource lists and/or interaction histories from time to time to delete irrelevant items. The problem was caused mostly by system's automatic unselective inclusion of all information objects employed by the user, even if the resources were not relevant to the project at hand. Second, some participants experienced difficulties understanding the user interface and the functionality of the system. Those users who were provided with brief (5–10 minute) face-to-face introductions did not mention this problem. However, participants who downloaded the system with minimal explanations, and had to learn how to use it though trial and error, reported initial confusion.

**Task Management and Email Use in UMEA**

Preliminary empirical evaluation of UMEA indicated that this tool was used separately from email. As mentioned above, the system allows the sending of messages from a project context by selecting an email address from the automatically compiled list of project-related contacts. However, participants did not use this functionality. This can be partly explained by the fact that some of the participants used email clients that were not supported by UMEA (the system only supported Microsoft Outlook). Another possible reason was that users did not see any tangible benefits from using email within UMEA because of the limited support for email-related activities (sending a new message to a person from an automatically created contact list was the only supported function). In everyday collaboration new emails do not constitute the majority of messages. Email messages are often sent as replies to previous emails and constitute a communication thread, which helps to retain the context of communication (Whittaker and Sidner 1996).

The second version of the UMEA system, which was developed to overcome some of the limitations of the first version, includes more email-related features. In this version, the items in the "Contacts" list are submenus. By selecting a contact the user has the choice of not only sending a message to the contact, but also of viewing (a) a prespecified number of the most recent messages received from the contact, or (b) a prespecified number of the most recent messages sent to the contact (see figure 10.4). The rationale for these new features is to allow the user to reply to project-related messages.

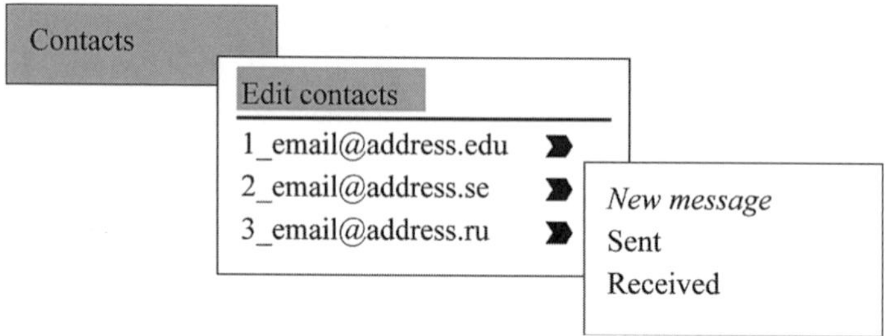


**Figure 10.4**
Extended email features of the second version of the UMEA system.

Even though the new version of UMEA supports more advanced access to email functionality from within a project context, this support is still basic. However, even this implementation of the system illustrates an example of the workspace-level design approach. If email communication is employed when the user focuses on a specific project and does not want to be distracted by information related to other projects, the user can perform some tasks, such as getting a list of recent messages received from a colleague or sending a new message to a person involved in the project, without switching to the email habitat. Future work in that direction can result in a more developed understanding of project-embedded use of email. The UMEA system can be further developed by implementing a number of additional features, such as linking email threads to a project, or the automatic compilation of project mailing lists.

The difference between the email-centric approach and the workspace-level approach (illustrated here by the UMEA system) regarding the integration of email and task management can be summarized as follows. According to the email-centric approach, the user's work on higher-level tasks is email-driven. Users are assumed to monitor incoming messages, switch between tasks when necessary, and bring additional resources to email if these resources cannot be accessed in the context of the email tool. The UMEA system, on the contrary, is based on the assumption that the use of email—as well as any other application—is determined by the goals of the user. The system aims to facilitate the use of information objects and the functionality of various tools, including email while carrying out a higher-level task, without forcing the user to switch between applications.

It is acknowledged that different approaches may be more suitable for different categories of users. For some users an extension of the email tool may be the best way to support their practices. However, at least some, and probably most, users can benefit from having certain email features available on demand. Some commercial software has taken steps in this direction. For example, a relatively recent extension of the standard functionality of Microsoft Office applications is the "Send to" command of the "File" menu. This command opens an empty email message with the current document as an automatically included attachment, and provides an on-demand use of email.

## Example System B: WorkspaceMirror

This section provides a second example of the workspace-level design approach, describing the empirical motivation, design, and evaluation of WorkspaceMirror (WM), an integration mechanism that allows an individual to share organizational hierarchies across PIM tools.

### Empirical Motivation

Many studies have observed the problems encountered by users in organizing information objects (e.g., Malone 1983; Whittaker and Sidner 1996). Since most previous studies in this area have focused on specific tools, such as email, the second author was motivated to perform an exploratory *cross-tool* study of personal information management practices for 25 users across their file, email, and bookmark collections (Boardman 2001, 2004; Boardman and Sasse 2004). The study provided evidence that users may benefit from sharing the folder structures used to organize items between PIM tools. Key findings included:

- Most participants organized files most extensively, with deeper folder hierarchies, and fewer unfiled items compared to the other collections. On average, participants had 49 file folders, as opposed to 37 in email, and 12 in bookmarks.
- Many of the users who filed items in two or more collections had created significant numbers of folders that appeared in multiple tool contexts. Such *folder overlap* suggests that certain user activities are cross-tool and involve the organization of multiple types of information. However, with

the current generation of PIM tools, each type of information must be organized separately.

• Several participants complained about the effort of managing multiple collections of personal information separately, and expressed annoyance that it was not possible to manage their files and email together in the same set of folders. For example, one commented: "They've got very distinct usages and purposes but to me it would be easy if I could have everything in one location."

• Some participants had attempted to manually perform *folder-mirroring*—maintaining identical folder structures across one or more collections. These participants reported that it was hard to keep the folder structures synchronized, and that they tended to diverge over time: "All of them [my folder structures] started off with an identical folder structure, but over time they've diverged somewhat." Therefore most had abandoned manual folder-mirroring because of the amount of effort involved: "I maintained my usability knowledge base [a set of folders mirrored between the web bookmark and email collections] for 6 months but it was too much hassle and I got out of practice."

• Some participants mentioned problems when looking for an item while they were not sure which collection it was in. In particular, retrieval problems were caused by the compromised ability to manage files as attachments within the email collection. Several participants also mentioned that retrieval problems were exacerbated by the existence of different organizational structures in each tool.

These findings lead to the question of what benefits might be offered by sharing one folder hierarchy between PIM tools. In other words, do users really need the flexibility to develop distinct classification schemes for different types of personal information? For example, would users be able to leverage organizational investment in their file system across to tools where they tended to develop fewer folders?

The study also provided evidence that sharing organizational structure between tools may not be appropriate. Folder overlap was in many cases partial, and often limited to certain types of folders such as those relating to projects. In other words, there was some variation in organizational behaviour across the three tools for many participants. Furthermore, some users did not rely on folders and instead relied on sort and search mechanisms, particularly in email.

### Design

In order to explore the potential of sharing folder structures between PIM tools, the second author designed a software prototype, WorkspaceMirror (WM), which allows users to mirror changes to folder structures between three collections of personal information: files, email, and web bookmarks (Boardman 2004; Boardman and Sasse 2004). In other words, if a change is made to the folder structure in one collection, it is replicated in the folder structures of the other collections. The prototype mirrored three types of structural change: (1) *creating a new folder, (2) deleting a folder, and (3) renaming a folder*. Note that each PIM tool still contained a distinct folder structure.

WM has been implemented on Microsoft Windows and synchronizes changes made to the folder hierarchies in three tools: (1) email folders in Outlook, (2) the user's document area in the file system, and (3) bookmark folders stored under "Favorites." The tool works in one of two modes: automatic or prompted. In prompted mode the creation, deletion, or renaming of any folder causes a dialogue box to be displayed asking the user if he wants to replicate the operation in the other two tools.

Note that WM should not be considered as an attempt to develop an alternative to hierarchical organization. Limitations of the hierarchy such as single-inheritance (Dourish et al. 1999) are beyond the scope of the design. Also, it should also be noted that the prototype does not provide alternative means for interacting with folder structures. The user interacts with the three PIM tools as before (e.g., via direct manipulation, or the command-line). The design can be considered as a step toward the full unification of personal information management that has been proposed in systems such as Lifestreams (Freeman and Gelernter, this volume) and Presto (Dourish et al. 1999). However, such *revolutionary* technologies have been criticized for a lack of evaluation (Boardman 2004; Boardman and Sasse 2004). In contrast, a prime aim of this work was to facilitate evaluation by pursuing an *incremental* design based on relatively modest changes to standard software. This has the advantage of enabling evaluation in real user workspaces with minimal disruption to the users concerned.

### Evaluation

An initial evaluation of WM was carried out with eight users to determine whether the design was workable. This was directed at investigating whether the folder-mirroring mechanism would help users manage multiple types of information more effectively. A major challenge was the lack of any accepted evaluation methodology regarding PIM tools (Whittaker, Terveen, and Nardi 2000). The limitations of traditional performance-based measures of usability for complex, ongoing, interleaved activities such as PIM (Dillon 2001), led the researcher to steer away from a task-based experiment. Instead the evaluation was based on a longer-term field study.

Eight colleagues tested WM in prompted mode for an average of 69 days each, providing feedback via diaries and weekly interviews. We also correlated this qualitative data with fortnightly logs of their evolving folder hierarchies to track their usage of any mirrored folders. The data was triangulated to build up a rich picture of the user's attitude to WM and investigate whether it influenced their PIM practices. The use of colleagues as participants is justified as follows. First, it was hoped that the study could leverage the existing trust between the researcher and his colleagues—avoiding possible privacy problems of working with strangers' personal data. Second, they were all technologically aware and ready to work with beta software. A third reason was pragmatic: it was easy to meet with them to carry out interviews and to install software.

Usage of WM varied widely between participants, partially owing to tool incompatibilities for some users, and is described in depth by Boardman (2004). Six of the participants mirrored folder creations between PIM tools (average 7 each, min: 1, max: 26). All mirrored events related to *folder creations*. No participants used WM to mirror a folder delete or folder rename event, except to test the prototype. Most mirrored folders were located high up in most participants' folder structures (average depth in the folder structure was 1.83 [SD: 0.89]). Across all participants, the most common types of mirrored folders were *project* (40%) and *event* (22%).[5] Participants varied in terms of which tools they performed mirroring between. The most common source collection was files (64% of mirrored folders), followed by bookmarks (21%), and email (14%). The most common trajectories were "*files to email*" (45% of all events), "*bookmarks to files and email*" (16% of all events), and "*files to bookmarks*" (13% of all events). The remaining two participants made no use of WM. However, they both ran WM on their computers to test its robustness, and they provided qualitative feedback.

### Qualitative Feedback: Pros and Cons of Folder-Mirroring

The aim of the evaluation was to investigate whether the participants would use WM to share folder structures between the three PIM tools. A range of positive and negative feedback was received regarding the tested version of WM. Two of the heaviest users observed and welcomed the increase in consistency between the folder structures over time and described how it helped them manage information for a variety of projects. Both suggested that mirroring lead to easier navigation, for example: "It's easier to navigate with a mirrored structure, compared to three different ones." Three participants who performed more limited mirroring also acknowledged the benefits of an increase in consistency.

Four participants indicated that mirroring was useful between all three tools, while the remaining four indicated that it was most worthwhile between files and emails. Note that all members of this second group placed little importance on mirroring folders to/from their bookmark collections.

A general theme mentioned by all eight participants was that mirroring should not follow a one-to-one mapping between PIM tools because of differing organizational requirements. In many cases, participants had more complex organizing requirements in their file collections compared to email and bookmarks. For example, one commented:

> It doesn't make sense to create an email folder for every single publication so I just have a single submissions folder that goes across the publications and has, let's say, at the moment maybe 30 entries or so. In my H-drive [file collection] on the other hand, every single publication is a project—and deserves its own folder because it consists of much more files than just the five emails.

Participants observed that there was not always a direct one-to-one mapping between their folder requirements in each tool. Seven participants suggested that mirroring was particularly appropriate for *top-level folders*. One said, for example:

> Images related to my project and all the substructure of that project . . . it's very difficult to see why you'd want to mirror all that [to files and bookmarks]. Once you've mirrored there [at the top level]—you might not want to mirror it further down. I think it would work at that level. Here are the projects I'm working on. Here are the emails about that project. And here are web links related to the project. That makes sense to me.

However, many participants welcomed the chance to reflect on the relevance of organizational decisions made in one tool to other contexts.

Occasionally mirrored folders were not always used for the storage of items in all tools, but the testers indicated that the improved organizational consistency outweighed the side effect of increased clutter. The users also reported lower management overheads and easier retrieval of filed items. However, no attempt has yet been made to confirm these results objectively.

Two participants noted difficulties in accommodating WM within an existing personal information environment where differing file, email, and bookmark folder structures had already been developed. One participant noted that he would need to perform a significant reorganization of his workspace to make WM worthwhile. Although he reported planning to do so, he had not done it over the course of the study. Another suggested that WM would be most appropriate when setting up a new computer:

> I'd say you get you'd get some seriously different results if you installed WM on someone with a brand new computer about to start to using it. . . . I think you'd get a very different dynamic, and you might even get a completely different usage out of the same person. . . . Most of my pre-organization had already occurred by then, reasonably quickly after purchasing the computer.

Feedback also included a number of design requests that are under consideration for future versions. This section focuses on the most common area of feedback—the need to make mirroring more selective. This points to a trade-off between *organizational consistency* (having the same folder structure in different tools) and *cross-tool organizational flexibility* (being able to organize different types of information in different ways). Several participants welcomed the increase in consistency, indicating that it made navigation easier. However, increasing consistency constrains users to organize different types of information in the same way. Overall, most participants favored flexibility over consistency. However, seven participants said that mirroring folders across all tools made sense in some cases—in particular, top-level folders. A key reason for the bias in favor of flexibility was the need for different organizational requirements between tools. For many participants, email and bookmarks tended to be based on shallow, one-layer folder structures, while files were organized within deep, branching structures. Therefore they saw little need to mirror all low-level file folders to email and bookmarks.

### Discussion

WM offers a second example of workspace-level design. The initial evaluation indicated the potential benefits of the design, although the trade-off between consistency and reduced flexibility warrants further investigation. The study indicates that folder mirroring has potential, especially for top-level folders. In this way it highlighted how information organizing, an important day-to-day user activity, is a cross-workspace activity, currently supported by application-specific functionality. WM illustrates a first step toward providing cross-workspace support for information organizing across multiple applications, and the potential benefits that may result.

The formative redesign of WM is outside the scope of this chapter. However, based on the response from the participants, the next step would certainly be to limit mirroring to top-level folders by default. Furthermore, participants varied in terms of which tools they found it useful to mirror folder structures between. Although overall files-to-email was the most common mirroring pattern, several participants mirrored mainly between files and bookmarks. Therefore, a customization facility to select the PIM tools between which to mirror would also be worth investigating.

## Conclusion

This chapter contrasts two design perspectives: (a) an application-centric approach, for example, extending the functionality of email to include task management features, and (b) a workspace-level approach, where the aim is to improve the integration of distinct applications. The difference between the approaches can be defined in terms of their relative foci. Whereas the email-centric approach, as a particular case of a more general application-centered approach, focuses on an individual *tool*, the workspace-level integration approach encompasses multiple tools.

Higher-level tasks transcend the boundaries of a single application and typically require coordination of multiple applications to work on an activity. In addition, a user will typically perform *multiple* activities within a digital work environment. Furthermore, users will often be interrupted, switch between activities, start new ones, resume, abandon, or suspend activities, and so forth. Environments need to be designed to support all these types of coordination. Therefore, the design of environments implies a design perspective different from that of application-specific design. This perspective received less attention and is less elaborated upon than application-centric design (see the introduction by Kaptelinin and Czerwinski, this volume).

Currently, much of the work on personal information environments is application-centric. In our view, this tendency could be usefully balanced with more attention to the design of the workspace as a whole. In this chapter we have argued that specific tools should not be studied, designed, and evaluated in isolation from the rest of the workspace.

Both the application-centric approach and the workspace-level approach have their respective advantages and disadvantages. As we discussed earlier in the chapter, an application-centric approach can offer the benefits of optimizing one specific user interface. For example, in the case of email, recent work has extended the inbox to act as a to-do list, and provided intuitive access to some task-related resources, such as messages, files, and web links. However, we have discussed how such email extensions, as well as increasing interface complexity, may also require the user to make a substantial investment of time and effort in manually linking resources to email. Thus, adding new functionality may have a side effect of making the monitoring of incoming messages more difficult. In addition, the usefulness of email as a task-management tool depends critically on how other tools are used; for instance, if the user relies heavily on web-based collaboration support, then email may constitute a relatively minor source of information for task management at the individual workspace level.

The workspace-level integration approach is based on the assumption that email, or any other application, is not the whole story. Instead, we urge that it should be considered a subhabitat within the wider workspace. In the case of email, this means that email should retain the primary function of providing a focus of attention for communicating with the "outside world."

This chapter presented two examples of mechanisms or "metatools" that improve integration between applications. Both systems described in this chapter illustrate the workspace-level design perspective. The systems themselves are relatively lightweight and can be learned quickly. Both systems let the user decide how to work, and do not prescribe how the users should go about their everyday activities. If the systems are not employed, users can follow their habitual work routines without experiencing any further inconveniences. The overall organization of a work environment remains flexible; users can make changes to their environments relatively easily. For instance, if the user decides to switch to another email program that he thinks is more consistent with his work practices, he can do that without a major restructuring of the workspace.

We do not claim that workspace-level integration is problem-free. The special-purpose integration systems described in this chapter do not explicitly suggest more advanced work practices to the user. Therefore, their usefulness may not be immediately apparent. Furthermore, the systems present new elements in the user's workspace, which require attention and learning. Even though the systems were deliberately designed to minimize extra cognitive load associated with their use, some effort will be required on the user's part.

It should be noted that although we have contrasted the pros and cons of the application-centric and workspace-level perspectives, these perspectives are not mutually exclusive. For instance, email could be extended with new functionalities *while at the same time* becoming better integrated with other tools. As this book indicates, there is a growing understanding in the HCI community that the traditional focus on individual applications is not sufficient. It reflects a fundamentally piecemeal approach in research and development, resulting in workspaces populated by massively complex applications, each attempting to provide a complete user habitat. However, as we have discussed, this can result in unused functionality, and coordination breakdowns. A balanced approach, combining design at both the application *and* workspace levels appears to be the only way to make digital work environments truly habitable.

## Notes

1. During the work on this chapter Richard Boardman was a graduate student at the Department of Electronic and Electrical Engineering, Imperial College London.

2. A general comment that can be leveled at the major of work in the field of PIM and task management in general is that there is too much focus on the needs of technically experienced users. Most empirical research and design has focused on the needs of knowledge workers.

3. Note that the terms application and tool are used interchangeably in this chapter.

4. Systems such as Bifrost (Bälter and Sidner 2002) or SNARF (Neustaedter et al. 2005) divide the inbox into several parts containing different types of messages. These systems are deliberately designed to make sure the user is aware of all received emails; they do not undermine but rather support maintaining a single focus of attention by suggesting optimal strategies of dealing with incoming messages.

5. These aggregate figures are biased toward those participants who mirrored more folders. Please see Boardman 2004 for more analysis on a user-by-user basis.

## References

Bälter, O. (1998). Electronic mail in a working context. Doctoral thesis, TRITA-NA-9820, Royal Institute of Technology, Stockholm, Sweden.

Bälter, O. (2000). A keyboard-level analysis of email message organization. In *Proceedings of the 2000 ACM Conference on Human Factors in Computing Systems,* pp. 105–112. The Hague, the Netherlands, April 1–6.

Bälter, O., and Sidner, C. (2002). Bifrost Inbox Organizer: Giving users control over the Inbox. In *Proceedings of the Second Nordic Conference on Human–Computer Interaction (NORDICHI'02),* pp. 111–118. Aarhus, Denmark, October 19–23.

Barreau, D., and Nardi, B. (1995). Finding and reminding: File organization from the Desktop. *ACM SIGCHI Bulletin* 27: 39–43.

Bellotti, V., Ducheneaut, N., Howard, M., and Smith, I. (2003). Taking email to task: The design and evaluation of a task management centered email tool. In *Proceedings of the CHI 2003 Conference: Human Factors in Computing Systems*, pp. 345–352. Ft. Lauderdale, Florida, April 5–10.

Bellotti, V., and Smith, I. (2000). Informing the design of an information management system with iterative fieldwork. *Proceedings of the Conference on Designing Interactive Systems: Processes, Practices, Methods, and Techniques*, pp. 227–237. New York City, New York, August 17–19.

Boardman, R. (2001). Category overlap between hierarchies in user workspace. In *Proceedings of the Eighth IFIP TC 13 International Conference on Human–Computer Interaction (INTERACT'01)*, Tokyo, Japan, July 9–13.

Boardman, R. (2004). Improving tool support for personal information management. Unpublished Ph.D. thesis, Department of Electrical and Electronic Engineering, Imperial College London.

Boardman, R., and Sasse, M. A. (2004). "Stuff goes into the computer and doesn't come out": A cross-tool study of personal information management. In *Proceedings of the 2004 ACM Conference on Human Factors in Computing Systems,* pp. 583–590. Vienna, Austria, April 24–19.

Boardman, R., Sasse, M. A., and Spence, B. (2002). Life beyond the mailbox: A cross-tool perspective on personal information management. Position paper for workshop "Redesigning Email for the 21st Century" at the CSCW 2002 Conference (New Orleans, Louisiana, November 16, 2002). Http://peach.mie.utoronto.ca/people/jacek/emailresearch/CSCW2002/submissions/UK-IC-boardman-sasse-spence-cscw2002-final.pdf.

Bødker, S. (1991). *Through the Interface: A Human Activity Approach to User Interface Design.* Hillsdale, N. J.: Lawrence Erlbaum.

Christensen, H., and Bardram, J. (2002). Supporting human activities—exploring activity-centered computing. In Borriello, G. and Holmquist, L.-E. (eds.), *Proceedings of the 4th International Conference, UbiComp 2002,* pp. 107–116. Lecture Notes in Computer Science 2498. Berlin: Springer.

Czerwinski, M., Horvitz, E., and Wilhite, S. (2004). A diary study of task switching and interruptions. In *Proceedings of the 2004 ACM Conference on Human Factors in Computing Systems,* pp. 175–182. Vienna, Austria, April 24–19.

Dillon, A. (2001). Beyond usability: Process, outcome, and affect in HCI. *Canadian Journal of Information Science* 26(4): 57–69.

Dourish, P., Edwards, W. K., LaMarca, A., and Salisbury, M. (1999). Presto: An experimental architecture for fluid interactive document spaces. *ACM Transactions on Computer Human Interaction* 6 (2): 133–161.

Dragunov, A. N., Dietterich, T., G., Johnsrude, K., McLaughlin, M., Li, L., and Herlocker, J. L. (2005). TaskTracer: A desktop environment to support multi-tasking knowledge workers. In *Proceedings of the 10th International Conference on Intelligent User Interfaces,* pp. 75–82. San Diego, California, January 10–13.

Ducheneaut, N., and Bellotti, V. (2001). Email as habitat: An exploration of embedded personal information management. *interactions* 8 (5): 30–38.

Fertig, S., Freeman, E., and Gelernter, D. (1996). Lifestreams: An alternative to the desktop metaphor. In *Conference Companion of the 1996 ACM SIGCHI Conference on Human Factors in Computing Systems (CHI'96),* pp. 410–411. Vancouver, British Columbia, Canada, April 13–18.

Gwizdka, J. (2002). Reinventing the inbox—supporting the management of pending tasks in email. In *Extended Abstracts of the 2002 ACM SIGCHI Conference on Human Factors in Computing Systems (CHI'2002),* pp. 550–551. Minneapolis, Minnesota, April 20—25.

Gwizdka, J., and Whittaker, S. (2002). Redesigning email for the 21st century. A CSCW'2002 workshop report. Http://emailresearch.org/.

Henderson, A., and Card, S. (1986). Rooms: The use of virtual workspaces to reduce space contention in a window-based graphical user interface. *ACM Transactions on Graphics* 5: 211–243.

Huynh, D., Karger, D., and Quan, D. (2002). Haystack: A platform for creating, organizing, and visualizing information using RDF. Http://haystack.lcs.mit.edu/papers/computer-network-2002.pdf/.

Kaptelinin, V. (1996). Creating computer-based work environments: An empirical study of Macintosh users. *Proceedings of the ACM SIGCPR/SIGMIS'96 Conference*, pp. 360–366. Denver, Colorado, April 11–13.

Kaptelinin, V. (2002). Putting work to email or putting email to work? Position paper for workshop "Redesigning Email for the 21st Century" at the CSCW 2002 Conference (New Orleans, Louisiana, November 16, 2002). Http://peach.mie.utoronto.ca/people/jacek/emailresearch/CSCW2002/submissions/UMEA-Kaptelinin_CSCW_2002_workshop.pdf.

Kaptelinin, V. (2003). UMEA: Translating interaction histories into project contexts. In *Proceedings of the 2003 ACM Conference on Human Factors in Computing Systems,* pp. 353–360. Ft. Lauderdale, Florida, April 5–10.

Kaptelinin, V., and Nardi, B. (2006). *Acting with Technology: Activity Theory and Interaction Design.* Cambridge, Mass.: MIT Press.

Lansdale, M. (1988). The psychology of personal information management. *Applied Ergonomics* 19 (1): 55–66.

Mackay, W. (1988). More than just a communication system: Diversity in the use of electronic mail. In *Proceedings of the 1988 ACM Conference on Computer-Supported Cooperative Work (CSCW'88),* pp. 344–353. Portland, Oregon, September 26–28.

Malone, T. (1983). How do people organise their desks? Implications for the design of office information systems. *ACM Transactions on Office Information Systems* 1 (1): 99–112.

Moran, T. (2003). Activity: Analysis, design, and management. In *Ivrea Symposium on Foundations of Interaction* Design, 12–13 November 2003, Italy. Http://www.interaction-ivrea.it/en/news/education/2003–04/symposium/index.asp/.

Nardi, B., Whittaker, S., Isaacs, E., Creech, M., Johnson, J., and Hainsworth, J. (2002). Integrating communication and information through ContactMap. *Communications of the ACM* 45: 89–95.

Neustaedter, C., Brush, A. J. B., and Smith, M. A. (2005). Beyond "From" and "Received": Exploring the dynamics of email triage. In *Extended Abstracts of the 2005 ACM SIGCHI Conference on Human Factors in Computing Systems,* pp. 1977–1980. Portland, Oregon, April 2–7.

Neustaedter, C., Brush, A. J. B., Smith, M. A., and Fisher, D. (2005). The social network and relationship finder: Social sorting for email triage. Paper given at the Second Conference on Email and Anti-Spam (CEAS 2005). Stanford, California, July 21–22. Http://www.ceas.cc/2005/index.html/.

Newell, A., Rosenbloom, P. S., and Laird, J. E. (1989). Symbolic architectures of cognition. In Posner, M. (ed.), *Foundations of Cognitive Science,* pp. 93–131. Cambridge, Mass.: MIT Press.

Norman, D. (1998). *The Invisible Computer: Why Good Products Can Fail, the Personal Computer Is So Complex, and Information Appliances Are the Solution.* Cambridge, Mass.: MIT Press.

Plaisant, C., and Shneiderman, B. (1995). Organization overviews and role management: Inspiration for future desktop environments. In *Proceedings of the 4th IEE Workshop on Enabling Technologies: Infrastructure for Collaborative Enterprises,* pp. 14–22. New York.

Raskin, J. (2000). *The Humane Interface*. Reading, Mass.: Addison-Wesley.

Robertson, G., van Dantzich, M., Robbins, D., Czerwinski, M., Hinckly, K., Risden, K., Thiel, D., and Gorokhovsky, V. (2000). The Task Gallery: A 3D window manager. In *Proceedings of the 2000 ACM Conference on Human Factors in Computing Systems,* pp. 494–501. The Hague, the Netherlands, April 1–6.

Segal, R., and Kephart, J. O. (1999). MailCat: An intelligent assistant for organizing email. In *Proceedings of the Third Annual Conference on Autonomous Agents,* pp. 276–282. May.

Smith, M., Cadiz, J. J., and Burkhalter, B. (2000). Conversation trees and threaded chats. *Proceedings of the 2000 ACM Conference on Computer Supported Cooperative Work*, pp. 97–105. Philadelphia, Pennsylvania, December 2–6.

Venolia, G., and Neustaedter, C. (2003). Understanding sequence and reply relationships within email conversations: A mixed-model visualization. *Proceedings of the 2003 ACM Conference on Human Factors in Computing Systems (CHI 2003),* pp. 361–368. Ft. Lauderdale, Florida, April 5–10.

Whittaker, S. (2005). Supporting collaborative task management in email. *Human Computer Interaction* 20: 49–88.

Whittaker, S., and Sidner, C. (1996). Email overload: Exploring personal information management of email. In *Proceedings of the 1996 ACM SIGCHI Conference on Human Factors in Computing Systems (CHI'96),* pp. 276–283. Vancouver, British Columbia, Canada, April 13–18.

Whittaker, S., Terveen, L., and Nardi, B. (2000). Let's stop pushing the envelope and start addressing it: A reference task agenda for HCI. *Human Computer Interaction* 15: 75–106.

Yiu, K. S., Baecker, R., Silver, N., and Long, B. (1997). A time-based interface for electronic mail and task management. In *Proceedings of the Seventh International Conference on Human–Computer Interaction (HCI International '97),* pp. 19–22. San Francisco, California, August 24–29.

# Conclusion

# 11

# Beyond the Desktop Metaphor in Seven Dimensions

Thomas P. Moran and Shumin Zhai

The ubiquitous use of the desktop metaphor as the primary means of interacting with information is perhaps the earliest, and arguably the most profound, landmark of user interface design. Ironically, such a success is both a great past achievement and a difficult future challenge to overcome. The computing technologies and user experiences available in our current web-driven world are evolving rapidly. In fact, the strict concept of the desktop metaphor is already a "straw man" notion, but it can help us characterize where we were and where we are going. We are already in midflight from the desktop to the next metaphor. Although we cannot be sure where we are going, we can discern different dimensions in which things are changing.

The research presented in this book represents some of the most promising recent efforts to move beyond desktop-metaphor-based computing. In this concluding chapter we reflect and comment on seven dimensions along which we see future integrated digital work environments changing, as experienced by users, from today's computing environment. Our analyses and speculations are based on the chapters in this book and our own research, as well as the HCI literature and information technology trends in general. We conclude this book in very broad strokes in the spirit of trying to capture major themes.

Here, in a nutshell, are the dimensions of change that we will examine:

1. The basic change is that personal information is being liberated from the constraints of the desktop metaphor. It is being dispersed in the networked world in what we might call a "personal information cloud."

2. Several other kinds of changes follow from the first. The desktop metaphor standardized, and thus limited, the ways information could be

presented. New ways of organizing personal information are spawning a great variety of new representations and visualizations.

3. The desktop metaphor was designed for a standardized computational form, that of the workstation and laptop. The proliferation of new forms of computing devices both requires and exploits the information cloud to allow information to "follow the user" rather than the existing forms.

4. The desktop metaphor is built around keyboarding and pointing. The multiplicity of devices of different sizes and functions forces designers to develop new modes and modalities of physical interaction techniques.

5. Not only is information being liberated from the desktop, but so also are software applications. Functional computations delivered as services from servers make these functions available independent of specific devices.

6. The desktop metaphor creates a personal office isolated from others except through limited channels. More and more personal information clouds are intersecting in richer ways to facilitate collaborating with other participants in large-scale social communities.

7. The desktop metaphor creates an arena focused on a variety of generic office tools geared to low-level interaction tasks. Future computational work environments should be centered instead around the user's meaningful activities, which requires an explicit representation of the concept of activity in the information cloud.

Note that these seven dimensions are not exhaustive; and they are dimensions of change, such as moving from rigid to more adaptive representations. But these seven seem most related to the body of work exhibited in this book. In what follows we reflect and comment on each of these dimensions, relate them to each other and to the chapters in this book, and conclude with a brief review on where we stand on the future of personal computing.

## Dimension 1: From the Office Container to the "Personal Information Cloud"

The desktop metaphor was originally invented to support office work. The metaphor is really a personal *office* metaphor. The metaphorical desktop itself is a display screen with various office-relevant objects—documents (overlapping windows), folders (icons), and tools (e.g., printer icons)—in a freeform arrangement. There is also a metaphorical file system organized as a hierarchy of folders and files, rather like file cabinets. Further, there is a metaphorical mail-based inbox, providing a route for messages and attached documents to enter and leave the office.

The dominant feature of the desktop metaphor is that information is *contained* in the office, in both a cognitive and a physical sense. Users understand that information objects have a place: on the desktop, in a folder, in the inbox, and so on. But there is also a physical reality to the containment notion—the digital information is actually stored in the physical memory of the personal computer. The metaphor enables the user to understand and manage the information in the computer's physical store. However, there is a growing trend to interact with information outside the metaphorical office. Workers in business settings have for a long time been using file servers to retrieve, back up, share, and archive information. The World Wide Web has made remote information accessible within the metaphorical office. Much information does not have to be stored in the office machine for it to be readily available. And people are not just retrieving, but also putting information on the web. Millions of people use hosted email services. The evolution of the web to "Web 2.0" is enabling people not only to retrieve, but also to create personal content and annotations on the web. So, personal information such as email is now commonly stored outside of the office machine.

But there is also a deeper cognitive trend in the way users understand how to manage their information. There is great cognitive comfort in the idea of *containment*—that a document is contained in some folder, a known *place* where it is located and can be found. The desktop metaphor is based on these familiar notions of containment and place. But these notions are being eroded by the ability to effectively search for information, first on the web and now on the desktop itself. Users do not have to be concerned about where information is if they can effectively get at it by search.

We do not believe that search will be the only method to locate information. There are strong individual preferences in relying on search. For example, some people do not create email folders at all, and rely on searching their inbox. Others are "frequent filers" (Whittaker and Sidner 1996). There are good reasons to pay the cost of manually structuring information, such as organizing and planning benefits (Jones et al. 2005).

Structuring information does not require containment; it only requires *reference*—the ability to create descriptions that can reference information objects. While this is inherently a more abstract notion than containment, people are gaining experience with the concept every day in using the web. The web emphasizes references (links) between pages and deemphasizes the notion that the information is contained in places (but it does not totally eliminate the notion of places, i.e., servers).

There is an interesting analogy between information and money. Money can also be kept in a place (at home or in a bank), or it can be placeless. Although there was also a great deal of cognitive comfort in keeping money "under the mattress," eventually most people gave up such a comfort and accepted the fact that their money is dispersed within financial institutions, which in turn loan and invest the money all over the world. It is practically unknowable where each individual's money precisely is. All that matters is that one can get it or transfer it on demand.

As users disperse and "destructure" their personal information, there is less need for the desktop metaphor to organize the information. We believe that the metaphor is being replaced by more abstract and sophisticated organizers, based on over a decade of experience of millions of people with information technology. Thus let us use the term *personal information cloud* to refer to the "working set" of information that is relevant to the individual and his work. We are not promoting this term as a profoundly new notion; it is just a convenient label for our use here. We do not claim that a "cloud" is a particularly useful metaphor for either users or designers. In contrast to the desktop metaphor, which was consciously designed by the first user-interface designers, the personal information cloud will probably not be "designed" at all, but rather will evolve as a set of organizing principles based on the collective experiences of those using and developing the web.

This collective personal information cloud is what people need to interact with, not with a particular device or metaphor; the latter are mediators of this interaction. There are several requirements the personal information cloud must meet in order to be useful:

1. *Personal:* It should contain most if not all information that is relevant to the individual and his activities.
2. *Persistent:* It should be preserved.

3. *Pervasive:* It should be always accessible from a variety of devices, programs, and services—that is, it should "follow the individual."

4. *Secure:* The information should be secure and private at an appropriate level. This is a significant issue when information is not held locally (although holding information locally is not in itself assurance of privacy in a networked world).

5. *Referenceable:* Each information object in the cloud should ideally have a unique ID (or permalink) and support a protocol for retrieval.

6. *Standardized:* The information needs to be in standard formats so that it is usable by a variety of devices, programs, and services.

7. *Semantic:* The cloud should be based on an extensible scheme of semantically rich metadata, so that it can be understood by a variety of programs and services in different contexts.

Many of the other dimensions follow naturally from this notion of a personal information cloud: new information representations, new device forms, and new interaction techniques. Social interactions and activity management can also be better enabled by a personal information cloud.

## Dimension 2: From the Desktop to a Diverse Set of Visual Representations

The most noticeable feature of today's personal computing environment is its visual interface, which is based on the desktop metaphor, and a set of GUI (graphical user interface) rules and conventions to represent information objects and regulate interaction behavior. As a virtual world, the "physics" of the conventional desktop to some extent resembles the real world, including constant scale, continuity, fixed place (of file location), and "Newton's first law" ("an object at rest stays at rest until acted upon by force" or "objects on the desktop stay where the user places them"). Today's desktop computing environments also organize information hierarchically into files within folders. Most computer users have lived digitally in this virtual world for more than a decade.

Much of this book is devoted to issues such as how successful is today's desktop interface, how users in fact use it (Ravasio and Tscherter, this volume), and, especially, what alternative representatives there are (Freeman and Gelernter's's chronological Lifestreams representation, Karger on Haystack, Robertson et al. on Scalable Fabric and the Task Gallery that use varying scale 2D projection and 3D objects to represent information objects respectively, Voida et al.'s work on extending the 2D desktop surface to wall displays so that montages of windows and objects can be continuously and visibly represented, and Kaptelinin and Czerwinski's introductions, all in this volume).

When the number of functions, programs, and files for an average user was relatively small, the desktop metaphor and the point-and-click style of GUI interface had an obvious advantage: users could interact with information objects by visual recognition and reaction, easing the burden of learning and memory. Furthermore, owing to de facto standardization, certain GUI conventions, even some unnatural ones (such as double-clicking to open a file), have become second nature to most users. However, the rapidly growing number of functions, applications, and files (hundreds if not thousands), puts strain on the desktop interface, at least in its conventional form. To relieve the strain, desktop search, which enables the user to find files in the local computer without navigating the desktop folder hierarchy, is gaining acceptance. Alternative or extended forms of information representation guided by different metaphors may also gain eventual acceptance. We do not believe that today's GUI conventions can be supplanted by one simple alternative representation having dramatically larger capacity, greater consistency, and the same level of ease-of-entry. More likely, in the future a variety of advanced visual representations may be adapted to specific problem domains and different device forms, complementing the basic conventional desktop metaphor.

## Dimension 3: From Interaction with One Device to Interaction with Information through Many Devices

The term "desktop" in computer jargon has multiple interrelated meanings. One is as the top-level "folder" in the hierarchical organization of files and applications in a personal computer. Another is as a set of visual representation conventions loosely guided by the metaphor. But the term also frequently refers to computers that take the form of a "workstation," typically resting on a desk (and by extension, on the lap). Leveraging the economies of scale, this form of computer (commonly known as the personal computer or PC) revolutionized computing and freed it from the much less accessible mainframe and timesharing computers. Personal computers give individual users the flexibility of installing and configuring their own software environments. Recall the discussions of dimension 1 on information containment in office metaphor: the drawback of relying on PCs as the sole information processor is that personal information is trapped in one fixed device (the PC), limiting mobility and flexibility. This is particularly evident for non-office-workers; recall Bardram's observation of the inconvenience of the location and form restriction imposed by today's desktop and laptop computers for doctors and nurses (Bardram, this volume).

While desktop and laptop computers will continue to be important platforms of personal computing, non-desktop computers, such as smart handsets, tablets, and electronic white boards, will complement today's unipolar desktop personal computers to a far greater extent than today. Consistent with visions of ubiquitous and pervasive computing, all networked digital devices and appliances in many different forms can potentially be connected and hence become interfaces to the personal information cloud. Potentially everyday objects or appliances (Norman 1998) can also be "powered" by the information cloud. For example, an electronic restaurant menu, once opened by a particular individual, can be connected to the individual's information cloud that keeps track of her diet history, preferences, and restrictions.

There are many user-interface design challenges when the same information can flow in and out of very different devices. How can the same information outflow from different physical devices have enough invariance in appearance and behavior, so that the user can easily identify it and interact with it? How can a unified and logically consistent user experience be provided independent of a device's specific form factor? What can be done to ensure the user has a coherent and consistent human-information interaction experience? For example, a user should be able to interact with his or her calendar events whether the computer at hand is a desktop PC or a smart handset. Separating the data model from its view has long been recognized as an important principle in computing in general and in user-interface design in particular (Wiecha et al. 1990). Initiatives at the W3 consortium in areas such as device independence may lay groundwork for achieving transformational user interfaces (Paterno and Santoro 2003; Calvary et al. 2003); but many difficult challenges call for further significant HCI research efforts. For example, can a truly usable user interface be designed independent of the specific form factors of a device? How can we counter the arguments that a good user-interface design has to consider the specific physical form factors of a device? Is there a fundamental set of interaction vocabularies that can be implemented in a variety of device forms so that information can be presented interactively on any device that supports such a set of vocabulary? These issues will be even harder to resolve than hardware-independent software development, which has proven very difficult.

Another important topic along the dimension of device diversity is the development of principles, technologies, and infrastructure to support teaming multiple devices with different input and output modalities to form a gestalt user experience, so users could opportunistically utilize the best features of more than one device or information channel to accomplish a task (Ahn and Pierce 2005; Yin and Zhai 2005).

## Dimension 4: From Mouse and Keyboard to a Greater Set of Physical Interaction Devices and Modalities

An integral part of the desktop interaction experience is the contribution of physical input devices, in particular the mouse as a pointing device and the keyboard as a device for inputting text and evoking commands (e.g., function keys). Almost all software today is designed to rely on these devices. As the personal information cloud model and multiple device forms begin to evolve, the mouse and keyboard can no longer be the only form of physical interaction device. However, the explicit or implicit assumptions of a pointing device and a keyboard are so broadly and deeply adopted in today's software development that even the Windows Tablet PC, which is quite similar to traditional desktop and laptop computers in form and size, is markedly more difficult to use than its predecessors. Developing novel, potent yet practical interaction methods that are suited to non-desktop forms of computing is a rare opportunity for the user-interface research field, a field that in general values novelty, often at the cost of practicality and real-world impact. Developing novel yet practical interaction methods is a difficult challenge, since the novel interaction methods are expected to match the performance of the mouse and keyboard, but without making use of the same long learning curve. Experienced computer users have spent years improving their typing and desktop interaction skills, so that even some artificial conventions have become natural to most users. For non-keyboard-based input methods to gain acceptance by users, deep research and careful design have to be invested in developing them. Leveraging users' existing desktop experience and skill, interaction methods that are "transplants" from the conventional desktop may provide a safe path. Paradoxically, such transplants are often poor replications of the desktop experience, inhibiting the full potential of non-desktop computing devices. For example, when using a pen to interact with a point-and-click style of a desktop graphic user interface, actions that are rather simple for a mouse-based interface, such as a double click, become more awkward, while the dexterity and expressive power of a pen go wasted.

Pen-gesture-based input methods have long attracted both researchers (e.g., Kurtenbach and Buxton 1994) and product developers (e.g., Go, Apple Newton, Palm Pilot, and Windows Tablet PC). Although pen-based interaction methods still have a long way to go before they can truly take advantage of the dexterity of the pen and yet be self-revealing enough to be compelling to novices, many research projects in the user-interface field show promise (Hinckley et al. 2005). In our own lab we have been developing interaction models that use pen-crossing action as a counterpart to mouse pointing (Accot and Zhai 2002; see also Apitz and Guimbretiére's work on CrossY, in Apitz and Guimbretiére 2004) and a new way of entering text and command using ShapeWriter (also known as SHARK shorthand). Shape writing takes advantage of the fluidity and dexterity of the pen in making gestures; the human ability in perceiving, remembering, and producing geometric patterns; and modern computing capabilities in processing statistical constraints to efficiently enter text and commands on nonconventional computers (Zhai and Kristensson 2003; Zhai, Kristensson, and Smith 2005).

As devices become more diverse, the interaction modalities may move beyond pointing, typing, or even pen input. Voice and eye-gaze are two modalities that may be taken advantage of in certain situations (Oviatt 2003). Multimodal interfaces could be particularly effective if contextual information can be drawn from sensing and the personal information cloud, so that these modalities are used cooperatively to their respective advantages.

Progress in the dimension of new input methods faces the challenge of overcoming users' existing mental models, skill sets, and habits. (This also holds for dimension 2 and perhaps many others.) Making changes concerning the interlock of user skills acquired under a set of conventions tends to be very difficult. Using the QWERTY keyboard as a prime example, Paul David argues for a "path dependence" or "lock-in" theory, dubbed qwertynomics, in which an accidental sequence of events may lock technology development into a particular irreversible path (David 1985). The opponents of qwertynomics argue that the qwerty keyboard has not been replaced because there is no convincingly superior alternative to the QWERTY layout, citing human factors research (Liebowitz and Margolis 1990). Regardless of the strength of arguments on either side, innovation concerning user interaction clearly has to either tap users' existing skills and behavior or offer dramatic advantages over conventional practice. Today new forms of computer devices clearly demand alternative input and output methods, but they have to be well researched to be successful.

### Dimension 5: Software and Computing Functions Move from Applications to Services

Today most of the computing functions are delivered through applications residing on the personal computer. An alternative approach is gaining momentum in the computer industry: server-based computing functions (services) delivered through the internet to a personal device, with internet search being the most successful example. Other examples include web-based email services. There are several factors that favor such a shift. First, the trend to being always connected (e.g., today's push in many cities for a municipal wireless local area network) enables the viability of the service model. Second, conventional applications have gotten too complex for most people to make use of or even to know about all of their functions. Web-based services tend to be much simpler and "under-featured," perhaps because services can't download huge bundles of code or because these services are young and not yet "enriched." Software services are forced to ask what is really needed, thus enforcing simplicity, which could mean more stable functions. Third, with AJAX (asynchronous java and xml) technologies, web user-interfaces can be very GUI-like, and therefore easier to use and more familiar in appearance and behavior. Fourth, unlike applications that are difficult to deploy frequently, services can be updated seamlessly (although software service providers really should be considerate of users' familiarity with their interface and refrain from forcing new looks and behaviors on the user every month). Finally, with services users tend to have more choices, since they're easier to find and try out; and potentially users can combine finer-grained services to their individual needs. The shift from applications to services obviously requires a different economic model for business (to date advertising has been the main economic enabler). It also has to overcome privacy and security hurdles.

The shift from application to services also is evolving in parallel with, but faster than, the evolution from personal desktop computing to the personal information cloud model. Together they may significantly influence the form of future integrated digital work environments. Software services should be able to adapt to a variety of individual devices as needed. In a ubiquitous computing world, a variety of devices, including desktop computers, handsets, specialized appliances, or in-car computers, could be used to accomplish a task. How could these devices team up effectively in an ad hoc fashion as the user moves around? Applications residing on these devices communicating with each other in a peer-to-peer fashion is one possibility (Newman et al. 2002). Another possibility is to support a variety of personal or public devices from software services. Based on personal identification sensing or user log in, services in the network could virtually track what devices are being used by an individual, coordinate these devices, and deliver information suited to each of the devices being used. Such a user- (ID-) centered integration approach has been demonstrated in our FonePal system (Yin and Zhai 2005, 2006) in which telephony voice menus are visually displayed on the user's computer screen via an instant messaging infrastructure based on the user's IDs.

## Dimension 6: From Personal to Interpersonal to Group to Social Interaction

The desktop metaphor supports the individual in managing his working set of personal information. But the individual doesn't live in isolation. Although personal information consists of information that is relevant to the person, most of it is not created by the person himself, but by other people. A person's communication with others, such as email or instant messaging, is not only personal, but interpersonal. The metaphor provides an inbox for such communication and also for exchanging information artifacts; but these communications are kept and managed on each person's desktop. Interpersonal interaction, by which we mean interactions targeted to specific other people, is not distinguishable from purely personal interaction. The desktop can accommodate a range of interpersonal tools. Collaboration (or interaction) with a group or team is where we begin to step outside the desktop metaphor. Collaboration is most often supported by some form of "place," such as a "teamroom," where information is shared. What makes such a place separate from the personal desktop is that the management of the place is shared with others. (Note that here we are not distinguishing how the place is supported architecturally, such as by client-server or peer-to-peer.)

The next level is to engage in more overt social interaction. One aspect of social interaction is to treat people as focal points in the personal information cloud. This is well illustrated by ContactMap and Soylent (Fisher and Nardi, this volume). ContactMap helps a person to explicitly manage his relationships with others, creating a personal social network. To do this we need persistent representations of people and their identities in the personal information cloud. Given people objects, we can organize information around people, such as a history of communications and shared objects. Notice the kinship with Lifestream (Freeman and Gelernter, this volume). Further, as illustrated in Soylent (Fisher and Nardi, this volume) we can use this same information to infer groupings of people into social and work contexts.

A second aspect of social interaction is making more information (which used to be personal or interpersonal) more easily available in a wider social context. There seems to be a trend here. More and more services are being created on the web that encourage people to disclose information publicly. People are putting out information and opinions on personal blogs that are available to an unknown public. People are contributing to various collaborative open-source projects, such as Wikipedia. People are tagging information, such as web pages and documents and photos, and making these tags public to create a system of social tagging for indexing information, often called "folksonomies." Thus more information in the personal information cloud is being made public to combine with that of others—creating public information clouds consisting of the intersections of personal information clouds. Perhaps this is a fad, or perhaps the web is evolving into a "culture of participation" where public information is created that is greater than the sum of personal contributions.

Important new social dynamics are emerging, and these must be taken into account, since they will strongly shape the future of integrated digital work environments.

## Dimension 7: From Low-Level Tasks to Higher-Level Activities

The desktop metaphor provides a set of generic tools for users to work on the information objects in the office. These tools, or applications, support a set of common low-level tasks, such as editing a document, sending an email, organizing a folder, and so on. It is up to the user to select tools and use these tools and objects to accomplish higher-level objectives, or *activities*. People think of work in terms of activities (Gonzalez and Mark 2004), for example, writing a book chapter, and over time perform a series of tasks to carry out the activities, for example, starting a new chapter file, gathering related materials in a folder, emailing the book editor, setting a due date in the calendar, editing the chapter, finding references in related papers, printing the chapter, and so on. The desktop metaphor affords great flexibility in organizing the activity, but it offers little help in managing the activity. The activity involves heterogeneous tools and objects scattered throughout the desktop. Many tools do not work well together; for instance, a reference in an email has to be cut and pasted into the chapter file lest it be forgotten.

Many chapters in this book can be seen as supporting work at the activity level. The Group Bar, Scalable Fabric, and the Task Gallery (Robertson et al., this volume) attempt to enhance the user's ability to manage their activities beyond individual windows and applications. Haystack (Karger, this volume) provides ways to express relationships between disparate objects to organize them better for activities. Lifestreams (Freeman and Gelernter, this volume) replaces the desktop with a stream of document-based actions that can be organized into activities. The notion of roles (Plaisant et al., this volume) can be seen as kinds of activities. UMEA (Kaptelinin and Boardman, this volume) is an explicit activity management system, and their WorkspaceMirror can also be seen this way, as indeed can their general notion of Workspace-Level Design. Kimura (Voida et al., this volume) is explicitly designed to support activities by representing them as montages of document images on a wall display. Finally, the activity-based computing system (Bardram, this volume) develops an explicit architecture and services to support activities in a hospital setting.

The notion of activity is an important concept across the social, behavioral, and management sciences. Most HCI researchers refer to activity theory's formulation of activity (e.g., Nardi 1996). But there are other relevant perspectives: distributed cognition (Hutchins 1994), linguistics (Clark 1996), and organizational behavior, which calls them *routines* (Pentland and Feldman 2005). Activity is also becoming an important analytic construct for understanding usage context in system design (Gay and Hembrooke 2003; Moran 2003; Moran, Cozzi, and Farrell 2005; Nardi 1996). But more important here is to see that people have to manage their activities and that integrated digital work environments need to support this activity management (Moran, Cozzi, and Farrell 2005).

Therefore, we agree with Bardram that the activity concept should be made a first-class computational construct that can be used to support human activity. Further, we believe that development of a standard representation of activity, called "unified activity" by Moran, Cozzi, and Farrell (2005), could provide a semantic foundation to enable integration across diverse work-support systems. A represented activity is straightforward. Activities are objects with some descriptions (objective, status) related to the people involved, the resources used, and the bounding events. Activities are also related to other activities (such as subactivities). Activity descriptions are fundamentally relational metadata for grouping and organizing elements around human activities (Dragunov et al. 2005; Kaptelinin 2003). How do activity descriptions relate to the personal information cloud? Activity descriptions are the part of the personal information cloud that organizes that information around the semantics of activity—how the information is used and what it is useful for—or the "personal activity cloud."

A standard activity construct can have many benefits. First, it provides objects around which to aggregate the resources to carry out activities, and also suspend and resume activities. Activities are shared information and thus can provide coordination and awareness among collaborators, as illustrated in the Bardram and Voida et al. chapters in this volume, and also by ActivityExplorer (Muller et al. 2004). Activities are explicit representations that people can operate on, thus providing a focus for reflecting on and planning activities. If activities are represented as they are carried out, then they provide a valuable record of *experience*, which can be reused ("how did George do it last month?"). Another powerful method of reuse is to create *activity patterns*, perhaps by "cleaning up" activity experience records to capture "best practices." It should be noted that activity representations are very different from descriptions of formal workflow process in that the former are malleable descriptions under the control of the people using them, and thus are adaptable to varying situations. Activity descriptions could complement workflow systems if properly integrated (Moran, Cozzi, and Farrell 2005).

There are at present only a few research prototypes of activity-support systems (Dragunov et al. 2005; Kaptelinin 2003; Moran, Cozzi, and Farrell 2005; Bardram, this volume; Voida et al., this volume), and these have produced as many questions as conclusions. There are many challenges to shifting users to an activity-centric mode of working. How are activity descriptions going to be created? Can they be automatically identified from monitoring action streams, as many chapters in this book discuss (Kaptelinin and Boardman, Voida et al., and Bardram, this volume)? It is well known that current automated methods are not accurate enough and require considerable manual "clean up" to make the results useful (Kaptelinin 2003). Can we do better? Can we create an attractive cost–benefit continuum? It would be extremely easy for users to create crude but useful activity descriptions (e.g., a threaded email conversation could be converted to an initial activity description by a single gesture). Activity descriptions would be further developed because they provide a flexible service for resource sharing, planning, and awareness. Another incentive for using activity descriptions is that they can be generated from activity patterns, providing an initial structure and advice. But can we make it easy enough to create useful activity patterns at a useful level of abstraction? And how can we make the patterns available in appropriate contexts? These are just a few of the remaining open questions.

## Where Do We Stand?

The theme of this book is that the computing world is moving beyond the desktop metaphor. It is not exactly clear where it is going, but the seven dimensions presented above articulate a design space that is being explored; they chart the course we are on. The diversity of these dimensions suggests that progress will not be uniform along all the dimensions. Research and industry will push forward on different dimensions based on creative insights and commercial opportunities.

We have observed that the desktop metaphor is a caricature of the current state, since we are clearly already well beyond the strict concept of the desktop. So, where do we stand? Let us consider each dimension separately:

1. *Personal information cloud:* Personal information has already started dispersing. Many users store their emails, calendar, and documents on the web. However, the correct shape of a personal information cloud model will take many years to evolve. What is not yet clear is who will provide the service to maintain and deliver the personal information cloud. The providers could be reputable corporations or open source organizations. Probably there will not be complete end-to-end host providers. Rather, the personal information cloud would be organized by a set of services that glue and coordinate a user's information from multiple hosts and servers.
2. *Diverse representations:* The conventional desktop metaphor and GUI continue to dominate, although it is increasingly complemented by desktop search and other new functions. New form factors for information devices are beginning to challenge the status quo and demand alternative forms of information representation.
3. *Device multiplicity:* We can already see many forms of computing devices, ranging from handsets to embedded computers in cars on the market. However, these devices are largely isolated from each other. Achieving a transformational user-interface design so that the diverse forms of devices can all be powered by the personal information cloud and deliver much greater value is still at the very early research stage.
4. *New interactions and modalities:* The use of voice as an interaction modality has finally developed into practical applications in telephony systems. Many other input methods (e.g., telephone-pad-based input) are alternatives to traditional mouse and keyboards and are already frequently employed by mobile users, although existing methods tend to be rather inefficient or even clumsy. User-interface innovations in this area have the ability to unlock the full potential of mobile and other forms of computing.

5. *Software as services:* Software services are rapidly gaining acceptance in the computer industry owing to market forces. Already enough services are available on the web for an individual to do serious work (and most of these are free, at least in limited forms), although some desktop functionality is still useful to glue all the services together. This dimension will mostly be led and driven by the intense competition in the information technology industry.

6. *Social interaction:* Social software is surprisingly popular. It is changing the way information is communicated (e.g., blogs), and it is changing the way we think of the web and large-scale social cooperation (e.g., Wikipedia). This dimension is based largely on early research efforts (e.g., wikis) and is now being driven mostly by innovative experiments and evolutionary progress based on wide adoption.

7. *Activity-centric computing:* The general notion that software should be more activity-centric is widely held. Current desktop environments are slowly evolving in this direction, as are some enterprise collaboration environments. Beyond such incremental changes, research is still mainly exploratory, such as the work exhibited in this book. There are research challenges in this dimension: the architecture for activity-centric computing, standards for activity representation, and the user experience being activity-centric versus being tool-centric and/or inbox-centric. From this research we can expect to see some public experiments and commercial offerings in the near future.

This book presents several research innovations that explore significant steps to the future beyond the desktop, as well as the rationale for the directions they represent. We have tried to add some perspective to the work here by laying out seven dimensions of change that they all participate in. Although some of the dimensions are strongly driven by the fast pace of commercial innovations on the web, all the dimensions present significant research challenges. Research can guide future integrated digital work environments by articulating human needs and capacities and exploring and evaluating technologies to meet them. The field of human–computer interaction has not had a greater opportunity to influence the broad computing industry, and indeed how people work and live in the world, since the desktop metaphor and graphical user interface were first developed.

## Acknowledgments

We thank our colleagues at the IBM Research for creating an intellectually stimulating environment and for many discussions that have shaped our thinking on the future of human–computer interaction.

## References

Accot, J., and Zhai, S. (2002). More than dotting the i's—Foundations for crossing-based interfaces. *Proceedings of CHI 2002: ACM Conference on Human Factors in Computing Systems, CHI Letters* 4 (1): 73–80.

Ahn, J., and Pierce, J. S. (2005). SEREFE: Serendipitous file exchange between users and devices. In *Proceedings of Mobile HCI*, pp. 39–46. Salzburg, Austria, September 19–22.

Apitz, G., and Guimbretiére, F. (2004). CrossY: A crossing-based drawing application. In *Proceedings of UIST—The 17th ACM Symposium on User Interface Software and Technology*, pp. 3–12. Santa Fe, New Mexico, October 24–27.

Calvary, G., Coutaz, J., Thevenin, D., Limbourg, Q., Bouillon, L., and Vanderdonckt, J. (2003). A unifying reference framework for multi-target user interfaces. *Interacting with Computers* 15 (3): 289–308.

Clark, H. H. (1996). *Using Language*. Cambridge: Cambridge University Press.

David, P. A. (1985). Clio and the Economics of QWERTY. *American Economic Review* 75: 332–337.

Dragunov, A. N., Dietterich, T. G., Johnsrude, K., McLaughlin, M., Li, L., and Herlocker, J. L. (2005). TaskTracer: A desktop environment to support multi-tasking knowledge workers. In *Proceedings of International Conference on Intelligent User Interfaces*, pp. 75–82. San Diego, California, January 10–13.

Gay, G., and Hembrooke, H. (2003). *Activity-Centered Design: An Ecological Approach to Designing Smart Tools and Usable Systems*. Cambridge, Mass.: MIT Press.

Gonzalez, V., and Mark, G. (2004). Constant constant multitasking craziness: Managing multiple working spheres. In *Proceedings of ACM CHI2004 Conference on Human Factors in Computing Systems*, pp. 113–120. Vienna, Austria, April 24–29.

Hinckley, K., Baudisch, P., Ramos, G., and Guimbretiére, F. (2005). Design and analysis of delimiters for selection-action pen gesture phrases in Scriboli. In *Proceedings of CHI 2005: ACM Conference on Human Factors in Computing Systems*, pp. 451–460. Portland, Oregon, April 2–7.

Hutchins, E. (1994). *Cognition in the Wild*. Cambridge, Mass.: MIT Press.

Jones, W., Phuwanartnurak, A. J., Gill, R., and Bruce, H. (2005). Don't take my folders away! Organizing personal information to getting things done. In *Proceed-*

*ings of ACM CHI2005 Conference on Human Factors in Computing Systems, Extended Abstracts* (short paper), pp. 1505–1508. Portland, Oregon, April 2–7.

Kaptelinin, V. (2003). UMEA: Translating interaction histories into project contexts. In *Proceedings of ACM CHI Conference on Human Factors in Computing Systems*, pp. 353–360. Ft. Lauderdale, Florida, April 5–10.

Kurtenbach, G., and Buxton, W. (1994). User learning and performance with marking menus. In *Proceedings of CHI: ACM Conference on Human Factors in Computing Systems*, pp. 258–264. Boston, Massachusetts, April 24–28.

Liebowitz, S. J., and Margolis, S. E. (1990). The fable of the keys. *Journal of Law and Economics* 33.

Moran, T. P. (2003). Activity: Analysis, design, and management. In G. C. S. a. S. B. e. Sebastiano Bagnara and Lawrence Erlbaum Inc. (eds.), *Symposium on the Foundations of Interaction Design*, Interaction Design Institute, Ivrea, Italy. To appear in *Theories and Practice in Interaction Design.*

Moran, T. P., Cozzi, A., and Farrell, S. P. (2005). Unified activity management: Supporting people in eBusiness. *Communications of the ACM* (December): 67–70.

Muller, M. J., Geyer, W., Brownholtz, B., Wilcox, E., and Millen, D. R. (2004). One-hundred days in an activity-centric collaboration environment based on shared objects. In *Proceedings of ACM CHI 2004 Conference on Human Factors in Computing Systems*, pp. 375–382. Vienna, Austria, April 24–29.

Nardi, B. A. (ed.). (1996). *Context and Consciousness: Activity Theory and Human–Computer Interaction.* Cambridge, Mass.: MIT Press.

Newman, M., Izadi, S., Edwards, K., Sedivy, J., and Smith, T. (2002). User interfaces when and where they are needed: An infrastructure for recombinant computing. In *Proceedings of ACM Symposium on User Interface Software and Technology*, pp. 171–180. Paris, France, October 27–30.

Norman, D. A. (1998). *The Invisible Computer: Why Good Products Can Fail, the Personal Computer Is So Complex, and Information Appliances Are the Solution.* Cambridge, Mass.: MIT Press.

Oviatt, S. (2003). Multimodal interfaces. In Sears, J. J. A. (ed.), *Handbook of Human–Computer Interaction*, pp. 286–304.

Paterno, F., and Santoro, C. (2003). A unified method for designing interactive systems adaptable to mobile and stationary platforms. *Interacting with Computers* 15 (3): 349–366.

Pentland, B. T., and Feldman, M. S. (2005). Organizational routines as a unit of analysis. *Industrial and Corporate Change* 14 (5): 793–815.

Whittaker, S., and Sidner, C. (1996). Email overload: Exploring personal information management of email. In *Proceedings of ACM CHI '96 Conference on Human Factors in Computing Systems*, pp. 276–283. Vancouver, Canada, April 13–18.

Wiecha, C., Bennett, W., Boies, S., Gould, J., and Greene, S. (1990). ITS: A tool for rapidly developing interactive applications. *ACM Transactions on Information Systems* 8 (3): 204–236.

Yin, M., and Zhai, S. (2005). Dial and see: Tackling the voice menu navigation problem with cross-device user experience integration. In *Proceedings of UIST 2005—18th ACM Symposium on User Interface Software and Technology*, pp. 187–190. Seattle, Washington, October 23–26.

Yin, M., and Zhai, S. (2006). The benefits of augmenting telephone voice menu navigation with visual browsing and search. In *Proceedings of CHI 2006: ACM Conference on Human Factors in Computing Systems*. Montreal, Canada, April 22–27.

Zhai, S., and Kristensson, P.-O. (2003). Shorthand writing on stylus keyboard. *Proceedings of CHI 2003, ACM Conference on Human Factors in Computing Systems, CHI Letters* 5(1): 97–104.

Zhai, S., Kristensson, P.-O., and Smith, B. A. (2005). In search of effective text input interfaces for off the desktop computing. *Interacting with Computers* 17 (3): 229–250.

# Contributors

*H. Ross Baker*
Chicago, Illinois

*Jakob E. Bardram*
Department of Computer Science
University of Aarhus
Denmark

*Patrick Baudisch*
Microsoft Research
Redmond, Washington

*Richard Boardman*
Google
Mountain View, California

*Mary Czerwinski*
Microsoft Research
Redmond, Washington

*Nicolas B. Duarte*
Penn State University
University Park, Pennsylvania

*Danyel Fisher*
Microsoft Research
Redmond, Washington

*Eric Freeman*
Walt Disney Parks and Resorts Online
North Hollywood, California

*David Gelernter*
Department of Computer Science
Yale University
New Haven, Connecticut

*Aydin Haririnia*
Ph.D. candidate, Biochemistry
University of Maryland
College Park, Maryland

*Eric Horvitz*
Microsoft Research
Redmond, Washington

*Victor Kaptelinin*
Department of Informatics
Umeå University
Sweden

*David R. Karger*
Department of Electrical Engineering and Computer Science
Computer Science and Artificial Intelligence Laboratory
MIT
Cambridge, Massachusetts

*Dawn E. Klinesmith*
SEMM—Department of Civil and Environmental Engineering
University of California, Berkeley
Berkeley, California

*Blair MacIntyre*
GVU Center, College of Computing
Georgia Institute of Technology
Atlanta, Georgia

*Brian Meyers*
Microsoft Research
Redmond, Washington

*Thomas P. Moran*
IBM Almaden Research Center
San Jose, California

*Elizabeth D. Mynatt*
GVU Center, College of Computing
Georgia Institute of Technology
Atlanta, Georgia

*Bonnie Nardi*
School of Information and Computer Sciences
University of California, Irvine
Irvine, California

*Catherine Plaisant*
HCIL/UMIACS
University of Maryland
College Park, Maryland

*Pamela Ravasio*
Department of Frontier Informatics
Graduate School of Frontier Sciences
University of Tokyo
Japan

*Daniel Robbins*
Microsoft Research
Redmond, Washington

*George Robertson*
Microsoft Research
Redmond, Washington

*Ben Shneiderman*
Department of Computer Science
University of Maryland
College Park, Maryland

*Greg Smith*
Microsoft Research
Redmond, Washington

*Desney Tan*
Microsoft Research
Redmond, Washington

*Vincent Tscherter*
PH Solothurn
Solothurn
Switzerland

*Leonid A. Velikovich*
Microsoft
Redmond, Washington

*Stephen Voida*
GVU Center, College of Computing
Georgia Institute of Technology
Atlanta, Georgia

*Alfred O. Wanga*
Silver Spring, Maryland

*Matthew J. Westhoff*
Severna Park, Maryland

*Shumin Zhai*
IBM Almaden Research Center
San Jose, California

# Index